Revolutionary Teamsters

Historical Materialism Book Series

The Historical Materialism Book Series is a major publishing initiative of the radical left. The capitalist crisis of the twenty-first century has been met by a resurgence of interest in critical Marxist theory. At the same time, the publishing institutions committed to Marxism have contracted markedly since the high point of the 1970s. The Historical Materialism Book Series is dedicated to addressing this situation by making available important works of Marxist theory. The aim of the series is to publish important theoretical contributions as the basis for vigorous intellectual debate and exchange on the left.

The peer-reviewed series publishes original monographs, translated texts, and reprints of classics across the bounds of academic disciplinary agendas and across the divisions of the left. The series is particularly concerned to encourage the internationalization of Marxist debate and aims to translate significant studies from beyond the English-speaking world.

For a full list of titles in the Historical Materialism Book Series
available in paperback from Haymarket Books, visit:
www.haymarketbooks.org/category/hm-series

Revolutionary Teamsters

The Minneapolis Truckers' Strikes of 1934

Bryan D. Palmer

Haymarket Books
Chicago, IL

First published in 2013 by Brill Academic Publishers, The Netherlands
© 2013 Koninklijke Brill NV, Leiden, The Netherlands

Published in paperback in 2014 by
Haymarket Books
P.O. Box 180165
Chicago, IL 60618
773-583-7884
www.haymarketbooks.org

ISBN: 978-1-60846-379-4

Trade distribution:
In the US, Consortium Book Sales, www.cbsd.com
In Canada, Publishers Group Canada, www.pgcbooks.ca
In the UK, Turnaround Publisher Services, www.turnaround-psl.com
In Australia, Palgrave Macmillan, www.palgravemacmillan.com.au
In all other countries, Publishers Group Worldwide, www.pgw.com

Cover design by Ragina Johnson.

This book was published with the generous support of
Lannan Foundation and the Wallace Global Fund.

Printed in the United States.

10 9 8 7 6 5 4 3 2 1

Library of Congress Cataloging-in-Publication data is available.

For Joan and Beth

Contents

Acknowledgements

This book grew out of my study of James P. Cannon and the development of Trotskyism in the United States. When a chapter on the Minneapolis teamsters' strikes in the second instalment of that yet-to-be-completed three-volume study grew to 225 pages, written as class-struggle showed some signs of revival in the United States, I decided to turn what I had written into a book of its own. For the Cannon project, I have incurred many debts, outlined in the acknowledgements to *James P. Cannon and the Origins of the American Revolutionary Left, 1890–1928*, and my more focused thanks in this volume complement those earlier statements of appreciation.

For financial support, I am greatly indebted to the Canada Research Chairs programme of the federal government of Canada, which has supported this, and other, projects for more than a decade. Trent University, which administers my Canada Research Chair, has always been accommodating and supportive. Since coming to Trent in 2000, I have benefited from a congenial research-environment and the material aid of the senior administration, which has always done what it could to advance my scholarship. I would especially like to thank the current and past Assistant Vice-Presidents of Research, James Parker and Neil Emery, as well as the current Vice-President, Academic and Provost, Gary Boire.

Peter Thomas and Sebastian Budgen encouraged me to publish this study in the *Historical Materialism Book Series*, and I am grateful for their support, resolute political commitments, and dedicated work in developing Marxist research and writing. David Broder has been an exemplary reader of my text, a copy-editor *extraordinaire*, whose meticulous attention to detail and scrutiny of my prose has improved this book immensely. I thank him for his efforts and insights, as well as for his patience and understanding. At Brill, I have benefited from the professionalism of its fine staff.

I am particularly thankful for the help I received from Tom Reid and Paul Le Blanc, who read drafts of this book and offered important suggestions for improvement. At the Prometheus Research Library, which has long supported my research on Cannon, providing much in the way of critical engagement with my study as well as material aid in advancing it, Emily Turnbull and Alison Dundy read a preliminary version of this book and prodded me with useful advice, helpful questions, and healthy (if sometimes ignored) scepticism. A Minneapolis expert on the events of 1934, David Riehle, graciously took time to look over this book in manuscript form, offering me his insights and pushing me to clarify certain matters. Tom Mackaman assisted my research of the Minneapolis daily press and other regional sources, and the Minnesota Historical Society gave permission for the reproduction of many of the photographs that appear in this book. I could not have secured access to these images without the gracious and tolerant help of Debbie Miller at the Minnesota Historical Society. Donna T. Haverty-Stacke also read an earlier, shorter, version of this study, offering me much useful commentary. Additionally, she kindly provided me with a copy of her forthcoming article on the 1940s trials and convictions of the Minneapolis teamsters' leaders, as well as much in the way of email-correspondence on this legal assault on the Socialist Workers Party and militant class-struggle trade-unionism, a subject that Joe Allen has also been researching and addressing. Audiences at the *Historical Materialism* Conference (York University, Toronto, May 2012), and at political forums and public lectures in March 2012 on 'Class Struggle Unionism and Beyond' at King's College, London, Ontario, Brock University, St. Catharines, and the Ontario Institute for Studies in Education, Toronto, listened to my thoughts on the significance of the Minneapolis teamsters' struggles and helped me to restate my arguments more effectively. Research in the extensive James P. Cannon and Rose Karsner Papers, archived at the State Historical Society of Wisconsin, and lightly drawn upon in this book, was facilitated by Jack Barnes, who is the owner of the copyrights in and to the Cannon Papers. He arranged for me to have uninhibited access to these materials, which, at the time, were restricted. The late Frank Lovell and the late Dorthea Breitman encouraged my research, and Dorthea provided me with bound volumes of *The Militant* and other materials which I have repeatedly pored over in reconstructing the history of the Minneapolis events of 1934.

To all of these people and institutions, then, and to others unnamed, I owe considerable debts. But my loudest and deepest thanks go to those who made the history I have tried to bring to life. And to those, in later generations, who will hopefully draw on this past to reclaim our futures.

This book is dedicated to two historians of different generations who have enriched my life in a myriad of ways and make me constantly aware of how fortunate I am to do what I do.

Figure 1. Strike-headquarters, 1934. Courtesy of Minnesota Historical Society, Carlos Hudson Estate.

Figure 2. The rally, 6 August 1934. Courtesy of Michael J. Irestone, Graphic Arts Institute & Graphic Communications Union, Minneapolis, Carlos Hudson Estate.

Figure 3. Vincent Ray Dunne, arrested and held at Stockade, State Fairgrounds, 1 August 1934. Courtesy of Minnesota Historical Society, with insert in possession of author, courtesy of Jean Tussey.

Figure 4. Carl Skoglund in the 1920s. Courtesy of Minnesota Historical Society.

Figure 5. Max Shachtman and James P. Cannon in police-custody, 26 July 1934. Courtesy of Minnesota Historical Society.

Figure 6. Grant Dunne (far left) and Albert Goldman (far right) meet Bill Brown, Miles Dunne, and Vincent Ray Dunne upon their release from military stockade, 2 August 1934. Courtesy of Minnesota Historical Society.

Figure 7. Women's Auxiliary members preparing food at the strike-headquarters commissary, with Mrs. Carle overseeing (four from the left). Courtesy of Minnesota Historical Society.

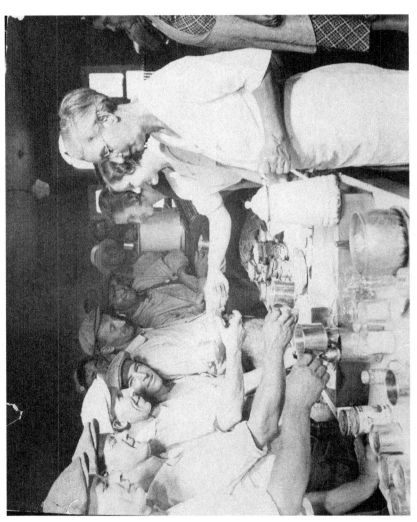

Figure 8. Women's Auxiliary members serving strikers food. Courtesy of Minnesota Historical Society.

Figure 9. Strike-gathering, with woman (possibly Marvel Scholl [Dobbs]) amidst the crowd. Courtesy of Minnesota Historical Society.

Figure 10. Strike crowd-scene, market-warehouse district. Dave Silverman, *Minneapolis Star*, courtesy of Minnesota Historical Society.

Figure 11. Special deputies in flight as strikers and police clash in the market, 21 May 1934. Courtesy of Minnesota Historical Society.

Figure 12. Prelude to the Battle of Deputies Run: police and a striker lay in the street after 21 May 1934 club battle. Associated Press photo, in possession of the author.

Figure 13. Battle of Deputies Run, 22 May 1934. Courtesy of Minnesota Historical Society.

Figure 14. Battle of Deputies Run, 22 May 1934. Associated Press photo, in possession of author.

Figure 15. Battle of Deputies Run: two women, 22 May 1934. Courtesy of Minnesota Historical Society.

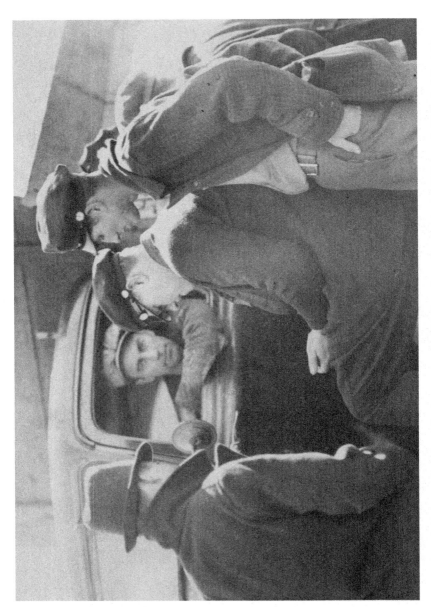

Figure 16. Strikers talking to a driver moving goods during the strike. Courtesy of Minnesota Historical Society.

Figure 17. Pickets in an open truck intercept a truck accompanied by a police-convoy, 20 July 1934. Courtesy of Minnesota Historical Society.

Figure 18. Fruit- and produce-truck overturned, with schoolboys, August 1934. Courtesy of Minnesota Historical Society.

Figure 19. Henry Ness memorial. Courtesy of Minnesota Historical Society.

Figure 20. Henry Ness funeral, 24 July 1934. Courtesy of Minnesota Historical Society.

Figure 21. National Guard seize the strike-headquarters, 1 August 1934. Associated Press photo, in possession of the author.

Figure 22. Minneapolis city-council chambers: sentries stand guard at the impeachment-hearing of Mayor Bainbridge, July 1934. Courtesy of Minnesota Historical Society.

Figure 23. Mayor A.G. Bainbridge, Father Francis J. Haas, Eugene H. Dunnigan, and Governor Floyd B. Olson, drafting a proposal to present to the strikers, 24 July 1934. Courtesy of Minnesota Historical Society.

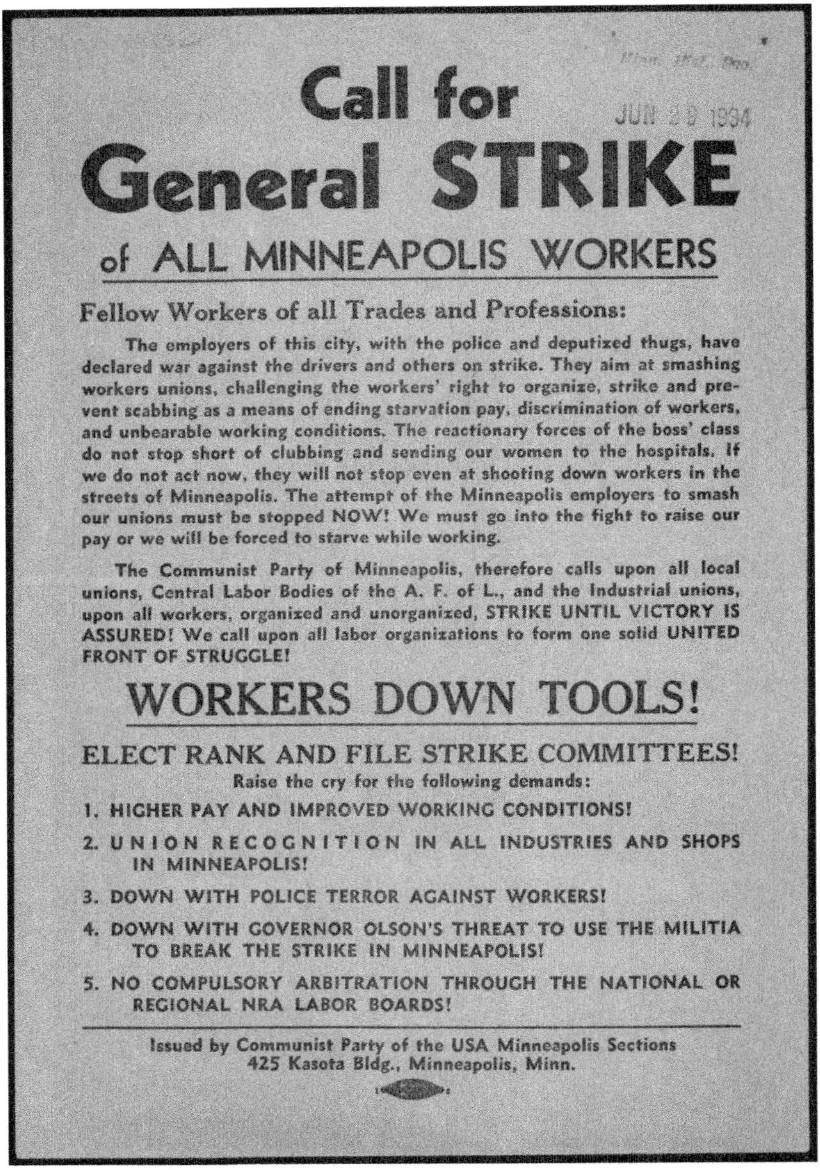

Call for
General STRIKE
of ALL MINNEAPOLIS WORKERS

JUN 2 9 1934

Fellow Workers of all Trades and Professions:

The employers of this city, with the police and deputized thugs, have declared war against the drivers and others on strike. They aim at smashing workers unions, challenging the workers' right to organize, strike and prevent scabbing as a means of ending starvation pay, discrimination of workers, and unbearable working conditions. The reactionary forces of the boss' class do not stop short of clubbing and sending our women to the hospitals. If we do not act now, they will not stop even at shooting down workers in the streets of Minneapolis. The attempt of the Minneapolis employers to smash our unions must be stopped NOW! We must go into the fight to raise our pay or we will be forced to starve while working.

The Communist Party of Minneapolis, therefore calls upon all local unions, Central Labor Bodies of the A. F. of L., and the Industrial unions, upon all workers, organized and unorganized, STRIKE UNTIL VICTORY IS ASSURED! We call upon all labor organizations to form one solid UNITED FRONT OF STRUGGLE!

WORKERS DOWN TOOLS!

ELECT RANK AND FILE STRIKE COMMITTEES!
Raise the cry for the following demands:

1. HIGHER PAY AND IMPROVED WORKING CONDITIONS!

2. UNION RECOGNITION IN ALL INDUSTRIES AND SHOPS IN MINNEAPOLIS!

3. DOWN WITH POLICE TERROR AGAINST WORKERS!

4. DOWN WITH GOVERNOR OLSON'S THREAT TO USE THE MILITIA TO BREAK THE STRIKE IN MINNEAPOLIS!

5. NO COMPULSORY ARBITRATION THROUGH THE NATIONAL OR REGIONAL NRA LABOR BOARDS!

Issued by Communist Party of the USA Minneapolis Sections
425 Kasota Bldg., Minneapolis, Minn.

Figure 24. Communist Party opposition to the strike-leadership: leaflet, June 1934.
Courtesy of Minnesota Historical Society.

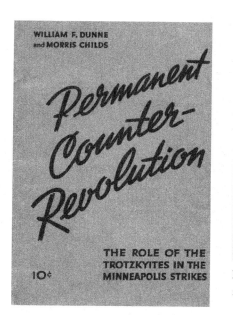

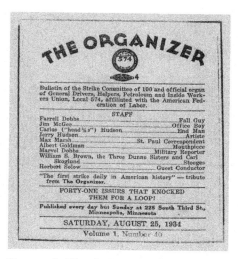

Figure 26. *The Organizer*, joke masthead, 25 August 1934. In possession of the author.

Figure 25. Communist Party opposition to the strike-leadership: pamphlet, October 1934. In possession of the author.

Figure 27. *The Militant*, 'Olson "Protects" the Strikers'.

Figure 28. Strike-coverage: *The Militant* and *The Organizer*.

Figure 29. Socialist Workers Party members after the Smith Act convictions. (Back row, left to right: Farrell Dobbs, Harry DeBoer, Edward Palmquist, Clarence Hamel, Emil Hansen, Oscar Coover, Jake Cooper; front row, left to right: Max Geldman, Felix Morrow, Albert Goodman, James Cannon, Vincent Ray Dunne, Carl Skoglund, Grace Carlson.) Courtesy of Minnesota Historical Society.

Figure 30. Marvel Scholl and Farrell Dobbs (far left) and Vincent Ray Dunne, Grace Carlson, and Carl Skoglund, 1948. Courtesy of Minnesota Historical Society.

Chapter One
Revolutionary Trotskyism and Teamsters in the United States: the Early Depression-Years

This book has a purposively mischievous title. *Revolutionary Teamsters* is about people whom we now have difficulty imagining. The coupling has the ring of the oxymoronic. Indeed, it is meant to pose a question and mark it with exclamation. For in the ballroom where revolutionaries and workers routinely dance, Trotskyists, with whom this book is concerned, and teamsters, often judged the least radical of working-class trade-unionists, are not usually seen hoofing it together. They just don't tango. If the latter are the leather-jacketed, cigarette-smoking clique gathered in the corner, demanding that all others give them a wide berth, the former are the proverbial wallflowers, metaphorically sitting alone on the sidelines. Tough guys think the two-step is for sissies; introverts and nerds are not on anyone's dance-card. Or so conventions would tell us.

Teamsters and revolutionary Trotskyists are thus not usually linked in discussions of the American working class. The International Brotherhood of Teamsters (IBT) is often recognised as a union that has managed to grow in the post-1970 doldrums-years of a declining US labour-movement. It is, however, also widely regarded as bureaucratically governed, corrupt to the point of being an embarrassment to advocates of trade-unions, and anything but a bastion of militancy. As early as 1940, the IBT amended its constitution, allowing its president full discretion in performing his duties, and providing 'fully and liberally' in the case of any expenses, including vacations and travel for him and his wife in the United States and abroad. In this same period, IBT officials were being prosecuted in New York for criminal acts. *Fortune* magazine wrote in 1941 that 'More than most American unions, the Teamsters' has been accused of crimes and offences against the public welfare, to say nothing of crimes and offences against its own members'. Things did not improve in the years after the Second World-War. Rank-and-file democracy-movements within the Teamsters have, indeed, signalled that there remain important currents of resistance struggling to the political surface of the IBT, but the legacy of gangster union-boss Jimmy Hoffa permeates the organised trucking industry, a brutal reminder of just how difficult it is to clean the house of labour once it has been compromised by racketeering.[1]

If the Teamsters are understood to be an eminently worldly organisation, tarnished by their many compromises of principle and shameful practices, Trotskyists are often seen in an entirely different light. Born in opposition to what they perceived as the degeneration of the revolutionary project in a Soviet Union undergoing Stalinisation, Trotskyists have historically been the most marginal of the forces of world-communism. At a time when many 'progressives' (as well as the vast majority of Marxists) regarded Russia with reverence, Trotskyists talked of the downside of Stalin's abandonment of world-revolution and retreat into the rhetoric and programme of 'socialism in one country', with its practical consequences of restrained activity that too often led to setbacks and defeats. And yet, complicating matters further, Trotskyists (or at least a critically important wing of the movement), insisted on defending the Soviet Union against imperialist attack, arguing that it retained significant components of a workers' state that demanded preservation and that differentiated it from capitalist political economies. Relentless critics of bureaucracy and refusing accommodation to all manner of 'lesser evils', Trotskyists have been the proverbial 'black sheep' of the fissiparous family-circles of the Left. Exiled and reviled, Trotsky and his followers were the first victims of Stalin's brutal machine of terror and repression within the Soviet Union, while outside of it they were hounded and loathed by the official Communist Parties, which largely remained obedient agents of the Communist International's directions. Trotskyists fought back in many ways, but their principal weapons were well-reasoned words of rebuttal and a consistent refusal

---

1. On early Teamster corruption, see Galenson 1960, pp. 469–71, quoting the May 1941 *Fortune* magazine, p. 97; and Jacobs 1957. The wider picture is presented in Friedman and Schwarz 1989; Franco and Hammer 1987; and Witwer 2003. On rank-and-file Teamster resistance to gangsterism and bureaucratisation, see Friedman 1982. Kim Moody's writings on US labour often allude to the Teamsters and democratic reform-movements. See, for instance, Moody 1988; 2007.

to abandon the first principles of revolutionary Marxism and Leninism that they insisted so many had jettisoned. This powerful arsenal of theory and commitment seemed unduly abstract. It did not always prevail over the state-apparatus of the Soviet Union and the long reach of the Communist International and its many advocates. Trotskyists were often dismissed as 'sectarian' hair-splitters, written off as ultra-left 'crackpots' whose criticisms could be ignored because there were more powerful left-wing forces capable of exercising an actual, albeit often compromised, impact in trade-union circles, be they labour advocates within federal or state-administrations, Socialist Party figures, or Soviet-aligned Communists. Written off as insignificant interlopers in working-class circles and social movements, Trotskyists were usually typecast as other-worldly, depicted as being too far removed from the supposed 'realities' of working life to intervene effectively in trade-union struggles and influence the activities and consciousness of American workers. All of this would lead one to believe that hard-nosed teamsters and wild-eyed Trotskyists would be a proverbial expression of the twain that will never meet. Historically, this was most emphatically not the case.

For teamsters and Trotskyists did dance in 1934. In Minneapolis, truckers and Left Oppositionists were locked in the embrace of a waltz that saw them gracefully circle and adroitly outmanoeuvre class-enemies among the employers, the police, and local authorities. It wasn't always slow-dancing. There were violent encounters, and there were those who saw in every reel a revolution in the making. In the end, an impressive mobilisation of truckers' strikes led by American Trotskyists established militant unionism in a city that was infamous as a bastion of the open shop. Far more than merely sectional struggles of one particular industry, the truckers' strikes of 1934 were explosive working-class initiatives that galvanised the entire spectrum of Minneapolis labour – skilled and unskilled, unemployed and waged, craft-unionist and unorganised, male and female – and polarised the city in opposing class-camps. As a result of this trio of workplace-actions in 1934, working conditions in the trucking industry improved, wage-levels were raised, and trade-union recognition was secured. This decisive class-struggle demonstrated to workers throughout the United States that unorganised labour was capable of making significant breakthroughs, and that trade-unionism could be used as a platform to address the interests of the entire working class. The Minneapolis events, along with similar Left-led struggles in 1934 – by auto-parts workers in Toledo and longshoremen in San Francisco – thus helped show the way towards the upsurge of mass-production workers, which by 1937 had signalled the arrival of a new centre of the American labour-movement, the Congress of Industrial Organizations. From this base-line of accomplishment, Trotskyists taught Jimmy Hoffa how to organise inter-state truckers, although they would later find the uses to which Hoffa put the skills that he learned from his Minneapolis mentors quite repugnant.[2]

How Trotskyists and previously unorganised teamsters came together in Minneapolis is the story of this book. It gives the lie to the conventional wisdom that Trotskyists were ineffectual in the real world of politics and labour-struggle because they could only relate to workers as abstract agents of revolutionary transformation. On the contrary, the coming together of teamsters and Trotskyists in Minneapolis in 1934 provides a concrete case of just what can be accomplished by workers guided by those who have a revolutionary perspective, even if the outcome achieved was never conceived as revolutionary. What was accomplished in this fusion of truckers and an organised group generally and rightly perceived to hold views far to the left of mainstream civil society is an inspiring indication of how determination, resilience, preparation, and inclusive solidarity can overcome seemingly unassailable forces of reaction. It reminds us that capital and its supporters in the state are not all-powerful, but can, indeed, be effectively challenged.

What occurred in Minneapolis in 1934 can not be reproduced in our own, quite different times. Neither, however, was it exactly *sui generis*. No historical event is entirely unique, or inevitable. In the general sense, it is important to believe that achievements like Minneapolis can, indeed, happen again, even if how such occurrences unfold will necessarily proceed on the basis of different realities and imaginative appreciations of *both* historical continuities *and* decidedly different circumstances, producing outcomes never entirely the same but advancing the cause of humanity in important and similar ways. Doing this, however, demands writing *finis* to what Mike Davis has referred to as an affliction of Western post-Marxists, lazy ruminations 'on whether or not "proletarian agency" is now obsolete'.[3] If we can get past this kind of *refusal* even to countenance the possibility of *revolutionary teamsters*, we might well be able to see the Minneapolis victories in 1934 as a reminder of how important resolute fortitude, principled leadership, and a well thought-out sense of tactics and strategy will always be in the struggle against capitalist inequality. This was what was developed over the course of the momentous Minneapolis working-class battles that rallied thousands to the cause of labour in the depths of the Great Depression, and this is a part of what will be required if future, necessary struggles are to be waged and won.

---

2. For brief comment on the Minneapolis events of 1934 and their significance, see Cochran 1977, p. 88; Friedman 1982, pp. 14, 18, 147, 156, 164, 263; Leiter 1957, pp. 41–2; Hoffa and Fraley 1975, pp. 59–62; Brill 1978, pp. 361–5; Franco and Hammer 1987, p. 51; Friedman and Schwarz 1989, pp. 76, 188; Sloane 1993, pp. 18–31.

3. Davis 2011, pp. 14–15.

Trotskyism in the United States is associated with two remarkable figures, both of whom would play specific roles in Minneapolis during 1934. James P. Cannon, a second-generation Irish-American revolutionary hailing from Rosedale, Kansas, whose Left labours included years as an itinerant agitator in the Industrial Workers of the World and a decade-long attempt to build a Leninist Communist Party in the United States, was American Trotskyism's founding figure. His public identification with Trotskyism, also known as the International Left Opposition, earned him expulsion from the Workers' (Communist) Party late in 1928. Max Shachtman, roughly ten years Cannon's junior, could not have been more different than the man who had been his revolutionary mentor throughout the 1920s. A Jewish New Yorker, Shachtman was comfortable with European cultures and languages, and was the pre-eminent translator of Trotsky's writings as he and Cannon combined to bring the critique of Stalinist degeneration into the United States workers' movement in the late 1920s and early 1930s.[4]

As indicated in an appendix at the end of this volume, which introduces the complicated history of American Trotskyism in the years 1928–33 to readers who require more background to contextualise the Minneapolis events of 1934, Cannon and Shachtman had a factional falling out as they played leading roles in founding the first Trotskyist organisation in the United States, the Communist League of America (Opposition), also known as the CLA, the League, or the Left Opposition. In this division, Cannon had as allies the Minneapolis Trotskyists, who will be featured prominently in the pages that follow: Vincent Raymond (V.R./Vince/Ray) Dunne; his two brothers, Miles and Grant; Carl Skoglund; and others. Ironically, Cannon's best friend and closest political ally in the endless factional jockeying within the Workers' (Communist) Party in the United States over the course of the 1920s was William F. 'Bill' Dunne, the oldest of the Dunne brothers. But Bill refused to follow his brothers and Jim Cannon into the trenches of Trotskyism, and in 1934 was assigned the party-task of attacking his former comrade and his younger siblings, caricaturing the militant Left Opposition leadership of the truckers' strikes as little more than a capitulation, a concessionary sell-out. Rank-and file teamsters, whose militancy became legendary in this period, thought otherwise. Some, like future Trotskyists Farrell Dobbs, Shaun (Jack) Maloney, and Harry DeBoer, would prove lifelong recruits to the ideas of the Left Opposition, won over to revolutionary politics as the teamsters' strikes of 1934 unfolded.

There will be those who will ask why another book on the Minneapolis strikes should be added to our already sagging shelves of writings on class-struggle in the 1930s in general, and on Trotskyism and the 1934 truckers' insurgency in

---

4. See Palmer 2007; Drucker 1994.

particular. At least three major relevant studies already exist: a contemporary journalistic account of striking insight, Charles Rumford Walker's *American City: A Rank-and-File History* (published in 1937); the detailed and largely reliable account of one of the leading actors in the strikes, Farrell Dobbs's *Teamster Rebellion* (from 1972); and, finally, Philip A. Korth's well-researched academic overview, enriched by oral history, *The Minneapolis Teamsters Strike of 1934* (which appeared in 1995).[5]

I have drawn on all three studies heavily, and I try to bring into my account many of the strengths of these previous volumes. But what follows also shifts gears, accelerating the study of Trotskyists and teamsters in ways not done in these other accounts. It interrogates the developments of 1934 on the basis of a more critical and Marxist analytical framework than is explicitly discernable in any of these texts, situating the rise and fall of the revolutionary Trotskyist leadership of the truckers within the framework of the uneven and combined development of class-relations in Minneapolis and the United States. Drawing heavily on Trotskyist sources that Dobbs knew well but did not cite methodically, and placing the revolutionary leadership of the insurgent teamsters at the centre of its narrative, it brings figures like James P. Cannon more to the forefront (he is mentioned on barely a dozen of Dobbs's almost two hundred pages; and hardly at all in Walker or Korth) in its account of the unfolding of the 1934 strikes. This adds significantly to the outline of events provided in Korth's study, which rests on oral recollections of Minneapolis-based participants and, as regards documentary material, scrutinises a far more conventional archive largely unconcerned with the Trotskyist leadership of the class-conflicts in Minneapolis. The sources I have used, and the resulting sensibilities, have important ramifications for our understanding of particular features of the strike, such as the ways in which women were drawn into class-battles that, superficially, might appear to be the sole terrain of men.[6] And while Dobbs's classic account of the truckers' upheavals of 1934 is largely accurate, it does, at times, need to be critically interrogated in terms of the leadership's occasional failures, especially with respect to its early inability to mount a revolutionary critique of Farmer-Laborism, which may have fed into a tendency to rely unduly on this political tendency's head spokesman, Governor Floyd B. Olson. There is, as well, the necessity to scrutinise the ways in which the successes of the Minneapolis General Drivers' Union may have conditioned practices on the part of its Trotskyist leadership that broke

---

5. Walker 1937; Dobbs 1972; Korth 1995.
6. What follows can thus be compared usefully with Faue 1991, for while I agree that the labour-movement in this period was gendered, I do not think the history of class-relations presents as stark a separation as that argued for in Faue's study, which also manages to understate the significance of the 1934 strikes to a startling degree.

from the theoretical and political insights that those very victories nurtured, and that came to be expressed in the founding document of the Fourth International – led by Leon Trotsky – namely *The Death Agony of Capitalism and the Tasks of the Fourth International.*[7]

It is axiomatic that any history is written in the context of specific times, but this is especially true of this account of the Minneapolis truckers' mobilisation of 1934. I have tried to produce a narrative of this epic class-struggle in ways that will animate contemporary readers. Like an unpublished study of the Minneapolis labour-movement in the 1930s,[8] moreover, I have followed the local newspapers closely in order to capture the considerable drama of day-to-day strike-events. This attention to detail, as well as the resulting appreciation of the tactical and strategic sophistication of the strike-leadership, means that this overview contains both a more elaborated outline of developments and a more sustained interpretation of specificities than is present in some previous writings, where the significance of the teamster-organising drive is given unduly short shrift.[9]

All of this means that, in comparison with the three best books on Minneapolis teamsters and their 1934 strikes, what follows stakes out often complementary, but nonetheless different, ground. It stands apart from an account written just after the events themselves, but before the Trotskyist leadership had been forced into retreat in the 1940s (that by Walker); it inevitably highlights the significance of the 1934 events in ways that are, perhaps, more pointed than does a summation of the struggle put together before the long downturn of the workers' movement beginning in the mid-1970s, striking a note of political urgency somewhat absent in this earlier treatment (Dobbs); and it necessarily has a tone and analytical trajectory dissimilar to that of an academic study of the 1990s seeking largely to recover the lost voices of an epic confrontation (Korth). As this book tries to emphasise, Minneapolis in 1934 matters because, in 2013, it has things to tell us, ways of showing that the tides of history, even in times that seem to flow against change, can be put on a different course.

Finally, implicit in this study is a slightly different understanding of the Minneapolis strikes of 1934 than is perhaps commonplace on the Left. The conventional wisdom is that the Minneapolis teamsters' struggles, along with other

---

7. I make use of two editions of this document throughout this text, both of which contain useful and different supplementary material: Trotsky 1973a, which contains introductory essays by Joseph Hansen and George Novack, as well as a number of relevant 1938 discussions with Trotsky; and International Bolshevik Tendency (ed.) 1998, an edition containing a number of insightful articles and commentaries relating to revolutionary trade-union work in specific periods reaching from the 1920s into the 1970s.

8. Tselos 1971.

9. Myers 1977 covers what is addressed in this book in seven pages (pp. 75–82).

major 1934 class-battles in Toledo and San Francisco, 'exhibited similar characteristics'. Bert Cochran listed what many take to be the common features of these critically important insurgencies:

> (1) They were led or propelled by radicals who maintained their position in the face of sustained barrages from employers, the press, public officials, and conservative AFL leaders. (2) All three were settled only after the opposing sides took each other's measure in physical tests of strength. Strikers, reinforced by masses of outside sympathizers and unemployed engaged in pitched battles with special deputies, strike-breakers, police, and National Guardsmen; bricks, rocks, street-paving and lead pipes against clubs, guns and tear gas. It was industrial war at its most raw. (3) Despite the hysteria against Communists and communism, and the featured charges in the press about conspiracies and plots to overthrown the government, the strikers enjoyed widespread support from the public, including sections of the middle class. The humiliations of the depression years had their effects. The political spectrum had shifted leftwards, and industrial barons and bankers had been knocked off their pedestals. They retained power but had lost some legitimacy. (4) The shooting down of strikers produced outcries for a general strike. The demand was actually pushed through in San Francisco over the opposition of old-line officials and would have been realized in Toledo and Minneapolis as well had the strikes not been settled before new incidents thickened the atmosphere. (5) Unlike so many poorly prepared and conducted NRA strikes, these were victorious. All three initiated the formation of strong labor movements in their locales and industries.[10]

All of this is true enough, up to a point. Yet – as what follows will show – Minneapolis, within this general depiction of these three 1934 mass strikes, actually stood out as distinct. Compared to the leadership of the American Workers' Party in Toledo, where the radical pacifist A.J. Muste figured decisively, and the Stalinist Communist Party's guiding role in the San Francisco general strike, the revolutionary Trotskyists orchestrating the Minneapolis truckers' strikes *were* somewhat different. First and foremost, this contingent developed organically, being more embedded in the industry than were the Musteites in Toledo or even the Communist Party in West-coast longshoring. Second, it proved undeniably more resolute and far-seeing in its preparations for class-battle. Third, there is no question that it was more effective in combating the anti-trade union Red-baiters and ensconced American Federation of Labor bureaucracy. Fourth, it was more adept at negotiating limited, transitional victories in the class-struggle. And, fifth, for all of these reasons, as well as aspects of its history in Minneapolis and its

---

10. Cochran 1977, p. 88. See also Preis 1964, pp. 19–43.

local relation to the trucking industry, the Trotskyist leadership of the teamsters' drive to unionise was more decisively in control of the events of 1934 than were other left-wing currents elsewhere. Precisely because all of this culminated in a highly successful and expansive industrial union-drive in the trucking sector, spearheaded out of Minneapolis and encompassing an eleven-state region, this Trotskyist cohort was also eventually targeted decisively by federal agencies, the conservative International Brotherhood of Teamsters officialdom, and even the Communist Party, as a force to be displaced and defeated. While powerful elements in the local business-community certainly did contribute much to this climate of Red-baiting, the trucking bosses did not defeat the Trotskyists and the teamsters' ranks: that was accomplished by the state and its labour-lieutenants in the trade-union bureaucracy, with a little help from some other less than wholesome quarters.

As I will suggest in concluding this account of teamsters and Trotskyists, the 1940s witnessed an ugly and ultimately successful assault on the leadership of the Minneapolis truckers and the gains they had registered in 1934. This campaign, launched in 1940–1 by the ostensibly labour-friendly, pro-union Democratic Party administration of Franklin Delano Roosevelt, took place as preparations for involvement in war were peaking, and the United States was about to enter into an alliance with the Soviet Union. Yet the attack on the Trotskyist leadership of the Minneapolis teamsters anticipated the anti-communist purges of the unions that were later a prominent feature of Cold War McCarthyism. Ironically, what was secured in Minneapolis had been great, but what was lost was also considerable. This helped to determine that the International Brotherhood of Teamsters, as a union, had a post-WWII history far more chequered, to put it mildly, than either the United Automobile Workers or the International Longshore and Warehouse Union, which owed their origins in Toledo and on the West coast, respectively, to the class-struggles of 1934.

Nonetheless, the teamster union-drive in Minneapolis in 1934 proved to be a breakthrough, not only for labour in the United States, but for the Trotskyist Communist League of America (Opposition). As is evident in what follows, this reciprocal great leap forward would not have happened without the painstaking patience evident in Ray Dunne and Carl Skoglund, who appreciated the protracted nature of labour-organising and class-struggle. As Cannon would later write, 'when our really great opportunity came in the trade union movement, in the great Minneapolis strikes of May and of July–August 1934, we were fully ready to show what we could do'.[11] What the Trotskyists did was remake the class-struggle in an important hub of regional American capitalism, then known as the

---

11. Cannon 1944, p. 138.

Northwest, a contemporary term I use in this study rather than the more current designation of Upper Midwest. This brought the unionism of the International Brotherhood of Teamsters out of its insular and complacent cocoon, with its deeply-entrenched resistance to organising any workers who could not present *bona fide* credentials as members of the 'trucking fraternity'. Trotskyists led one of the first and most successful battles for the kind of industrial unionism that would come to be associated with the vibrant Congress of Industrial Organizations in the later 1930s. The Trotskyist/teamster connection made 'Minneapolis' a rallying cry for combative workers across the United States. This seemingly incongruous alliance, which consolidated the possibility of *revolutionary teamsters*, advanced the agenda of the working class and helped to establish 1934 as one of the unforgettable years of labour-upsurge in America.

Chapter Two
The Mass Strike

In 1934, Louis Adamic put the finishing touches on the second revised edition of his book *Dynamite: The Story of Class Violence in America*, first published in 1931. Three years later, however, Adamic saw the United States differently than he had in 1930–1. Sending the manuscript off to his publisher, Harper and Brothers, Adamic confessed that he had 'rewritten comparatively few pages', but that his study was nonetheless 'almost a new book'. Adamic now sensed, like an old lumberjack in John Steinbeck's *In Dubious Battle*, that the United States was seething with class-anger. 'I feel it in my skin', said the grizzled logger in Steinbeck's novel, 'Ever' place I go, it's like water just before it gets to boilin''. Unlike Steinbeck's fictional old-timer, Adamic predicted more than he anticipated the class-upheavals of 1934, his words less metaphorical and more categorical. 'America will be', he wrote, 'the scene of thousands of bitter disputes between labor and capital and between radical or revolutionary and conservative (in many cases racketeering) labor unions'. Furthermore, Adamic took his stand alongside strikes which he knew would inevitably be ensnared in violence, regarding them as of 'paramount importance' in charting a new path for the development of class-relations in the United States:

> American labor is faced with the *immediate* necessity of breaking up the oligarchy of the A.F. of L., and overhauling that organization to be able to meet the new problems, and of ridding itself of

the NRA-supported company unions, which lately have been formed by the industrialists for the purpose of preventing regular unionization. Both of these aims can be achieved *only* by an avalanche of rank-and-file strikes with full union recognition as their chief objective. Should any considerable number of strikes be successful, recognition of unions would be followed by campaigns, under new leadership, for the organization of unions along industrial lines; which eventually, I hope, will lead to the formation of a new movement, a *real* American labor movement, fresh, radical, and revolutionary, along industrial and political lines – a realistic *American* movement of the producing masses....

Adamic was not far wrong. With the sheer number of strikes per million workers more than tripling figures from the late 1920s and doubling those of 1930–1, 1934 marked a watershed-year in the history of US class-conflict. If rank-and-file militancy was crucial to this escalating pace of industrial battle, the violence of the struggles of 1934 was equally evident. The year opened with the *New York Times* complaining in February that arrests, injuries, and even deaths on picket-lines were all too common. Over the course of 1934, more than fifty workers were killed as a consequence of their involvement in strikes. Federal troops occupying strike-districts, criminal syndicalist charges levelled against workers who would not bend the knee to powerful employers, and legal injunctions of a broad, sweeping character that were aimed at limiting the labour-revolt – all of this only exacerbated fundamental class-tensions. It also called into question the impartiality of the state in general, and the Democratic US President, Franklin Delano Roosevelt, and his early New Deal administration in particular.[1]

James P. Cannon, leader of the Trotskyist Left Opposition in the United States, saw things very much as had Adamic, but with a slight twist. Cannon, like Adamic, sensed in 1933 that class-relations in the United States were about to take a new turn. He, too, understood that nothing less than the very future of the American workers' movement was at stake. Yet Cannon resisted resolutely the tendency, possible to read between the lines of Adamic's text, to downgrade the importance of the entrenched business-union milieu. He parted company with the arguments of the Communist Party in this period, maintaining that new, revolutionary unions had to be established as a challenge to the class-collaboration rampant among leaders of the mainstream labour-movement. This had the effect of removing militant workers from those conservative American

---

1. Adamic 1934, pp. vii, ix, 456–7; Steinbeck 1947, pp. 66–7, quoted in Bernstein 1970, p. 126; Edwards 1981, pp. 134–8; Brody 1972, p. 242; Green 1972; Preis 1964, p. 17, quoting *New York Times*, 11 February 1934; Hugo Oehler, 'The New Deal: A New Stage in the NRA', *The Militant*, 30 December 1933.

Federation of Labor (AFL) unions where, as Cannon rightly suggested, much of the class-battle of 1933–4 was inevitably going to be fought. In September 1933, Cannon wrote in *The Militant* that 'the Left Wing's place is in the A.F. of L. unions'. Acknowledging that different unions and situations presented complex, even contradictory problems, and that there could be no universal formula suitable for all circumstances, Cannon nonetheless insisted that, 'the *main* direction of working-class movement *at the present time* is into the conservative unions'. Therefore, it was mandatory to work within these organizations and to push forward the struggle. Arguing that the ossified AFL leadership would not 'organize the masses of unskilled workers in the basic industries for effective struggle', Cannon called on revolutionaries to be in the forefront of mobilisations that could well culminate in a new and more vibrant trade-union movement:

> The resurgent struggles of the masses, following the inevitable collapse of the Roosevelt program and the disillusionment of the masses who are now captivated by it, will very probably break out of the formal bounds of the A.F. of L. and seek expression in a new trade union movement. But in order to influence such an eventuality the revolutionaries must connect themselves with the live process of the movement at every stage of its development.

Adamant that, in 1933–4, 'The center of gravity...is unquestionably in the conservative mass organizations', Cannon declared unequivocally, 'That is where we must be'.[2]

It was not long before Cannon found himself in the middle of the struggle for Adamic's '*real* American labor movement'. 'The hour has now struck when we are to be put to a new test', he wrote on 29 July 1934 in the pages of the *The Organizer*, the daily strike-bulletin of Minneapolis's Local 574 of the International Brotherhood of Teamsters (IBT). Aware that 'The eyes of the labor movement of the whole country are upon us', and that 'workers everywhere are looking to us', Cannon exhorted striking workers to 'resist every effort to strip us of our fighting strength'. Promising to 'bring the employers to terms which make it possible for us to live like human beings', Cannon helped to lead workers 'imbued not only with an unshakeable conviction in the justice of [their] cause, but with an iron resolve to fight to the last ditch'.[3]

As Cannon wrote these words, longshoremen had already tied up West-coast ports from Bellingham, Washington to San Diego, California. The San Francisco

---

2. James P. Cannon, 'The Left Wing's Place is in A.F. of L. Unions', *The Militant*, 2 September 1933. See, also, for an even more explicit rejection of Stalinism's Third Period advocacy of what Cannon called 'paper unions', as well as a critique of AFL fetishism, 'The Left Wing Needs a New Policy and a New Leadership', *The Militant*, 16 September 1933; Cannon 1944, pp. 142–3. See also Muste 1935a; 1935b; Swabeck 1935.
3. Cannon 1958, pp. 78–80.

general strike, involving 125,000 workers at its peak, was led by the then relatively-unknown Harry Bridges, elected in 1933 to the Executive Committee of Local 38–79 of the International Longshoremen's Association (ILA), affiliated with the American Federation of Labor. Heavily influenced by the Communist Party, and quite possibly a clandestine member, Bridges worked closely with Sam Darcy, the Party's District-Organiser in California. In spite of the Comintern's Third Period insistence that Red-led unions were the proper vehicle for revolutionaries to utilise in advancing the class-struggle, Bridges, with Darcy's backing, found himself at the head of a mass strike, inside an ostensibly 'social-fascist' union, the ILA. Bridges and Darcy were thus forced to rely less on their Communist Party connections in the anti-AFL, Stalinist-led Marine Workers' Industrial Union, and, instead, engage in building solidarity among the mass of maritime workers. The eruption of the San Francisco general strike thus brought to the fore the contradictions inherent in the sectarianism of Third Period Stalinism. Within the mass strike galvanising West-coast labour, as Robert W. Cherny has shown, those Communist Party figures adhering rigorously to the Comintern's position, such as Seattle's Morris Rapaport and Moscow emissary Harrison George, were pitted in a contest against Darcy, who had emerged as a 'premature Popular Frontist' and, implicitly, Bridges. Rapaport and George denounced the failure to bring the Party, as the true leader of all revolutionary forces, to the fore, deploring the apparent California policy of giving 'fascist' (the state) and 'social-fascist' (AFL leaders) forces a pass and focusing the attack on the ship-owners. American Communist Party head Earl Browder prevaricated, waiting on the outcome of the strike, poised to denounce Bridges and Darcy if things went badly downhill, but prepared to restrain his repudiations if it appeared that the general strike might bring the Communist Party some laurels. As we will see, the militancy and solidarity exhibited in the San Francisco general strike did precisely this.

Nonetheless, no clear-cut victory emerged in the bloody contest, although no less a figure than William Z. Foster noted that the trade-union tops in the AFL cut the general-strike call 'to pieces as quickly as possible' resulting in a 'formal loss' for the waterfront-workers. As a serialised account in *The Militant* concluded, Stalinist leadership of the strike was not without both strengths and weaknesses, not to mention some obvious contradictions:

> In connection with the strike we must analyze the role of the Stalinist party. In the ranks of the waterfront workers they were an important factor and were in many ways responsible for the militancy displayed. But their past weighed heavily on them. They were still of the belief that the A.F. of L. was a company union in which there is little use to struggle. It is true they did not take this attitude as far as the I.L.A. was concerned. In that union they instructed their membership to work from within. On the other hand, in the seamen's

organization they made no effort to penetrate but brought to the forefront, in opposition to the A.F. of L. unions, their own Marine Workers Industrial Union. Within the ranks of other A.F. of L. unions, having no organized fraction their influence was small in spite of the militancy of the rank and file. Also in the I.L.A. their refusal to build a genuine left wing composed of all militants and progressive elements narrowed their base considerably. The *Western Worker* in its attacks was equally bitter both towards the bureaucrats and towards elements in the radical movement who would not endorse the policy of the C.P.

Pointing out that this organ of the Party became the official strike-paper on the waterfront, *The Militant* noted that this 'openly put the label of communism on the leadership', sacrificing the interests of the masses and isolating not only those directing the strike, but also those many radical workers committed to an all-out fight against the bosses and their hirelings, be they vigilantes, police, or Guardsmen. Whether it registered in the *Western Worker* becoming the *de facto* voice of the strikers, or the hope that a federation of waterfront-unions would consolidate under the Communist Party's leadership through splits in the ranks of the AFL unions and the breaking off of a sizeable chunk of the ILA membership, it appeared that the Stalinist priority was less a generalised advance of working-class interests than promoting the Party and its particular agenda. This played directly into the hands of the conservative American Federation of Labor bureaucracy, which was able to break the militant backbone of the strike. Yet, as the post-mortem in *The Militant* stressed, "The labor movement in San Francisco in spite of the defeat of the general strike and the 'red' raids is not crushed. The unions are growing, the spirit of struggle is increasing, and the need for industrial unionism as the next step is being hammered home more and more".[4]

---

4. Writing on the San Francisco general strike is voluminous, and includes Eliel 1934; Quin 1949; Kimeldorf 1988; Nelson 1988; Selvin 1996. A useful recent study, on which I draw, is Cherny 2002. In addition, *The Militant* published a number of articles on the San Francisco events, including: 'A.F. of L. Moves Against Pacific Dock Strike', 23 June 1934; 'A.F. L. Misleaders Betray Frisco General Strike', 21 July 1934; 'Lessons of the General Strike in Frisco', 18 August 1934, by Jack Weber; and a four-part serialisation, the last instalment of which is quoted above: Jim Osborn and Dick Ettlinger, 'The History of the Frisco General Strike', 22 September, 29 September, 6 October, 13 October 1934. See, as well, Foster 1939, p. 197. More charitable is Cochran 1977, pp. 61, 88. It is instructive to compare the Stalinist critique of the leadership of the Minneapolis strikes of 1934 with Trotskyist criticism of the leadership of the San Francisco general strike. The latter is far more balanced. Note, for instance, that while the Communist Party critic, William F. Dunne, would denounce his three brothers – Ray, Miles, and Grant – for failing in Minneapolis to call for a general strike to bring down the Farmer-Labor Governor, Floyd B. Olson, no such demand to oust the Governor of California was being made during the San Francisco general strike. Instead, as Cherny notes, Darcy was attempting to have the liberal Lincoln Stephens run on the Party's ticket and, failing in that endeavour, to

The Trotskyist assessment of the 1934 San Francisco general strike, while critical, placed the accent on the upheaval's militant, rank-and-file character. Frank Lovell [Frederick J. Lang] struck this interpretive note in his general study, *Maritime: A Historical Sketch and A Workers' Program*, writing: 'It was a real rank-and-file strike, with the 'leaders' swept along in the flood'.[5] Angered by the injustices of the 'slave-market' 'shape-up', a hiring system that saw crowds of men gather at designated locales like San Francisco's Embarcadero every morning at six o'clock, the stevedores grew increasingly aggrieved by the daily ritual of supplication. The foremen's eyeballing of those huddled in hopeful expectation of a day's pay was a degrading experience that too-often ended in the humiliation of rejection. Even when chosen, a set number of hours of work was not always the end of it: many lead-hands demanded sycophancy if the 'hiring' was to be renewed, while there were also those whose expectations of bribes or other favours were transparent. Flocking to the ILA, dock-labourers pushed reluctant union-officials to abolish the 'shape-up' and replace it with the hiring hall, precipitating a bitter strike on 9 May 1934. The Waterfront Employers' Association was a formidable foe, however, and one dedicated to keeping the ports as free from the taint of unionism as possible. It resisted the workers' demands and imported seventeen hundred strikebreakers, many of them university-students. This unleashed a generalised working-class anger, and many teamsters supported the longshore picket-lines; they refused to move goods from the docks even when successfully unloaded by scab-labour. Soon, the strike had idled unrelated industries in other states. It also affected the spectrum of maritime labour, with ten unions involved. Thousands of sailors, marine firemen, water-tenders, cooks, stewards, and licensed officers linked arms with the striking longshore-

orchestrate CP support for the socialist Upton Sinclair and his End Poverty in California movement. That, too, proved a dead end, and Darcy was then strong-armed into running himself, 'exposing' Sinclair. Anything but an enthusiast, Darcy recalled, 'Swallowing hard I set about executing the decision'. There was, however, no attempt during the general strike to demand the ousting of the sitting Governor, as William F. Dunne demanded in Minneapolis. Indeed, Harrison George wrote to Communist Party head Earl Browder to complain about what he labelled the economism of the general strike, and its lack of politicisation. 'If the role of the State is even mentioned, I have not heard of it' he reported in disgust. See Cherny 2002, pp. 20–2, and for Dunne's sectarianism, discussed below, see Dunne and Childs 1934. Dunne's co-author of the Communist Party pamphlet denouncing the Trotskyist leadership of the Minneapolis 1934 strikes, Morris Childs, was a graduate of Moscow's Lenin School, where he was recruited by the Soviet secret service to spy on his revolutionary classmates. Later he served as a courier for the Russians and, as a leading official in the American Party, became an informant for the Federal Bureau of Investigation in the 1950s. As arguably United States communism's most infamous double agent, Childs was fêted by both antagonists in the Cold War, receiving the Order of the Red Banner in 1975 and the Presidential Medal of Freedom in 1987.

5. Lovell 1945, p. 83.

men. San Francisco became a hotbed of working-class solidarity; pitched battles raged between union-pickets and armed police. ILA officials did their utmost to get their membership back to work, but they often found themselves booed off podiums, their protocols of labour-peace rejected by acclamation in rowdy rank-and-file meetings. The first week of July saw an Independence Day attempt to open the port of San Francisco, seven hundred police armed with tear-gas and sawed-off shotguns accompanying five truckloads of strikebreakers. Strikers and their supporters attacked the cop-escorted convoy, and 25 people were hospitalised. Two days later, the crowds larger and the police more trigger-happy, the melée had a more tragic denouement, leaving 115 injured, and two strikers and an onlooker dead. California's governor declared a 'state of emergency'. Almost two thousand National Guardsmen were soon on the scene, nested atop a barbed-wire enclosed Embarcadero with machine-guns trained on potential hot-spots of confrontation. Armoured cars patrolled the streets adjacent to the docks, where scabs now unloaded freight and moved it to warehouses with impunity.

The violence of the conflict and the utilisation of the armed might of the state to break the resolve of the longshoremen soon backfired. San Francisco's labour-movement rallied to the cause of the seemingly beaten dock-labourers. Roosevelt's appointed mediators in the National Longshore Board dropped the ball time-and-time again, conveying to strikers and sympathisers that they were thoroughly out-of-touch with what was unfolding in San Francisco. The writer Robert Cantwell reported that 'the moves made by the government arbitrators and the employers...have been at once wonderful and meaningless, perfectly organized in detail and childish in purpose.... they have brought on the general strike'. A mass funeral for the workers killed on 5 July 1934 drew thirty thousand workers and their supporters into the streets, in a solemn procession. Within days, more than twenty unions had voted, largely unanimously, to strike. These early advocates of the mass strike were soon joined by others in the conservative Central Labor Council, where delegates from 115 unions met on the inauspicious date of Friday 13 July 1934 to debate the pros and cons of a general strike. By Monday morning, San Francisco was eerily quiet, as trolleys and taxis stopped running, theatres and bars closed their doors, and industrial plants and small shops found that business as usual was impossible. Upwards of one hundred and thirty thousand workers declined to come to work, and window-placards in downtown stores declared 'Closed Till the Boys Win'. The Labor Council, its cautious leadership quaking in fear as the mass strike seemed to be taking on a life of its own, did its utmost to isolate and marginalise the radicals, force crucial sectors of striking workers back to their jobs, and exempt some workers on the grounds they were providing essential services. Labour-officials even organised 'strike-police'. They kept pickets from intimidating those who had been sent back to work. Vigilante-thugs, orchestrated by a Citizens' Committee of five hundred prominent San Franciscans, raided outposts of radical labour, smashing up offices, beating militant workers' leaders, disrupting the mobilisation, and generally sowing seeds of discord. Under a barrage of newspaper-propaganda, in which the strike was assailed as a 'Communist-inspired and led revolt against organized government', and anti-strike tirades by Roosevelt's National Recovery Act chief, General Hugh S. Johnson, the San Francisco uprising was nipped in the bud. Immense pressure was put on the ILA to submit all the issues in the strike, including the demand that a hiring hall replace the hated 'shape-up', to arbitration. It was soon clear that the workers' revolt was flagging. Workers in a variety of unions drifted back to their jobs. William Green, president of the American Federation of Labor, disowned the general strike.

Things dragged on for another ten days, but the longshoremen finally conceded to arbitrate all issues. They were back on the docks, unloading ships, on 27 July 1934. The outcome, after two-and-a-half months of struggle, was something of a draw. The hiring hall was won, but it was to be operated jointly by the ILA and the waterfront-employers through a Labor Relations Committee of the two parties. If the union selected the dispatcher, it was understood that longshoremen were to be placed 'without favouritism or discrimination' based on 'union or non-union membership'. Employers insisted on the right 'to have dispatched to them, when available, the gangs in their opinion best qualified to do their work'. They could also introduce 'labor saving devices' and 'methods of discharging and loading cargo … best suited to the conduct of … business'. Workers, in turn, secured the understanding that six hours constituted a day's work and thirty hours made up a week's work, averaged monthly. Given the intensity of the bouts of labour that constituted the working day on the docks, this was not as much of a victory as it would have seemed in other occupational sectors, but the longshoremen also won concessions on wage-rates and overtime. Moreover, they had successfully drawn tens of thousands of workers into a general strike, sustaining a wave of militancy, and catapulting into national prominence the young Communist-inclined firebrand of the Pacific coast, Harry Bridges. Combative and unyielding, West-coast longshoremen would soon gain a reputation as volatile vectors of class-struggle, their trade a nursery of radical thought and militant direct-action tactics.[6]

---

6. The above paragraphs draw on many sources, among them: Robert Cantwell, 'San Francisco: Act One', *New Republic*, 25 July 1934; 'Government by Strike', *Business Week* (21 July 1934), pp. 7–8; Bernstein 1970, pp. 259–98; Brecher 1974, pp. 189–200; Preis 1964, pp. 31–3; Goldberg 1958, pp. 130–62; Schwartz 1986, pp. 81–114; Larrowe 1956; 1972; Quin 1949; Kimeldorf 1988; Nelson 1988.

Toledo, Ohio, seemed worlds away from San Francisco's Embarcadero. A glass and auto-parts centre, with a population of roughly 275,000, Toledo was less than half the size of the more cosmopolitan West-coast port. Its concentration of independent auto-parts suppliers depended on sales to the large Michigan firms that dominated car-production in the United States, especially Chrysler. The Toledo formula for success was simple: a low-wage, non-union workforce turned out selected vehicle-components more cheaply than could the larger automobile-plants. Electric Auto-Lite, which produced lighting, ignition, and starting systems, dominated the Ohio auto-parts supply-sector. Auto-Lite had been founded by Clem Miniger, a hated business-huckster and financier with an estimated fortune of over eighty million dollars. When the economic collapse of 1929 decimated the Toledo economy, driving automobile-producer Willys-Overland into bankruptcy and throwing its twenty-eight thousand strong workforce into unemployment, Miniger's Ohio Bond and Security Bank closed its doors. Thousands of depositors were left in the lurch. Antagonism to the conspicuously rich escalated as Toledo became a centre for the pugnacious unemployed-movement. Mobilising the jobless would soon intersect, in 1934, with the struggle for trade-union rights and protections among those who managed to hang on to employment. As Auto-Lite paid less than National Recovery Administration wage-minimums, ostensibly because of a 'misinterpretation' of the government-agency's codes, working-class resentment reached fever-pitch. Disgruntled workers paraded with strike-placards reading, 'We don't need Dillinger – We have Miniger', while the Auto-Lite magnate hired a private police-force to guard his home.[7]

The organization of the Toledo unemployed was the work of the American Workers' Party (AWP), led by A.J. Muste, a Christian minister with a strong record of left-wing activism. Having opposed the First World-War, he had been drawn into the post-war strike-upheavals and political ferment of 1919, his Christianity increasingly informed by Marxism. In the 1920s, Muste served as the Director of the Brookwood Labor College, a training center for labour-activists that was part-funded by American Federation of Labor unions. Formed in 1933, the AWP grew organically out of the Conference for Progressive Labor Action (CPLA). As left-leaning intellectuals sympathetic to labour and affiliated with Brookwood and the CPLA came increasingly to promote paths of intervention in the unions that seemingly steered a course between 'procapitalist labor bureaucrats and communists', Muste and those within his progressive circle formed the AWP, a heterogeneous body with a politics to match. It harboured a longstanding and leading layer of old-style labour-educators and activists, whose approach was invariably

---

7. See Bernstein 1970, pp. 218–19; Preis 1964, pp. 19–20.

compromised by their classically centrist orientation. As Cannon argued forcefully, as early as 1931, the progressives could not, in actuality, be a third force
between communism and capitalism: their political trajectory always tended
to follow the lead of already-insurgent workers, perhaps even prodding them
to further militancy, only, at the decisive hour, to press the rising masses back
into the containments of convention.[8] This had been made abundantly clear to
Cannon, Arne Swabeck, Max Shachtman, Hugo Oehler, and other Trotskyists in
the Illinois coal-fields in the early 1930s, where Muste, Tom Tippett, and a corps
of Brookwood Labor College instructors charted a particular course of alliance
with elements in the Progressive Miners of America that tended to thwart the
realisation of a class-struggle leadership.[9] Yet the AWP was itself a product of
the working-class ferment of 1933–4. Rank-and-file militants in the unions and
the unemployed-movement where the Musteites had been campaigning were
both influencing the politics of the old CPLA types as well as pushing the new
party to be more resolute in its stands against capitalism. The result was that as it
was born the AWP was being pressured in the direction of revolutionary politics.
Muste and those around him were propelled to the left.[10]

Between 1929–34, then, conditions were changing rapidly. This necessitated
a shifting of tactical gears with respect to how the Left Opposition related to
figures such as Muste, and organisations like the AWP that showed signs of
containing within their midst both 'proletarian revolutionists' and 'reactionary
scoundrels and fakers'. When Cannon and the Communist League of America
(CLA) were functioning as an external opposition to the Communist Party, it was
not possible to enter into blocs with Muste's progressives against the Party. But
as the CLA discarded its external-opposition stand, and sought to build a new
party and a new international, Trotskyists had more leeway in terms of who they
could orient towards and even, in certain circumstances, align with. Stalinist
Third Period sectarianism isolated the Communist Party more and more from an
increasingly radicalising reformist milieu, in which Muste and his followers were

---

8. Cannon's position on the CPLA is outlined in a number of articles in *The Militant*, reprinted in Stanton (ed.) 1981, especially 'The Communists and the "Progressives"',
pp. 130–4; 'Limits of the United Front', pp. 337–41; and 'The Struggle Against Left Reformism', pp. 348–9.

9. Much of the critique of the Musteites in the Progressive Miners of America was
generated by Hugo Oehler, a trusted Cannon field-operative working among the miners
in the early 1930s. For a brief published statement, see Hugo Oehler, 'Prospects of Development of the Progressive Miners', *The Militant*, 13 May 1933. For internal discussion of
the Musteite influence in the PMA, inseparable from Left Opposition criticism of CLA
member and PMA leader Gerry Allard, see National Executive Committee, CLA, Minutes,
8 September 1932 and 29 September 1932, Box 32, File 8; 12 January 1933, Box 32, File 9,
George Breitman Papers, Tamiment Library, Bobst Library, New York University.

10. Cannon 1944, pp. 112, 140, 169–71. See also the comments of Ted Grant in Evans
(ed.) 1976, pp. 93–6.

leading elements. Cannon and his comrades thus necessarily adapted to the new contours of the political landscape. As the CLA leader wrote, the progressives in Muste's milieu were 'weather cocks. The decisive factor is the pressure of the masses. From this it follows that the most important aspect of the united front tactic is not 'negotiations' [with the progressive reformists] but widespread and intelligently-conducted agitation'.[11]

However small their numbers, the American Workers' Party had a significant impact on the wave of union-drives that swept through Toledo's auto-parts plants in the summer of 1933 and continued into 1934. Leading the charge was the AFL's Federal Labor Union 18384. A number of plants were struck, but the walkouts ended with minor concessions and vague assurances that negotiations would continue. The companies were buying time; the workers grew increasingly disenchanted. By March 1934, an industry-wide strike-threat had necessitated the intervention of Roosevelt, whose mediations led to the establishment of the Automobile Labor Board under Columbia University economist and National Recovery Administration apparatchik Leo Wolman. At Auto-Lite, the employer took a particularly hard line against unionisation, ordering the AFL business-agent off the premises and, according to Local 18384, discriminating against its members. In mid-April 1934, Auto-Lite workers walked out for the second time in less than two months. The strike was anything but a resounding expression of solidarity: more than half the employees remained at their jobs and the plant, as well as others in the auto-parts sector, was kept open. Strikebreakers were hired, supplementing the core working group that refused to join the labour stoppage.

It was at this point that the AWP entered the picture. Louis Budenz, Executive Secretary of the Party and Muste's second-in-command, was directing the strike-strategy of Local 18384 by the end of April 1934. The Lucas County Unemployed League, led by the young Musteites Ted Selander and Sam Pollack, coordinated the increasingly close relations of Toledo's jobless masses and the striking auto-parts workers. Young AWP recruits and future Cannonists like Art Preis threw themselves into the battle. Mass picketing of strikers and Unemployed League members blocked scabs and supplies from entering the Auto-Lite factory. When injunctions prohibited such militant activity, Selander and Pollack defied the judicial order, were repeatedly arrested, and filled the courtroom with their supporters. The noisy throng forced the judge to back off, issue a 'no decision', and release the arrested rabble-rousers. Selander, Pollack,

11. See Cannon et al 2002, pp. 63–6, 430–1, 585, 590, 604; James P. Cannon, 'The Communists and the Progressives', *The Militant*, 1 April 1931; Arne Swabeck, 'Results of the Illinois Miners' Revolt', *The Militant*, 15 May 1931; Cannon 1944, pp. 170–1; Hentoff 1963, pp. 56–90; Budenz 1947, pp. 103–13; Rayback 1966, p. 318.

and their supporters, hundreds-strong, returned immediately to picket-duty, the young AWPers resuming their leadership of the unemployed, whose support for the strikers bewildered White House correspondents. One newsman wrote that it was common to see the unemployed 'appear on the streets, fight police, and raise hell in general'. In Toledo, however, the unemployed charted a new path: 'they appeared on the picket lines to help striking employees win a strike, though you would expect their interest would lie the other way – that is, in going in and getting the jobs the other men had laid down'. Under militant class-struggle leadership, Toledo politics was making for unprecedented, and remarkably effective, alliances. Budenz continued the crusade to reinstate 'peaceful mass picketing' and the 'smashing of the injunction'. Auto-Lite production continued as armed company-guards and special deputies patrolled the perimeter of the plant and stockpiled weapons inside what was quickly becoming a militarised compound.

Crowds surrounding the Auto-Lite plant soon swelled to six thousand, growing daily. On 23 May 1934, Budenz was arrested at the mass picket and hauled off to jail. With ten thousand picketing workers and their allies howling derision, a deputy beat an elderly strike-supporter 'unmercifully'. A six-day-long 'Battle of Toledo' erupted. Fighting broke out in the mid-afternoon and continued until midnight. Angry workers laid siege to the factory; fifteen hundred strikebreakers were imprisoned. The scene was one of almost medieval tumult: windows were smashed with stones and bricks, many of them launched from giant slingshots improvised from rubber inner-tubes; fire-hoses were used by those trapped inside the plant to drive the angry workers back. When every window in the factory had been smashed, one striker shouted: 'Now you have your open shop'. Cars in the plant's parking lot were overturned, doused with petrol, and torched. Guards and scabs barricaded doors and beat back invading platoons of strikers and their unemployed allies, who nonetheless managed to fight their way into the Auto-Lite premises three times to engage in combat. From the roof, company-guards showered the surging crowd with tear-gas canisters; when the supply of corporate bombs ran low, the stock was replenished by a Cleveland munitions-firm.

The next day, nine hundred Ohio National Guardsmen arrived on the scene. While they were able to evacuate many of the fifteen hundred strikebreakers trapped inside the Auto-Lite building (they looked a 'sorry sight', according to local press-reports), their presence merely inflamed an already explosive atmosphere. Women jeered 'the landing of the Marines', while soap-boxers, many of them veterans sporting First World-War medals, offered impromptu lectures on how the troops were breaking the strike. This was the calm. Battle-storms punctuated the talk of unions and what honourable soldiers should and should not be doing. The strikers' ranks faced a hail of Guardsmen bullets, which left two dead. 25 were wounded, including ten troopers who required medical treatment. As darkness enveloped the Auto-Lite plant, and martial law was imposed in the immediate vicinity of the factory, roving bands of workers clashed with the National Guard, driving their armed antagonists back into the refuge of the workplace, which had suffered some $150,000 in physical damage. As four additional companies of National Guardsmen were deployed, the 'Battle of Toledo' became the largest display of military power in the peacetime history of the state of Ohio. Talk of a general strike spread among Toledo's trade-unionists, encouraged by the Communist Party. The next days saw more skirmishes, including a weekend-clash on 26 May 1934, but unemployed-leaders like Selander had been swept up in a National Guard dragnet, held incommunicado. The *New Republic* surveyed the carnage and concluded that for all of the Roosevelt administration's promises of labour rights, 'The sorry American scene in Toledo finds its setting in broken promises of the New Deal'.

It was not until 31 May 1934 that some quiet was restored. Muste, ill-at-ease with the violent course the Auto-Lite struggle was taking, apparently played a role in engineering class-peace, caucusing with local authorities to advocate a compromise, whereby the company would keep the factory closed, the National Guard would withdraw, and the AFL union would take responsibility for ensuring that picket-lines remained peaceful. By this time, 85 of the 103 AFL unions affiliated with Toledo's Central Labor Union had voted in favour of a general strike. There was little appetite for this, however, among conservative trade-union officials. At a monster rally of forty thousand at the Lucas County Courthouse Square on 1 June 1934, these labour-leaders remained mute on the threatened mass strike, instead opting to assure the militant gathering that a victory had been achieved and Roosevelt would come to the aid of the Auto-Lite strikers. With the promise of concessions, the militancy of the strikers and their supporters in the AWP and the Unemployed League appeared to have achieved a breakthrough in Toledo. The final settlement at Auto-Lite won Local 18384 a modest wage-increase and, more importantly, secured the AFL union exclusive bargaining rights in the struck plant and in other factories involved in the six-week confrontation. To be sure, the back-to-work conditions insisted that the Auto-Lite plant's reopening would proceed through a hierarchical rehiring process: pre-strike employees who worked during the stoppage were to be hired first, strikers second, and scabs third. Muste and Budenz opposed this obvious blow to the union, and found themselves impolitely dismissed by an American Federation of Labor officialdom that now clamped down on control of the strike and its settlement. The AWP and the Unemployed Leagues, which had shored up the Auto-Lite strike when it was obviously flagging, were deemed expendable as the AFL local's membership secured its right to jobs, even though this meant working alongside blacklegs and turncoats. Something of the direct-action tactics of the AWP rubbed off on the workers, however. When it appeared that Auto-Lite was dragging its heels in rehiring strikers, crowds amassed outside the factory-gates. Their intimidating presence, and recollection of the damage that could be inflicted on the company, forced the hand of management, which conceded jobs to all of the strikers immediately. Big winners from this titanic clash of labour and capital were 275 members of the International Brotherhood of Electrical Workers at Toledo Edison, who piggybacked off the Auto-Lite workers' militancy to gain a 22 percent wage-hike and union-recognition. These victories wrote *finis* to any mobilisation for a general strike, but they paved the way for ongoing union-victories in the automobile-industry. Before the year was out, 19 more auto-parts plants in Toledo would fall to union-organisers. A General Motors plant was rocked with the first successful strike in the history of this corporate giant, the opening blow in what proved to be a long and taxing effort to establish trade-unionism in the open-shop bastions of the automobile-industry.[12]

The mass strike was thus a historical phenomenon, emerging out of the particular social conditions of the US working class in 1934. In the words of one report in the *New Republic*, resort to such mobilisations grew out of the belief that 'It is . . . now or never labor must establish its rights; it must be demonstrated that without the workers' consent no activity can be carried on; it is believed that those who do not "hang together will hang separately"'. The mass strike, and its highest expression, the general strike, thus revealed the capacity of American labour in this period to mobilise in combative ways, but it also reflected the importance of Left leaderships embedded in the unions but quite different to the ensconced bureaucracies that so often directed rank-and-file actions within mainstream organisations. For this reason, the response of many business-publications to the 1934 general-strike movement was one of exaggeration and political scaremongering. In a July 1934 editorial, 'General Strike', *Business Week* deplored the San Francisco 'outrage' as little more than 'insurrection', 'in one word, revolution'. The voice of capital was shrill in its denunciation of 'Government by Strike', insisting that 'a general strike cannot win. If it is complete, the public smashes it; if it isn't complete, it is futile'. Organised labour, *Business Week* pontificated, must surely learn 'the tragic peril of following radical leadership'. What this dismissive condemnation missed was the extent to which the mass strikes of this era were often waged within mainstream AFL unions by

---

12. The above paragraphs draw on 'Labor: Bricks, Bats & Blood', *Time*, 4 June 1934; an oral-history collection, Korth and Beegle (eds.) 1988; 'What is Behind Toledo', *New Republic*, 6 June 1934; 'The General Strike', *New Republic*, 25 July 1934; Rosenzweig 1975; Robinson 1981, pp. 52–4; Muste 1967a; 1967b; 1935b; Bernstein 1970, pp. 205–29; Brecher 1974, pp. 200–2; Preis 1964, pp. 19–24; Levinson 1956, pp. 66–7.

disgruntled, non-revolutionary workers, who then discovered that allies, agitators, and advisers from a variety of revolutionary organisations were ready to back their cause. The torch of militancy in 1934 was lit by particular kinds of workers, usually those who had little connection with and even less faith in a complacent layer of trade-union functionaries loyal to traditions of privileged and respectable labour. Once the spark of conflict was ignited, Communists, Musteites, and Trotskyists might come to play critically important roles, and their influence registered in important, if limited, victories. The origins of the mass strike, nonetheless, lay in the particular conditions long experienced by sections of the working class that had been ill-served by the conservative hierarchy of unionism in the United States. Rather than the old crafts – building tradesmen, members of the railway-brotherhoods, and other skilled workers – leading the way, the 1934 upheavals featured longshoremen and coal-heavers, truckers, textile-mill operatives, and machine-tenders.[13]

The post-Labor Day 1934 walkout of hundreds of thousands of cotton, fabric, silk, and wool-workers closed mills in Alabama, Georgia, North and South Carolina, Tennessee, Virginia, Pennsylvania, Massachusetts, New Jersey, Maine, Rhode Island, New Hampshire, and Connecticut. These striking wage-earners made an emphatic point: this explosion of class-resentment was a new uprising of workers no longer willing to accept industrial disenfranchisement. Punctuated by riots, bombings, shootings, and employer-intransigence, as well as militant and roving picket-lines known as 'flying squadrons', the general strike in the textile-industry ended badly. The strikers were defeated, and often found themselves and their families evicted from company-housing. Hundreds of mills closed the factory-gates to those who had dared to march defiantly out of them weeks before; in spite of Roosevelt's pleas, strikers were blacklisted. Starvation stalked many mill-towns. Novelist Martha Gellhorn wrote from North Carolina at the end of November 1934, claiming that in the aftermath of the mass strike, workers lived 'in terror of being penalized for joining unions'. According to her, the bosses were 'in a state of mingled rage and fear against this imported

---

13. For background on the craft/operative differentiation, see Montgomery 1987. For a discussion of the upheaval in the American Federation of Labor in the early-to-mid 1930s that outlines both the call within the AFL to organise the unorganised as well as the general failure of this initiative to achieve concrete advances, see Levinson 1956, especially pp. 49–78. Levinson concludes that, 'The A.F. of L. campaign had been a complete failure, except in the Toledo sector, where the rank and file ignored both the Wolman board and the A.F. of L., struck against the Electric Auto-Lite Company, refused to permit the smashing of their ranks by injunction and the militia, and finally won a 5-per-cent wage increase, a six months' contract, and the death of a company union' (p. 64) For the *Business Week* commentary, see 'Government by Strike' and 'General Strike' (21 July 1934), pp. 7–8 and 36.

monstrosity: organized labor'.[14] Not every mass strike, then, ended in working-class victory. The mass walkout of textile-workers in 1934 suggested, contrary to the ideological posturing of *Business Week*, that where involvement of revolutionary agitators affiliated with Left organisations was weakest, so too were the chances of specific successes lessened.[15] But regardless of the outcome, the general strike did declare, loudly and proudly, a new mood of labour-insurgency. As Clifford Odets's 1937 proletarian play, staged by the Group Theatre in New York, emphatically declared, many workers discovered in this period that the only answer to their worsening conditions was 'STRIKE, STRIKE, STRIKE!!!' This rallying cry traversed the land in 1934.[16]

As Rosa Luxemburg had noted in 1906, 'If anyone were to undertake to make the mass strike generally as a form of proletarian action and object of methodical agitation, and to go house-to-house canvassing with this "idea" in order to gradually win the working class to it, it would be as idle and profitless and absurd an occupation as it would be to seek to make the idea of the revolution or of the fight at the barricades the object of a special agitation'. No mere 'isolated act', such strikes were not conjured up as a calculated move in the class-struggle, 'called at will'. Rather, they emerged out of the increasing attractiveness, to many workers, of class-struggle, militancy being cultivated by decades of discord that, in 1934, found expression 'in the consciousness of the mass of proletarians', often endorsed and supported by small but influential groups of revolutionaries. As the Communist International had learned since the Le Havre mass strike of 1922, however, the general strike was neither an automatic outcome of the spontaneous eruption of class-grievance, nor was it easily mobilised. The painful experience of failed general strikes meant that the mistakes of revolutionary trade-unionists, syndicalists, and communist and socialist parties were exposed alongside the treacherous misleadership of a conciliatory layer of labour-bureaucrats. This instilled in revolutionary leaders like Leon Trotsky and James P. Cannon the need 'to pay the utmost attention to the problems of mass action'. It was incumbent upon all revolutionaries, wrote Trotsky, to 'prepare down to the last detail the very possibility of mass action by means of large-scale and intense agitation; and to fit the slogans to the readiness and the ability of the masses to act'. For his part, Cannon, schooled in the Industrial Workers of the World's militant commitment to the mass strike, also came to appreciate the dualism of this kind of upheaval, which could be, in revolutionary circumstances, a possible opening volley in a far-reaching class-war. More likely, nonetheless, was that in non-revolutionary circumstances, the mass strike might take on a more limited

---

14. Bernstein 1970, pp. 298–317; Brecher 1974, pp. 209–19; Levinson 1956, pp. 73–6.
15. Cannon 1985; Muste 1967b.
16. Odets 1937, pp. 45–6; Brecher 1974, pp. 209–19.

purpose, one in which the victories would be transitional rather than transformative. Cannon thus understood that

> the general strike is not to be played with carelessly or fired into the air to see what will happen. It must be well organized and prepared. Its limitations must be understood and it must aim at definite, limited objectives. Or, if the aim is really to challenge the government, the general strike cannot be confined to one locality and there must be the conscious aim to supplement the strike with an armed struggle.

As we will see, this sober judgement about what different kinds of general strikes could accomplish was a good part of what led to the success of Trotskyists in Minneapolis in 1934.[17]

Among the literati of the early-to-mid 1930s, picketing, strike mobilisations, and the violence of class-struggle were now important staples of a writer's representational arsenal. This was particularly evident in Charles Rumford Walker's 1937 *American City: A Rank-and-File History* and Meridel Le Sueur's 1934 short story, 'What Happens in a Strike'. Walker sought to portray 'the dynamics of social change' that were fermenting below the surface of America's archetypal urban centres, while Le Sueur addressed 'the drama forming from deep instinctive and unified forces of real and terrible passion'. Both writers drew their inspiration from an actual time and place, focusing on the labour-capital divide running through Minneapolis, Minnesota. In 'Notes for Life-Story of a Truck-Driver', assembled for his book, Walker referred to 'the complex machinery of class warfare', in which members of the General Drivers' Union were sergeants in a thousands-strong 'strike army'. This regiment fought what Walker judged 'two of the bloodiest and most ingeniously ruthless strikes in American labor history'. Le Sueur's notebooks from 1934–5 convey her sense of artistic imperative, the necessity of capturing in a 'huge novel' the drama of these class–conflicts and the 'suffering' associated with this 'great awkward surging ... social movement':

> There is a strike going on in Minneapolis. I feel anxious ... eager to see what is happening ... I feel it is a real emergent world ... Emergent ... coming from the past ... into the future. It is the point of emerging violence ... it is the point of departure of growth.

Le Sueur looked at what was happening in 1934, and knew that 'you damn yourself forever not getting into it'. She feared being 'left out', withdrawing and not really seeing anything, so that her writing would be little more than a 'hoax'.

---

17. See Luxemburg 1971, pp. 17, 51, 92; Trotsky 1977, pp. 278–80; Cannon 1934a. See, for a range of commentary: Crook 1931; Goodstein 1984; and on the significant events in Le Havre, Barzman 1997.

As a writer, Le Sueur felt tested by class-struggle: 'I am determined to get IN to have an experience with it, in it and not just look at it'.[18]

For tens of thousands of workers, 1934's 'bitter, explosive episodes of...labor struggle' were, indeed, a decisive turning point. As Arthur Schlesinger, Jr. noted many years ago, the truckers' strikes in Minneapolis in 1934 represented, alongside the advances registered in Toledo and San Francisco, small victories in a working-class upheaval that was more often than not characterised by defeat. They helped inaugurate a transformation of the US labour-movement. In Saul Alinsky's words, these tumultuous battles – crucial events in the making of Adamic's realistic movement of the American producing classes – constituted 'the revolutionary handwriting on the walls of American industry'. It was this climate of mass strikes and class-polarisation that convinced John L. Lewis to ride the cresting conflicts of 1934 into the later 1930s creation of the mass-production unionism known as the Congress of Industrial Organizations. 'Lewis watched the unrest and flareups of violence through the summer of 1934' Alinsky claimed, and he could not help but notice that, 'Blood ran in Minneapolis'. In the summer of 1934, the Communist League of America found itself at the centre of this Minneapolis upheaval, in which Trotskyists 'led a general strike of truck drivers into a virtual civil war'.[19]

---

18. Walker 1937; Le Sueur 1934; 1945, pp. 289–97; Charles Rumford Walker, 'Notes for Life-Story of a Truck-Driver', Box 1, File 'American City: Preliminary Prospectus and General Notes', Charles R. Walker Papers, Minnesota Historical Society, St. Paul, Minnesota (hereafter CRW Papers, MNHS); Meridel Le Sueur, Box 26, 'Notebooks: Volumes 8, 1934–1935', pp. 12–18, Meridel Le Sueur Papers, Minnesota Historical Society, St. Paul, Minnesota (hereafter Le Sueur Papers, MNHS).

19. Schlesinger Jr 1958, pp. 385–419; Alinsky 1947, p. 72; Milton 1982, p. 52; Dray 2010, pp. 433–40.

Chapter Three
Uneven and Combined Development: Class-Relations in Minneapolis

The Marxist concept of uneven and combined development arose out of an obvious need to address the complexities of capitalism's transformative capacities and revolutionary responses on a global scale. Was proletarian revolution *only* possible in the most advanced capitalist economies? Or could it actually break out and exercise its multiple emancipations in areas of the world dominated by agrarian peasant-production, but clearly altered fundamentally by intense pockets of highly concentrated, often monopolistic, industrial-capitalist development? Within the Second International, a debate raged among the European revolutionary movement over precisely this question. Russia teetered on the brink of insurrection. The crisis of the Tsarist *ancien régime* accelerated daily, with the devastations wrought by the First World-War making everyday life in the Russian Empire increasingly untenable. Revolutionaries puzzled through and argued about what *could* be done, weighing in the balance the structures of economic determination and the agency of the conscious, subjective forces advocating radical change. Was it necessary for societies to proceed through a bourgeois-democratic era, nurtured in the hegemony of capitalist market-relations, *before* working-class revolution could liberate humanity? Some claimed this 'stagist' sense of possibility was, in fact, an iron law of historical politics. Alternatively, there were those, such as Lenin and Trotsky, who insisted that in an epoch of imperialist decay, the global peripheries of capitalism offered unique opportunities. A numerically constrained, but socially expansive, workers' movement, leading an alliance involving other oppressed social layers, could defeat autocracy precisely because this ossified ruling order was centred in the atrophied, ever weakening class-power of feudal remnants and the politically stunted, not yet consolidated, authority of the nascent bourgeoisie. A mature period of capitalist bourgeois democracy might be leapfrogged and a workers' republic created in these conditions of previously unexplored possibility. The audacity of Bolshevik leaders like Lenin and Trotsky, theorists as well as architects of revolution, was decisive in the working-class victory of 1917. As Trotsky noted in his *History of the Russian Revolution*, 'The privilege of historical backwardness – and such a privilege exists – permits, or rather compels, the adoption of whatever is ready in advance of any specific date, skipping a whole series of intermediate stages'.[1]

Since neither the United States in general, nor Minneapolis in particular, faced a crisis of potentially revolutionary proportions in 1934, there is no sense in which the theory of uneven and combined development, pertaining to global capitalism's capacity to combine the most advanced industrial forms and backward remnants from earlier, even feudal eras, in a specific political economy, can be applied mechanically, here. In what follows, there is no suggestion that any stage in a process of development, necessary or not, could be 'skipped', and revolution thereby realised. That said, much of Trotsky's insight can be usefully transferred to an analytical assessment of the intensification of class-struggle in certain circumstances, of how it could be mired in a kind of stasis only to erupt in relatively unprecedented explosiveness. What is at stake in such conceptual understanding, then, is most emphatically not an argument about revolutionary development *per se* or about dispensing with certain levels of achievement – with which the theory of uneven and combined development was originally concerned – but rather what the uneven nature of class-struggle in one locale, combined with the historic necessity of redressing imbalances in the social relations of production, could produce.

In this sense, the class-struggle in Minneapolis, in which 1934 signalled a decisive breakthrough, can be understood within Trotsky's framework of 'the privilege of historical backwardness', this backdrop of uneven and combined development. By 1934, the combined development of a particular kind of regional capitalism, which had reached a conjuncture of stagnation, as well as the unevenness of the balance of class-forces, in which class-struggles of specific kinds had culminated in contradictory outcomes, produced a situation overripe for a dramatically disruptive resolution. Minneapolis in 1934 was thus an expression of a historical

---

1. Trotsky 1932, p. 5. See also Löwy 1981; Novack 1972; Le Blanc 2005.

impasse in which fundamental contentions were poised to clash in what proved to be a momentous resolution, and the ultimate transcendence, of an inherently unstable, antiquated régime.[2]

One part of this process has been uncovered by Elizabeth Faue, whose feminist account of women, men, and the labour-movement in Minneapolis between 1915 and 1945 presents something of a Golden Age of community-based, often radical and socialist, trade-unionism in the Minnesota metropolis during the era of the First World-War. A twelve-week telephone-operative strike in 1918–19 serves to illustrate the importance of women's involvement in class-struggle in this era. Faue's account places stress on the exuberant 'spirit of carnival and celebration' animating 'flapper-militants' who 'gave public voice to long-held grievances'. Community and neighbourhood seemed critically important in such struggles. They developed alongside the growth of influential ethnicity-based organisations, consumer-cooperatives, organising drives among textile-workers, the increasingly public face of class-conscious militant women speaking from rostrums created by a variety of political, labour, and reform-bodies, and the rising challenge that the Industrial Workers of the World posed to the archaic but entrenched American Federation of Labor. A labour-socialist coalition elected machinists' leader Thomas Van Lear as mayor for a two-year term in 1916–18. Lear and William Mahoney, editor of the *Minnesota Union Advocate*, helped found the Working People's Non-Partisan League, with which many radical women and working men affiliated. At this time, organised labour in Minneapolis peaked, with a total membership approaching thirty thousand, of whom sixteen hundred were women.[3]

Class-power in Minneapolis was, nonetheless, reflective of uneven and combined development. The old empire of wood, minerals, and wheat that had sustained Minnesota throughout the late nineteenth century and that had catapulted Minneapolis into becoming a regional metropole was declining. In the words of *Fortune*, 'the lusty, pioneering, growing youth of Minneapolis was over'.[4] Labour's strengths feeding off the growth of this empire, both in terms of the availability of jobs and wages as well as the political confidence that flowed from this kind of material possibility, were on the wane. Added to this, the economic disruptions of the post-WWI reconstruction period, combined with the

---

2. Although the insights of Trotsky's analysis of uneven and combined development have usually been applied to understanding the revolutionary possibilities inherent in underdeveloped or developing political economies, its applicability to particular – albeit specifically structured – industrial-capitalist contexts, like Minneapolis in 1934, is evident in the general method of Trotsky's conceptualisation. See, for instance, Trotsky 1939.

3. See Faue 1991, pp. 21–68, which contains much useful evidence on the nature of the Minneapolis workforce in the years 1915–35.

4. 'Revolt in the Northwest', *Fortune*, 13 (April 1936), p. 113.

1919–20 Red Scare and assault on organised labour, ended a chapter in working-class initiative. With veterans returning from Europe and demanding jobs that were disappearing fast, and the climate of class-relations spiralling downward, with an increasingly powerful capital hostile to all forms of radicalism and even the mildest expressions of trade-unionism, the tide of class-relations was turning. In Minneapolis, this shift was abrupt and decisive. It decimated the radical, community-based labour-progressive coalition-politics that Faue illuminates. Trade-union memberships wilted, living standards deteriorated, radical visions receded. As a pugnacious employers' movement mobilised and seized the initiative, labour's multiple voices became both fewer in number and more subdued. Faue chronicles these losses, which included what she terms 'a kind of amnesia about how [to] build an inclusive labor movement'.[5]

It is striking how quickly and decisively these changes in class relations occurred in Minneapolis. For the city was most emphatically *not* a stronghold of working-class power in the 1920s. The decade opened with a May Day parade in which a donkey figured prominently. 'I and all my relatives work in an open shop', read the large placard sported by the ass.[6] Indeed, Minneapolis in the mid-1920s was remarkably quiescent: it was known nationally as a stronghold of opposition to unions, its reputation as an open-shop town exceeding even that of Detroit and Los Angeles. The city's anti-union employers gathered in the Citizens' Alliance, founded in the opening decade of the twentieth century. There they worked in concert to blacklist labour-organisers; keep tabs on radicals; and hire spies, company-guards, and strikebreakers.[7]

A *Special Weekly Bulletin* sated the employers' appetite for anti-unionism with steady servings of ideological pronouncement and reports on unions served up by a network of industrial stool-pigeons. Many of these worked for the 'Marshall Service' of Kansas City, which placed operatives inside unions. A typical correspondence between this detective agency and a Minneapolis milling company reported: 'Our Number Fourteen, who is at present in Minneapolis, will be elected Secretary of Local No. 92 at the next regular meeting and will then be in a position to wreck the Union and put it out of business or will be able to let the Union continue and assume control of it and we wish your instructions as soon as possible what course we shall pursue'. By 1920, labour was in retreat, and the

---

5. Faue 1991, p. 57. See also the underappreciated and unpublished study Tselos 1971, pp. 1–58, which recognises and details the importance of the declining empire of resource-extractive Minnesota, a point also stressed in Walker 1937, pp. 9–44. Also useful is a recent study Smemo 2011, which contains useful background to the developments of the 1930s.

6. Latchem 1920.

7. For a general introduction to such Citizens' Alliances/Committees, see Silverberg 1941. A superb study of the Minneapolis Citizens' Alliance from 1903–47 is Millikan 2001.

employers' anti-union, open-shop drive was in high gear. Not surprisingly, in the period reaching from 1920 to the 1934 teamsters' strikes, the Citizens' Alliance largely had its way with an – admittedly, complacent and often compromised – AFL craft-unionism; less than nine percent of the city's workers were affiliated with such trade-bodies. Wage-rates were low, rising by only two percent in Minneapolis over the course of the 1920s, compared to over eleven percent nationally. Strikes were rare. When industrial unrest did happen to rear its head, it soon found itself smacked down by the advocates of organised capital in the Alliance, who boasted that they were undefeated in their contests with workers' organisations. Finally, and not surprisingly, this weakness of urban, organised labor in Minnesota's major productive and distributive centre translated into a conservative Republican stranglehold over municipal and county-politics.

Epitomising this reactionary and aggressive capitalist mobilisation, and its economic and political grip on Minneapolis before 1934, was A.W. Strong, a self-made man who founded the Citizens' Alliance and believed he had created a kind of 'industrial salvation'. Strong, according to Charles Rumford Walker, 'spoke of the labor leaders he had fought with a reserve of hatred which only strict Christians employ against wilful heretics'. If labour, then, was weak and beaten into submission in Minneapolis prior to the labour-upsurge of 1934, capital was undeniably and correspondingly strong, or at least so it seemed: 'equipped with both economic power and the spirit of evangelism, the Citizens' Alliance of Minneapolis [was] no ordinary employers' organization. . . . it possessed centralized committee control, a disciplined membership, a permanent staff of highly paid functionaries, the backing of the Minneapolis banks, the cooperation of the police, and one of the most thorough labor spy organizations in the country. It was a redoubtable antagonist for any rank-and-file rebellion'. Small wonder, then, that Minneapolis workers were regarded as defeated and demoralised as they entered the 1930s, the city known as 'the worst scab town in the Northwest'. As Cannon later wrote in his *History of American Trotskyism*, 'Minneapolis wasn't the easiest nut to crack. . . . it was a town of lost strikes, open shops, miserably low wages, murderous hours, and a weak and ineffectual craft-union movement'.[8]

There were, however, 'privileges' associated with this historical backwardness. They registered in the strangely uneven nature of class-politics in Minneapolis. If, on the one hand, labour-organisation on the job and within the municipal political arena was stunted and deformed by Citizens' Alliance opponents as well as the exclusiveness and political myopia of craft-unionism, this was offset, on the other hand, by a variety of countervailing developments. Labour's very

---

8. The above two paragraphs draw on Spielman 1923; Tselos 1971, pp. 1–45; Millikan 1989; 2001; Quam and Rachleff 1986; Korth 1995, pp. 13–22; Walker 1937, pp. 59, 84–7, 187–92; Rachleff 1989, pp. 205–6; Cannon 1944, p. 142; Schlesinger Jr. 1958, p. 386.

failures meant that there were spaces for radicalism to breath, for it could not be suffocated by mainstream counterparts almost entirely lacking in strength. The Industrial Workers of the World left its militant stamp on Minneapolis, through which tens of thousands of migratory timber-workers and field-hands had passed over the course of the first quarter of the twentieth century. Third partyism had deep roots in the state, particularly in rural Minnesota, where Scandanavian immigrants drew on the social-democratic heritage of their homelands and adapted it to the agrarian populism of the WWI-era Non-Partisan League. In the 1920s and 1930s, this was reflected in the electoral support given to the Farmer-Labor Party (FLP), which won the endorsement of significant numbers of urban workers and displaced the Democratic Party as the voice of capitalist opposition to the entrenched Republicans. In 1930, 38 year-old Floyd Bjorsterne Olson was elected the first Farmer-Labor governor in the United States. Olson campaigned under the banner, 'Minnesota Needs a Change!' While he was originally elected proclaiming that he was not a 'bitter radical and theorist, but a well-balanced progressive', he was, like so many others, moving leftward over the course of the depressed economic years of the early 1930s. 'I am not a liberal', he declared in 1934, 'I am what I want to be – a radical'. The influence of organised labour may well have been, as Walker noted in *American City*, 'at its nadir', but a 'rather startling contradiction in the arena of class forces existed in Minneapolis between the years 1930 and 1934. Labor by joining hands with the farmer had won a measure of political power. But meantime labor's economic power lagged'. Olson himself urged downtrodden workers in sectors like the trucking industry to 'organise and fight for their demands'.[9]

Further to the left of this radical populism, Minneapolis also harboured working-class revolutionaries. They later proved to be the conscious, subjective element needed to take this context of uneven and combined development in such directions as to transcend its contradictions. Again, precisely because the mainstream AFL-dominated labour-movement was so weak, communists were able to exercise an important influence. Over the course of the 1920s, the Workers' (Communist) Party, its members concentrated among the largely Scandinavian and German building and metal-tradesmen, supported and then broke from the Farmer-Labor Association. Expelled from this body in January 1925, Communists resurfaced within its ranks in 1928. Vincent Raymond Dunne was a longstanding secretary of Minneapolis's Twelfth Ward Farmer-Labor Party Club, and was chosen as a delegate to the 1928 state-convention of the Farmer-Labor Association. When he ran for Senate on the Communist ticket, however, Dunne was promptly stripped of his Farmer-Labor credentials, expelled from this body as

---

9. Dobbs 1972, p. 43; Tselos 1971, pp. 59–77; Gieske 1979; Valelly 1989; Mayer 1951; Lefkovitz 1935, pp. 36–40, 70; Walker 1937, pp. 85–7.

unceremoniously as he would soon be dumped from the Workers' (Communist) Party. Communists also presented a significant left-wing challenge to the conservatives in the Central Labor Union, necessitating a 'Red purge' of the assembly in 1924. When, in November 1928, Cannon and his supporters were expelled from the Communist International for embracing Trotsky's critique of Stalinism, Minneapolis was a source of strength for the nascent dissident-movement that culminated in the founding of the Communist League of America (Opposition) in 1929. By the end of November 1928, some 27 Minneapolis revolutionaries had been expelled from the Communist Party, USA. Among them were Carl Skoglund and the Dunne brothers, Ray, Miles, and Grant, all of whom would figure prominently in the 1934 labour-revolt.[10]

In this context of uneven and combined development, then, Minneapolis was poised, in 1934, to erupt in class-warfare. The fifteenth-largest city in the United States in 1930, Minneapolis's population of roughly 465,000 was divided, rather brutally so, into class-camps of the haves and the have-nots. For the latter, the prospects appeared to worsen day-by-day in the early 1930s.

Minneapolis's rural hinterland, for instance, was decimated by the Great Depression, with farm-income more than halved between the late 1920s and 1932. Foreclosures drove families from homesteads, many of them finding their way on to crowded city relief-rolls. As Meridel Le Sueur's 1939 novel *The Girl* suggested, migrants to the city, many of whom were single young women looking for the employment-opportunities of an urban environment, faced a plethora of problems. They might, indeed, find jobs in the gendered labour-market – as domestics, waitresses, switchboard-operators, machine-operatives, secretaries, or clerks – but such jobs paid poorly and were now decisively cut off from the labour-movement. The percentage of the workforce that was female had risen over the course of the years 1910–35, to be sure, but women's industrial employment had stagnated, blocking certain possibilities and elevating the importance of non-union work for both men and women. In 1932, fully 86 percent of Minneapolis manufacturing plants were losing money. Key industries like flour-milling and meat-packing were operating at 65 percent capacity. If the cost of living had, indeed, dropped 20 percent, pay-rolls had crashed even lower, to 35 percent of pre-Depression levels. Minneapolis workers, men and women, organised and unorganised, were ravaged by the usual maladies of the era: wage-cuts, job-losses, stretch-outs, and attacks on any and all who advocated alternatives to the uninhibited reign of capital. Within urban Hennepin County, by the winter of 1932–3, some 68,500 were unemployed, those persons dependent on

10. Dobbs 1972, pp. 25–35, 44; Cannon 1944, p. 144; Palmer 2007, pp. 347–8; Korth 1995, p. 39; Gieske 1979, pp. 97, 111–12, 115; Tselos 1971, pp. 54–5; Draper 1963, pp. 96–126; Weinstein 1969, pp. 272–323.

public assistance swelling to 120,000 in number; in 1934, almost one in three people in Minneapolis and Hennepin County were reliant on some kind of dole.

Workers with jobs were either working less hours for less pay, or more hours for strikingly little money. In the Twin Cities of Minneapolis-St. Paul, over 60 percent of those with jobs were not able to count on more than $20 weekly. The comparable figure for those earning below this amount in 1928 had been only 28 percent. Among workers who were putting in long hours – barbers, filling-station attendants, and the like – the 59–60 hour work-week was coupled with wages of 38 cents an hour. Male 'breadwinners' in the pivotal Minneapolis trucking sector, which sustained the city as a distribution-hub of the Northwest, supported families on weekly wages of $12–$18, but they worked anywhere from 54–90 hours. Unionised workers fared little better: the number of dues-paying members of labour-organisations halved over the course of 1929–33, plummeting to seven thousand. So desperate was the quest for work that many trades could not maintain the union-scale of wages. Within the Central Labor Union, acrimony erupted as AFL unionists clashed over lowering standards and breaches of fundamental labour-principles. Class-struggle was subdued, but when overt conflicts were forced on workers – mainly in the building trades, by employers demanding to stretch hours out and shrink workers' pay-packets – the resulting strikes were more often than not defeated. If there were signs in 1934 that Minneapolis had weathered the Great Depression storm, there was also great fear, especially among the Citizens' Alliance crowd, that Roosevelt's provisions for labour in the National Recovery Act contained 'real dynamite', a charge that might blow apart their cherished open-shop town. This threatened to slow what one timber-baron thought was Minneapolis's destiny: to become the 'greatest peasant capital in the world'.[11]

In the midst of this devastation, the Communist Party took the opportunity on May Day, 1930, to call for mass demonstrations against all enemies of labour, including 'agents of imperialism' like 'the officialdom of the American Federation of Labor, the Farmer-Labor Party, the Socialist Party, etc.' It singled out former comrades, demonising 'Trotskyites [who] have become a tail to this corrupt capitalist class bureaucracy and are carrying on the same work of attacking the working class and its organization'. In its struggle to build Red-led Unemployed Councils and its focus on trade-unionism among the 'production workers' of the unorganised flour-mills and company-union dominated meatpacking industry, the Twin Cities Communist Party was both sectarian and adventurist, gaining little headway on either front. George Powers, Trade Union Unity

---

11. The above paragraphs draw on Le Sueur 1978; Tselos 1971, pp. 59–113; Faue 1991, pp. 21–46, 58–68; Walker 1937, pp. 79–92, quotes from pp. 82, 85.

League Secretary in Minneapolis, and Party functionary Karl Reeve incited a crowd of five hundred jobless people to storm the Gateway Meat Market after a 25 February 1931 Hunger Demonstration. The brazenness of the food-rioters met with the 'secret satisfaction' of the Minneapolis dispossessed, who appreciated this daring act of expropriation and food-redistribution. Nonetheless, the actions of the Party leaders who were involved squandered any possibility of the militant direct action of the crowd translating into advances in consciousness among the unemployed. As three desperate rank-and-filers were arrested after the mass attack on the supermarket, the Communist Party was nowhere to be seen. Powers, Reeve, and others disappeared as the crowd marched menacingly on the retail-outlet. They made themselves scarce as the arrested were sentenced to ninety-day terms in the workhouse. Earl Browder then distanced the Party from such attacks on stores, claiming that they were 'isolated actions of food seizures which are not approved by the masses'. The Party's defensive arm, the International Labor Defense, failed to take up the cause of the food-rioters officially. Minneapolis's Republican mayor banned all Communist assembly and used this edict to raid the headquarters of the Communist League of America, which eventually had to close its doors. Trotskyist meetings were broken up. As Carl Cowl reported in *The Militant*, 'chagrin was felt at the manner in which the party shamefully deserted the workers', and those arrested 'felt the bureaucrats had betrayed them'. They apparently resolved 'never to be made scapegoats again'. When a movement to build a Minneapolis Central Council of the Unemployed emerged in the difficult winter of 1933–4, the organising drive, in which Ray Dunne figured prominently, was punctuated by Stalinist verbal assaults on all 'social fascists' connected with it. Communists did little better among established trade-unionists. They apparently shunned the American Federation of Labor. Few new recruits were members. The Party had no presence to speak of in the labour-organisation that would figure centrally in the 1934 strikes, the largely enfeebled General Truck Drivers' and Helpers' Union Local 574 of the International Brotherhood of Teamsters, Chauffeurs, Stablemen, and Helpers. First organised in the early 1920s, Local 574 struggled throughout the opening years of the Depression. It had a membership of between 75 and 175 in 1933, its activity concentrated among half-a-dozen taxi-drivers who owned their own cabs, a coal-company 'which recognized the union for the purpose of getting union business', and possibly a few other marginal enterprises. Affiliated with the larger Teamsters' Joint Council, whose full-time organizer, William [Bill] S. Brown, was also the president of Local 574, the Union was anything but a hotbed of activity. Many remembered the defeat of a 1916 truckers' strike, in which the Citizens' Alliance spent $25,000 in order to crush Minneapolis's teamsters. Things did not get any better in the years that followed. Farrell Dobbs claimed that up to 1934 'not a single Teamster strike had been won in [Minneapolis] for some twenty years'.[12]

Charles Rumford Walker nonetheless suggested that Depression-era Minneapolis was a 'city of tension'. The longstanding erosion of the resource-empire on which the open-shop city's good fortunes rested created a myriad of difficulties, exacerbated by the economic downturn of 1929. By the 1920s, the timber-lands, mining ranges, and agricultural prairies of the Northwest that had sustained the growth of Minneapolis were showing signs of economic fatigue. As a regional empire of bountiful harvests, the Northwest's day had been and gone. The demand for steel sputtered, and iron-ore from the Mesabi Range was no longer in high demand; the centre of the lumber-industry shifted to the Pacific Northwest; and the Panama Canal displaced the railroads that converged in the Twin Cities as a transportation-centre of what was increasingly a global, rather than American, economy. When the Great Depression lowered the boom on this slow economic bust, it left Minneapolis reeling. *Fortune* concluded that 'Minneapolis has outgrown the northwest, from which it must live, and now that the days of expansion are over its classes are fighting among themselves for what is left'. Walker laid stress on this apparently inevitable clash of class-forces: 'If the workers and farmers, the lumberjacks, shovel stiffs and factory operatives – rank-and-file builders of the empire – failed for the most part to share in the imperial spoil or to influence the confident policies of their masters in the period of the empire's

---

12. 'One Thousand Teamsters Are Denied Rights', *Minneapolis Labor Review*, 16 June 1916; Tselos 1971, pp. 88–9, 92, 99–102, citing Earl Browder, *Daily Worker*, 6 March 1931; Carl Cowl, 'With the Opposition in Minneapolis', *The Militant*, 9 January 1932; William Kitt, 'St. Paul Packing Strike', *The Militant*, 16 December 1933; C.F., 'United Front at Minneapolis: Labor Organizations in Unemployed Fight', *The Militant*, 23 December 1933; *Minneapolis Labor Review*, 30 September 1932; Walker 1937, p. 85; Dobbs 1972, pp. 36–9; Mayer 1951, p. 185. Membership estimates for Local 574 one year before the 1934 upheaval vary, with Dobbs citing the lowest figure of 75 (Dobbs 1972, p. 65). The president of the Minneapolis union, William (Bill) Brown, offered his assessment of the membership as slightly larger, numbering 90, while union-militant and later Socialist Workers Party member, Shaun (Jack) Maloney, estimated the dues-paying ranks at 175. Carl Skoglund noted in a 1955 interview that there were only 65 members of the General Drivers' Union in 1931. See Charles Rumford Walker, 'A Militant Trade Union, Minneapolis: Municipal Profile', *Survey Graphic* (January 1937), 29, Box 1, Folder: 'Newspaper clippings and magazine articles, Local 574 strike, 1934', CRW Papers, MNHS; Shaun (Jack) Maloney interviewed by Sol Salerno, Peter Rachleff, Don Seaverson, 1–4 April 1988, Oral History Interview Transcript, p. 72, in Shaun (Jack) Maloney Biographical File, 1911–99, David J. Riehle Papers, Minnesota Historical Society, St. Paul, Minnesota (hereafter Riehle Papers, MNHS); Shaun Maloney interviewed by Martin Duffy and Chris Miller, 30 May 1979, Box 2, File: '1934 Teamsters Strike', Transcript, pp. 1–10, in Shaun Jack Maloney Papers, Minnesota Historical Society, St. Paul, Minnesota (hereafter Maloney Papers, MNHS); Carl Skoglund interviewed by Fred Halstead, 25 March 1955, Transcript, p. 14, Box 2, Riehle Papers, Minnesota Historical Society, St. Paul, Minnesota (hereafter Riehle Papers, MNHS).

expansion, they began to challenge both in the period of its decline'. In this analytical insight, Walker grasped, albeit in gendered ways, the peculiar volatility
of class-relations in Minneapolis at a specific conjuncture of uneven and combined development. 'The depression', he argued, 'rapidly ripened these historic
difficulties in a space of three years', resulting in 'an explosive... spring of 1934'.
Appreciating that, 'A successful challenge is never made against a ruling group
while it is historically young, powerful, and progressive', Walker suggested that
ruling capitalist interests in Minneapolis in 1934 were themselves, ironically, as
backward as the labour-forces that they had, for decades, been keeping under
their thumb. 'Consciousness of unassailable power for a generation with a slow
decay of its substance left them not as persons but as an economic group both
arrogant and a little stupid'.[13] This opened the door of 'privilege' to those revolutionaries able to seize the opportunities presented by labour's resentments at its
backward state. And since the Communist Party was, in some ways, the mirror-
image of the Citizens' Alliance, itself also 'both arrogant and a little stupid', it was
the Communist League of America (Opposition) that seized upon the possibilities presented by Minneapolis's particular uneven and combined development
of class-relations.

---

13. Walker 1937, pp. 86–7, 24; 'Revolt in the Northwest', *Fortune*, 13 (April 1936),
pp. 115–16.

Chapter Four
Trotskyists Among the Teamsters: Propagandistic Old Moles

The notion that Trotskyists would lead working-class Minneapolis out of the barren desert of class-quietude and the open shop, and into a year of strikes and battles for union-recognition in 1934, would have seemed fanciful indeed in 1930–1. And yet the seeds of conflict had been germinating, all the while being cultivated by conscious if cautious agents of labour's cause. As a London costermonger told Henry Mayhew in the mid-nineteenth century: 'People fancy when all's quiet that all's stagnating. Propagandism is going on for all that. It's when all's quiet that the seed's a growing'. Like Marx's revolutionary old mole, the preliminary work of burrowing into the social relations of society, so that seemingly dormant forces might arise and leap from their somnolence to exclaim a new social order, was thoroughgoing.[1]

Even in the inner circles of the American Left Opposition, where Minneapolis was recognised as one of the League's 'mainstays . . . easily one of [the] best branches and . . . most active units', there was little inkling of what was in the making. In 1932, New York's national leadership of the CLA worried about the capacity of the Minneapolis branch to defend its views in mass meetings and in work among the unemployed. Left Opposition member C.R. Hedlund, a railway-engineer, had misjudged the situation when agreeing to serve on the Minneapolis Mayor's Unemployment Relief

---

1. Mayhew 1968, p. 20; Marx 1968, p. 170.

Committee, a class-collaborationist body composed of businessmen, politicians, and a few prominent labour-leaders. The Communist Party was seemingly besting the Left Opposition in public debate and in dominating the selection of delegates chosen to attend an important conference called to free America's pre-eminent class-war prisoner, Tom Mooney. As late as March 1933, Trotskyist political activity in Minneapolis seemed focused on the Communist Party and its municipal campaign to back a 'Workers' Ticket' in local elections. Vincent Raymond Dunne, when asked by a sardonic employer who respected his work-skills but had little regard for his commitment to organising coal-drivers 'how he was making out', replied 'truthfully that progress was almost nil'.[2]

Albert Glotzer, closely aligned with Max Shachtman in what was something of a factional hothouse in the Communist League of America (Opposition), chose to make much out of how Cannon supporters Ray Dunne and Carl Skoglund had seemingly misdirected work in the coal-yards in the winter of 1932, placing the organisational accent on bringing the truck-drivers into Local 574 rather than concentrating their efforts on 'the more exploited' coal-yard helpers. Furthermore, Glotzer chastised Dunne and Skoglund for 'fraternization' with the bosses, claiming that when the drivers celebrated the formation of a grievance-committee with a 'stag party' or 'beer bust' they invited the employers to attend and allowed them the floor to speak while suppressing political work by comrades. Skoglund answered these allegations, noting that Glotzer seemed unaware of the complexities of trucking work in the coal-yards, where drivers responsible for providing and outfitting their own trucks also hired helpers, both of these working contingents drawing their earnings in a 75/25 percent split of the monetary intake. In addition, men were hired by the hour in the yards. Through organising the drivers, Skoglund and Dunne had as their purpose the 'demand that these workers be employed more steadily and also that the drivers refuse to load their trucks without more help'. Workers' meetings, Skoglund insisted, were never attended by bosses, and it was only at the amusement 'stag' that they were present. They demanded the right to speak in response to a satirical reading by Miles Dunne which 'pictured the conditions of the workers'. If, as Glotzer implied, a CLA comrade had insisted on being 'mechanically forced on the platform to advertise' Left Opposition politics, the result would have been 'discharge of some of our comrades'. Skoglund and Dunne stressed, instead, that their work in the coal-yards was of a protracted nature. They were building contacts 'for future work', introducing the drivers and helpers to *The Militant*,

---

2. See National Executive Committee, CLA, Minutes, 20 January 1932; 18 August 1932; 24 October 1932, File 7, Box 32; 18 March 1933, File 10, Box 32, George Breitman Papers, Tamiment Institute, Bobst Library, New York University, New York, New York (hereafter, GB Papers); Kramer 1942.

and preparing for the seasonal layoffs that beset those working in the coal-yards every spring. 'What work was done this year will … be borne in mind by these workers, thereby making it easier to talk organization next year', Skoglund concluded presciently. A young Cannon protégé, Sam Gordon, recalled that he first talked to Dunne, Skoglund, and Oscar Coover in June 1932, and came away from the conversation highly impressed with the foundation that had been laid for developments in the Minneapolis coal-yards: 'I remember that on parting I glowed with confidence at the prospect for their trade work and our League as a class-struggle organization'.[3]

Time once pontificated that 'the big boys in Minnesota labor are three little men, the Dunne brothers'. The eldest of these small-of-stature siblings was Vincent Raymond Dunne, born in 1889 in Kansas City, Kansas, but raised in rural Little Falls, Minnesota. When Ray's father, a streetcar-mechanic, suffered a debilitating injury and could no longer earn a living in the city, the family was forced to move to a grandparents' Minnesota farm. Self-educated, and influenced early in his life by his older brother and Cannon ally in the Workers' (Communist) Party of the 1920s, William F. (Bill) Dunne, V.R. had a long history as a rebel-worker behind him when Minneapolis erupted in class-war in 1934. Raised in a poor, Irish Catholic family, a young Ray was witness to Bill's dressing down by the parish-priest for his 'worldliness' (he had been caught reading the forbidden Victor Hugo to his brothers). Ray was expelled from a catechism-class for his failure to close his ears to his older brother's blasphemous behaviour. Disgraced in the eyes of his parents, Ray's intellectual curiosity was piqued and he became an avid reader. His schoolroom, however, was to be the workers' movement. Forced into the labour-market at the age of fourteen, Dunne went to work as a lumberjack in Montana. There, he first read Darwin's *Origin of Species*. An attraction to the ideas of philosophical materialism soon translated into a politics of class-struggle. Like Cannon, Dunne was drawn to the Industrial Workers of the World (IWW), but the business-panic of 1907 tightened the knot on employment-prospects and forced Dunne on the tramp. He caught rats in Seattle in order to scrape together meal-money from the nickel-bounty the city was offering for each rodent. Not yet out of his teens, he was arrested in California for delivering a political speech. He wandered the Southwest, ending up in

---

3. See Albert Glotzer, 'Report on National Tour', 11 April 1932 and Carl Skoglund to the National Committee, 'The Coal Drivers in Minneapolis', 18 April 1932, both in Cannon et al. 2002: pp. 205–7 and 216–18. Swabeck's correspondence to Skoglund around Glotzer's allegations led to heated accusations of factional abuse of office on the part of Shachtman and Glotzer. See National Executive Committee, CLA, Minutes, 18 April 1932; 'Statement by Albert Glotzer', 25 April 1932, File 7, Box 32, GB Papers; Sam Gordon in Evans (ed.) 1976, p. 64. The 'stag' referred to is undoubtedly the 'beer bust' described by Farrell Dobbs in *Teamster Rebellion*: Dobbs 1972, pp. 48–9.

Louisiana cutting pine in the swamps. A vagrancy-charge earned Dunne a stint on an Arkansas chain-gang, convincing him that life on the road was not for him. Returning to Minnesota, he settled in Minneapolis in 1908, where he married and raised a family which included, from time to time, a number of adopted children. Working in a variety of jobs, most of them associated with the trucking industry, V.R. Dunne eventually joined the Socialist Party and, in 1919, gravitated to the emerging communist underground. Prodded by Bill, who would figure prominently in the upper echelons of the Party hierarchy over the course of the 1920s, Ray, who clearly respected his brother's views on the necessity of joining the Workers' (Communist) Party, eventually broke decisively from his elder sibling over the question of Stalinism. No family-bond remained, as Bill and Ray parted paths in 1928: 'As each considers political opinions more important than blood', one journalist wrote in 1942, 'they have since referred to each other as complete strangers'. When Bill was assigned the party-task of assailing his brothers' leadership of the teamsters' strikes in 1934, Ray refused to attend his hostile public harangues, letting it be known that 'this Stalinist bootlicker has nothing of importance for me to hear'.

Nonetheless, the future Trotskyist had been a well-known Communist in 1920s Minneapolis, easily identifiable as one of the city's most notorious 'Reds' in the Central Labor Union (CLU), the Farmer-Labor Party, and municipal and state-politics. Dunne was fired from one job during the First World-War for refusing to buy war-savings stamps. He was apparently blacklisted by the Wells-Fargo Express Company for handing out copies of the *Appeal to Reason*, but his skills as a driver were much in demand during the wartime labour-shortage. Known as a good worker who got along with his fellow workers, as well as an advocate of trade-unionism and revolutionary politics, Dunne managed to land another job within a few months. From 1921 to 1933, Ray worked for the Delaittre-Dixon Coal Company; he started in the yards as a coal-heaving helper, but graduated to driver, dispatcher, and weighmaster. This latter position, in which Dunne assigned drivers for the delivery of fuel-orders and weighed each load of coal to ascertain that it was properly fulfilled, allowed Ray to take the initiative in helping to organise an AFL local of stenographers and bookkeepers. This, in turn, eased him into the CLU as a delegate. DeLaittre-Dixon, run by a scion of the old Minnesota lumber-industry, had a touch of Tory paternalism running through it, and Ray's politics were tolerated, treated with bemusement. Dunne's value to the firm was undeniable; his intelligence and reliability apparently trumped his public radicalism, and the family-enterprise may not have been fully aware of Ray's role in aiding in the organisation of white- and pink-collar workers. His bosses undoubtedly saw Dunne as a trucker's advocate who, while up to no good, was achieving very little.

This enlightened complacency faded, however, as the DeLaittre-Dixon inter-ests merged in 1933 with some smaller coal-yards to form an expanded Ford-controlled firm known as Fuel Distributors. After Dunne took an afternoon off to be a featured speaker at an anti-fascist rally *and* lead an unemployed-march on City Hall, the manager gave him his last pay-cheque and told him he was done. 'This embarrasses us', the company-spokesman told Dunne, 'and we must let you go'. From earnings that might approach $175 monthly, Vincent Raymond Dunne was reduced to scrounging for odd jobs, dependent mostly on support from friends in the labour-movement and on relief. As Walker writes, at this point in time,

> Probably four or five hundred workers in Minneapolis knew 'Ray' personally. Scores had worked with him in the coal yards, talked with him, eaten with him, known his wife, his brothers, and his friends. They formed their own opinions – that he was honest, intelligent, and selfless, and a damn good orga-nizer for the truck drivers' union to have. They had always known him to be a Red; that was no news.

Deliberate, sober, unobtrusive, known as a respectful listener more likely to extend the analysis of others or to amplify opinions and perspectives, V.R. Dunne could also demolish the foolhardy with mordant wit or argue down a crowd with reason, logic, and the conviction of his ideas. Resembling Humphrey Bogart, Dunne had something of the soft-spoken deliberation of the popular actor's screen-persona. A regular guy who 'smoked union-made cigarettes' and 'was fond of the movies', the oldest of the Minneapolis Dunne brothers was seen as a respected unionist 'with an intimate knowledge of the coal yards...'. His integ-rity and often-tested physical courage were admired to the point that workers would follow Dunne's lead. Ray, then, was the 'big Dunne', but as a later portrait in *Harper's Magazine* explained, 'he seldom bothered to hold union office, pre-ferring to rule by the force of his personality and the demonstrable accuracy of his judgment'.[4]

Not unlike Marx's revolutionary old mole, and in line with the London coster-monger who told Mayhew that even when nothing appeared to be happening on the agitational front, radicals were at work, Dunne was a propagandist of quiet times. When James Rorty pigeon-holed Vincent Raymond Dunne in 1936, the

---

4. The above paragraphs draw on 'National Affairs: Three Little Men', *Time*, 7 July 1941; U.S. Military Intelligence Reports: Surveillance of Radicals in the United States, 1917–1941, Reel 32, Series 2667, Seventh Corps Areas-Omaha, Nebraska, HQ, File 0248, Series 2667–53, June 1934, Minneapolis Truck Drivers' Strike, 'Report of J.M. Moore', 4 pp; Kramer 1942, pp. 388–95; Dobbs 1972, pp. 29–30, 32, 47, 49; Tselos 1971, pp. 203–7; Walker 1937, pp. 160, 192–7.

quiet times were over, and Minneapolis had experienced a taste of his 'finely disciplined energy'. Rorty tended to believe the 'slightly built, leanly muscular workman in his early forties' who had the 'brow and eyes of an Irish intellectual', when he told the roving analyst of industrial-capitalism's increasingly unstable social ecology that 'we were within two or three years of a decisive employer-worker show-down'. Another commentator, the left-wing literary critic F.O. Matthiessen, was similarly impressed, convinced that Ray Dunne 'was devoted to the values of culture, and determined that the workingman should share them'. Matthiessen thought Dunne 'the nearest America had come to producing a Marxist in the selfless tradition of Lenin'.[5]

Ray Dunne was thus often seen as 'the brains, the directing genius' of the organising drive that broke the back of Minneapolis's open-shop traditions. Anything but the 'blazingest ball of fire' that he was described as in *Time*, Dunne actually 'preferred a behind-the-scenes role'. This suited the characters, personalities, and talents of the two other Dunne brothers who worked with him among the teamsters. They complemented Ray wonderfully. Miles (Micky/Mick) Dunne, for instance, was the most gregarious of the three Trotskyist Dunne brothers, an effective orator who enjoyed the limelight. An aspiring actor said to possess dashingly good looks, Mick Dunne was forced into coal-driving to make a living. In time, he would grow into the role of union-executive, relishing the trappings of office in a way that would have been quite foreign to Ray Dunne. Convivial and something of a fashionable dresser, Micky mixed well with the truckers and coal-yard workers, with whom he liked to share a drink and talk fishing, hunting, boxing, and football. To Miles, then, fell the task of 'buttering up' those it was considered diplomatic to appease or flatter and 'his vitriolic tongue was helpful against stubborn enemies', including his brother Bill, whom Miles enjoyed heckling occasionally. Not surprisingly, Miles was the most comfortable of the Dunne brothers in the role of public speaker, a budding union-figurehead capable of serving in a variety of organisational positions as the situation required. The last Dunne brother among the Minneapolis truckers, Grant, was arguably the face of teamster militant toughness: in negotiations with bosses and bureaucrats, politicians and police, he bluffed and bellowed; on a picket-line he was intrepid, defiant, and resolutely calm; his legendary scowl was threatening. Injured in the First World-War, Grant Dunne suffered through bouts of depression, and relied on the extroverted Miles to bring him out of his periodic despondency. Unlike Ray,

---

5. Rorty 1936, p. 196; Matthiessen 1948, pp. 87–91, and for a disparaging review of Matthiessen's book, P.B. 1948. See also Jacobs 1965, pp. 44–60, which details a New York bohemian student's introduction to the Minneapolis Trotskyists, Ray Dunne setting a standard of toughness and associated with proletarian revolutionaries.

he rarely picked up a book. When trouble was brewing, Grant Dunne 'was of the greatest use'. There was to be trouble aplenty in Minneapolis in 1934.[6]

The Dunne brothers made for good mainstream press. Small, dark, and wiry, they were the archetypal 1930s labour-movement 'tough guys'. A Minneapolis policeman and future sheriff of Hennepin County, Ed Ryan, remembered the Dunnes as 'soft spoken, gentlemanly little fellows, but tougher than hell'.[7] Journalistic attention focused on their role in the teamsters' strikes of 1934. But they alone did not lead the truckers. Also vitally important were two other figures, Carl (Skogie) Skoglund and William S. (Bill) Brown.

Skoglund was arguably the decisive strategist of the two.[8] Equally important, he was always well-liked and respected by his workmates, who revered his intellect and his strategic good sense. Five years Ray Dunne's senior, many in the coal-yards looked up to the husky Skogie, and even Dunne considered him his mentor, acknowledging his leading role in the 1934 strikes. Born the son of Swedish serfs, Skoglund came to the United States around 1911. Not yet thirty, he had racked up a reputation in Sweden as a militant trade-unionist and a mutinous leader of a conscripted soldiers' protest. Blacklisted for his activism, he fled the Old World for the New, hoping to find work. He brought with him to the United States the politics of Scandinavian social democracy, but he originally lacked sufficient language-skills in English to challenge the arbitrary dictates of the railway-camp bosses who barked orders as Skoglund laid ties for the Northern Pacific. Fed-up with the foreman's autocracy, Skoglund packed up his meagre belongings and moved into lumberjacking. A falling pine-tree crushed his foot, leaving Skoglund bed-ridden for nine months. Thereafter, the lumbering Swede walked with a decided limp. Having used his period of confinement and recovery to learn English, Skoglund moved to Minneapolis. He found work at the Pullman yards, drew on his early apprentice-training as a skilled worker, and eventually qualified as a first-class mechanic, earning relatively high wages. A good part of Skoglund's income was expended on workers' causes, generosities to workmates

---

6. Kramer 1942, pp. 388–98; Valelly 1989, pp. 104–5, 116.

7. 'National Affairs: Three Little Men', *Time*, 7 July 1941; Ryan quoted in Korth 1995, p. 116.

8. Shaun (Jack) Maloney stresses Skoglund's pre-eminent role in developing the strategy of how best to organise truckers in Minneapolis in 1934 and, later in the 1930s, throughout the Northwest in the interstate campaigns led by Dobbs. Among the Minneapolis Trotskyists, Maloney regarded Skoglund as 'the grand old man of the bunch'. See Maloney interviewed by Martin Duffy and Chris Miller, 30 May 1979, Transcript, pp. 1–10, Box 2, File '1934 Teamsters Strike', Maloney Papers, MNHS; Maloney interviewed by Salerno, Rachleff, and Seaverson, 1–4 April 1988, Transcript, pp. 65–76, 88; 5–9 April, Transcript, pp. 123–5, in Maloney Biographical File, 1911–99, Box 1, Riehle Papers, MNHS. Also File 'Skoglund-Weissman Interviews, undated' and File 'Skoglund-Halstead Interview, 1955', Box 2, Riehle Papers, MNHS; Skoglund Centenary Committee 1984.

in need, and his growing library of radical tracts. Widely known as a militant, he was elected district-chairman of the shopmen's strike-committees in both 1919 and 1922. Neither conflict saw a victory for the workers. Skoglund weathered the first 1919 union-defeat, but his good fortune ended with the railroad shopmen's strike of 1922. When the lengthy national battle wound down, with labour-organisation crushed and the establishment of a company-union, Skoglund again faced the blacklist. He made his way to the coal-yards and worked there as a driver, employed by the same firm for nine years. Always aligned with the revolutionary movement, Skoglund was a member of the IWW, but also affiliated with the Socialist Party's Scandinavian Federation, becoming its state-chairman in 1917. Together with other left-wingers, he gravitated instinctually to communism, and became a founding member of the Workers' Party in 1921. Over the course of the 1920s, he was a leading figure in the Workers' (Communist) Party in Minneapolis, a left-wing delegate to the Central Labor Union. Nationally, he knew of Cannon and his caucus, of course, but he was more often aligned with William Z. Foster. When Cannon and others were expelled from the Party in 1928 for embracing Trotskyism, however, Skoglund, like Vincent Ray Dunne, demanded that the Party explain itself. For this, he and his Minneapolis comrades were summarily expelled. An outcast among the long-marginalised 'Reds' of known Minneapolis revolutionaries, Skoglund settled into the coal-yards, another Trotskyist mole among the teamsters.[9]

Their burrowing was anything but easy. Trying to move the American Federation of Labor General Drivers' Local 574 to action was difficult work. It was bad enough that Skoglund, who briefly secured a position on the Executive Board of 574, advocated an organising campaign to bring new members into the wilting local sometime in 1930–1, but when he suggested organising all the workers in the yard rather than admitting into the Union only the drivers and their paid helpers, he was chastened for stepping outside the bounds of national teamster-policy. Word spread that Skoglund was a 'radical troublemaker', and inside the Union he was attacked as 'a red, IWW, communist and a disrupter of the movement'. Local 574's conservative business-agent, Cliff Hall, may have refused to accept dues from him and, fed up, Skoglund even withdrew from the General Drivers' Union for a time, disgusted with the behaviour of the local IBT leadership. But it was not possible to freeze Skoglund out, and he soon fought his way back into Local 574. As Harry DeBoer later recalled: 'He was generous and

---

9. Tselos 1971, pp. 202–3; U.S. Military Intelligence Reports: Surveillance of Radicals in the United States, 1917–1941, Reel 32, Series 2667, Seventh Corps Areas Omaha, Nebraska, HQ, File 0248, Series 2667–53, June 1934, Minneapolis Truck Drivers' Strike, 'Report of J.M. Moore', 4 pp.; Walker 1937, pp. 30–2; Dobbs 1972, pp. 30–3. On the 1922 shopmen's strike, see Davis 1997.

a nice fellow and most of the fellas knew him and if he asked you to join a union, you pretty much had to. You knew he was serious about it. He understood what the workers would have to face'. Skogie continued to talk union among the men; they listened. One autumn-morning in 1933, Skoglund was warned by his employer that if he insisted on fomenting discord among fellow coal-drivers, he would no longer be on the payroll. 'After that I said to myself, I got to put on my fighting clothes and organize a union here', Skoglund later said; 'Even if you are a revolutionist and know what it's all about, you're apt to put things off. Well, right now I couldn't, or I'd be out on my ear'.[10]

It was at this point that the Trotskyists among the teamsters joined up with Bill Brown. This proved a boon for the Left Opposition, now aligned with an established union-leader who was developing 'sound class instinct'. Brown had a history, throughout the late 1920s and early 1930s, of going along with the local IBT leadership, and he had acquiesced in the Red-baiting of Skoglund in 1931. But eventually, he turned away from the likes of Cliff Hall, tiring of their routinised refusal to organise the trucking industry. As Brown committed himself more and more to the cause of the truckers, he blossomed as a militant labour-leader. Farrell Dobbs described him as 'a fighter by nature and a gifted speaker, one of the best mass agitators I ever heard'. Shaun (Jack) Maloney recalled that Brown, who liked to drink almost as much as he enjoyed delivering his famous one-liners against the bosses, was 'an agitational speaker out of this world ... [he] could really whip things up'. As Cannon said, somewhat tongue in cheek, Brown being on the ground as a Minneapolis truckers' leader was 'a fortunate circumstance. ... Fortune favors the godly. If you live right and conduct yourself properly, you get a lucky break now and then'.[11]

Vincent Raymond Dunne and Skoglund had been diligently trying to create a lucky break for some time. They basically worked in tandem inside the Central Labor Union for many years. Dunne was the public face of the agitational duo, largely because he was an American citizen and Skoglund, an immigrant, lacked official documentation. They had been thinking through the necessity of organis- ing the trucking industry in Minneapolis since before their expulsion from the Communist Party late in 1928, recognizing the decisive role that the industry's

---

10. Dobbs 1972, pp. 40–3, 47, 62; Walker 1937, pp. 88–9; DeBoer quoted in Korth 1995, p. 60. On the conservative, cautious obstructions of Cliff Hall, see Maloney interviewed by Duffy and Miller, 30 May 1979, Transcript, pp. 12–13; 4 June 1979, Transcript, 2, Box 2, File '1934 Teamsters Strike', Maloney Papers, MNHS; Skoglund interviewed by Halstead, 29 March 1955, Transcript, p. 15, Box 2, Riehle Papers, MNHS.

11. Cannon 1944, p. 144; Dobbs 1972, p. 54; Maloney interviewed by Salerno, Rachleff, Seaverson, 1–4 April 1988, Transcript, pp. 83–5, 88, 115, Box 1, Maloney Biographical File, 1911–99, Riehle Papers, MNHS; Maloney interviewed by Duffy and Miller, 16 August 1979, Transcript, pp. 13–14, Box 2, File '1934 Teamsters Strike', Maloney Papers, MNHS.

four thousand, largely unorganised drivers played in the economic life of the city. With Dunne's ties to truckers and the coal-yards consolidated before his firing in 1933, and Skoglund and Miles Dunne working in the General Drivers' Local 574, the groundwork for a breakthrough was being laid as early as 1931. Skoglund, Ray Dunne, and Martin Soderberg purchased some trucks with which they hauled coal, and Mick Dunne had a battered-up vehicle that he shared with a couple of buddies. Grant Dunne, thrown out of work as a plumbing estimator, also managed, with Ray's help, to get hired as a coal-driver. Over the next three years, the DeLaittre-Dixon Fuel yard became a centerpiece of underground union-activity. As V.R. Dunne recalled:

> In the yard we were in, I think it was seven to ten different people that were quite well known to myself. Some of them were members of the party, some were not [but it]...was very carefully handled.... [I]t took us three years to do it. I'm sure the employers knew it. They just laughed at it.

The formation of a volunteer organising committee, in which the three Dunne brothers, Skoglund, and Martin Soderberg were the initial recruits, was eventually supplemented as Farrell Dobbs, Harry DeBoer, Kelly Postal and others joined. Some of these pro-union forces were brought into contact with the Dunnes and Skoglund, ironically, after the DeLaittre-Dixon merger created the larger enterprise and amalgamated a number of coal-yards. But as Ray Dunne later insisted, the Executive Board of Local 574 wanted nothing to do with these militants:

> We tried to get into 574. They didn't want us in there, because they had a couple of drivers and one coal yard: that's all they wanted. They said, come one at a time with your problems. We'll take care of them in the Union. You pay your dues. They weren't for organizing all the inside workers; they were afraid of all of our people.

Brown was tiring of the lethargy of the AFL officialdom that sat atop the International Brotherhood, kept the General Drivers' Local 574 of which he was president weak and ineffectual, and constrained the Teamsters' Joint Council, where Brown was ostensibly an organiser. According to Ray Dunne, 'Bill Brown was opposed to the executive committee of 574 who was opposed to taking us in. He hated them for that'. Appointed an 'international organiser' by Teamster boss Dan Tobin in 1933, Brown decided to live up to his billing. Newly-invigorated in this position, Brown was following his own inclinations. One journalist described him as 'a cop-fighting, roistering truck driver who, on the side, was president of the puny teamsters' local'. But Brown was also spurred to action by Miles Dunne, whose company he preferred to the staid local union-bureaucrats who did little more than knuckle under to the Teamster autocrat Tobin, an Irish-Catholic immigrant brought up in the coal-yards of Boston. Tobin's view of trade-unionism valued paid-up dues and rank-and-file deference. He distrusted militants and change, and was especially hostile to communism, which he saw as destructive of 'the Church, Mass, the beads, and the good Father...'. Tobin was thus the International Brotherhood's far-off voice of organisational temporising and timidity. Strikes, under Tobin's leadership, were a last resort for any Teamster local. Minneapolis militant Shaun (Jack) Maloney later quipped that, 'Tobin would give up his wife rather than give up strike benefits, and he thought a lot of his wife'. A classic self-conscious 'labour-aristocrat', Tobin 'would rather wear a business suit and negotiate over the leg of a chicken than on a picket line on a street'. Brown came to appreciate that if the teamsters of Minneapolis were to advance, it would almost certainly be over Tobin's objections and against considerable resistance from the head offices of the Union. Dunne remembered that Brown and his brother Miles were 'a certain type. They loved a good time; they were very humorous people'. And this shared attraction to sociability provided a political opening. Mick Dunne and Bill Brown became bosom drinking companions, and as they occupied their favoured tavern-tables, Brown heard about what the Trotskyist moles had been doing. It seemed that the teamsters' union Brown had presided over for six years might become something more than merely 'puny'.[12]

While far more militant than the conservatives on the Executive Board of Local 574, Brown was anything but a Trotskyist. A committed Farmer-Laborite, he took up political ground far closer to the mainstream than his new found Left Opposition allies. Yet he could see that Ray Dunne and Carl Skoglund were doing more in their quiet, clandestine organising than what the Tobin-constrained Brotherhood would ever willingly undertake on its own initiative. 'I decided to work with a few men in the union who knew *how* to organize', Brown recalled a few years later; 'They were the Dunne boys, who were working in the coal yards at the time, and Karl Skoglund. Conditions were lousy and there was plenty of sentiment for a union'. Brown worked on the only Local 574 Executive Board member who showed signs of coming to life as the Dunne-Skoglund volunteer organising committee drew truck-drivers and coal-helpers to its ranks in the autumn of 1933, vice-president George Frosig. Together, Brown and Frosig pressured their reluctant counterparts on the Executive Board, while

---

12. The above paragraphs draw on Korth 1995, pp. 53–6, 74, which contains much direct interview-quotations from Vincent Ray Dunne and others; Cannon 1944, pp. 144–5; Dobbs 1972, pp. 54–6; Kramer 1942, p. 392; Dray 2010, p. 433; Skoglund interviewed by Halstead, 25 March 1955, Transcript, p. 14; 29 March 1955, Transcript, p. 15; 23 April 1955, Transcript, pp. 21–2, Box 2, Riehle Papers, MNHS; Maloney interviewed by Duffy and Miller, 30 May 1979, Transcript, pp. 10–11; 24 July 1979, Transcript, pp. 18–21, Box 2, File '1934 Teamsters Strike', Maloney Papers, MNHS.

the Dunne brothers, Skoglund, and their growing number of union-advocates in the coal-yards carried on an underground campaign. Brown surreptitiously gave his blessings as early as the spring of 1933.

A union was crystallising from the bottom up, in spite of AFL foot-dragging. Its demands and aspirations were becoming staples of conversations among coal-heavers and truck-drivers. Teamsters' wages had actually worsened under the National Recovery Act code's minimums, with 40 cents an hour becoming standard over the course of a working week, hours often being cut back. This resulted in reductions in weekly wages, $16 becoming the new, and lower, standard. For the first time in the history of the Minneapolis truckers, moreover, a push for unionisation included all workers in the industry, drivers and their helpers as well as the hourly-paid shovel-men in the yards.

Dunne and Skoglund weighed up the options and decided to proceed with deliberation and caution. They kept the lid on militant talk of job-action at the end of the coal-season in 1933, when some in the yards wanted to strike in protest against Dunne being fired. Walking out when orders for fuel were tapering off, the Left Oppositionists rightly argued, would only play into the hands of the employers. Correspondence from Tobin to the Union's Minneapolis business-agent continued to erect roadblocks to slow the momentum of the union-drive, and was especially adamant that strike-action was not to be entered into without exhausting all other avenues of negotiation. Nonetheless, the 'door had been opened . . . a crack; it would take the pressure of the coal workers to push it wide open'.[13]

---

13. The above paragraphs draw on Walker 1937, p. 89; Dobbs 1972, pp. 54–7; Tselos 1971, pp. 208–10; Miles Dunne, 'Story of 544', *Northwest Organizer*, 27 February 1941. The conservative American Federation of Labor's response to developments in the Minneapolis trucking industry, which included three strikes, culminating in the massive July-August 1934 work-stoppage discussed below, has historically been one of understating the significance of these momentous class-struggles. See, as one example, the official AFL history of labour in the state, Lawson 1955, pp. 117–18, which reduces the history covered in this book to one restrained paragraph.

Chapter Five
January Thaw; February Cold Snap: The Coal-Yards on Strike

The Dunne-Skoglund partnership helped revive trade-unionism's prospects in Minneapolis. By November 1933, *The Militant* reported that the General Drivers' Local 574 was on the upswing, with membership having quadrupled since September. Communist League of America speakers were increasingly active, with National Executive Committee member Arne Swabeck delivering a number of talks in Minneapolis in early November 1933 and branch-members C.R. Hedlund, William Kitt, and Oscar Coover speaking at Left Opposition Open Forums in January 1934. Local subscriptions to *The Militant* were increasing, and Minneapolis readers of the Trotskyist newspaper apparently outnumbered all other League strongholds save for New York City.[1]

What kept workers in the coal-yards on the job? All talk turned on the weather. Normally the coldest month of the year, January in Minneapolis seldom saw the mercury rise above freezing. Yet in 1933–4, the winter was unseasonably warm. January temperatures averaged 39 degrees Fahrenheit, and a late-month thaw produced spring-like conditions. Nobody was ordering coal for their slumbering furnaces. Company-practices added the insult of idleness to the already long-established injury of low wages and long hours. By hiring surplus, individually-owned rigs and paying

1. Cee-Kay, 'Minneapolis Branch in Action', *The Militant*, 11 November 1933; Cee-Kay, 'Swabeck Meetings in Minneapolis', *The Militant*, 18 November 1933; 'Minneapolis Open Forum', *The Militant*, 30 December 1933; '569 Subs!', *The Militant*, 10 February 1934.

drivers on commission and carrymen by the tonne of coal hauled in heavy bas-
kets to the bins of specific customers, employers exacerbated an already deteriorating situation. As drivers, helpers, and shovel-men awaited assignment in
the yard's 'doghouse', a heated shack in which men gathered to play cards and
grouse about their conditions, the air was thick with grievance. Throughout the
trucking industry, whether it be in the grocery or taxi-sectors, workers were being
mercilessly squeezed into destitution. Many working in transport had to go on
the public-relief rolls in order to provide for their families. Across the country,
moreover, labour seemed to be on the march. Emboldened by the seeming guar-
antees of the National Industrial Recovery Act (NRA), whose Section 7(A) ostensibly provided the right to organise a union, workers were joining the AFL and
striking for rights and improvements. In practice, the NRA delivered little, and in
Minneapolis as in other centres, Regional Labor Boards were established to temper the rising antagonism of class-hostilities. These Boards did what they could
to avert strikes, but in Minneapolis they were confounded by the ideological
rigidity of the Citizens' Alliance, which claimed that all 'bargaining' with labour
must take place through individual discussions of employment-conditions. In
the coal-yards, the Dunne brothers and Carl Skoglund had to keep the increasingly perturbed ranks on something of a short leash as talk of strike-action grew
more and more agitated.[2]

Twenty years later, Skoglund recalled how the Trotskyist nucleus in the
coal-yards pressured Local 574's reluctant Executive Board to request sanction
for strike-action from the International, knowing that this approval would be
denied; press for a leaflet to be issued and distributed setting a definite date
for a mass meeting of all coal-drivers and yard-men, the topic of discussion to
be the organisation of an industrial union in the trucking sector; and getting
Miles Dunne placed on the IBT payroll, so that he could make arrangements for
the agitational rally and get the ball rolling by preparing a flyer announcing the
event. With Brown and Frosig supporting these initiatives inside the Executive of
Local 574, things moved quickly, and six hundred workers out of one thousand
employed in the coal-yards showed up for a boisterous meeting on the first Friday of February 1934. Local IBT bureaucrats did their best to dampen the spirits
of the assembly, declaring, 'If you should go on strike, you would be defeated
before you start'. Hundreds of workers who had come to the meeting expecting
to join the Union, witnessed a teamster-officialdom that prevaricated and proce-
durally blocked any attempt to pass motions relating to organising the coal-yards
or strike-action. Skoglund noted how it was 'necessary to steel the ranks for a
real battle against, not the companies, but also against the bureaucrats and to
educate them as to the nature of these bureaucrats'. As frustrated rank-and-file

2. Korth 1995, pp. 58–61; Dobbs 1972, pp. 49–53.

workers littered the floor of the meeting with torn-up union application-cards and membership-books, the dissident volunteer organising committee finally secured passage of a motion that another meeting be convened in two days time, on Sunday afternoon. The Dunne brothers, Skoglund, and others antici-pated that 'no bureaucrats would be present at that meeting, since they only work[ed] the regular week'. This proved correct, and the Sunday gathering, less well attended than its predecessor, unanimously endorsed a Monday morning, city-wide strike.[3]

The planning and foresight of the Trotskyist moles among the teamsters, as well as the weather, produced the long-awaited green light for a coal-yards strike. A cold snap had dropped temperatures well below freezing over the course of the first week of February, and orders for coal began to pile up in the dispatchers' offices of various companies. Wasting no time, the volunteer organising commit-tee of Local 574, its demands long in place, and the vote to strike secured at the second mass meeting, prepared for a walkout if the companies refused to grant union-recognition. The coal-yard workers had a list of other demands, but their primary consideration was forcing the bosses to deal with union-organisation. In the heat of the emerging battle, most other considerations were relegated to secondary status. The most intransigent of these 'dock-retailers' rejected the General Truck Drivers' and Helpers' Union unceremoniously. Their spokesman, J.B. Beardslee of the Pittsburgh Coal Company, declined even to meet with Bill Brown at the offices of the Regional Labor Relations Board. 'Mr. Brown means just exactly nothing to me', snorted Beardslee contemptuously. If some of the coal-yard owners were less bellicose, Beardslee and other Citizens' Alliance stal-warts nonetheless managed to thwart any possibility of the companies meeting with union-representatives. Brown and Local 574 had no choice but to strike, yet they did so with a wily minimalism. They let it be known that they demanded only that the Union was to be the agent of its declared members who worked on the trucks and in the coal-yards. Workers who were not part of the Union would be free to bargain with employers themselves, and there was no demand that all workers in the industry be unionised. Local 574 presented itself as the public voice of reason and compromise, painting its opponents among the coal-operators into the corner of intransigent ideologues. With the Regional Labor Relations Board seemingly powerless to cajole the coal-companies to even meet with union-representatives, the February 1934 coal-yards strike was shaping up as an out-and-out battle between capital and labour.[4]

---

3. Skoglund interviewed by Halstead, 23 April 1955, Transcript, pp. 22–3, Box 2, Riehle Papers, MNHS; 'Fight with Tobin and Teamsters' Joint Council', in File 'American City: Minnesota Miscellaneous Notes (2)', 11 pp., typescript, Box 1, CRW Papers, MNHS.
   4. Korth 1995, pp. 61–3.

Dunne and Skoglund were well aware of what was at stake in this historic, albeit limited, contest. A defeat for the insurgent coal-yard workers would have been a timely boost for the open shop, a setback not only to one sector of the trucking industry but to the entire Minneapolis working class. Victory, in contrast, opened the door to future possibilities. Bill Brown summed up the situation: 'if we win it will be like a red flag to a bull. The workers will come to us and we can organize the whole damn industry'. As we have seen, Dunne and Skoglund had been preparing for this moment for years. And they had the coal-company owners, however much their bluster gave the appearance of absolute power, about as close to where they wanted them as it was possible to imagine. March was approaching and the coal-season about to end; orders needed to be filled, and dispatched by truckers and their helpers, if the companies were to be paid. Finally, Dunne and Skoglund knew as fact what the coal-barons and their anti-union Citizens' Alliance brothers-in-arms did not believe: they actually had the workers in the yards behind them.[5]

The organisation of the strike was exemplary, Walker describing it three years later in his *American City* as 'surprising, detailed and painstaking'. Before the workers walked off the job, the leaders left their trucks locked inside the coal-yards. Picket-captains received a map of the fuel-distributors of Minneapolis and mimeographed instructions of their tasks and responsibilities as strike-leaders. Because the coal-yards covered ten square miles of territory, and involved dozens of individual enterprises, the decision was made to concentrate stationary picket-lines at the largest depots and maintain only a skeleton-presence of strikers at the other yards. Telephone-contact was arranged between those posted at the coal-docks and a centralised strike-committee. Picket-captains were entrusted to make necessary shifts of the strikers' forces as situations changed. A rank-and-file union-member suggested that these mass pickets be supplemented by a 'cruising picket squad', later to be known as 'flying squadrons', composed of teams of four or five strikers who patrolled the coal-yards and delivery-routes in cars and trucks, and awaited instructions from the strike-leadership as to any coal being moved through the streets of Minneapolis. At least one member among each group of these 'roving strikers' was thoroughly familiar with the operation of a coal-truck, and as these bands of cruising pickets monitored city-streets, they confronted and disabled scab-trucks. Tracking down the strikebreaking delivery-units, one of the flying pickets would jump on the running board, reach inside the cab, pull the emergency-brake, and occupy the driver in 'warning' conversation. A second striker then pulled the dump-lever, depositing the load of coal in the middle of the street. If the scab-driver proved particularly obnoxious, his truck might be commandeered and his load of coal taken to a working-class neighbourhood

---

5. Walker 1937, pp. 89–92; Korth 1995, p. 64.

where it would be dumped with the understanding that needy scavengers would make off with the highjacked fuel in short order. Within three hours of the strike being called, 65 of the 67 coal-yards in Minneapolis had been closed up 'as tight as a bull's eye in fly time' and 150 coal-dispatching offices were shut down. A local newspaper reported that, 'not a wheel is turning'. Routes into and out of nearby St. Paul had been sealed and the 'well organized, mobile, fighting picket line' had 'swept the streets clear of scabs'. Relief coal-deliveries were run out of one coal-yard, sanctioned by the Union, which appointed its own weighmasters, including Vince Dunne. Local 574 provided the drivers and picket-escorts, all paid at union-rates, the dispatching done under written authority of the General Drivers' organisation. In this way, relief-recipients, the Orphans' Home, and municipal hospitals received their necessary heating supplies, but 'the Strike Committee had complete command of the machinery of coal distribution in the City'. As Dunne wrote to *The Militant*, 'The methods used and the manner in which the organization work was carried out, stands as a model for the benefit of those who will take up the vast work that lies just ahead'.[6]

The speed, audacity, and effectiveness of the Dunne-Skoglund-Brown led strike rallied the mass of previously unaffiliated drivers and helpers to the cause of Local 574. According to one driver, who recalled being initiated into the clandestine ranks of the Union by Carl Skoglund, the initial vote to strike had been taken by a mere 34 coal-yard workers. Yet when the strike commenced on 7 February 1934, hundreds of workers supported the walkout. Nightly meetings kept the strikers' morale high. Forty years later, truck-driver Chris Moe exclaimed: 'we went out and tied up the town. I just got like a fanatic, like a religion. I didn't care what happened'. Insisting that only 150–200 workers were on strike, the companies perhaps believed that they could get coal deliveries back on track by agreeing to a settlement mediated by the Regional Labor Relations Board, whereby a modest wage-hike would be granted if they did not have to meet formally with Local 574's representatives. The companies wanted to reduce the issue of union-recognition to a perfunctory acknowledgement that the General Drivers' Union now commanded the support of a number of their employees. Indeed, W.W. Hughes, Executive Secretary of the Regional Labor Board, negotiated the terms on which the coal-yard owners could save face by coming out of the strike-defeat with their anti-union principles largely intact. The coal-dealers threw in the

---

6. Vincent Raymond Dunne, 'Coal Yard Workers Win Strike in Minneapolis', *The Militant*, 24 February 1934; *Minneapolis Journal*, 7 February 1934; Walker 1937, p. 90; Tselos 1971, pp. 210–11; Dobbs 1972, p. 56; Mayer 1951, p. 189. Maloney later claimed that it was Harry DeBoer who developed the roving pickets. See Maloney interviewed by Duffy and Miller, 4 June 1979, Transcript, p. 15, Box 2, File '1934 Teamsters Strike'; 'Minneapolis Teamster Strikes', Box 4, File 'Miscellaneous Notes and Clippings, 1940s–1980s', Maloney Papers, MNHS.

towel after two-and-a-half days, but the concessionary rag, as Dunne, Skoglund, and Brown well knew, had been tossed in their face. No contract would be signed, the employers retained the right to hire and fire, and all coal-yard workers were to be 'engaged, retained, or discharged solely on the basis of merit'.

And yet for Local 574, a victory of sorts had been achieved. Wages had been increased slightly, but more important was the refusal to yet again have trade-unionism beaten into submission. As Dunne insisted, 'workers have demonstrated their power. They have forced recognition of the union while ON STRIKE, a victory of no mean proportions, in the present state of the local drivers' unions'. Cognisant of the intransigence of the open-shop bosses, the defeatist and accommodationist role of the Regional Labor Relations Board, and the necessity of generalising the organising drive to all workers in the trucking industry, Dunne stressed that the brief February 1934 strike in the coal-yards left much important work undone. As a demonstration of *rank-and-file* militancy and an indication that the open-shop era in Minneapolis was drawing to a close, however, the winter-walkout had been something of a 'whirlwind ... battle which electrified the whole city and tied up every coal yard tight as a drum'. Miles Dunne reported to the Central Labor Union, on behalf of a strike-committee composed of himself, Bill Brown, Carl Skoglund, and the now enthusiastic (but formerly reluctant) Teamster business-agent, Cliff Hall. The coal-yard strike, Miles Dunne insisted, had established that American workers were, indeed, willing to fight for their rights. 'A week ago Minneapolis was not paying much attention to the coal drivers', the official organ of the CLU, the *Minneapolis Labor Review*, proclaimed, 'Today organized and militant they are a mighty factor in the industrial world'. Jumping on the organisational bandwagon, a slew of trade-union skates gushed about the prospects of working-class mobilisation. One of them characterised Skoglund as 'the General'.[7]

The February 1934 strike was an education in the class-struggle. Among the 'Things the Minneapolis Coal-Yard Workers Won't Forget', Vincent Raymond Dunne listed: the dumping of coal in front of notorious anti-union yards; the picket-line fights with police; how mass picketing became a reality, not 'an empty slogan'; the growing body of workers joining the Union; and the effective prohibition of the movement of coal in Minneapolis during the work-stoppage. Dunne also stressed the support of other teamsters, especially the twelve-hundred-member Ice Wagon Drivers' Union, which, 'in spite of their officials, decided to go out in sympathy'. Indeed, the three-day strike was notable precisely because it had been waged without AFL officialdom's seal of approval or

---

7. The above paragraphs draw on Vincent Ray Dunne, 'Coal Yard Workers Win Strike in Minneapolis', *The Militant*, 24 February 1934; *Minneapolis Labor Review*, 16 February 1934; Korth 1995, pp. 61–7, 76–8; Dobbs 1972, pp. 56–7; Skoglund interviewed by Halstead, 23 April 1955, Transcript, p. 24, Box 2, Riehle Papers, MNHS.

material support. As Cannon later stressed, the Minneapolis Trotskyists constituted an 'Organizing Committee', but none of them were, in fact, officers of the
Union. Rather, they were 'a sort of extra-legal body set up for the purpose of
directing the organization campaign', although undertaking their coordination
of the strike 'virtually over the head of the official leadership of the union'. As
Farrell Dobbs suggested, 'a situation of dual leadership was taking place within
the changing union'. Early in January, 1934, Bill Brown had tested the waters
with Dan Tobin and the International Brotherhood of Teamsters' headquarters, learning that the labour-officialdom atop the union wanted nothing to do
with militant job-actions, and was prepared not only to withhold strike-funds
but, if necessary, to revoke the General Drivers' Union's charter. Tobin, having
responded to Brown bluntly, bypassed the local president, and wrote an open
appeal to 574's membership, cautioning them about the ill winds that blew
in the wake of walkouts, reminding IBT members of the bitter pills organised
labor had to swallow when it chose to come up against recalcitrant employers,
a legal system not stacked in its favour, and police who had little sympathy for
workers' struggles. If this were not enough, even prior to Brown being in touch
with Tobin, the IBT boss had communicated with Central Labor Union figures,
pressuring them to twist the arm of Local 574's leadership and get it to clean
its house of communists and their sympathisers. A month later, Cliff Hall and
Brown wrote to Tobin informing him of the imminence of a strike and asking
for endorsement. It was a futile request. Tobin's assistant replied on 7 February 1934. The initial advice involved the usual run-arounds, stressing the need
to work with the Roosevelt administration to pressure the coal-dealers to meet
with union-representatives. With this an unlikely scenario, Tobin refused support on the grounds that, 'these men have not been members of your organization for six months', stressing that they were thus ineligible for 'strike benefits'.
By the time that Tobin's missive reached Minneapolis, the strike's effectiveness
had been established and a settlement was in the offing. Less than a week later,
the elections ordered by the Regional Labor Relations Board demonstrated how
decisively the Union had rallied the coal-drivers and shovel-men to its banner.
Among a 900-strong total workforce eligible to vote (the employers provided
the lists of certification), 780 cast ballots, of whom roughly 77 percent, or 600,
voted to join Local 574. This display of strength no doubt weakened the coal-
dealers' resolve to lay-off or fire union-activists *en masse*. They did blacklist some
of the leading militants, but this only added committed bodies to the ranks of
a newly invigorated General Drivers' Organizing Committee. Many of the new
union-recruits were young men, schooled by the Dunnes and Skoglund in the
basics of class-struggle. As Local 574 grew, so too did the Minneapolis branch of
the Communist League of America: between February and May 1934, its ranks
doubled from about thirty to over sixty.

One of the leading activists in the coal-yards strike, and a recent convert to Trotskyism, was Farrell Dobbs, a 27 year-old militant whose aspirations to study political science and law at the University of Minnesota were terminated by the economic collapse of the 1930s. Dobbs, who worked for one of the most recalcitrant anti-union yards, the Pittsburgh Coal Company, first contemplated labour-organising as he heaved coal with Grant Dunne on a November afternoon in 1933. Within weeks, he was part of the small group around the Dunne brothers and Carl Skoglund who formulated what were to be the initial demands of the General Drivers' Union: recognition of Local 574; increased wages; shorter hours; premium-pay for overtime; job-protection through a seniority-system; and improved working conditions. From that point on, Dobbs was a marked man among the coal-operatives, and he would be one of those victimised in the aftermath of the February strike. 'I was among those who got the ax in coal', Dobbs later remembered, but he promptly teamed up with Carl Skoglund, who taught him the ropes of labour-organising and introduced him to the politics of the Communist League. According to a jaundiced military-intelligence report, Dobbs was 'not particularly bright, but is a blind follower of the Dunne Brothers. He considers himself one of the "tough boys" in the organization'.

Ray Dunne offered an immediate assessment of what had been accomplished by the coal-yard workers in February 1934: 'The bosses had to swallow their insolent slander that "the men can't organize", "they can't stick" – they saw UNION organization – they saw them STICK – more than that, they saw them FIGHT'. In the months to come, Local 574's ranks swelled as workers in the trucking industry turned up at weekend union-socials or Sunday-night forums, button-holed a 574 representative, paid their dues, and asked impatiently when they would be going on strike. By the end of April 1934, some two to three thousand workers in the broad trucking sector were sporting Local 574 buttons. That number ballooned to seven thousand in the summer. Another round in the Minneapolis class-war was in the making.[8]

---

8. The above paragraphs draw on: Vincent Raymond Dunne, 'Things the Minneapolis Coal-Yard Workers Won't Forget', *The Militant*, 24 February 1934; Korth 1995, pp. 63–7; Cannon 1944, pp. 144–5; Mayer 1951, p. 189; Dobbs 1972, pp. 56–7, 62; Dobbs 1975, pp. 37–41, with quote on dual leadership, p. 41; Farrell Dobbs, 'Funeral Address', *Northwest Organizer*, 9 October 1941; 'The Coal Strike of 1934 – Birth of a Great Union', *Northwest Organizer*, 24 February 1934; 3 March 1934; Smemo 2011, pp. 24–5, quoting Tobin to Brown, 6 January 1934; Tobin to Local 574, 6 January 1934; Tobin to Roy Weir, 4 January 1934, all in 'Minneapolis Teamsters Strike, 1934: Selected Documents, 1928–1941', Microfilm 494, Minnesota Historical Society, Manuscript Collection, St. Paul, Minnesota; Tselos 1971, pp. 211–14; Walker 1937, pp. 89–92; Miles Dunne, 'Story of 544', *Northwest Organizer*, 27 February 1941; Kramer 1942, p. 392; Vallely 1989, pp. 105–7; Bernstein 1970, p. 234; Preis 1964, pp. 24–5. On Farrell Dobbs, see Dobbs 1972, pp. 17–21, 62; U.S. Military Intelligence Reports: Surveillance of Radicals in the United State, 1917–1941, Reel 32, Series 2667, Seventh Corps Areas Omaha, Nebraska, HQ, File 0348, Series 2667-53, June 1934, Minneapolis Truck Drivers Strike, 'Report of J.M. Moore', four pages.

Chapter Six
Unemployed-Agitation and Strike-Preparation

With the coal-yards strike settled, Minneapolis Trotskyists lent their support to the city's upholsterers, whose
uphill fight to secure union recognition stalled in the
morass of NRA Labor Board 'negotiations'. According to
The Militant's report, the upholsterers were betrayed by
AFL officials and led into more than one cul-de-sac by
the usual New Deal obfuscations. 'The outcome to date
has demonstrated the inadequacy, the hopeless futility,
of the begging tactics of the local's leaders in all previous struggle', wrote Carl Feingold from Minneapolis.
Anything but impressed with the union-bureaucrats'
'dickerings with employers through politicians and
lawyers, their emphasis upon "legal defense" in court
cases and injunctions coming out of the struggle, [and]
their failure to maintain mass picketing consistently
when experience showed that as often as it was used
gains were made by the workers', Feingold considered
the upholsterers' imbroglio a sad illustration of where
illusions in Roosevelt's New Deal would lead.[1]

February's drop in temperature not only strengthened the coal-yard workers' hand. It also precipitated
an uprising of the unemployed. Estimates suggested
that there were some thirty thousand jobless in the
winter of 1934. In desperate need of fuel for heating,
Minneapolis families dependent on municipal relief
besieged the city's Public Welfare Department, demanding 'emergency-orders' for food and coal. Court-house
demonstrations culminated in a 'near-riot' and the

1. C.F., 'Mpls. Labor Notes', *The Militant*, 24 February 1934.

arrest of one protester. The unemployed-movement, seemingly dormant, was given 'a new lease on life'. The Communist Party's Unemployed Councils revived, but a Trotskyist-led attempt to create a broader united-front movement – the Minneapolis Central Council of Workers (MCCW) – also coalesced and grew. It aimed to unite around a common agitation-programme the unemployed, local unions, and cooperatives, as well as the Socialist Party, the Farmer-Labor Party, and the Communist League of America. With the purpose of coordinating the struggles of both the employed and unemployed workers, the MCCW began, in February 1934, to discuss concrete actions and plan a conference.[2]

It proved difficult for the MCCW to crack the hegemony of the Communist-led Unemployed Councils and their umbrella-organisation, the United Relief Workers' Association (URWA), which dominated the struggles of the jobless in Minneapolis.[3] The revolt of the unemployed peaked in the first week of April 1934, as mass demonstrations led by the URWA challenged the city's Welfare Board and attacked 'the starvation program of the Roosevelt NRA administration'. Protesting the ending of the Civic Works Administration (CWA), which had provided jobs and wages for the unemployed, and its replacement with a 'scheme of work relief on a pauper basis', huge crowds gathered at the Minneapolis Court House to demand a 40 percent increase in relief-rates; continuation of the CWA on a cash-basis; no forced-labour programmes; and immediate support for all dismissed CWA workers. A battle ensued, with police and protesters clashing and tear-gas canisters raining down on the crowd, only to be thrown back, crashing through the windows of the Court House, where the City Council was meeting to hear the demands of a committee of 23 leaders of the angry unemployed. All 23 were eventually arrested, as were many others, charged with disorderly conduct. Seven workers and eight police sustained injuries. The Trotskyists in the MCCW tried to intervene in these events, but were largely rebuffed by the sectarian leadership of the URWA, which preferred to denounce all of those opposed to their policy of organising the unemployed in a 'united front from below', bypassing direct connections with established trade-unions and non-Communist Party workers' organisations. As League member William Kitt noted in *The Militant*:

> The Minneapolis Central Council of Workers has as its corner stone the idea that the interests of the organized and the unorganized, the employed and the unemployed workers are identical. It is convinced that the policy of the united

2. C.F., 'Mpls. Labor Notes', *The Militant*, 24 February 1934; Dobbs 1972, p. 67. For a discussion of American Federation of Labor activities around unemployment in the 1930–4 period, see Lawson 1955, pp. 415–63.

3. For brief comment on the Communist-led unemployed-movement, see Faue 1991, pp. 64–6.

front from organization to organization will enable the workers to cope with the problems that confront them. It believes that the struggle of the unemployed has only begun and it attempts to bring the entire working-class movement to the active support of the unemployed.

These ideas, and others congruent with them and highlighting the differing approaches of the Communist Party and the Communist League of America, were being bandied about in Open Forums and in talks sponsored by the Left Opposition delivered by League spokesmen like Max Shachtman and Vincent Raymond Dunne. Among the coal-yard workers, in particular, and the Minneapolis trucking workforce in general, there was less and less willingness to accept Stalinist 'demagogy and factual distortion'.[4]

The Communist League of America rode the wave of militancy that was cresting in Minnesota in 1933–4. Minneapolis labour seemed uncharacteristically combative in April 1934. Three hundred unionised ice-wagon drivers were ordered back to work by the Regional Labor Board, a battle that also halted delivery of relief-coal to needy families. May Day was celebrated by thousands of unemployed, who rallied at the Municipal Auditorium and marched to City Hall, which was protected by a police-guard. Street-railway workers, claiming that 77 of their number had been dismissed because of union-affiliation, threatened a strike in mid-May and were closely aligned with the Trotskyist-led truck drivers. Across the city, workers prepared for a major confrontation.[5]

The Farmer-Labor Governor, Floyd Olson, seemed a veritable loose cannon of radical shots fired at a faltering capitalism. Deluded reactionaries saw Olson paving the way to a Soviet Minnesota. In a futuristic political tract, published in St. Paul, Minnesota in 1934, Robert C. Emery outlined how a fictional John Hansen returned to Minnesota after thirty years' absence. He found Minneapolis in 1964 to be a virtual police-state, an 'ultra soviet regime' in which private property had been collectivised, basic freedoms abolished, and progress halted. Hansen's brother explained that Minneapolis was now called Olsonia:

> It was done as a tribute to Governor Floyd B. Olson, who was in office when you left. What Lenin was to Russia, Govern Olson has been to Minnesota. He is called 'the founder of the faith'. It was during his third campaign for governor

4. William Kitt, 'Minneapolis Workers Fight Starvation Program', *The Militant*, 14 April 1934; William Curran, 'Shachtman on Tour: Minneapolis', *The Militant*, 14 April 1934; Bill Curran, 'Role of Unemployed Labor in Union Fight', *The Organizer*, 11 August 1934; Dobbs 1972, p. 67.

5. 'Ice Workers Ordered to End Strike', *Minneapolis Journal*, 1 April 1934; 'Vote on Ice Peace Tonight', *Minneapolis Journal*, 2 April 1934; 'Ice and Fuel Delivered As Strike Halts', *Minneapolis Journal*, 3 April 1934; 'May Day in Minneapolis', *Minneapolis Journal*, 1 May 1934; 'Issues in Two Labor Disputes', *Minneapolis Journal*, 14 May 1934; 'Strike Vote of City Streetcar Men Delayed', *Minneapolis Journal*, 16 May 1934.

that his liberal supporters first presented their public ownership program, which was the opening wedge from which everything else has grown.[6]

Olson had, indeed, made loose-lipped suggestions, in the midst of the severe economic dislocations of the Great Depression, that private ownership may well have been saddling Minnesota with an unmanageable burden. At a 1934 convention of the Farmer-Labor Association, he asked, 'should not the government own all those industries which have to do with the obtaining of raw materials and transforming them into necessary products?' The Governor suggested that public ownership of such resources could, perhaps, be understood as part of the 'ideals of this movement' of Farmer-Laborism that he and his audience were engaged in building, the end-result of which was 'an ultimate co-operative commonwealth'. This, however, was a case of Olson's rhetoric running ahead of his actual politics. No sooner had he departed the convention than he was backtracking, appalled at the supposed misrepresentation of his views, and deeply troubled that there were those in his audience who had interpreted him to be endorsing nationalising idle factories to employ the jobless, or state-takeovers of banks and businesses. James Rorty had no trouble sizing up Olson's pronouncements as 'a kind of political, quasi-Social Democratic hot-cha – enough to get ... headlines in the morning papers, but nothing more'. Olson, preparing a run for the Senate, was not about to do much more, Rorty thought, than 'make fierce Populist faces'.[7]

Olson's seeming radicalism put him at odds with the conventional Republican mainstream in Minnesota. The Governor was often at war with his own conservative state-senate, welcoming farmers protesting the rising tide of mortgage-foreclosures and upstaging Roosevelt with a statement to a politicians' conference that he supported conscripting wealth if it would 'put the people back to work'. From the steps of the State Capitol, Olson told a throng of unemployed people in April 1933 that if conditions in the United States could not be improved, he hoped 'the present system of government goes right down to hell'. Much of this was, however, little more than bombast, and Olson was committed to keeping the lid on explosive class-relations, using moderate reform to effect 'orderly constructive change'.[8] Trotskyists like Dunne, Skoglund, and Dobbs knew this intuitively, but they chose, unlike the Communist Party, to focus their early approach to Governor Olson not on his shortcomings, but on placing strategic stress on the Farmer-Labor Party leader's ostensible pro-union sympathies, which could

6. Emery 1934, p. 22.
7. Walker 1937, pp. 67–8; Rorty 1936, p. 186. See also, Leif H. Gilstad, 'Pfaender Sees Power Behind Olson Throne', *Minneapolis Journal*, 15 May 1934; Gilstad, 'Farmer-Labor Analyzes Platform, Denies Interest to Take Over Factories', *Minneapolis Journal*, 18 May 1934.
8. Walker 1937, pp. 65–8; Mayer 1951, p. 187.

be exploited to build labour-organisation among the truckers. As Minneapolis teamsters flocked to the expanding ranks of the General Drivers' Union, Local 574, Dunne and others invited (indeed, pressured) a reluctant Olson to speak at a 15 April 1934 rally at a large local auditorium, the Shubert Theatre. Olson made no appearance, which was itself a statement. But he did send his secretary, Vince Day, a self-proclaimed, if somewhat oddly-placed, philosophical anarchist, to read a statement. Olson's message to the teamsters was, in Farrell Dobbs' words, 'even better for the union' than any appearance could have been. It distinguished workers' unions from company-unions, railed against the 'vested interests' that always did their utmost to thwart labour organisation and sustain 'their reign of exploitation of the working man and woman', and championed workers for having utilised their collective strength to weather 'gun fire, injunctions, and prosecution by malicious propaganda'. Olson's message closed by urging Minneapolis labour to 'follow the sensible course and band together for your own protection and welfare'. These words would come back to haunt the Farmer-Labor Governor.[9]

Olson's words of encouragement had been preceded by fighting speeches delivered by Bill Brown and Miles Dunne, as well as an organisational report by Grant Dunne. They were followed by Carl Skoglund, advising the workers on what lay ahead, preparing the ground for the formulation of demands and a formal strike-vote. On 30 April 1934, its ranks having swelled to some three thousand, Local 574 voted to target selected trucking employers with demands for a closed shop, a wage-minimum of 56 cents an hour for a 40 hour working week, with overtime to accrue thereafter, translating into an average wage of $27.50 a week. Caught off-guard, the trucking bosses, their every move monitored closely by Citizens' Alliance stalwarts, dug in their heels and refused to deal with workers except on an individual basis. The Alliance had already convened the city's employers, organising the trucking bosses in an association of 166 firms. This core-group bought into the view that communism was running rampant in Minneapolis and strike-action was tantamount to a Soviet revolution. Alliance forces began conversations with the mayor and the police on the necessity of standing fast against the unionisation-drive, and took steps to set up an anti-strike headquarters at a prominent downtown hotel. The clash between the truck-drivers and their bosses was shaping up as a titanic and irreconcilable conflict. Labour and capital sparred at the Regional Labor Board, but the bickering achieved nothing and negotiations, such as they were, soon collapsed. Brown declared that if a walkout was necessary, the insurgent truckers would 'tie up every wheel in the city'. A strike-date was set for 16 May 1934. As in the

---

9. Dobbs 1972, pp. 64–5; Tselos 1971, pp. 215–16.

previous coal-yard strike, the Communist League of America leadership had its
eye firmly on the calendar and the ways in which climate worked to the benefit
of a possible work-stoppage. Anne Ross noted in the *New Republic* that the 'strike
was timed for May because the movement of vegetables, gasoline, etc., was then
at its height'.[10]

If the Citizens' Alliance anticipated Armageddon and did what it could to
insure the victory of the just, Local 574, with the Dunne brothers, Skoglund,
Brown, and Dobbs leading the way, went about its preparations for the coming
strike with methodical efficiency. The 'Organizing Committee' of the General
Drivers' Union, with its Left Opposition nucleus largely outside of any structured
AFL officialdom, was responsible for a number of initiatives in the months leading up to the possible mid-May strike. All of these preparations were driven by
a fundamental recognition

> that the bosses would never recognize the union. Their record proved it. Nor
> would they grant the workers any concessions unless we forced them to do so.
> We prepared *at the very beginning* for a fight which we knew was inevitable.[11]

Skoglund stressed from the outset that it was only by 'all the sections of the
trucking industry *acting together*' that the General Drivers' Union would 'have a
chance of winning anything for any one of them'. This meant that Local 574 would
be battling the Citizens' Alliance, the combined forces of the trucking industry
bosses, *and* the AFL Teamsters hierarchy. The International Brotherhood's president Dan Tobin was insistent that if the so-called 'inside workers' were brought
into the Union, this was a breach of the traditional craft-jurisdictions in the trucking industry: only drivers and helpers who rode with them could be organised.
Dock-loaders, warehousemen, clerks, dispatchers, checkers, traffic-managers and
other workers – all critically important to the varied parts of integrated trucking operations – were, in Tobin's view, ineligible for union-membership in Local
574. Yet Skoglund, the Dunne brothers, and the rest of the organising committee did a masterful job in exploiting the Minneapolis teamsters' designation
of themselves as a 'General' Drivers' Union. Workers were grouped in sections
that met together, drafting particular kinds of demands and identifying a wide
range of grievances, some of them peculiar to specific occupations or areas of

10. Tselos 1971, pp. 216–17; Dobbs 1972, pp. 66–7; Mayer 1951, p. 204; Walker 1937,
pp. 90–1; Korth 1995, pp. 79–88; Anne Ross, 'Labor Unity in Minneapolis', *New Republic*,
25 July 1934, p. 284. For the details of the pre-strike discussions and developments, see
the many articles in *Minneapolis Journal* of 1–14 May 1934, with Brown quoted in 'Peace
Effort Fails; Drivers Strike Nears', *Minneapolis Journal*, 12 May 1934, and the final union-
meeting and strike-vote outlined in 'Workers to Vote Tonight on Walkout if Negotiations
Fail', *Minneapolis Journal*, 14 May 1934.
11. Walker 1937, p. 94.

the transportation-industry. Among the 'departments' of the Union were ice, coal, transfer, market-wholesale grocery, package-delivery, department-stores, furniture-outlets, independent truck-owners, building materials, excavation, and sand and gravel. Contrary to the ideological posturing of the Tobin hierarchy, this collectivity of sections did not weaken craft-'strength', the illusion of which was maintained only by keeping the teamsters' local unconscionably small and ineffective. Rather, a union united around the particularities of sectional realities and the solidarities growing out of general principles managed both to be powerful enough to extract important gains from the employers at the same time as recognising the necessity of grappling with definite differences in the industry. The Trotskyist leadership thus reinvented Local 574, as recent student of the truckers' mobilisation Kristoffer O. Smemo suggests, refashioning it as a mass, industrial union rather than a selective craft-organisation.[12]

As a strike threatened in April and May 1934, Tobin did his utmost to scotch the mass influx of new members into the General Drivers' Union, many of them much-maligned 'inside workers'. He suspended the Minneapolis local from the International and denied it the right to strike, insisting that the general organising of an industrial union of all those employed in the trucking industry must cease and that negotiations with employers should continue through the auspices of the Regional Labor Board of Roosevelt's NRA. When he could not dam the flow of workers into the rising industrial union, and with his business-agent, the ever-cautious Cliff Hall, holding back payments of *per capita* taxes on new members to International headquarters, Tobin pulled out the stops and did what he could to besmirch Local 574 within the local AFL-dominated Central Labor Union. An AFL official was dispatched to Minneapolis to threaten the CLU, which was advised that if it continued to seat General Drivers' Union delegates, its charter would be revoked. At a heated CLU meeting, it was supposedly suggested from the floor that the AFL emissary be tossed out of the hall on his head. Through all of this, the General Drivers' Union acted with moderation and restraint, and its delegate withdrew from the CLU voluntarily, pre-empting a vote on the Local's expulsion. With the strike looming, Local 574 concentrated its efforts on the main union-organising front, and cultivated informal support among its many sympathetic contacts inside the Central Labor Union, which was induced to go on the record in favour of Local 574's strike-demands, boxing a number of AFL figures into supporting the seemingly inevitable teamsters' rebellion.[13]

---

12. Smemo 2011, p. 27, drawing on Charles Rumford Walker, 'Notes for Life-Story of a Truck-Driver', Box 1, File 'American City: Preliminary Prospectus and General Notes', Box 1, CRW Papers, MNHS. See also 'Organizational Structure 574', 6 pp. Typescript, in File 'Notes Local 574 and Strike', Box 1, CRW Papers, MNHS.

13. Walker 1937, pp. 94–5; Korth 1995, pp. 88–90; Dobbs 1972, p. 67.

These machinations paled in significance to the actual organisational sophistication and foresight of Skoglund, Vincent Raymond Dunne, and others. They
had been sketching out a series of mobilising procedures in Communist League
of America discussions for several years. Their crucial contribution to the 1934
industrial-union drive was to establish rank-and-file committees among all sectors of the trucking industry, so that the coal-yards, drivers and helpers, gas and
oil-workers, market and food-store workers, warehousemen, shipping-room
employees, packers, checkers and weighers, dispatchers, and counter and platform workers were all involved in the development of the Union and the formulation of strike-demands. Skoglund recalled meetings of 34 different sections
of transport-workers, among them those employed in lumber and petroleum,
ready-mix concrete, wholesale groceries, and package-delivery. Out of these distinct gatherings, came a number of possible contract-demands around wages,
hours, and conditions.[14]

As the momentum increased, with a Teamster local galvanising mass support
among its previously unorganised constituency, the informal and proliferating
organising committees actually supplanted the General Drivers' Union Executive Board, comprised largely of 'old line labor-skates'. Attempts to monitor the
voluntary organising committee, composed of Communist League of America
members and their militant allies, proved futile. Ignoring Tobin's dictates, and
breaking down the barriers that had divided the ostensible jurisdictions of
different unions, the Minneapolis General Drivers' Union was charting a new
form of 'rank-and-file democracy' within the petrified shell of a local affiliate
of the American Federation of Labor. Cannon stressed how diligently his comrades worked 'through the Central Labor Union, by conferences with the labor
skates as well as by pressure from below, to put the whole labor movement in
Minneapolis on record in support of these newly-organized truck drivers; worked
tirelessly to involve the officials of the Central Labor Union in the campaign, to
have resolutions passed endorsing their demands, to make them take official
responsibility...the official unions of the American Federation of Labor found
themselves in advance in a position of having endorsed the demands and being
logically bound to support the strike'. As Ray Dunne explained in the pages of
The Militant, the strategic importance of the trucking industry in Minneapolis
seemed to have escaped the notice of most AFL trade-union leaders, who looked
upon the mobilisation of the General Drivers' Union as something that was getting 'in the way' of 'official' labour-movement work. Dunne insisted,

14. Skoglund interviewed by Halstead, 24 April 1955, Transcript, p. 27, Box 2, Riehle
Papers, MNHS.

This attitude must be changed. It is a menace to the whole labor movement. The General Drivers can and must be made the corner stone for the trade union structure as a whole. This corner stone is not yet in place. The entire workers movement will see to this job and bring the unions into action to this end.[15]

It was a particular case of what Arne Swabeck saw as a general pattern of new trends in the labour-movement. A fresh influx of union-members, according to Swabeck, was opening the door to an unprecedented stage of working-class militancy. Pointing out that, 'The center of gravity of the trade union movement is still within the A.F. of L.', Swabeck argued that, 'A continuation of its policies and betrayals will unmistakably lead to the possibilities of new militant unions emerging. But such moves can become successful only after the rank and file thoroughly absorb the experiences after a period of crystallization of forces and a better understanding of the purposes and tasks of militant unions. Above all', Swabeck stressed, 'it can become successful only under the direction of a conscious left wing movement'. With 'new mass numbers in the unions... defending the unions,... fighting for their recognition, [and] driving them into action on a large scale', Swabeck concluded, 'the leaders who yield to the company unions and accept the class collaboration... instituted by the NRA' were about to be displaced.[16]

Had the Minneapolis Trotskyists confined their initiatives to simply effectively organising the trucking industry in anticipation of a protracted and difficult struggle, they would have accomplished much, but also would have left the workers they were leading into battle vulnerable on a number of fronts. Beyond working to neutralise conservative labour-leaders and to develop sympathy, support, and material aid among other unions, the Dunne brothers, Skoglund, and Dobbs missed few opportunities to develop allies among the rank-and-file. The informal organisation-committees became a training ground for strike-leaders, and old hands among the Trotskyists worked with younger, up-and-coming militants to develop speaking skills among the volunteer-organisers who showed signs of oratorical promise. These novice soap-boxers were given some instruction and pointers and then sent into local unions to explain the General Drivers' campaign and to consolidate and deepen support for the truckers' cause, learning the art of agitation as they practiced it. A coordinated effort was undertaken to have Local 574's publicity featured prominently in the *Minneapolis Labor Review*, official organ of the AFL's Central Labor Union (CLU). The

---

15. R [Vincent Ray Dunne], 'Minneapolis Union Prepares for Action', *The Militant*, 12 May 1934; Dobbs 1972, pp. 60–1, 67; Cannon 1944, pp. 145–6.
16. Arne Swabeck, 'New Trends in the Trade Union Movement', *The Militant*, 12 May 1934.

editor, Robley D. (Bob) Cramer, figured prominently in the intelligence-reports on radicals that surfaced in the aftermath of the teamsters' strikes, an informant writing:

> Volumes could be written about the radical activities of this labor leader. He is not a member of the Communist organizations by reason of the fact that as editor of the official journal of the Central Labor Union of Minneapolis, he does not dare join.... He is, nevertheless, present at most of their meetings; is one of the most vitriolic and inflammatory speakers against capitalism and has rendered immeasurable assistance to the General Drivers' Strike leaders, advising them constantly.

This report overstated Cramer's radicalism. The labour-editor was well ensconced in Farmer-Laborite circles, had Olson's ear, and operated largely within the mainstream of the CLU. Sincere in his conviction that 'the working man' deserved a 'square deal', Cramer was, nonetheless, incapable of committing himself to an all-out war pitting the forces of labour against their capitalist adversaries. Cramer's capacities, limited though they may have been, were put to good use by Skoglund, Dunne and others. With Cramer's help, the Trotskyist leadership of Local 574 cultivated critical support among the militant Farmers' Holiday Association, a body that had galvanised rural Minnesota in its opposition to farm-foreclosures and by fomenting milk-strikes aimed at extracting higher prices from the creameries. Farmers regularly trucked produce, livestock, and other wares into the city, and their support for teamsters shutting down the trucking industry was crucial. The Holiday Association's president John Bosch was well connected to the Communist League of America, harboured considerable antipathy to the urban capitalist overlords, and assured Local 574 of his organisation's full support in the event of a strike.

Finally, as we have seen, the Left Opposition learned directly from the Toledo Auto-Lite union-drive, especially with respect to the Musteites' sustained and successful organisation of the Unemployed Leagues, and their important contribution to picket-lines and strike-support. CLA members were active in the unemployed-movement in Minneapolis, and Ray Dunne and railwayman Trotskyist C.R. Hedlund, in particular, made use of their contacts to spread the word that 'Local 574's strategy included the organization of an unemployed section of the union once it had been consolidated'. A plan for how to fight for relief-provisions for the strikers, should the job-action be protracted, was discussed. Leaders of the unemployed-movement were drawn into discussions of strike-strategy and made to feel that they were an integral part of the mobilisation, rather than second-rate 'country cousins'. Few strikes could boast of the outreach that had been undertaken in Minneapolis in the spring of 1934. Eric Sevareid, a cub-reporter for the *Minneapolis Star*, concluded that the Dunne brothers 'organized the strike as none had been organized before in American labor history'. Even police conceded, retrospectively, that 'The strike was beautifully organized'.[17]

Preparing the ground for the pivotally-important strike that would actually *prove* to workers that industrial unionism could be victorious against the employers, the politicians, and the conservative American Federation of Labor officialdom, thus proceeded on many levels. Orchestrated by the Communist League of America leadership of Local 574, this sophisticated strategy was premised on the need to expose and neutralise those forces, such as Tobin and Olson, who could publicly claim to be supportive of workers' struggles but who were, in actuality, important props of the *status quo*. As against Tobin and the AFL bureaucracy – exercising a decisive grip on the International Brotherhood of Teamsters, the local Teamsters' Joint Council, and even extending into the broader Minneapolis Central Labor Union – the mobilisation of the General Drivers' Union and its strike had to be done in such a way as to highlight the antagonistic class-interests of labour and capital. Dunne, Skoglund, and others were aware that the class-struggle waters could easily be muddied with claims that the Trotskyists leading the union-drive coveted the highly paid sinecures of the trade-union tops. Dobbs would later write that overcoming 'bureaucratic obstacles' at the local and national levels of trade-unionism was fundamental to the success of the 1934 organising drives and strikes. Referring to Cliff Hall, Tobin's voice in Minneapolis teamster-circles, and other AFL 'worthies', Dobbs noted that it was understood among the Trotskyists that they were 'expected to be hostile toward the projected strike action'. It was crucial, then, to keep the momentum of mobilisation and the direct line of workers' attack focused on the trucking companies and their resistance to trade-unionism. Rather than harping on about Tobin's and Hall's routinised foot-dragging and obstructionism, their approach was to lead workers into struggles that would then *reveal* the failure of conventional trade-union officials. As Dobbs recalled, the conscious intent 'was to aim the workers' fire straight at the employers and catch the union bureaucrats

---

17. The above paragraphs draw on Miles Dunne, 'Story of 544', *Northwest Organizer*, 27 February 1941; Dobbs 1972, pp. 58–68; U.S. Military Intelligence Reports: Surveillance of Radicals in the United States, 1917–1941, Reel 32 – Series 2667 Seventh Corps Areas – Omaha, Nebraska, HQ, File 0348, Series 2667-53, June 1934, Minneapolis Truck Drivers Strike, 4 pp.; A Rail, 'Minneapolis Rail Workers Organize', *The Militant*, 12 May 1934; Sevaried 1976, p. 57; Ed Ryan quoted in Korth 1995, p. 117; Maloney interviewed by Duffy and Miller, 24 July 1979, Transcript, p. 11, Box 2, File '1934 Teamsters Strike', Maloney Papers, MNHS.; Maloney interviewed by Salerno, Rachleff, and Seaverson, 5–9 April 1988, Transcript, pp. 168–9, Box 1, Maloney Biographical File, 1911–99, Riehle Papers, MNHS; Skoglund interviewed by Halstead, 24 April 1955, Transcript, pp. 29–30, Box 2, Riehle Papers, MNHS.

in the middle. If they didn't react positively, they would stand discredited'. Similarly with regard to Governor Olson: the Left Oppositionists were well aware that he presented a balance-sheet that contained both pluses and minuses: given his political base in the Minnesota Farmer-Labor constituency, he could ill afford to be openly hostile to trade-unionism, and to act as an overt strikebreaker would cost him his political career. Yet in an unambiguous showdown between capital and labour, Olson was just the kind of figurehead who could tap into his seeming status as a friend of working men and women to take over the leadership of any strike and divert it into compromise and conciliation, siphoning away the potential of truly meaningful material advances and dampening down the possibility of workers developing radical, or even revolutionary, consciousness.[18]

This sophisticated set of understandings and the consequent stance towards the likes of Tobin, Hall, and Olson, meant that the Trotskyists guiding the teamsters' insurgency in 1934 were constantly manoeuvering their more conservative trade-union and reformist counterparts into situations where these 'alternatives' either had to stand with workers at least rhetorically, or else expose their vulnerabilities. The Shubert Theatre mass rally of mid-April 1934, in which Local 574's strength was consolidated, a strike-vote was first taken, and a broad strike-committee elected, was a case in point. Discussions inside the leading bodies of the General Drivers' Union, its organising committee and Executive Board, revealed a split between conservative Teamster union-officials like Cliff Hall and Miles Dunne, Skoglund, and Brown. The former stood the usual ground of timidity. Not wanting to spend the $66 required to rent a large public hall, these chronic objectors argued, in effect, against having a mass meeting of insurgent truckers. Their opponents 'spoke up on the necessity of securing a larger hall', and eventually carried the day. Brown and the Left Oppositionists then worked on Olson to speak at the rally on 'The Right to Organize'. Realising that the Farmer-Labor Governor would draw 'a big turnout to the meeting', and that he would have no choice but 'to go on record in support of the union campaign', Brown, the Dunne brothers, Dobbs, and Skoglund then reaped the benefits of Olson's public statement, delivered *in abstentia* by his aide. To be sure, the fly in this principled ointment of class-struggle leadership was understating the extent to which Olson would inevitably turn against working-class interests if labour's momentum pushed and accelerated the battle between truckers and employers in ways that seemed to threaten the stability of the capitalist order. In threading the needle of pressuring the Farmer-Labor Governor in ways that advanced the cause of Local 574 and that would ultimately expose Olson's politics of capitulation to and servicing of capitalist interests, the Minneapolis Trotskyists

---

18. Dobbs 1972, pp. 43–5.

undoubtedly neglected to hammer home relentlessly how this seeming advocate of the producers was bound to turn against the very plebeian constituency that had propelled him into office. This failure also registered, in later and tense periods of negotiation, in figures like Dobbs investing too much faith in Olson's assurances that specific collective-bargaining provisions would, indeed, be sacrosanct, when the populist governor was obviously trying to straddle both sides of the class-fence in the interests of re-establishing much-needed socio-economic order.

Nonetheless, this shortcoming aside, the Left Oppositionists guiding the General Drivers' Union were, indeed, capable of criticising Olson when the Governor clearly took actions that undermined the effectiveness of Local 574's strikes. The Minneapolis Trotskyists thus *generally* exhibited an acute understanding of how most effectively to negotiate the many contradictions – political and economic, organisational and ideological – at play in the complex weave of relations affecting the local class-struggle in 1934. This organisational acumen was a product of the Communist League of America, whose leading members and secondary cadre conceived the plans behind the union-drive and developing strike strategy, implementing them over the course of the spring and summer of 1934. It led one teamster-militant, recruited to Trotskyism in the midst of these battles, and appreciative of what they won for the Minneapolis working class, to declare: 'We couldn't have done it without a disciplined revolutionary party'.[19]

19. The quotes in above paragraphs are from Dobbs 1972, pp. 63–5, and, citing Harry DeBoer, p. 187. For a brief, useful discussion of the Trotskyist approach to trade-union matters in Minneapolis in 1934 that addresses critically their approach to Governor Olson, see Knox 1998a. Although not entirely in agreement with his manner of presenting Trotskyist/Farmer-Labor Party relations in the years 1934–8, I find the discussion in Smemo 2011 instructive, especially in terms of Trotskyist concessions made in 1936–8. This large matter is essentially beyond the parameters of this book.

Chapter Seven
The Women's Auxiliary

In this period of strike-preparation in April–May 1934, one development of particular significance involved women. Especially important was the explicit, conscious, and successful creation of an organised contingent of working-class women supporting the male trucking industry workforce. Cannon stressed that the Minneapolis Trotskyists 'took a leaf from the Progressive Miners of America and organized a Women's Auxiliary to help make trouble for the bosses'. His own positive assessment of and experience with the women of Illinois mining communities may well have prompted him to suggest a similar initiative to his Minneapolis comrades.[1]

The idea of a Local 574 Auxiliary was first bandied about in the living room of Clara and Grant Dunne, at a meeting where Ray Dunne, Miles Dunne, Carl Skoglund, and Farrell Dobbs proposed that Clara and Dobbs's wife, Marvel Scholl, undertake to organise women associated with the Union's members. They agreed to do so, although neither had 'ever made a speech, public or otherwise', and they were well aware of the difficulty of the task. Skoglund, who apparently first proposed the formation of the Women's Auxiliary, was, according to one of his young recruits, committed to an industrial unionism that was 'equal for everyone ... including women. His expression was "women

---

1. Cannon 1944, p. 149. On the Illinois-based Progressive Miners of America and their Women's Auxiliary movement, see Young 1947; Hudson 1952; Bernstein 1960, pp. 358–66; Booth 1996; Merithew 2006; Thoreau Weick 1992.

hold up half the sky" and they're entitled to ... half the jobs'.[2] This was a long way from happening in Minneapolis in the 1930s, and Dobbs, who initially presented the idea of bringing women into the struggle to a general-membership meeting of Local 574, faced resistance from some in the entirely male ranks of the insurgent drivers, helpers, and yard-workers. Many men were uneasy with the thought of wives, sisters, girlfriends, and mothers suddenly becoming a part of their union-activities, which they regarded as separate and distinct from the domestic sphere. They wanted their 'night out' with the union-boys to be untainted by women's presence. It was all they had ever known. When Dobbs suggested the notion of a Women's Auxiliary, it was accepted, but without much in the way of enthusiasm. He was subjected to 'needling' for having seemingly broken ranks with the unwritten code of unionism as an expression of male sociability. But this male opposition to women encroaching on the public sphere of waged work and its collective struggles was quickly broken down as Marvel Scholl and Clara (Holmes) Dunne explained to various workers' committees how women could undertake a variety of crucial and important tasks in the event of a strike. Those involved in picket-duty or confrontation with police and scabs needed sustenance; the injured or the arrested required care; and the families of strikers had to be visited and their support encouraged. Women and their domestic and occupational skills could be put to good use at strike-headquarters and in the community. Scholl and Dunne appeared almost nightly before small groups gathering at the Central Labor Union to discuss what needed doing in preparation for the inevitable May conflict. Later, in July 1934, the Women's Auxiliary distributed two thousand invitations to women to participate in a mass protest-parade and rally demanding union-rights in the trucking industry. Women were also in touch with Marvel Scholl and Clara Dunne,[3] telephoning them at home,

---

2. Maloney interviewed by Salerno, Rachleff, and Seaverson, 1–4 April 1988, Transcript, p. 65, Box 1, Maloney Biographical File, 1911–99, Riehle Papers, MNHS.

3. I stress the leading roles of Dunne and Scholl, who embraced Trotskyism like their husbands, because according to the documents I have consulted, their significance in the Women's Auxiliary is unrivalled. They were also elected as President (Dunne) and Secretary-Treasurer (Scholl) of the Auxiliary, arguably the most important administrative posts. Other women, of decidedly different political orientations, no doubt contributed much, and the Women's Auxiliary, as a broad union-organisation, encompassed a diversity of political views. The wife of IBT bureaucrat Cliff Hall, for instance, was elected Vice-President of the Women's Auxiliary, and it is possible that the wife of Minneapolis Milk Drivers' Union business-agent Patrick J. Corcoran (an ally of Tobin in this period) was one of a small group of Auxiliary trustees. During the 1934 mobilisations in the trucking industry differences between women such as Dunne and Scholl, on the one hand, and Hall, on the other, might have been suppressed in the upheavals of the moment, but in the aftermath of the strikes of 1934, the Women's Auxiliary was apparently disrupted as conservative women launched attacks on Local 574's leadership. This resulted in the Women's Auxiliary being wound down, an unfortunate development that raises obvious questions about autonomy and control. On the election of Auxiliary officers and

telling them what they might do as cooks, waitresses, nurses, or office-workers. Husbands began to talk to wives, young men to girlfriends, sons to mothers.

Cannon would later capture this process (and perhaps help to consolidate it), in an imaginative fictionalisation of a striker's letters to his country girlfriend. The column, 'Letters to dere emily [sic]', would become a routine fixture in Local 574's daily strike-bulletin, *The Organizer*.[4] It outlined – through the presentation of an intimate, but routine, correspondence – how young men could break out of understanding trade-unionism as a masculine enclave, by representing just how discussions with women could, indeed, address work, politics, labour-organisation, and strikes. The Women's Auxiliary grew out of just this kind of dialogue, where Cannon's fictions paralleled everyday happenings, all of which reinforced a conscious attempt on the part of the Trotskyist leadership of the General Drivers' Union to transcend a gendered bifurcation of the working class that was, in the trucking sector, both longstanding and deeply rooted. Eventually the Women's Auxiliary would be meeting every second and fourth Monday of the month, and women were introduced to 'a whole new world . . . outside [the] home'.[5]

The contributions of Women's Auxiliary members, as originally proposed, were decidedly gendered as traditional, nurturing, female roles – staffing a union-commissary or a first-aid station and handling telephones, for instance – and Clara Dunne recalled somewhat contemptuously that, 'No one from the woman's auxiliary sat on the meetings of the main [union] committee. It was "no women allowed". We did what they wanted us to do, if they wanted us to run errands'. The mainstream press contributed to this view, likening the role of women in the strike to traditional understandings of women's place in any combat-situation: 'Their wives', declared the *Minneapolis Journal* in reference to strikers' spouses, 'like the wives of men in war, are behind the firing lines'. This

preparations for the 6 July 1934 mass parade and rally, see 'Auxiliary Elects Officers', *The Organizer*, 25 June 1934; and, on the Auxiliary's demise, Shaun (Jack) Maloney's note appended to 'The Organizer: The Secret of Local 574', Box 3, Maloney Papers, MNHS.

4. Cannon's column may well have been inspired, as David Riehle has suggested to me, by a popular WWI book by Edward Streeter, *Dere Mable: Love Letters of a Rookie* (Streeter 1918), which collects fictional letters written by a doughboy to his girlfriend. The Streeter book went through 13 printings.

5. The above paragraphs draw on Scholl 1975; Dobbs 1972, pp. 68–9; *The Organizer*, 2 July 1934; Lasky 1985, quoting Marvel Scholl, p. 196; Faue 1991, p. 72. Cannon's 'Letters to dere emily', first appeared in *The Organizer*, 20 July 1934, with Cannon recently having arrived in Minneapolis, and the column was no longer being written by September 1934, with Cannon's return to New York. Over twenty 'dere emily' entries (a couple had Emily writing to Mike) appear in *The Organizer*, and below I quote from them and offer further evidence of why they can be attributed to Cannon. The only acknowledgement of Cannon writing this column that I have seen appears in a casual handwritten note by Shaun (Jack) Maloney, appended to a document, 'The Organizer: The Secret of Local 574', Box 3, Riehle Papers, MNHS.

condescending view of the Women's Auxiliary, in Clara Dunne's case filtered through the perspective of certain late twentieth-century feminist expectations, registers in recent scholarly commentary on the Minneapolis labour-struggles of 1934. It is countered somewhat by Marvel Scholl's recollections. She noted, in 1975, that women were not always excluded from participation, and at a decisive meeting endorsing the strike, 'there were many women in the hall, and although their vote didn't count because they were not union members, when the motion for a secret ballot was voted down and a hand ballot approved, these women raised their hands as high as the men, and sang "Solidarity Forever" as loudly'. Skoglund recalled in a 1955 interview how the commissary changed its fare on a doctor's advice, providing balanced meals for strikers, many of whom were living on what was available through the union-kitchen. He stressed that this effort 'to change the type of food so as to maintain good health' meant that it was 'possible for strikers with families to bring them down to the headquarters to eat, thereby bringing the whole family into the fight'.[6]

Elizabeth Faue and Marjorie Penn Lasky nonetheless represent the Women's Auxiliary of Local 574 as rooted 'in conservative gender ideology'. These feminist studies present an often nuanced assessment of the dual nature of the Women's Auxiliary: on the one hand, it undoubtedly arose partly as an expression of a confining domesticity, in which a separate sphere of stereotypical femininity was assumed by male trade-unionists, who then subordinated 'women's work' to the cause of the labour-movement, extending and perhaps even tightening the straitjacket of traditional gender-roles and masculine dominance; yet women also experienced liberation in their involvement in the Women's Auxiliary and, especially as class-struggle escalated, found themselves transgressing orthodox understandings of women's place.[7]

An 'Auxiliary Member' writing about the important role of women in the May 1934 strike of General Drivers' Union Local 574 noted that women 'trained in office work took over the routine' tasks at strike-headquarters, as well as giving 'their heart and soul to the feeding of hungry droves of men'. She also acknowledged how women raised money for the Commissary Relief Fund. 'The necessity of feeding the families of the men on strike until they would again be able to draw wages', she stressed, 'was brought home to us very forcibly' during the

---

6. Clara (Holmes) Dunne quoted in Korth 1995, pp. 175–6; 'Strikers Turn Garage into Headquarters ... Wives Take Places Behind Lines to Make Meals', *Minneapolis Journal*, 16 May 1934; Dobbs 1972, pp. 68–70; Skoglund interviewed by Halstead, 24 April 1955, Transcript, p. 30, Box 2, Riehle Papers, MNHS; Scholl 1975, p. 21, whose views are similar to those expressed by Pauline DeBoer in 1971 in Trimble (ed.) n.d., especially pp. 73–6. See also Le Sueur, 'Notebooks, 1934–1935, Volume 8', p. 18, Box 26, LeSueur Papers, MNHS; Redfield 1984, p. 40.

7. Lasky 1985, especially p. 200; Faue 1991, especially pp. 12–13, 72.

strike. But for all of this, 'Auxiliary Member' began and ended her article, entitled 'Women Active on Firing Line', with evidence suggesting something other than gendered traditionalism. Women-pickets, she stressed, had put their bodies on the line, and suffered serious injury. Writing at the end of May 1934, 'Auxiliary Member' claimed that, 'Three of our members were seriously injured in riots with police. One's life was despaired of for several days. Another was taken to the hospital with a very seriously fractured ankle'. None of this gave 'Auxiliary Member' cause to pause. Women's place, she insisted, was 'Into the Class Struggle!' She agreed with others that 'the power of women' needed to be felt more strongly and more directly in active class-mobilisation. Concluding that 'their place is right alongside the men', 'Auxiliary Member' urged women to put their shoulders to the wheel and fight 'for their birth-right'.[8]

What is, perhaps, understated in Faue's and Lasky's representations of the Minneapolis Women's Auxiliary is the extent to which the Trotskyist leadership of the 1934 truckers' uprising struggled with their own time-bound gendered limitations. They present Skoglund, for instance, as pushing the idea of a women's auxiliary largely because he was like 'most union men' and worried that women would undercut class-struggle by pressuring their husbands to avoid or abandon strike-action because it would threaten domestic security. They label this the 'nagging wife syndrome'. This language is, in and of itself, far more derogatory than the more nuanced formulation of the gendered problem that it caricatures. Fine lines of distinction are warranted in balancing distinct interpretive orientations. Scholl, for instance, presents the issue with much more subtlety than either Lasky or Faue, acknowledging that as strikes dragged on and domestic reserves dwindled, working-class wives inevitably faced the hard consequences of husbands going without pay-cheques. Then began a domestic 'back-to-work campaign', with 'the hungry faces of his children [breaking] the will of many a formerly loyal union man'. Skoglund and other Local 574 leaders were, indeed, sensitive to the ways in which strikes caused working-class families immense financial hardship, but the reason for advocating the formation of a Women's Auxiliary was not, as Faue seems to suggest, revealing of 'implicit fears that women could not or would not hold the line against employers'. Rather, as Dobbs made explicit in his *Teamster Rebellion*, Skoglund's position flowed from his insistence that, 'Instead of having their morale corroded by financial difficulties they would face during the strike', women should 'be drawn into the thick of battle where they could learn unionism through firsthand participation'.[9]

8. Auxiliary Member, 'Women Active on Firing Line', *The Militant*, 2 June 1934; Dobbs 1972, pp. 68–70.
9. Contrast Scholl 1975, p. 21 and Dobbs 1972, pp. 68–9 with Faue 1991, p. 72 and Lasky 1985, p. 186. See also 'Ladies Auxiliary Give Benefit Dance', *The Organizer*, 25 June 1934;

Organs of Local 574, like *The Organizer*, tended to appeal to women to join the Auxiliary to 'further the cause to which your husband is fighting',[10] but there were other public statements making it eminently clear that mobilising women was central to all class-struggle. Such organising was not merely an appendage to a masculine cause, but was an essential component of the widening solidarity emblematic of insurgent labour in 1934. Cannon posed the matter in just this way as Local 574 prepared to do battle with the trucking bosses in May of that year:

> It is not a strike of the men alone, but of the women also. The Minneapolis Drivers' Union proceeds on the theory that the women have a vital interest in the struggle, no less than the men, and draws them into action through a special organization.... To involve the women in the labor struggle is to double the strength of the workers and to infuse it with a spirit and solidarity it could not otherwise have. This applies not only to a single union and a single strike; it holds good for every phase of the struggle up to its revolutionary conclusion.

Alluding to the ways in which the Progressive Miners of America had effectively developed and benefited enormously from the organisation of a militant, class-struggle Women's Auxiliary movement, Cannon claimed that, 'The grand spectacle of labor solidarity in Minneapolis is what it is because it includes also the solidarity of the working-class women'. Writing in August 1934, under the pseudonym 'Old Timer', Cannon saw the creation of the Women's Auxiliary by the General Drivers' Union as one example of how this organization was 'blazing new labor paths', doing so because its Trotskyist leadership had learned from other struggles, like those waged by the Progressive Miners: 'Local 574 is one of the very few local unions that have understood the necessity of organizing the women and making their organization a vital part of the strike machinery', Cannon wrote, adding that labour was not a male monolith, and that fully fifty percent of the working class was made up of women. Like the organisation of the trucking industry in Minneapolis, the Women's Auxiliary movement was undoubtedly a work in progress, an attempt to take the incomplete and imperfect organisation of all workers and extend it, against historically-embedded limitations, into new spheres of possibility. No doubt, this attempt to mobilise women in a class-struggle sense faltered upon the shoals of entrenched chauvinisms, but it also registered advances as certain strikers' wives left their homes to work

---

'Auxiliary Elects Officers' and 'Domestic Service Department', *The Organizer*, 16 July 1934; 'Commissary to Move', *The Organizer*, 17 July 1934; 'Ladies Auxiliary Notes', *The Organizer*, 20 July 1934.
   10. *The Organizer*, 2 July 1934; 9 July 1934.

closely with their husbands in the cause of trade-unionism and develop deeper ties with other working-class women. One such woman, the wife of truck-driver Roy Bauman, soon became active in the Auxiliary, preparing food and coffee for strikers; leaving a copy of Local 574's newspaper *The Organizer* in an empty bottle on the doorstep to educate the milkman in trade-union principles; and listening intently to the informal talk and public addresses at strike-headquarters. Even more than Roy, Mrs. Bauman came to believe in the spring and summer of 1934 that '*strike(s) had to be won*'.[11] This was the articulation of the Women's Auxiliary's accomplishment, and it would, in the months to come, contribute significantly to the teamsters' rebellion.

11. James P. Cannon, 'Minneapolis Shows the Way: Learn from Minneapolis!', *The Militant*, 26 May 1934; Old Timer, '574 Strike Methods Are Blazing New Labor Paths', *The Organizer*, 18 August 1934. For another 'Old Timer' article in which Cannon recognised the energy, resilience, enthusiasm, and intelligence of 574's strike-activity, attributing this working-class mobilisation to both the General Drivers' Union and the Women's Auxiliary, see 'Drivers' Strike Reveals Workers' Great Resources', *The Organizer*, 11 August 1934, reprinted in Cannon 1958, pp. 86–8. On the Baumans, see Walker 1937, pp. 145–52.

Chapter Eight
Rebel-Outpost: 1900 Chicago Avenue

On 12 May 1934, the General Drivers' Union called a mass meeting at the Minneapolis Eagles Hall. The turnout to the evening-rally was large, boisterous, and impressive; the assembled workers heard resounding speeches from Bill Brown and others solidifying support for the strike, which was to begin three days later. Many women from the Auxiliary were present, and Marvel Scholl pledged their support in what all knew was going to be a difficult battle. The meeting adjourned to 1900 Chicago Avenue, a newly established strike-headquarters 'where women and men alike joined in putting the finishing touches on preparation for the walkout'.[1]

The old garage at 1900 Chicago Avenue, a former stable, was a dark, flat, two-storied building, four hundred feet wide and a block long. Surrounded by office-buildings, the comings and goings at 1900 Chicago Avenue in mid-May 1934 attracted copious comment from the neighbourhood's resident doctors, lawyers, and businesspeople. They could not quite believe what they were seeing as a parade of workmen and strange assortments of wives and middle-class volunteers congregated at the garage and came and went in oddly jubilant groups. The long-vacant building was now 'electric with activity'. The shock was perhaps greatest when a large sign, emblazoned with the foot-high words, 'Strike Headquarters of General Drivers' Union

---

1. Dobbs 1972, pp. 69–70; Walker 1937, p. 97.

Local 574', was suspended above the doorway. 'Nothing will happen', the liberal onlookers assured themselves, their voices perhaps betraying a hint of disbelief in their own confident proclamations. 'This will be settled square and above board.... This is a civilized city. This will be settled over the table'. But the very transformation of the empty garage at 1900 Chicago Avenue was itself an indication that suggestions of inevitable class-compromise were wishful thinking. It had been rented by the General Drivers' Union, knowing that a large strike-headquarters would be needed. The building's transformation was a physical statement of the Trotskyist leadership's preparation for and anticipation of what was truly at stake in Local 574's struggle for union-recognition. And it most certainly was not the calm that the business-residents of Chicago Avenue had come to regard as their due.[2]

On the eve of the strike, the old garage at 1900 Chicago Avenue was a 'beehive of activity' as union carpenters and plumbers installed stoves, sinks, and serving counters in the commissary, a former car-wash area that had been whitewashed. Local unions, friendly grocers, and sympathetic farmers lined up to supply foodstuffs and materials, and landlords and the municipal-relief officers had been pressed to make allowances for workers who might need accommodation or aid. Butchers' workmen cut meats to prepare sandwiches. A striker recalled, decades later, hauling a truckload of wieners to the strike-kitchen, and remembered that the Farm Holiday Association brought in 'pigs, cattle, chickens and everything else'. There was 'a spirit for union in them days', he concluded. Marvel Scholl acknowledged the Sunday chicken-dinners, the stews served, and the vegetables and meats prepared in the kitchen, but her most visceral memories were of spam, the canned, precooked ham-concoction staple that Minnesota's Hormel Foods turned out in profusion, the very sight of which still managed to make her nauseous decades later. 'To this day', she wrote in 1975, 'I will not eat spam'. As Cooks' and Waiters' Union members advised Women's Auxiliary volunteers on the ins and outs of serving four to five thousand people daily meals, a stout proletarian overseer, Mrs. Carle, barked out orders and dismissed middle-class ladies, whom she distrusted as incapable of following her plebeian direction. They perhaps found jobs setting up cots in part of the floor-space on the garage's upper level, so that strikers and supporters could get some sleep between shifts on the pickets.

---

2. Le Sueur 1934, pp. 329–30; Korth 1995, p. 91; C.H., 'Sidelights from the Great Battle of the Minneapolis Workers', *The Militant*, 16 June 1934; Walker 1937, p. 99; A Striker, 'How the Strike Was Organized', *The Militant*, 2 June 1934.

The first floor of the garage used older structures, such as the tool-crib, establishing the Women's Auxiliary in a general office where typing and mimeographing was done, and new members could be signed into the Union. Written instructions for all of those on picket-duty were distributed, and captains named. Charts of city-streets and a cartography of picket-locations, organised throughout the city in fifteen separate districts, was set up in the 'nerve-centre' of the strike-headquarters as Vincent Raymond Dunne and Farrell Dobbs oversaw dispatching of pickets from the first floor. They took over a suite of offices that had been a part of the original structure of the garage, relying on a bank of telephones staffed by volunteers, a short-wave radio used to monitor police-calls, and a courier-service of half-a-dozen teenagers on motorcycles. A temporary auditorium with a stage outfitted with a loudspeaker-system rigged so that it could project throughout the garage and on to the street outside the building, where crowds might gather to hear announcements, guest-speakers, and musicians, allowed for nightly meetings of two to three thousand people inside the headquarters. Thousands more were able to listen to the proceedings on adjacent pavements. An impromptu roadway was roped off through the centre of the building, meaning that cars and trucks could be pushed into and out of the headquarters, their motors turned off to avoid carbon-monoxide fumes. There, they were serviced by a crew of twelve to fifteen mechanics, essential to the maintenance of the vehicles that would keep the mobile pickets 'flying'; stores of petrol had been secured, and a tyre-repair service lined up. Donations of money and vehicles came from across the city and throughout the state, bankrolling the costs of all of this. The Union received $15,000 before 20 May 1934. The powerful milk-drivers' union provided $2,000, and Governor Olson managed to cough up $500 for the General Drivers' Union.

Most impressive of all, perhaps, was the section of the garage devoted to first aid. Dr. H.P. McCrimmon, Mrs. Vera McCormack, two interns from the University of Minnesota hospital, and three trained nurses, headed up a large corps of volunteers in the strike-headquarters' makeshift emergency 'hospital', the existence of which, more than any other element of the now thoroughly-transformed garage, indicated that Local 574 expected and was prepared for the worst. An organised guard was entrusted the responsibility of monitoring the building and its surrounding streets in the event of police-intrusions, and ensuring that strike-supporters were sober and orderly. A sign on the wall of the headquarters proclaimed: 'No drinking. You'll need all your wits'. A troop of four armed watchmen reputedly kept a roof-top vigil. Indeed, the elaborate preparations evident at 1900 Chicago Avenue suggested what Charles Rumford Walker described as an impressive 'strike machine', a centralised 'brain core of military operations'. A Strike Committee of 75 people was established to oversee all activities.

Cannon praised the garage-headquarters as 'a fortress for action'. Less laudatory was the *Minneapolis Tribune*'s assessment: 'The strike headquarters are everything but a fort...and might easily be converted into that should occasion come'. The local newspaper, something of a mouthpiece for the employers, suggested that the extensive strike-preparations undertaken by the Union indicated that Minneapolis was on the verge of a 'far reaching affair, covering all the city and all its business and industry.... Even before the start of the strike at 11:30 P.M. Tuesday, 15 May 1934, the "General Headquarters" organization set up at 1900 Chicago Avenue was operating with all the precision of a military organization'. Indeed, press-coverage of the strike-headquarters generally stressed the 'surprising discipline' of 'an order almost military'. One of the Dunne brothers, proudly showing off the Union's capacity to monitor police-radio station-calls through a short-wave system, smiled when commenting to a *Minneapolis Journal* reporter, 'Pretty well organized, don't you think'. Dobbs offered a more understated view: 'On the whole the union was...ready for action'.[3]

---

3. The above paragraphs draw on A Striker, 'How the Strike Was Organized', *The Militant*, 2 June 1934; Lasky 1985, pp. 187, 190, 193; Walker 1937, pp. 99–103; Walker, '1900 Chicago', and 'Ray Dunne', in File 'American City Strike Notes: Dobbs, Skoglund', Box 1, CRW Papers, MNHS; Cannon 1944, p. 148; James P. Cannon, 'Minneapolis Strike – An Answer to Its Defamers', *The Militant*, 16 June 1934; Scholl 1975, p. 21; Anne Ross, 'Labor Unity in Minneapolis', *New Republic*, 25 July 1934, p. 284; Dobbs 1972, pp. 69–75; Le Sueur 1934, pp. 329–31; Korth 1995, pp. 90–1; 'Strikers Turn Garage into Strike Headquarters; Chiefs Snap Orders in Military Style', *Minneapolis Journal*, 16 May 1934; Rorty 1936, p. 190; Jacobs 1965, p. 53.

Chapter Nine
The *Tribune* Alley Plot and the Battle of Deputies Run

The first three days of the strike – Wednesday, Thursday, and Friday – seemed like a sleepy Minneapolis Sunday. A 'holiday atmosphere' prevailed. Clashes between strikers, non-union drivers, and police were, certainly, evident, but on the whole the situation was relatively peaceful, and the city uncharacteristically quiet. Strike-headquarters at 1900 Chicago Avenue combined serious purpose and discipline, on the one hand, with an exuberant festivity, on the other. 'Whole families went down there', recalled one Minneapolis workingman, 'It was a perpetual picnic'.[1]

The economic life of Minneapolis, however, was paralysed.[2] Unionised milk, brewery, coal, and ice-wagon truckers were allowed by Local 574 to conduct their business. As the sheriff later testified, however, the General Drivers' Union 'had the town tied up tight'. Trucking employers would later make much of the fact that the strike, strictly speaking, was conducted against only eleven firms. In 120 of the 166 trucking firms identified by the Citizens' Alliance as operating in Minneapolis, apparently no-one had walked off the job; drivers were able to report to work should they be needed. They were not needed, for the most part, precisely because all trucking ground to a halt. Dobbs boasted: 'Nothing moved on wheels without the union's permission'.

---

1. Korth 1995, pp. 135–6.
2. See, for instance, 'Strike Threatens Food Supply of City: Law and Order Mass Meeting is Called', *Minneapolis Journal*, 17 May 1934.

There were, of course, specific concerns that were defiant in their reaction to the closure of the streets, among them the city's newspapers. The Minneapolis dailies were particularly insistent that they suffer no interruption in their dissemination of the news, and on the first day of the city-shutdown they arranged for police-escorts to guard their routes. An incomplete list of businesses affected by the strike included: general and department-stores, groceries and bakeries; cleaners and laundries; meat and provision-houses; the construction-sector; all wholesale-outlets; factories; gas and oil-companies, including stations and their attendants; breweries; truck and transfer-dock facilities; warehouses; and delivery-services. The pivotal central market-district was tied up particularly effectively, *The Militant* describing it as 'closed like a tomb'. Five thousand strikers gathered at the Chicago Avenue headquarters, and pickets were sent out to strategic locations, while flying squadrons of vehicle-dispatched union-members toured the city and kept in regular communication with Ray Dunne, Farrell Dobbs and other strike-leaders. Farm-deliveries of vegetables were turned back at the city-limits, where some fifty entry-points were guarded by strikers. When trucks inside Minneapolis tried to move merchandise under police-escort, they were intercepted and usually successfully turned back. Some trucks were seized, and driven to the Chicago Avenue garage, where the area was soon crowded with vehicles loaded full of livestock, tobacco, coffee and tea, coal, and hay. Petrol-station attendants were, at best, reluctant participants in the economic shutdown, but thought better of strikebreaking after an angry group of pickets lassoed a pump and then hauled it bumping down the street. Less dramatic, but equally effective, was the teamsters' tactic of driving large trucks into a gas-station, lining them up around the pumps, locking their doors, and walking away, 'bottling [the fuel-dispensing outlet] up completely'. Eventually, Tanker Gas, owner-operator of six filling stations, resorted to a restraining order prohibiting Local 574 and figures associated with it, including Brown, Vincent Ray Dunne and his brother Grant, Farrell Dobbs, Robley D. Cramer and others, from 'molesting, damaging, or in any way interfering' with its business.

Charles Rumford Walker described the scene at 1900 Chicago Avenue: 'Men stood all day at four telephones which poured forth information to them and registered calls for strike help from every corner of the city. Picket captains were under instruction to phone every ten minutes from a known point, such as a friendly cigar store in their picket district, or a bar, or a striker's home'. As pickets put in fifteen-hour days, a reserve-army of strikers, never less than four to five hundred in number, camped out at the Chicago Avenue garage, eating, sleeping, and listening to detailed reports broadcast over the microphone. Women's Auxiliary members kept the coffee and sandwiches coming.

The strike immediately divided the entire city, as 'class lines [were] tightly drawn'. Workers supposedly supported the General Drivers' Union in overwhelming numbers, reportedly as high as 95 percent, constituting 65 percent of the population of Minneapolis. The remaining 35 percent were conflicted, running the gamut from vaguely sympathetic but questioning to vehemently hostile. Even private secretaries working for bosses inside the bowels of the Citizens' Alliance decided they had a side in the dispute, surreptitiously passing 1900 Chicago Avenue information and documents they deemed helpful to the strikers. They were part of what Farrell Dobbs described as a 'spontaneous intelligence service' that telephoned in reports of scab-activities. University-students from Greek fraternities packed up their baseball-bats and joined the police and the Citizens' Alliance, but there were others from the college who 'pitched in to help the union', including a young Eric Sevareid and his friend, Dick Scammon, son of the University of Minnesota's Dean of Medicine. Scammon, a giant of a young man, was blessed with acute intelligence, a prodigious memory, and a precocious interest in politics. At six-foot-four and two hundred and sixty pounds, Scammon could 'swing a club' if he had to, and was a welcomed addition to the legion of strike-supporters that came from outside the ranks of traditional labour-movement advocates. Divisions aside, there was no question that the mid-May 1934 truckers' strike was shaping up as 'the most imposing display of labor solidarity and militancy Minneapolis [had] ever seen'.[3]

---

3. For quotes and information in the above paragraphs see 'Minneapolis Shows The Way', *The Militant*, 26 May 1934; Walker 1937, pp. 97–9; Tselos 1971, pp. 219–22; Korth 1995, pp. 92, 137–8; Bernstein 1970, p. 236; 'Problems of the Truck Strike', and 'Strike Ties Up Truck Movement', *Minneapolis Journal*, 16 May 1934; 'Gas Stations to Re-Open, Defy Threats', 'Strike Threatens Food Supply of City', and 'Both Sides Explain Positions in Strike', *Minneapolis Journal*, 17 May 1934; 'Strike Riots Flare, 20 In Hospital', *Minneapolis Journal*, 19 May 1934; Sevareid 1976, pp. 57–8; Dobbs 1972, pp. 74–6. Richard Scammon was a member of the Socialist Party's Minneapolis branch in 1934. He graduated from the University of Minnesota in 1935 with a degree in political science, went on to complete a Master's degree in the same subject at the University of Michigan, and studied for a time at the London School of Economics. An expert on elections and polling, Scammon, who had moved from the Left into the Democratic Party, headed up the Presidential Commission on Regulation and Voting Participation in 1963–4. Later, he collaborated with Ben Wattenberg in producing two books *This USA* (published in 1966) and *The Real Majority* (in 1970), both of which indicated a rightward-moving political trajectory. The first study proclaimed that the United States had achieved substantial progress, and tried to deflect attention away from 1960s protests around civil rights, urban riots, and the anti-war mobilisations of youth. In the 1970 book, Scammon and Wattenberg warned that the Democratic Party, seemingly moving to the left, was on a collision-course with 'middle America'. They stressed that it was necessary for Democrats to address social issues such as 'law and order' and busing in ways that were more empathetic to the values and aspirations of middle-aged moderates. Scammon eventually took his interest in politics and electoral behaviour overseas, becoming an observer of elections in such countries as the Dominican Republic, Vietnam, and El Salvador. He died in 2001 at the

The 166 trucking firms under the anti-union umbrella of the Citizens' Alliance were at first committed to playing a waiting game. The largest among them attempted to cajole small businesses, like the plethora of city-bakeries, to run bread-trucks through the gauntlet of flying pickets, or to wait until regional farmers broke strikers' lines and liberated the central market. 'Big Business was going to use the small farmers to pull their chestnuts out of the fire', noted a report to *The Militant*, 'using them as pawns to open up the market. They wanted the farmers to do something that the big produce importers and distributors, the packing trust, the fruit trust, and the milling trust did not dare do themselves'. As this tactic failed miserably, the General Drivers' Union appeared to have gained the upper hand. Among organised labor in Minneapolis-St. Paul, even in bastions of AFL conservatism, the instinctive reaction was now to jump on the bandwagon of supporting the strike: building tradesmen, street-railway workers, and printers offered aid and the use of their members' skills. Talk of sympathy-strikes was widespread. Delegations of most of the city's unions made their way to 1900 Chicago Avenue: 'Use us, this is our strike', was their common refrain. Cab-drivers actually struck on Friday 18 May 1934. Unorganised factory-labourers cheered the flying pickets as they cruised city-thoroughfares. Unemployed-organisations threw their weight behind the striking truckers; the jobless would soon gain a reputation as having 'fought like tigers' beside their employed teamster-counterparts. 'The whole labor movement of Minneapolis was now on the defensive', explained Walker, 'They sensed that a decisive defeat for the striking truck drivers meant the beginning of the end for organized labor in Minneapolis'. Cannon extended the analytic canvas optimistically: 'Today the whole country looks to Minneapolis', he wrote in *The Militant*; 'Great things are happening there which reflect a strange new force in the labor movement, an influence widening and extending like a spiral wave. Out of the strike of the transport workers of Minneapolis a new voice speaks and a new method proclaims its challenge'.[4]

As the Citizens' Alliance, something of a shadow-cabinet of the unnamed trucking employers' council, fumed, all of this prodded power to action. A thousand businessmen convened to lay plans for opening the streets to trucks. One

---

age of 85. I am indebted to David Riehle for pointing out Scammon's 1934 Socialist Party membership. For further information on Scammon, see his obituary, 'Richard Scammon; Elections Expert, Political Advisor', *Washington Post*, 30 April 2001.

4. 'Zero Hour 11:30; Union to Mass 2,000 Pickets', *Minneapolis Journal*, 15 May 1934; F.K., 'Minneapolis Shows the Way: Building Trades in Sympathy; Womens Auxiliary Active in Fight; General Strike Growing; Workers' Spirit Soars', *The Militant*, 26 May 1934; James P. Cannon, 'Learn from Minneapolis!' *The Militant*, 26 May 1934; Walker 1937, pp. 110–11; Dobbs 1972, pp. 74–6.

of their number reported on how the good citizens of Winnipeg had kept petrol-stations up and running during that city's general strike in 1919. This now-consolidating employer's council rebuffed an attempt by Governor Olson to orchestrate a compromise-settlement, in which Local 574 would withdraw its demand for a signed contract. Instead, it called on a 'mass movement of citizens' to 'see to it that we are not dictated to by a mere handful'. Police-Chief Mike Johannes combined with Citizens' Alliance ideologues to recruit strikebreakers, designating them 'special police' and 'deputies'. Skoglund claimed that 'one notorious non-union employer' headed up the drive to entice these anti-union 'specials', while 'an insurance company' executive was second-in-command. Many of those drawn into the role of strikebreakers were 'middle-class', but some were also unemployed workers 'who saw in this a way of making a few dollars'. Others were apparently hired directly out of jail-cells, as 'ex-crooks, murderers, and all the scum of the city' were rounded up to shore up the local cops. Railway-man Communist League of America member, C.R. Hedlund, later named local hold-up artist Dick Daniels as one of the 'deputies' with a particularly unsavoury past. Olson thought the selection of these 'special city police officers' lacked discrimination, protesting that such ill-advised and lax recruitment would probably result in physical injury to Minnesotans, including innocent parties. But who was innocent in Minneapolis in May 1934? 'Keeping the streets open', took on the force of a religious conviction for those in most positions of constituted authority; in the evangelical crusade to break the strike, there were merely those aligned with order and those arrayed against it. Mayor A.G. Bainbridge authorised putting 500 new police on the municipal payroll. Yet there was evidence of popular resistance: the American Legion rebuffed an official police-request to organise a corps of 1,500 volunteers; when the Citizens' Alliance approached the Veterans of Foreign Wars to put together a contingent of 'special deputies', it received an impolite response to 'this asinine request'. City-thoroughfares grew tense. Police wiretapped telephones at the Chicago Avenue strike-headquarters; Dunne and Dobbs, alerted to the eavesdropping, dispatched pickets in code. On the third day of the strike, the cops were more aggressive. Only 18 arrests had taken place on the first two days of the job action, but on Friday 18 May 1934, the numbers taken into police-custody soared to over a hundred and fifty. Fines of $50 were handed out promiscuously, and 17 of those brought before the courts received workhouse-sentences of from 10 to 45 days. A Committee of Forty prominent businessmen and citizens formed, tasked with putting together an 'army of peace'. It was to march under orders to defend Minneapolis against the riotous disorder fomented by 'professional agitators and communists'. Colloquially known as the 'Law and Order Committee', this body rallied a rag-tag assembly of fifteen hundred 'salesmen, clerks, and patriotic golfers', whipped into frenzy against 'red dictators' bent on starving the 'city into submission'. Another Committee of 25 prominent trucking employers was empowered to act in negotiations with the strikers.[5] The stage was set, on Saturday 19 May 1934, for a clash of irreconcilably opposed class-forces.

The City Market became the designated battle-zone. Produce-distributors, animated by fears that their perishable goods would rot in the market-stalls if not moved, used scabs to load trucks on the Saturday morning. A large contingent of cops, supplemented by blackjack and club-wielding 'special deputies', fought with unarmed strikers and their flying-picket reinforcements. The barehanded workers were no match for the better prepared and numerically superior strike-breaking force, which numbered 425. In the riotous clash, picket-captains, strikers, and supporters, were routed, many of them sustaining serious physical injury. Eighty trucks of produce were removed from the market. As the defeated picket-forces straggled back to 1900 Chicago Avenue, where their broken noses and shattered limbs were tended to, an impromptu meeting of Local 574 dashed off a letter of protest to Olson, withdrawing its delegates from settlement-discussions and threatening to 'throw out a general call for every worker in Minneapolis and vicinity to assist us in protecting our rights and our lives'. Nursing wounds and channelling their anger, workers settled into their fortress-like headquarters and planned for the inevitable escalation of the struggle on Monday, Sunday being a day in which little would move on the embattled streets. 16 workers and four cops convalesced in the hospital. Letters to the editor of the *Minneapolis Journal* began to bemoan the tyranny of trade-unionism: 'Are we going to be ruled by a mob in this town?' asked 'Minneapolitan'. 'Are we to allow the mob to tell us if we can buy gasoline for our cars? Are we going to allow them to prevent our food supplies moving through normal channels..... The time has come for direct action', concluded this irate citizen, 'if our authorities are not going to allow us the freedom of our American citizenship'. Governor Olson made loud noises about calling in the National Guard to preserve order and protect citizens. If necessary, Olson declared, he would establish a military government that would 'take over all the machinery for distribution of foods and necessities'. Moreover,

---

5. On the close connections of the Minneapolis and Winnipeg 'Citizen's' committees, see Kramer and Mitchell 2010, pp. 15, 46–7, 170. Note also Tselos 1971, pp. 219–22; 'Board of 40 Named to Aid Police Heads', 'Sluggings, Property Damage Mark City Strike Violence', 'Pickets Jailed', and 'Olson Begins Overtures for Peace Meet', *Minneapolis Journal*, 18 May 1934; 'Leaders Not Optimistic of Settlement', *Minneapolis Journal*, 19 May 1934; Walker 1937, pp. 100–11; Skoglund interviewed by Halstead, 24 April 1955, Transcript, p. 28, Box 2, Riehle Papers, MNHS; Rorty 1936, p. 194; William Kitt, 'A Lesson in "Law and Order"', *The Militant*, 2 June 1934; C.H., 'Sidelights from the Great Battle of the Minneapolis Workers', *The Militant*, 16 June 1934; Korth 1995, pp. 90–5; Dobbs 1972, p. 77.

if the National Guard proved incapable of taking 'full charge of the city', Olson continued, he would not hesitate to induct more men into the service.[6]

Perhaps emboldened by their Saturday-morning victory, the Citizens' Alliance and municipal police-forces upped the ante that evening, utilising one of their stool-pigeons (supposedly a badge-carrying Burns Detective Agency hireling) who had ingratiated himself with the General Drivers' Union leadership. James O'Hara appeared at the Chicago Avenue headquarters, his credentials as an active worker in a Minneapolis ward on behalf of the Farmer-Labor Association vouched for, and seemed an able and committed strike-supporter. He was, in fact, an *agent provocateur*. 'I used to watch him', Grant Dunne later remembered, 'and think him one of our best men. He was there twenty hours a day, and always busy'. Somehow, this agent of the Alliance and the police managed, on Saturday evening at about ten o'clock, to take over the dispatcher's mike. O'Hara called for two or three cars from the battery of cruising pickets awaiting assignment to line up. He added for good measure (and against the usual practice of excluding women from dangerous assignments to conflicts that could well involve physical confrontation), 'This is a little job we have to do tonight, and some of you women pile in there with the men'. Then the industrial spy arranged for the cars to be sent to Newspaper Alley, where the *Tribune* and the *Journal* had loading docks from which bundles of daily papers would be packaged for distribution across the city. Notorious for their opposition to the strike and their relentless efforts to maintain truck-distribution with police-escorts, the newspapers were logical targets for the flying pickets. But *Tribune* alley was also a cul-de-sac, and the perfect setting for a police-ambush. When the unsuspecting strike-support group drove into the loading area, the dead-end passage was sealed off by police and 'special deputies'. The men and women of the Union were immediately cornered, and their opponents showed no mercy. Beaten with saps and night-sticks, and pistol-whipped, a half-dozen had to be sent to the municipal hospital. Skoglund sat through the night with the wounded who could be treated at the Chicago Avenue headquarters' emergency first-aid station. He recalled the carnage vividly:

> They brought the women in, and the other pickets from the *Tribune* Alley, and laid them down in rows in strike headquarters. All the women were mutilated and covered with blood, two or three with broken legs; several stayed unconscious for hours.... When the strikers saw them lying round with nurses

---

6. Tselos 1971, pp. 222–3; Korth 1995, p. 94; Dobbs 1972, pp. 77–9; 'Strike Riots Flare, 20 in Hospital: Trucks Move, Battles with Police Follow', *Minneapolis Journal*, 19 May 1934. 'Direct Action: Letter to the Editor', *Minneapolis Journal*, 19 May 1934; 'Where Both Sides Stand in Truck Strike', and 'Police Rout Strikers in Pitched Battles; Gardeners Run Gauntlet; Plans Laid out To Take Control of Food Delivery', *Minneapolis Journal*, 20 May 1934.

working over them, they got hold of clubs and swore they'd go down and wipe up the police and deputies. We told them, no, the Alley was a trap. 'We'll prepare for a real battle, and we'll pick our own battleground next time'.

And so began in earnest the marshalling of the pro-union forces. 'The fellows were wild there for a couple of days', Skoglund confessed. 'You'd see men all over headquarters making saps and padding their caps for battle'. Two police-officers barged into 1900 Chicago Avenue, claiming a scab-driver had been kidnapped; beaten senseless, their departure was in an ambulance. They were, perhaps, looking to rescue O'Hara, who turned up at the scene of his crime the next morning and was immediately seized, searched, and, begging for mercy, confessed that he worked for the police. Meanwhile, the old garage was abuzz with the sound of hacksaws cutting lead-piping, and two-by-twos being formed into club-lengths. Cheers no doubt went up when a truckload of wooden saps manufactured for the 'deputies' by the Clark Woodenware Company was hijacked, the weapons instead being brought to 1900 Chicago Avenue. An elderly supporter of Local 574 tore out the spokes of the stairway-banister in his house, donating the club-like spindles to strike-headquarters, transporting them in a child's wagon. A picket-captain, Shaun (Jack) Maloney, analysed the changing mood of the strikers after the *Tribune* Alley massacre:

> In my opinion the weekend activity at 1900 Chicago was prompted not only in anticipation of what was ahead but actually by what had [occurred] .... the employers were ready and determined to kill if needed to maintain their control. I was determined to make them prove it and so it was with so many men at that time. They knew what to expect on Monday or the next day and they were ready to 'go for broke'.

With a thousand National Guard troops poised to be summoned into Minneapolis's strike-torn streets, and Police-Chief Johannes swearing in police-officers by the hundreds, the General Drivers' Union knew full well what it was up against. Talk of a general strike circulated throughout working-class Minneapolis.[7]

The Communist League of America leadership of the strike-committee did not agitate for a violent confrontation, but rather, expecting that this was inevitable, prepared for it. Rather than be herded into a space that suited the police and the 'special deputies', they decided that it would be better that they themselves determine the battleground and then, with the element of surprise

7. Walker 1937, pp. 107–11; Cannon 1944, p. 150; Dobbs 1972, pp. 79–82; United States Senate 1936, pp. 44–5; Bernstein 1970, pp. 236–7; Scholl 1975, p. 21; A Striker, 'Minneapolis Shows the Way', *The Militant*, 26 May 1934; Korth 1995, pp. 95, 128; Schlesinger Jr. 1958, p. 387; Maloney interviewed by Duffy and Miller, 10 July 1979, Transcript, p. 3, 'Minneapolis Teamsters Strike 1934', Maloney Papers, MNHS.

working in their favour, engage their adversaries on a playing field that was at least somewhat levelled. Farrell Dobbs explained: 'We selected the market where there would be plenty of room'. The Central Labor Union AFL building was, as it happened, strategically located at the edge of the market-district, and its 'coffee station' had been established since the beginning of the strike, with cruising pickets dropping in for refreshment and talk. Over the course of Sunday 20 May 1934, hundreds of vehicles stopped in at the CLU building, their five or six Local 574 members/supporters ostensibly ducking in for an coffee. When the cars and trucks departed, however, they carried only the driver and perhaps one or two other passengers. In this way, unbeknownst to watching police and Citizens' Alliance informants, six hundred union-advocates, armed with clubs, were congregated in the AFL hall's basement. Small union picket-lines marched outside the market from four o'clock on the Monday morning, and unidentified strikers and allies fanned out so that they encircled the district. At the Chicago Avenue headquarters, nine hundred men waited in anticipation. Women's Auxiliary members took over almost all normal strike-headquarters functions. In addition, knowing that if the police decided to use firearms, the strikers would need to engage them at close quarters so as to minimise their use of guns, Local 574's strategists had a truck with 25 pickets stationed ready to drive into the middle of the police's forces in the market, splitting the armed cops. Driven by a fearless teamster, Bob Bell, the truck bore a sign proclaiming 'All organized labor help spring the trap. Rid the city of rats'. The resulting hand-to-hand combat, Dobbs, the Dunne brothers, and others felt, would neutralise the police's use of small arms, shotguns, and rifles, because they either could not be drawn effectively or else their discharge would endanger everyone involved in the melée, police and 'special deputies' included. The army of redressers – strikers, supporters, sympathetic workers from other unions, and legions of the unemployed – was poised for battle, readied 'to give the cops some surprises'. Behind the scenes, the strike-leadership pressured Olson to keep the National Guard out of sight, stressing to the Farmer-Labor Governor that if troops were, indeed, to take over the city and distribute foodstuffs, this would inflame the situation and quite possibly unleash even worse violence.[8]

Discipline was, perhaps, a little less rigorous among the police and the 'special deputies'. Feeling their oats after Saturday's exploits, the cops and their 'citizen's army' were overly confident of their capacity to physically rout pickets. Drawn to what they imagined would be another unequal contest, some of the professionals, Greek fraternity-boys (entire chapters of whom were said to have 'rushed down to scab headquarters', their 'atrophied social appetites'

8. On the union's preparations, see Dobbs 1972, pp. 82–3; Walker 1937, pp. 113–14; Korth 1995, p. 98.

hungry for a taste of humiliating their social inferiors), paid thugs, and employers who joined the ranks of the 'specials' were perhaps overtaken by 'a sort of gala holiday spirit'. Young playboys from the fashionable Lowry Hill district had been strutting about the Citizens' Alliance headquarters at the West Hotel and the Committee of 25's Hennepin Avenue rooms. These 'foppish' first citizens enjoyed their 'deputisation', revelling in a kind of 'Skull and Bones high spirit', according to Arthur Schlesinger, Jr. 'Booted, six-shooters at belt...the flashier of them strode about...getting the heft of new ax handles'. They looked forward to what was undoubtedly touted as the 'liberation' of Market Square, and on Monday morning some of them appeared dressed for sport. A football-helmet could be discerned bobbing about among the crowd of 'specials'. One socialite, Alfred Lindley, came decked out in jodhpurs and a polo-hat. The sight of this élite garb infuriated strikers and their plebeian allies, many of whom, no doubt, thought that for people like this, 'the business of clubbing down working-class sheep' was 'a bit of a lark'. Polo-hats became symbols of class-antagonism. Adding 'fuel to the flame' of underlying resentment, they would be, along with the badges of the 'special deputies', prizes to be seized in the Market Square battles and then taken back to strike-headquarters, where they were jocularly put on display. At dawn, the police and the motley crew of this deputised 'law and order brigade' milled about the market, awaiting the action. They had underestimated their adversaries.[9]

Minnesota's stormy Farmer-Labor congressman, Francis Shoemaker, given to grandstanding and other acts of adventurism that were anything but appreciated by the strike leadership,[10] nevertheless provided a sense of the anger evident among the strikers and their sympathisers. He appeared at the market around six o'clock in the morning, and was one of the first to be arrested. Brandishing a broom-handle, he harangued and threatened 'coppers', 'scabs' and others, warning them that if they were caught in 'alleyways' and 'rat traps' they would get a thrashing in retribution for the violence they had inflicted on those lured into *Tribune* Alley on Saturday night. Shoemaker was promptly taken into police-custody, charged with disorderly conduct, jailed, and then released on bond later that day. He missed the main attraction, a pitched battle that began soon after Shoemaker was hauled away by the police. Fighting commenced at an almost ritually understood announcement of the hostilities. Scab-trucks drove into the

---

9. Dobbs 1972, p. 83; Kramer 1942, pp. 392–3; Schlesinger, Jr. 1958, p. 387; Cannon 1944, p. 150; C.H., 'Sidelights from the Great Battle of the Minneapolis Workers', *The Militant*, 16 June 1934; Korth 1995, pp. 95, 122; Walker 1937, pp. 113–16, 121; Maloney interviewed by Duffy and Miller, 10 July 1979, Transcript, pp. 5–11, Box 2, File 'Minneapolis Teamsters Strike 1934', Maloney Papers, MNHS.

10. Shoemaker was actually banned from strike-headquarters. See Dobbs 1972, pp. 88–9, 111.

market, their windows screened with chicken-wire, and pulled up to the loading docks. Hauling a few, token crates, one of the trucks started to move out, and was immediately set upon by the strikers, who forced the driver to flee on foot. Disciplined pickets separated the 'special deputies' from the police, and then the Union's reserves began marching on the market, four abreast, clubs dangling at their sides, a menacing and seemingly endless onslaught. An initial contingent came from the basement of the nearby Central Labor Union, followed by a second phalanx from the Chicago Avenue strike-headquarters. The 'socialite specials', expecting 'a little picnic with a mad rabble', began 'to get some idea what the score was'. They 'broke into headlong flight with hardly a scuffle'.

Engaged almost entirely with uniformed police, Local 574's forces made sallies against the surrounded cops, separating a few out from the ranks, and withdrawing when they had to evacuate their injured to safety. Police and pickets battled, with the cops getting the worst of it; boisterous bystanders cheered on the strikers. With the 'deputies' dispersed, the police needed fresh infusions into their beleaguered ranks, and cops were rushed to the market from various Minneapolis precincts, swelling police numbers by fifteen hundred. But the strikers and their supporters were at least their equal in number, their ranks bolstered by sympathetic onlookers joining the fight. For two hours, it was a stand-off as pickets charged police, cops regrouped, and then retaliated. Rocks, clubs, and other debris were thrown at the police. Frustrated, trapped, and much the worse for wear, the police eventually unholstered their firearms, and pulled out sawed-off shotguns when one of their number was slashed in the face with a knife. This was the signal for Bob Bell to come barrelling into the police 'like a bat out of hell, with his horn honking'. As the cops scattered and Local 574 members leapt from the truck, the fighting intensified. 'It was almost a civil war', remembered one Minnesota striker, badly beaten by the police in the ensuing affray.

Meanwhile, Clara Dunne and Marvel Scholl headed a Women's Auxiliary protest of five to seven hundred people. Marching by the mayhem at the market, they proceeded to City Hall, defiantly breaking 'every traffic rule in Minneapolis'. Upon their arrival, they demanded to meet with the Mayor, who refused to see even a small delegation. The women nonetheless stirred up a scare amongst civic officials. Gun-toting police barred them from the seat of municipal power, but the crowd gathered on the pavements heard a fiery speech from Auxiliary member Frieda Charles, and learned of the women's demands: fire the Chief of Police, Mike Johannes; withdraw all 'special deputies'; and stop interfering with pickets.

Gradually, an assistant police-inspector oversaw the withdrawal of the police from the market-district, their orderly retreat aided by a contingent of 'special deputies'. No trucks had moved. More than thirty cops were injured, the bulk of them requiring hospitalisation; on the strikers' side, the injury-tally was much less, including a broken collar-bone, some broken ribs, and at least one seriously broken head. Bandaged workers unlucky enough to run into cops on Minneapolis streets after the affray were unceremoniously arrested. Johannes put the entire Minneapolis police force on 24-hour duty, and the Citizens' Alliance intensified its recruitment of 'special deputies'. Newspapers carried reports of appeals for an end to the violence, and 12 prominent Minneapolis citizens petitioned Washington to act decisively in what, they insisted, constituted an emergency-situation. Suggesting that the Regional Labor Board intervene in the conflict, end the strike, and 'restore peace and security to the citizens of Minneapolis', this contingent was distressed that 'a concentrated camp by several thousand strikers had resulted in various manufacturing plants being shut down'. Professing little faith in the abilities of Governor Olson to restore calm, this Group of Twelve feared that calling out the National Guard would 'result in further disorders, possible bloodshed or loss of life'. Particularly irksome was the threat of 'sympathetic strikes...launched by milk, ice, and coal wagon drivers'.

Indeed, trade-unions, outraged by the day's events, rallied to the standard of Local 574. The city's building trades, thirty-five thousand strong, declared a sympathetic general strike. Electricians, urged to establish solidarity with the truckers by two Communist League of America members, Oscar Coover and Chester Johnson, marched in a body to 1900 Chicago Avenue, placing themselves at the disposal of the voluntary strike-committee. The painters' union did likewise. Iron workers soon declared themselves on strike. Other unions opted for subterfuge: they proclaimed that their members were 'on holiday' as long as the General Drivers' Union members were walking picket-lines. Meridel Le Sueur's notebooks capture, in their cryptic and chaotic condensation of the moment, something of its explosive context:

> There was the strike...the headquarters women working men singing Annie Laurie radio going...young men in front...The mass meeting going on down town...Now they are meeting thousands...with the feeling broken down completely of getting into a middle-class society...and the language was racy and vulgar and that peculiar smile of the worker...knowing...he has not gotten into the money world.

Round one had gone to Local 574, and the class-struggle in Minneapolis was widening.[11]

---

11. The above paragraphs draw on A Striker, 'Minneapolis Shows the Way: Militant Mass Picket Line Routs Scabs, Cops, Special Deputies, and Thugs and Stops All Commercial Transport; Building Trades in Sympathy Strike; Women's Auxiliary Active in Fight; General Strike Sentement [sic] Growing; Workers' Spirit Soars', *The Militant*, 26 May 1934; Auxiliary Member, 'Women Active on the Firing Line', *The Militant*, 2 June 1934; A Sym-

On the Tuesday morning, 22 May 1934, huge crowds gathered in the market. Estimated at twenty to thirty thousand in number, the assembled mass of humanity at first had something of the carnivalesque about it. Many 'holidaying' workers were present. News-photographers were everywhere, and a local radio-station was set up to broadcast live from the day's events. The picture-houses had cameramen there to shoot newsreels of the day's activities, which would serve as shorts in cinemas showing feature-length films. Yet the standoff between the adversaries was anything but light-hearted. The two sides, both having taken up their positions in the market before dawn, defiantly stood their ground for several hours. The police made it clear they intended to keep the streets open and, with 'special deputies' in profusion, promised to have 1,500–2,000 patrolling the market-district. Learning from their defeat in the streets on Monday, the 'special deputies' were organised militarily into sections, each one to be accompanied by a uniformed police-officer. Employers announced that they would be moving perishables out of market-warehouses. Local 574 was committed to stopping all such trucking activity. It had the support of the vast bulk of Minneapolis's workers, organised and unorganised, employed and unemployed, on strike or just taking a short 'vacation'. But given the huge numbers present, there was not to be the same kind of coordinated planning that had gone into the General Drivers' Union's strategic use of its ranks on Monday. As Dobbs later noted, 'A planned battle was almost impossible on that day'.[12]

Accounts vary as to what happened. In one telling, things unfolded quickly. A crate of tomatoes kicked off the mayhem. As it appeared that a scab was about to load up a truck, the wooden produce-container was seized by a picket and thrown through a plate-glass window. The window shattered, shards of glass spraying on to the pavement. 'Instantly', in Dobbs's words, 'it became a free for all'. Strikers and sympathisers attacked the sections of deputies. Uniformed police, vastly outnumbered, laid back, for a time, as the Union's supporters thrashed the volunteer 'citizen's army', which was especially targeted by wrathful advocates of the workers' cause. Indeed, one newspaper-report claimed that 'At no time was

---

pathetic Striker, 'Support from Other Unions', *The Militant*, 2 June 1934; Maloney interviewed by Duffy and Miller, 10 July 1979, Transcript, pp. 1–28, quote on civil war at p. 3, 'Minneapolis Teamsters Strike 1934', Box 2, Maloney Papers, MNHS; Maloney interviewed by Salerno, Rachleff, and Seaverson, 1–4 April 1988, Transcript, p. 119, Maloney Biographical File, 1911–99, Box 1, Riehle Papers, MNHS; Mayer 1951, p. 198; Dobbs 1972, pp. 83–7; Walker 1937, pp. 113–17; Scholl 1975, p. 21; Korth 1995, pp. 97–8; Tselos 1971, p. 227; 'Strikers Fight Pitched Battle, 37 in Hospital, Officer Stabbed', 'Shoemaker Jailed After Strike Row', 'Group of 12 Appeals to Washington', and 'Building Trades Vote Sympathy Walkout to Involve 35,000', *Minneapolis Journal*, 21 May 1934; Meridel Le Sueur, 'Notebooks, Volume 8, 1934–1935', dated entry 29 May 1934, p. 18, Box 26, Le Sueur Papers, MNHS.
    12. Tselos 1971, p. 224; 'Shoemaker Jailed After Strike Row', *Minneapolis Journal*, 21 May 1934; Walker 1937, pp. 117–18; Dobbs 1972, pp. 87–8.

there any real clash between regular police and strikers', as the latter group concentrated their rage on the 'deputies', whom they considered strikebreakers. Picket-captain Shaun (Jack) Maloney confirmed that the cops were largely a non-presence: 'they did not participate.... I did not see a ... [uniformed police-man] involved that Tuesday morning, not a one'. There were, of course, inevi-table skirmishes with the 'harness-bulls' – the working-class designation of the police – but these fights never escalated to the level of violence directed at the 'specials'. At first reluctant to use guns, the cops were no match for the pickets, union-supporters, unemployed, and other Local 574 sympathisers, many of whom carried clubs, lead-pipes, baseball-bats, saps, and rubber lengths of hose filled with sand and plugged with lead. Matters only became more confused when a second detail of police arrived on the scene, seemingly without instructions as to what orientation to take toward the volunteer 'citizen's army'. Led by retired 'colonels' and 'majors', the 'deputies' were, by all accounts, quickly dispersed, many of them dropping their clubs and badges, seeking to blend anonymously into the hostile crowd. Another first-hand description of the Tuesday confronta-tion stressed that these morning-fights merely heralded the battle to come. The *grand finale* broke out at about noon, the precipitating incident being a club-war between two women, a pro-union female laying out her 'deputised female' assail-ant. This led to 'a roar that was heard for blocks'. Bill Kitt described what fol-lowed, as a crowd of Local 574 pickets and sympathisers surged into the street:

> The specials made no effort to stem the tide but turned and fled, tossing away
> their clubs and badges as they ran. Many were cornered in stalls and blind
> alleys and laid out three deep. Clubs swung everywhere as the fighting pick-
> ets surged irresistibly through the rows of stalls smashing down all opposi-
> tion. Several truckloads of deputies attempting to escape were surrounded
> and transferred to the mounting casualty list. In desperation the regular cops
> drove their cars into the ranks of the strikers in a vain effort to stop them.
> Ambulances worked overtime taking away the specials.

Kitt closed his account colloquially: the 'deputies', fifty of whom were injured, were 'completely licked'. Meridel Le Sueur confided to her notebooks that the businessmen who looked forward to a class-battle with the truckers 'found out it was a bloody matter to defend their marketing world'.

Regardless of how it originated or when it actually began, all accounts suggest how forcefully the hated 'special deputies' were routed. A Minneapolis Labor Board report of 13 May 1934 declared that as soon as the battle broke out, 'rocks and clubs [were] flying through the air'. The 'deputies' dispersed, many of them falling or being knocked down, while 'the mob ... trampled those underfoot while others kicked the prostrate forms'. 'A Striker' wrote to *The Militant* that, 'The cowardly sluggers [took] to their heels and [ran]'. Their dress and demeanour nonetheless marked them out as obvious class-enemies, and, in one case, the consequences were fatal. C. Arthur Lyman, vice-president of the American Ball Company and the long-serving attorney for the Citizens' Alliance, was a 44-year old father of four with quite extensive military and field-artillery volunteer-service. A leader in the Minneapolis Community Fund and the Rotary Club, as well as a central figure in Saint Mark's Church, Lyman was a member of Kappa Alpha fraternity. When strikers and 'specials' clashed, Lyman apparently sought cover in a grocery-store. In spite of his experience in military training, he had come to the market in footwear anything but suitable for the circumstances. Mrs. George Fahr, wife of a University of Minnesota medical-school faculty-member and a rare women's voice on the employers' committee (she had signed the Group of Twelve's appeal to Washington), described Lyman and the attack at the market:

> I saw Arthur Lyman come, being pushed forward by the crowd and trying to push the strikers back. The floor of the market was cobblestone, and Arthur had worn mountaineering boots with metal cleats in them. Nothing would have been more lethal than those boots were, and the strikers pressed upon him and he slipped and went down and they were on him like a pack of wolves.

His skull fractured in the violent market-fracas, Lyman was rushed to hospital, but was pronounced dead a few minutes after he was admitted. The Citizens' Alliance hung a framed parchment on its walls, dedicated 'In Memoriam to Arthur C. Lyman, who fought for his country abroad, and who knew how to fight and die for the same principles at home'.

The pillar of respectable Minneapolis society was one of two 'special deputies' to die as a result of injuries sustained in what would come to be remembered as 'The Battle of Deputies Run'. The other fatal casualty of 22 May 1934 was Peter Erath. Having moved to Minneapolis from the countryside, Erath was of more plebeian stock than Lyman, working as a labourer before setting up a marginal-coal and wood-hauling business. Like Lyman, Erath suffered a fractured skull and loss of blood, but hung on under the care of General Hospital physicians for a few days before succumbing to his injuries.

Those 'specials' who tried to stand their ground in 'The Battle of Deputies Run' were driven back to their headquarters, where they tended to the incapacitated, armed themselves with guns, and faced off anew against a jeering crowd. The damage inflicted was extensive. 'Our fellows were beaten up and bleeding and in a terrible condition', one 'deputy' later reported. Among the crowd, cheers erupted whenever a fleeing 'deputy' was knocked to the ground. Police, often acting with restraint, could barely contain their contempt for the 'volunteer specials' who proved so inept in the heat of battle; the 'harness bulls' were less vilified than these scorned 'deputies'. A letter to the editor in the *Minneapolis Journal* stated: 'it is a well known fact that the strikers as well as their friends held the regular police in high regard and esteem, while they looked upon the special police as nothing but mercenaries'. The hiring of these 'special' strikebreakers, according to this commentator, turned public sympathy away from the employers. 'The damn fools who went out as deputies got what was coming to 'em', snorted many Minneapolis citizens who otherwise claimed to be above aligning with either capital or labour in the spring of 1934.[13]

There were casualties on both sides, of course, and many fighting for the cause of Local 574 suffered injury. A striker known as 'Big Harold' had his scalp ripped back from his forehead to the crown of his head, and was stitched up at 1900 Chicago Avenue by Dr. McCrimmon and Marvel Scholl. The only anaesthesia available came out of a whisky-bottle. Minor skirmishes continued throughout the day and night, and pickets, according to one source, 'continued to mop up, or settle individual accounts in alleys and bars' until ten o'clock on the Tuesday evening. Some cops supposedly went into hiding for as long as twelve hours, resurfacing only when it was clear that the hand-to-hand combat had run its course. But 'The Battle of Deputies Run', an intense and deadly confrontation, was essentially over in short order. And it left the General Drivers' Union in command of the situation, seemingly unchallenged. 'In less than an hour after the battle started', Dobbs claimed in *Teamster Rebellion*, 'there wasn't a cop to be seen in the market, and pickets were directing traffic in the now peaceful district. For good measure all police were run out of the vicinity of the strike headquarters and they were kept away for the duration of the walkout'. According to Bill Kitt, 'the strikers had complete control'. It was even claimed that Local 574 prevented looting and property-damage by patrolling the market-district

---

13. The above paragraphs draw on Walker 1937, pp. 117–21, 176; Meridel Le Sueur, 'Notebooks, Volume 8, 1934–1935', dated entry 29 May 1934, p. 18, Box 26, Le Sueur Papers, MNHS; 'Statement Made by Labor Bd, 13 May, Battle of Deputies Run', p. 12, and 'Skoglund', [typescript of Skoglund's notes on 'Battle of Deputies Run'], File 'American City Strike Notes: Dobbs, Skoglund', Box 1, CRW Papers, MNHS; Maloney interviewed by Salerno, Rachleff, and Seaverson, 5–9 April 1988, Transcript, pp. 133–5, Maloney Biographical File, 1911–99, Box 1, Riehle Papers, MNHS; A Striker, 'At the Minneapolis City Market – "The Battle of Deputy Run"', *The Militant*, 2 June 1934; Hagen E. Johnson, 'Strike Viewpoints: Letter to the Editor', *Minneapolis Journal*, 27 May 1934; William Kitt, 'A Lesson in Law and Order', *The Militant*, 2 June 1934; Dobbs 1972, p. 88; Korth 1995, pp. 99, 119–27; Tselos 1971, p. 225. Mrs. Fahr's approving commentary on her friend Arthur Lyman can be contrasted with the less laudatory appraisal in C.H., 'Sidelights from the Great Battle of the Minneapolis Workers', *The Militant*, 16 June 1934. For a discussion of Lyman, see 'Rites Set Tomorrow for Young Business Man Serving as Special Officer', *Minneapolis Journal*, 23 May 1934; and for Erath, 'Special Policeman Injured in Strike Riot is Near Death', *Minneapolis Journal*, 25 May 1934.

and keeping the remnants of the fighting crowd in check. Bill Brown, prone to hyperbole, was adamant that

> we could have taken over the city after the Battle of Deputies Run. We controlled it. All that would have been necessary 'to seize power' would have been to urge a few thousand strikers to capture the Court House. That would have done it .... the union might have made me soviet mayor, huh? and Skoglund over there commissar of police.

This was the Citizens' Alliance's worst nightmare, one that its forces believed reflected the aims of the General Drivers' Union's Trotskyist leadership. But it was entirely beside the point to those, like the Dunne brothers, Skoglund, Dobbs, and other CLA members, who were 'revolutionaries enough to tell the difference between a militant strike and a revolution'. What they wanted was 'a truck drivers' union in Minneapolis'. Unlike Teamster boss Dan Tobin, who ordered the General Drivers' Union to seek arbitration rather than continue the fight, they would never abandon this basic purpose of building a union.[14]

14. Scholl 1975, p. 21; Walker 1937, pp. 118–27; Kitt, 'A Lesson in Law and Order', *The Militant*, 2 June 1934; Mayer 1951, p. 200; Korth 1995, p. 99; Dobbs 1972, pp. 88–91. Note the discussion of dual power in Redfield 1984, pp. 16–17. After the May 1934 violence, the issue of arbitration and federal conciliation or mediation was ever-present, an explicit attempt to derail the militant leadership of the insurgent truckers. The first mediator sent into the fray was B.M. Marshman, Commissioner of Conciliation of the United States Labor Department, who appeared in Minneapolis on 22 May 1934. See 'U.S. Sends Mediator to Strike Scene: Conciliator Will Act If Board Fails', *Minneapolis Journal*, 22 May 1934; 'Mediator Marshman Hopes for Way Out in Strike Impasse', *Minneapolis Journal*, 23 May 1934.

Chapter Ten
May 1934: Settlement Secured; Victory Postponed

As the forces opposing the Minneapolis truckers' union-organising gathered in the aftermath of the Battle of Deputies Run, the most rabid of the city's anti-union employers contemplated how best to fight back. Some wanted to throw more police into the field and move trucks at any cost. Others apparently proposed luring the strike-leadership into ostensible negotiations at their West Hotel headquarters, but then to arrange a mass arrest. Such die-hards yielded nothing to Governor Olson. The state's leading official, shaken by the violence in Minneapolis's market and attacked by sources such as the *Chicago Tribune* for having served as 'an invitation to disorder', requested a temporary, 24-hour truce. As a show of strength, Local 574 called a mass rally on the evening of Wednesday, 23 May 1934, at which well over five thousand men, women, and children roared their approval for the General Drivers' Union and its ongoing struggle. Armfuls of circulars headed 'NO SURRENDER' had called on them to gather together at the civic Parade Grounds. Furious applause greeted every speaker, save for Olson's lieutenant-governor, K.K. Solberg, whose wishes of 'God speed' produced only stony silence. 'There was a wild free spirit abroad that night at the Parade', according to Left Oppositionist C.R. Hedlund, 'a spirit surging with hope' that 'welded together a solidarity of the workers of Minneapolis'.[1]

---

1. Walker 1937, pp. 122–7; Korth 1995, pp. 99–102; Dobbs 1972, pp. 90–1; 'Conciliator Will Act If Board Fails', and 'Both Sides Avoid Major Encounters', *Minneapolis Journal*, 22 May 1934 (evening edition); 'Begin Canvas on Orders of Federal Board', *Minneapolis*

As the armistice held in check the violence that had marked the Monday and Tuesday, 'cops and businessmen, white-faced with venom', stared in hatred at the union-advocates handing out leaflets or the small groups of pickets who remained on the streets. Moderates among the trucking owners prevailed, however, and agreed that they would not try to transport goods if the Union consented to remove the mass pickets and negotiate through the Regional Labor Board. As a 'stick' to complement the 'carrot' of his truce, Olson put the National Guard, 3,700 strong, on alert, although as a concession to an angered union-leadership he agreed to continue to keep the militia harnessed indoors. Amidst reports that the National Guard had dispersed crowds of striking workers at the Toledo Electric Auto-Lite plant, using bayonets and machine-guns to quell the riotous and militant crowd, Olson ordered units of Guardsmen from outside Minneapolis into the city. Companies were mobilised from Owatonna, Jackson, Hutchinson, Austin, Northfield, Stillwater, and Aitkin. Reports in the press focused on their field-equipment of 'rifles, machine guns, and gas and chemical warfare implements'. There was also much talk, fuelled by Chief of Police Mike Johannes, that military authority would be necessary to deal with the influx of 'communists and sluggers' into Minneapolis from Detroit, Chicago, St. Louis and elsewhere. State-officials had apparently been informed that, 'a large number of lawless and desperate characters were drifting into the city from all parts of the country in an effort to take over the strike for their own purposes'. Never substantiated, such claims of a 'Red menace' about to overrun Minneapolis exacerbated tensions and extended the pressure to bring the strike to an end.[2]

Over the next few days, the Dunne brothers, Skoglund, Brown, and others parleyed with the trucking bosses, facilitated by government-mediators, but they never abandoned their insistence that they be constantly protected by pickets from police-intimidation and the threat of arrest. With Regional Labor Board officials passing notes from the employers' committee and the General Drivers' Union back and forth between the parties, it at first appeared that nothing would come of the 'diplomatic shuttle between combatants', now ensconced at the Nicollet Hotel. As the truce was extended from one day to two, however, progress began to be made, with the employers yielding on the Union's demand that all workers be reinstated. Local 574's committee took a page from the history of the earlier coal-yard strike and simply withdrew the demand for the closed shop,

Journal, 23 May 1934; C.H., 'Sidelights from the Great Battle of Minneapolis Workers', *The Militant*, 16 June 1934.

2. 'Johannes to Reject Any Proposals to Extend Armistice', 'Reds and Sluggers in City, Chief Says', 'Troops Smash Strike Siege at Toledo Plant', and 'Plans to Resume Motor Transport in City at 9 PM – Regional Board Rushes Efforts, Abandons Formal Sessions to Confer with Groups', *Minneapolis Journal*, 24 May 1934; 'Fresh Troops Relieve Guard in Toledo Riot', *Minneapolis Journal*, 25 May 1934.

asking for other provisions that established *de facto* recognition of the Union. While this concession would, of course, limit the decisiveness of any outcome, it largely took the anti-union wind out of the employers' sails. The organising committee was adamant that the business-committee's insistence that any strikers 'guilty of any crime' would not have to be taken back was merely an attempt by the bosses to keep 'the opportunity to frame and convict on false charges any man whom they wanted to get rid of in the union'.[3]

The Law and Order Committee of the Citizens' Alliance, popularly dubbed the 'Low and Odor' by workers sympathetic to the truckers and their union-drive, offered $20,000 for information leading to what the strike-leaders unsentimentally referred to as the apprehension 'of the exterminator of a couple of rats'. Indeed, in the aftermath of the May strike, concerted efforts, stretching over months, were made to try and convict a Local 574 striker and a youthful 'mentally deficient' union-supporter for the murder of Arthur Lyman. Both cases, widely regarded as frame-ups, ended up in legal 'no-bill' decisions or acquittals. In the last such effort, launched in the autumn of 1934, Happy Holstein, a Chippewa truck-driver and leading figure in the Strike Committee of 100, was arrested. This prompted the formation of a militant Trade Union Defense Committee, which bailed Holstein out of jail on a $10,000 bond, secured by putting the Milk Drivers' Union hall up as collateral. Meanwhile, as representatives of labour and capital discussed how to get Minneapolis moving again, the City Council erupted in a testy row over who should foot the bill for paying the 'special police'. With 43 arrested strikers and Local 574 supporters still in jail, unable to cough up the required $200 bail, the first of approximately two hundred trials began in the courts, pickets and others facing a variety of charges from disorderly conduct to assault. Dozens would be convicted, but the bulk of those brought to trial had their charges dismissed; when found guilty, strikers often received terms in the workhouse, ranging from 10 to 45 days.[4]

In the end, the sticking point for the employers, as it had been for Dan Tobin, was the issue of 'inside workers'. As James Rorty noted, 'The employers immediately saw the implied threat: if Local 574 took in chicken pickers and fruit

3. Dobbs 1972, pp. 89–91; Korth 1995, pp. 99–102; 'Workers Committee Will Submit Peace Proposals to Union but No Recommendation', *Minneapolis Journal*, 25 May 1934.

4. Walker, 1937, pp. 122–7; Walker, 'Holstein Frame-Up', in File 'Notes Local 574 and Strike', Box 1, CRW Papers, MNHS; 'Riot Trials Open; First of 200 in Court', *Minneapolis Journal*, 25 May 1934; 'Truck Driver Gets 45 Days', *Minneapolis Journal*, 27 May 1934; Dobbs 1972, pp. 89–91; C.H., 'Sidelights from the Great Battle of the Minneapolis Workers', *The Militant*, 16 June 1934; Korth 1995, pp. 99–102; and on later attempted 'frame-ups' involving those charged with the murder of Lyman, see Dobbs 1973, pp. 18–23; 'Minneapolis Notes: Plot Frame-Up in Mpls', *The Militant*, 23 June 1934; 'Minneapolis Bosses Plot Frame-Up of 574 Leaders', *The Militant*, 8 December 1934; *Minneapolis Labor Review*, 23 November 1934. Note also 'The "Low and Odor" League', *The Organizer*, 25 June 1934.

handlers, what was there to prevent their encompassing the entire body of unorganized workers in the city, building a union, a one-big union, that would hold the destinies of Minneapolis in its powerful hands?' Industrial unionism, the rallying cry of Minneapolis militants, had strong opponents among the bosses as well as within the AFL officialdom. Pressed by Governor Olson, Roosevelt's mediators, and a recalcitrant employers' committee, the Trotskyist leadership of Local 574 conceded that an agreement that essentially conferred union-recognition, arbitration of wages and hours based on past concessions, and reinstatement of all strikers, was a limited victory that sacrificed 'no fundamentals'. Governor Olson worked both sides of the Nicollett Hotel, and, along with Regional Labor Board officials, drafted a paragraph that seemed to give the Union what it needed on the issue of recognition: 'All members of the General Drivers and Helpers Union Local No. 574 in dealing with employers may be represented by the officers of such Union'. The wording – *may* – was, indeed, inconclusive, but Olson assured the General Drivers' Union that the settlement covered all workers that it considered among its ranks. In discussions with the employers, however, Olson allowed them to cherish their view that they held the upper hand in determining the basic parameters of who was included in the settlement. A subsequent paragraph in the agreement read: 'The term "employees" as used herein shall include truck drivers and helpers, and such other persons as are ordinarily engaged in the trucking operations of the business of the individual employer'. This seemingly left the definition of 'trucking operations' all-too open-ended and, as such, could well exclude 'inside workers' from union-protections and representations. But it was also possible to interpret the settlement's wording more inclusively. A third clause, moreover, established that all disagreements had to be resolved through a Board of Arbitration. Again, there was a lack of precision in the language used to develop resolution, which would ultimately prove contentious.

As a package, these and other clauses, in spite of ambiguity, left the General Drivers' Union's leaders thinking that they had made significant advances. They were convinced that the settlement achieved, for all intents and purposes, union-recognition, setting up a means of handling disputes, paving the way towards realising collective-bargaining rights in the trucking industry. After a strike that had polarised Minneapolis, leaving one prominent citizen and another 'special deputy' dead, a 'progressive governor' caught between a rock and a hard place, its local police physically defeated, and thousands of National Guardsmen readied for perhaps worse battle – 'eleven days of the fiercest class warfare in the Northwest', according to one author – postponing the final conflict that would ultimately resolve the meaning of industrial unionism in the city's critically important trucking industry seemed, to many, a not-unreasonable option. 'Recognizing the need for recoupment and consolidation of actual gains as a basis for future struggle', the strike-leadership urged acceptance of the Labor Board-orchestrated agreement at a Local 574 ratification-meeting. It did so with a frank acknowledgement that what had been achieved by the General Drivers' Union, while a monumental breakthrough, was by no means a complete victory. No written collective-bargaining document was signed between the Union and the employers, since this Local 574 demand had been dropped. What stood in its stead was a consent-order issued by the Regional Labor Board and signed by both parties, neither of which had reached agreement about what constituted 'trucking operations'. Reliance on arbitration, agreed to by both the employers and the General Drivers' Union, suggested weaknesses among both camps, displaced fundamental disagreements, and postponed a decisive final reckoning of the dispute between workers and employers.

At issue in the way in which arbitration was understood by labour and capital, respectively, was a fundamental divergence of class-perspectives. Employers insisted that arbitration would only be entered into when employees at a particular trucking concern expressed their firm-specific complaints relating to wages and conditions, which would then be submitted to the Regional Labor Board to be arbitrated by a panel containing, among others, representatives of Local 574 and the specific trucking company. This individual-firm resolution-mechanism effectively nullified the existence of the Union, since it refused to cede to the recognised body of organised labour in the trucking industry the right to arbitrate issues of wages and conditions on behalf of its membership, restricting all arbitration to cases involving specific workers within individual firms. The General Drivers' Union saw arbitration as operating very differently. Local 574's view was that the Board of Arbitration be a standing body empowered to arbitrate general issues of wages and conditions of employment within the trucking sector.

None of this, however, was sufficiently clear at the time of the May settlement. For the leadership of the Union, as well as the majority of truckers and helpers who stood behind them, what had been secured seemed enough, although it was all-too-apparent that future struggles were inevitable.[5]

---

5. The above paragraphs draw on Rorty 1936, p. 191; Walker 1937, pp. 124–8; Mayer 1951, pp. 196–200; Scholl 1975, p. 22; 'Terms of Strike Peace', and 'Thousands Back at Work, Moving Mountains of Goods', *Minneapolis Journal*, 26 May 1934; 'Labor Board to Arbitrate Strike Issues', *Minneapolis Journal*, 27 May 1934. Korth 1995, pp. 98–104, 136–40 presents a useful perspective on the imbroglio regarding arbitration. Local 574 militant and strike-picket captain Shaun (Jack) Maloney, would later insist that Olson 'flat out double-crossed us' and that the Farmer-Labor Governor hoodwinked the strike-committee on the meaning of 'inside workers'. See Maloney's interview with Salerno, Rachleff, and Seaverson, 5–9 April 1988, Transcript, pp. 136–7, Box 1, Maloney Biographical File, 1911–99, Riehle Papers, MNHS.

There were workers who demanded that picket-lines be re-established, and that the strike continue to a more clear-cut resolution. Sources as divergent as the *Minneapolis Journal* and the Communist Party insisted that ratification of the settlement, which took place over a marathon Local 574 session lasting many hours, was, in fact, in jeopardy. Militants clamoured for a general strike to be called, while opposition to ending the confrontation was, at times, quite strong. Yet in the end, as the *Minneapolis Journal* reported,

> The strike leaders favored acceptance and urged the men to realize that it offered the union some important concessions. The plea was made that the agreement is 'an important first step' and it was pointed out that rejection meant a long and perhaps uncertain battle. It was the plea of the strike leaders that finally brought ratification by the big crowd.

The insurgent truckers trusted the Dunnes, Carl Skoglund, Farrell Dobbs, and Bill Brown, who had established a national reputation as resolute rank-and-file leaders. A Trotskyist leadership reviled by the Citizens' Alliance as hell-bent on the revolutionary creation of a Soviet Republic, had, in fact, pursued an uncompromisingly and militantly effective strike-strategy. Rather than lead workers into what could well have been a lethal confrontation with armed National Guardsmen, a battle that could easily have been lost, and that would almost certainly have resulted in a nullification of the achievements secured in the Nicolett Hotel negotiations, Local 574's leaders thought it was time to consolidate what had, at considerable cost, already been secured.

The major result was a massive influx of previously unorganised workers into a nascent union: by the summer, the General Drivers' Union could boast a membership of seven thousand. Even more importantly, the Minneapolis working class had faced down a formidable adversary, and done so by demonstrating a decisive refusal to be cowed by the usual array of ideological scapegoating and baton-wielding gendarmes. As Cannon wrote in *The Militant*:

> What is out of the ordinary in Minneapolis, what is most important in this respect, is that while the Minneapolis strike began with violent assaults on the strikers, it did not end there.... 'Business men' volunteering to put the workers in their place and college boys out for a lark – as special deputies – to say nothing of uniformed cops, handed over their badges and fled in terror before the mass fury of the aroused workers.... Here was a demonstration that the American workers are willing and able to fight in their own interests. Nothing is more important than this, for, in the last analysis, everything depends on it.

'This was an example of mass action', Cannon concluded, 'which points the way forward for the future victorious struggles of the American workers'. In spite of *not* formally calling for a general strike, Minneapolis's Trotskyist vanguard had, indeed, mobilised what constituted an overwhelming municipal work-stoppage and had, in a few short months over the course of the winter and spring of 1934, brought thousands of workers into an American Federation of Labor union that had resisted organising the unorganised. None of the other epic labour-battles of 1934 had achieved as much.[6]

When a Citizens' Alliance stalwart, an old slouch-hat concealing his countenance and an oversized raincoat draping his physique, sneaked into the Monday, 28 May 1934 mass ratification-meeting of the General Drivers' Union, he was aghast at what he saw. 'There were thousands and thousands of bums and hoodlums and Communists there', he insisted. 'Agitators worked the crowd up to the highest pitch of mob fury. They shouted, sang, and yelled. It was really horrible'. Prominent Minneapolis citizens, some of them having served as 'special deputies', demanded new laws to curb the wanton violence of the strikers, and denounced Olson as having 'called a meeting of the striking truck drivers at the theatre and told them to tighten their belts, arm themselves, and take what they wanted'. Rumours circulated, even making their way to Roosevelt's Department of State, that Minneapolis had been overrun by fifteen hundred Communist-imported, strike-supporting thugs from Chicago. 'Hopped up on cocaine', they were ostensibly the type responsible for killing Arthur Lyman. Rather than confront the actuality of class-war in the City Market, a public space described by élite matron Mrs. George Fahr, as 'right in the heart of Minneapolis … right in your lap', many opponents of trade-unionism needed to conjure up an enemy that was imposed on them from outside of their customary social relations. Reality and fantasy had clearly converged. The Battle of Deputies Run confirmed the class-hatred that now had many of the well-to-do firmly in its irrational grip. Face-to-face encounters with proletarian insurgency drove the dagger of fear and loathing deep into many a bourgeois bosom. Among the frenzied 'mob', however, perceptions were often, ironically, more sedate. Many thought that 'Minneapolis in time might [now] be made a tolerable place in which to live', and the next morning they went back to their workplaces, the drivers and helpers of Local 574 among them doing so, for the first time, under the modest terms of what they considered their first 'union-contract'. Robley Cramer used the *Minneapolis*

---

6. The above paragraphs draw on *Minneapolis Journal* quoted in Dunne and Childs 1934, pp. 19–20; James P. Cannon, 'Learn from Minneapolis!', *The Militant*, 26 May 1934; Cannon 1944, pp. 152–3; Dobbs 1972, p. 100; Korth 1995, p. 88. 'K.', in a telegram to *The Militant*, 26 May 1934, stated that 'The Communist League has raised the slogan of general strike throughout the twin cities and sentiment for it is spreading like wildfire', but V.R. Dunne always maintained that this call for generalised work-stoppages was never made, precisely because it would have drawn conservative AFL leaders into the strike-committee and inevitably compromised the capacity of Trotskyists to lead the struggle to a positive conclusion. For a fuller discussion of this point, see Tselos 1971, pp. 230–3.

Labor Review to trumpet the view that the strike and settlement constituted 'the greatest victory over the Citizens' Alliance in the history of the city'. Cannon wrote more prudently that, 'The spirit of victory and achievement was in the air, although no attempt had been made by the leadership to exaggerate the gains of the first battle'.[7]

Cannon and the national leadership of the Communist League of America had been kept informed of Minneapolis developments in the first six months of 1934 largely by mail. A strike in New York hotels and restaurants, led by B.J. Field, a mercurial Left Oppositionist, had preoccupied Cannon, Shachtman and other New York-resident League leaders during Minneapolis's coal-yards work-stoppage in February. As Field proved impossible to bring under League discipline, leading the culinary and hostelry-workers to defeat, the distant battle of Northwest truckers, helpers, and coal-heavers, which appeared to be making good headway, was, perhaps, left to its own devices. When a fresh confrontation broke out among the Trotskyist-led Minnesota teamsters in mid-May 1934, Cannon and the rest of the National Executive Committee in New York were again involved in a number of other developments. They were aware of the ongoing struggle to consolidate the General Drivers' Union, to be sure, but they perhaps had an incomplete understanding of what was about to unfold. The extent to which Local 574, and its Trotskyist leadership, was on the verge of becoming national news had not registered decisively.[8]

The Battle of Deputies Run changed all this, for the 22 May 1934 clash in Market Square put Minneapolis truckers and their struggle on the front pages of major metropolitan newspapers, where it was considered alongside the coverage of mass strikes in Toledo and San Francisco. More importantly, perhaps, sensational newsreels

> showed combat scenes filmed during the Tuesday battle. Workers everywhere reacted enthusiastically to the news. Audiences in movie houses broke out in cheers at the sight of pickets clubbing cops for a change, since in most strikes it was entirely the other way around.

Offsetting the finger-pointing that followed in the wake of B.J. Field's ill-advised direction of the New York hotel-workers, his eventual expulsion from the

---

7. Walker 1937, pp. 127–8; Korth 1995, pp. 99–101, 126; Tselos 1971, pp. 232–3, quoting Robley and *Minneapolis Labor Review*, 1934; James P. Cannon, 'Union Recognition Gained by Militant Minneapolis Battles: Victory is an Inspiration to Workers Everywhere', *The Militant*, 2 June 1934.
8. National coverage of events in Minneapolis began in May and reached into August. Among many sources, see, for instance, coverage in the *New York Times*, 22–25 May 1934; 10 July 1934; 16 July 1934; 18 July 1934; 21–22 July 1934; 27 July 1934; 5 August 1934; 12 August 1934.

Communist League of America, and the ultimate breakup of the union-drive in the food and entertainment-sector, developments in Minneapolis garnered the American Left Opposition considerable credibility among trade-unionists. Cannon would later note that after the Field fiasco, there were those ready to write the Trotskyists off in terms of their 'contacts and forces' in the labour movement. The Minneapolis organising drive re-established a sense that 'The Trotskyists mean business.... Serious people were attracted to the League, and our whole membership was stiffened with a new sense of discipline and responsibility toward the organization'. All of this combined to impress upon Cannon and others in New York 'their first inkling of the full scope of the Teamster strike'. As the Minneapolis truckers' strike negotiations unfolded quickly in the aftermath of the violence at the market, with the National Guard mobilised to be a serious threat to the Union, the future of working-class interests in the Northwest hung in the balance.

It was apparent to both Local 574's established informal leadership, as well as Cannon and others in New York, that Olson, Roosevelt's Labor Board officials, and the employers were manoeuvring striking workers, relying on making contradictory assurances to the opposed parties, ambivalent language in the settlement, and other such trickery to re-establish bourgeois order in Minneapolis. Knowing full-well that, with the Left Opposition now associated with one of 1934's most dramatic class-battles, there would be criticism galore directed at Local 574 from naysayers as divergent as the Communist Party and the Citizens' Alliance, the New York-based National Executive Committee understood that it needed both to help in Minneapolis and to 'take responsibility' for the strike's outcome. Communication by mail was obviously not sufficient, if the Communist League of America leadership was to offer guidance and support to its Minneapolis comrades in Local 574. The fledgling organisation was anything but financially stable, Cannon noting that 'we were still so poor that we couldn't afford a telephone in the office'. Yet the League went to the extraordinary expense of flying Cannon to Minneapolis. It was probably the veteran-revolutionist's first time on an airplane: as a Wobbly agitator, he rode trains to get to strikes, and even as a high-ranking Communist *en route* to Comintern gatherings in Moscow over the course of the 1920s, his transatlantic travel and traversing of Europe was done by steamship and railroad. Cannon walked into a meeting of the organising committee at 1900 Chicago Avenue, looked at Carl Skoglund, and asked rhetorically, 'What the hell kind of trouble are you getting us into now'. It was a Cannonesque kind of ice-breaker, and Skogie's smile conveyed to the young militants in the room that this new arrival from New York was their 'kind of people'.[9]

---

9. Dobbs 1972, pp. 92–4; Cannon 1944, pp. 134–5, 150–1; Harry DeBoer in Evans (ed.) 1976, pp. 90–2.

Cannon's role was, undoubtedly, to shore up the voluntary organising committee's sense that a limited victory was worth seizing in late May 1934. Ray Dunne and Carl Skoglund had come to the conclusion that they had erred in not involving the national leadership more directly in the events unfolding between January and May 1934 in Minneapolis. A part of their reluctance stemmed from a sense that Cannon was overwhelmed, in New York, with 'troubles in the center', a reference to the conflicts that had long raged on the National Executive Committee, as detailed in the Appendix to this volume.[10] This factional impasse, pitting Cannon and his allies, including the proletarian current active in the teamsters' insurgency, against Max Shachtman and his supporters, many of them concentrated among the New York youth, skewed the political judgement of Trotskyist teamsters' leaders. Dunne, Skoglund, and other Minneapolis supporters of Cannon regarded these intra-Left Opposition battles as emanating from 'a petty-bourgeois grouping'; the resulting factionalism had, indeed, stymied the Communist League of America. If the consequences of this organisational strife tended to be concentrated in New York, and were most often associated with international issues, the negative reach of these difficulties, what Cannon would later refer to as 'the dog days' of American Trotskyism, extended into the Minneapolis situation.[11] With Dunne and Skoglund reticent to load 'onto New York local problems that would only add' to Cannon's difficulties, the Trotskyist-led teamsters' uprising was deprived, for a time, of important political leadership that would later prove decisive in moving the mobilisation forward and keeping it decisively on track. Dunne later acknowledged that the Minneapolis Trotskyists had committed a 'grievous mistake' in not keeping Cannon and the New York leadership informed of the 'fast-developing' situation in the truckers' insurgency. In this, Dunne and Skoglund not only made a wrong judgement, but they did so on the basis of an inadequate understanding of the situation in New York, which had been altered somewhat by signs of Cannon and Shachtman coming together in their opposition to B.J. Field's disappointing performance as a hotel-workers' strike-leader.[12] Dunne and Skoglund were thus almost certainly unaware of faint, but hopeful, signs that the Shachtman-Cannon impasse of 1931–3 was about to be transcended in the new context of 1934's mass struggles. More critically, however, their failure to keep the New York CLA centre fully aware of what was unfolding in Minneapolis meant that the leaders of Local 574 did not receive a great deal of input from Cannon and others, at a crucial time during the May negotiations that would bring the second truckers' strike to its conclusion.

10. A thorough introduction to this factional context is provided in Cannon et al. 2002.
11. Cannon 1944, pp. 80–100.
12. Cannon 1944, pp. 126–35.

Agreements were reached between Governor Olson, Local 574 representatives such as Farrell Dobbs and Bill Brown, and the Employers' Advisory Committee, in which the crucial ambiguities around the Union's right to represent specific workers and reliance on arbitration (which was also weighed down with uncertainty) papered over the irreconcilable differences between the General Drivers' Union and the Citizens' Alliance. When Cannon did appear at 1900 Chicago Avenue, on either Thursday or Friday, 24/25 May 1934, he was immediately made a part of the strike-settlement negotiations, caucusing with the Dunnes, Skoglund, Dobbs, and Brown. But the foundations of a settlement were largely in place, and, as Philip A. Korth later concluded, 'Peace spread over Minneapolis like a cheap veneer, thinly masking both workers' dissatisfaction and suspicion, and employers' determination never to bargain with the union'.[13]

Vincent Raymond Dunne recalled, years later, that it was Cannon's capacity to relate the local needs of the General Drivers' Union and the ways in which these affected and fit with nationwide developments in the class-struggle and the well-being, influence, and growth of the Communist League of America that was 'almost completely new and strange'. What clearly impressed Dunne was Cannon's capacity to draw certain lessons from his past experiences that could then be assimilated to the particularities of specific, and distinctly new, situations. Cannon had an instinctive aversion to the false promise of state-orchestrated labour-boards and processes of arbitration. He abhorred professional mediators. 'They came into Minneapolis all greased up for another standard performance', he would later note contemptuously. Cannon also seemed particularly adept at reinforcing his comrades' inclinations not to capitulate to AFL officials like Cliff Hall and the Local 574 Executive Board members influenced by him, all of whom would have willingly given Governor Olson 'a free hand' in the negotiations.[14]

---

13. Dobbs 1972, pp. 93–4. It is difficult to pin down precisely when Cannon arrived in Minneapolis, and while Dunne and Childs 1934, pp. 19–21 is factually inaccurate and sectarian in its presentation, there is a believable assertion that Cannon was in meetings with Ray Dunne and Carl Skoglund as Grant Dunne and Bill Brown addressed the Friday ratification-meeting. Korth's statement appears on pp. 104–5 of Korth 1995.

14. Dobbs 1972, p. 93; Cannon 1944, p. 157. Shaun (Jack) Maloney always stressed how Olson's attacks 'were always on the union first and the Citizens' Alliance last', but this position may well have grown out of Cannon's post-May 1934 interventions. It did not seem entirely borne out by the trust invested in Olson by Dobbs in May 1934, as suggested above. Finally, Maloney insisted that 'Local 574 was opposed to arbitration', except on a one-time basis, relating to wage-issues, when the limited concession of arbitration could be used to secure a strike-settlement. Again, this seems to have been a position that emerged out of Cannon's post-May 1934 involvement in Local 574, for it does not apply to the resolution of the second teamsters' strike. For Maloney's positions, see his interview with Duffy and Miller, 4 June 1979, Transcript, pp. 2–14, Box 2, File 'Minneapolis Teamsters Strike 1934', Maloney Papers, MNHS; and an informal note on arbitration appended to Specktor 1984 in Box 4, File 'Miscellaneous Notes and Clippings', Maloney Papers, MNHS.

Indeed, it was Cannon's approach to Olson that was most noteworthy. 'Floyd Olson was undoubtedly the leader of the official labor movement in Minnesota', Cannon later wrote, 'but we did not recognise his leadership'. Cannon's adroitness, however, lay in his understanding that Olson could be pressured, albeit only so far, to exercise his influence positively for the General Drivers' Union. Pushed beyond where he was prepared to go, Cannon understood that the Governor would then be backed into a corner where he would have to mobilise the National Guard in a 'naked strikebreaking action'. It was one thing for Local 574's forces to best the Minneapolis police and their despised 'deputies' in open street-battle. It would have been something quite different to confront armed state Guardsmen, whose ties to strikers and local supporters were undoubtedly weaker than those of local police, and whose capacities to exercise restraint with their weapons would necessarily have been considerably less than those of the home-grown cops. This dilemma, as well as pointed Communist Party criticism that the strike-settlement flowed from the leadership of Local 574's fear of battling the National Guard, no doubt prompted some in the Trotskyist ranks to suggest that this 'ace in the hole of American capitalism' could well be neutralised by a concerted campaign to proselytise among these 'young workers dressed in soldiers uniform'. In the absence of any such revolutionary activity preceding the calling out of the National Guard in Minneapolis in May 1934, the situation was, perhaps, posed in more starkly oppositional terms. On the one hand, Olson had no appetite for escalating the Minnneapolis truckers' strike into a seeming test of state-power. On the other, Cannon and the Trotskyist leadership of the strike appreciated that, if pushed beyond certain limits, Olson would necessarily be forced to do just this. Knowing full well that the strike had been organised in order to secure the diverse workforce associated with the Minneapolis trucking industry the protections of trade-unionism, it would have been an adventurist (and defeatist) folly to lead militant workers into a revolutionary confrontation with the state.

Cannon thus served as a voice of realism in the strike-settlement negotiations. He understood that

> Every strike is a compromise in the sense that it leaves the bosses in control of industry and free to exploit the workers. The best settlement only limits and checks this exploitation to a certain extent. Realistic leaders do not expect justice from the capitalists, they only strive to extract as much as possible for the union in the given situation and strengthen their forces for another fight.

Knowing from his experience as an itinerant agitator in the class-struggle army of the Industrial Workers of the World, and well aware of the Communist Party's trade-union record, Cannon appreciated that 'revolutionary workers have been distinguished by a singular one-sidedness in regard to strike and trade union strategy'. Having led and organised many a militant strike, American revolutionaries had nonetheless 'seldom succeeded in maintaining a stable union'. How and when to settle strikes so as to keep alive the momentum of industrial unionism in a clearly non-revolutionary situation was thus entirely new territory for 'modern militants'. Cannon made use of his experience in the US class-struggle, as well as his understanding of the protracted nature of revolutionary organisation, which he was learning in the school of Trotskyism, to place his own stamp on the uprising of the Minneapolis truckers.

An editorial in *The Militant* stated unequivocally that the gains in Minneapolis in May 1934 were fourfold: defeat of the capitalist open-shop offensive; union-recognition; proven leadership; and appreciation of the coercive role of the capitalist state, even if its main functionary was an ostensible advocate of a 'Farmer-Labor' coalition. The issue for revolutionaries, this editorial made clear, was not 'Revolution', the groundwork for which had not yet been prepared in 1934. Rather, what was critically necessary was the tactical capacity to win immediate gains that might serve as a transition to revolutionary possibilities. Within an unfolding class-struggle, nothing was more important, from a working-class point of view, than the difficult dialectic of realising short-term advances so that the actual balance of class-forces in capitalism might be tipped in the direction of the proletariat. This embodied painstaking attention to detail in building trade-unionism in a rabidly hostile climate, ongoing organisation and the cultivation of militancy, and a discerning assessment of the totality of actualities comprising any given moment.

> In Minneapolis we had a strike and a leadership which, when viewing it as a whole, its militancy, its thoroughness of organization, its loyalty to the class and effective policy is unequalled in recent labor history. For the first time in this present period the entirely correct method of mobilizing every member and every worker involved in a solid phalanx resulted in preventing a single wheel from moving and in routing not only the scabs but also the police and special deputies.... [T]he Minneapolis struggle came as a turning point, cutting a deep wedge into the capitalist offensive and into the attempt to crush the strike movement by force.... At this moment the essential issue is working class organization – trade union organization – as preparation for the much greater class battles to come. The real test of the revolutionists lies today in their ability to establish such organizations and to weld them firmly into a movement against the class enemy.... [T]he strike ... gained the central objective – union recognition. It is one of the first of the new unions to gain actual recognition.... The Minneapolis strike was not a revolution. It fell short of being a revolution.... [I]t is ... strikes such as the one in Minneapolis that begin to prepare the basis for the upsurge which is still to come. It is the organizations of the

kind...built in Minneapolis which hold promise of far greater working-class victories. In that strike, and due to its able leadership, the workers involved received a valuable lesson and gained a real understanding not only of what the role of the capitalist state is – and more specifically the capitalist state with a farmer-labor governor – but they also received a lesson and an understanding in the first fundamentals of how to begin to cope with that state.

Given that the Trotskyist organising committee of Local 574 achieved all of this with such 'a rapid sweep' that the General Drivers' Union 'counts today some 7,000 members and is gaining new recruits daily', Cannon was convinced that the settlement in May 1934 represented a historic advance, not only for the mobilised truckers, but also for the Communist League of America.

Yet, Cannon also placed a much-needed accent on not representing the outcome as an absolute victory. This was a tendency with a long history among conservative business-union officialdom. It was also not unheard-of for Communist Party trade-union figures to exaggerate the advances registered in particular struggles. Such an orientation usually backfired, however, because of its refusal to acknowledge concessions made and gains not decisively secured. Thus, the 25 May 1934 ratification-meeting, convened and addressed by the strike's Left Opposition leaders, among others, contrasted sharply with 'the snake-oil seller's pitch with which the AFL officials had presented the coal settlement the previous February'. The strikers were given the straight goods: the settlement was presented frankly as 'a compromise with the bosses', and what it did and did not accomplish was 'forthrightly and fully discussed'.

When all was said and done, however, Cannon was adamant that 'the indubitable establishment of a new union where none existed before' was, in spite of concessions made and ambiguities that unfortunately prevailed, a considerable achievement, one that reverberated throughout the country. 'The labor movement of Minneapolis has been restored to new life by the emergence of Local 574', Cannon insisted. This local achievement also extended the Union's significance nationally. 'The working class of the entire country has been inspired by a new example and enriched by a fresh experience which constitutes a real contribution to the burning question of trade unionism'. Those sage but quiet advocates of proletarian revolution who had been denigrated even within the Communist League of America during the height of dog-days factionalism as little more than 'Cannon's hand-raisers' were now 'universally recognized as among the most important Trotskyist militants in America'. In Sam Gordon's later words,

> They had helped make Minneapolis a union town. They had forged a cadre that was to prove impregnable in the struggles to come. Their fame reached out to wherever there were Trotskyists in the world.

Cannon, in 1934, was less effusive, if unambiguously laudatory:

> Honest and loyal workers everywhere will acknowledge an indebtedness to
> the group of Minneapolis militants at the head of Local 574 who organized this
> magnificent movement, steered it through the strike and the settlement, and
> still remain at its head. The work they have done already is bound to influence
> future developments of the left-wing labor movement on a national scale. And
> they are not finished yet.[15]

The Communist Party, not surprisingly, accepted nothing of this interpretation.
It proved constant in its carping. It was unrepresented in the leadership of the
strike, of course, but it also had very few members among the thousands of strikers, possibly one or two and certainly no more than a half-dozen. Yet it was not
shy in its attempts to intervene in the struggle. Before the General Drivers' Union
voted to strike, a Stalinist leaflet circulated among the truckers, denouncing Mick
Dunne and Carl Skoglund as 'agents of the bosses' and 'traitors'. With a strike-
committee of 75 already formed, the Communist Party called for 'rank-and-file
leadership' to counter the 'undemocratic' authority that it saw ensconced in
strike-headquarters. Two days before the Battle of Deputies Run, the Communist
Party, the Unemployed Council, and the International Labor Defense marshalled
their forces and demanded to address a mass meeting of the strikers at 1900
Chicago Avenue. The Dunne brothers, Skoglund, and Dobbs reputedly had to
hold back rank-and-file strikers from attacking Minneapolis Communist Party
figurehead, Sam K. Davis, as he berated the leadership of the General Drivers'
Union. Strikers ripped up Stalinist circulars in anger. In the aftermath of the
strike-settlement, this Communist Party attack heightened. Articles in the *Daily
Worker* proclaimed the strike a defeat and denounced its leaders. Browder
addressed a Minneapolis mass meeting in June 1934 on the general-strike wave,
idealising the struggle unfolding in San Francisco and painting a rather dismal
picture of the Toledo Auto-Lite Strike and the local teamsters' insurgency. The
Dunnes came in for particular derision. 'Is their settlement any better than that
made by the Social-Fascists everywhere else?', Browder asked, as the crowd of
seven hundred and fifty, dominated by Communist Party members, reacted with
telling silence. Claiming that the settlement contained 'an endorsement of the
Company Union', Browder had apparently gone too far, and his remarks failed to
draw applause. All of this, according to a report in *The Militant*, 'was even too raw

---

15. The above paragraphs draw on Tselos 1971, pp. 232–3; Dobbs 1972, pp. 90–8; 'The
Minneapolis Strike: Editorial Note', *The Militant*, 9 June 1934; Clem Forsen, 'Tactics at
Minneapolis', *The Militant*, 30 June 1934; C.H., 'Strike Sidelights', *The Militant*, 30 June
1934; James P. Cannon, 'Minneapolis Strike – An Answer to its Defamers', *The Militant*,
16 June 1934; Al Dasch, 'Strikes and the National Guard', *The Militant*, 30 June 1934; Sam
Gordon in Evans (ed.) 1976, p. 64; Cannon 1944, pp. 151–62.

for the hard-boiled Stalinists ... to swallow'. Cannon took special aim at Stalinist misrepresentation of the settlement, noting caustically that it was the success of the Minneapolis teamsters' uprising, and its patient and efficient leadership, that necessitated a Communist Party assault on what had been accomplished. 'Here's a strike that wasn't wrecked, here's a new union that is still alive and going strong after the strike', Cannon bellowed. For 'the Stalinist quack doctors of trade unionism', so acclimatised to 'their patients always' dying 'Something must be wrong!' As Cannon insisted, the Communist Party, 'specialists in the art of losing strikes and breaking up unions' were 'bitterly disappointed with the Minneapolis situation'. It was not surprising that the Stalinists would 'work overtime to discredit the strike and the union and blacken the names of the organizers and leaders'.

Cannon nonetheless found it nauseating that the dirtiest job of 'slandering the Minneapolis movement and all connected with it' had been assigned to his old friend and brother of the leaders of the organisational drive, William F. Dunne. Dunne's denunciation, at first voiced in speeches and articles in the *Daily Worker*, was later published in a coauthored pamphlet appearing under the title *Permanent Counter-Revolution: The Role of the Trotzkyites in the Minneapolis Strikes*. Claiming that the militant workers '*had just begun to fight*', Dunne argued that the Trotskyist leadership of Local 574 suppressed 'the mass sentiment for a general strike' and turned a victory into defeat. 'The exposure and defeat of Olson should have been the central political objective of the Minneapolis struggle', according to Dunne, and driving the Farmer-Laborite from office was 'the basic necessity for winning the economic demands for the Drivers' Union and the rest of the working class'. Instead, Cannon and the Dunne brothers, who were written off by their elder sibling as mere 'comedians' of the class-struggle (also as 'palookas', 'traitors', and 'fools or crooks, or both'), engineered a shameful capitulation. It left Olson firmly entrenched in the Governor's mansion, the Central Labor Council demagogues 'never put to the test of actually mobilizing strike action in support of the auto drivers', illusions in Roosevelt's NRA strengthened, employers breathing easy, and the teamsters and unemployed 'who bore the cruel brunt of the struggle' left as the losers. '[T]he workers were cold-decked by James P. Cannon, his lieutenants in the leadership of the union, and Governor Olson and his Farmer-Labor Party henchmen in control of the Minneapolis Trades and Labor Assembly', Dunne claimed, assailing the 'incurable opportunism' of 'the Trotzkyite position' and 'its priests and altar boys'. Insisting that when Olson cocked the trigger of the National Guard, Cannon and the Dunnes retreated in cowardice, Bill Dunne wrote that this sorry record of appeasement constituted 'another miserable page in the history of class collaboration in the labor movement.... With one gesture the Trotzkyite leaders nullified the days and nights of heroic struggle by thousands of workers'. Dunne concluded that the May strike and settlement of General Drivers' Union Local 574 was 'one of the most serious recent setbacks suffered by the working class [,] ... a needless retreat engineered by spineless and unprincipled leaders'. The Cannon-Dunne leadership, in Bill Dunne's representation, was responsible for a venal surrender.[16]

Dunne and the Communist Party did highlight some shortcomings of the Trotskyist leadership of the Minneapolis teamsters' uprising in May 1934. Stronger stands could have been taken against Olson, his harnessed use of the National Guard, and his duplicitous role in the obvious ambiguities inherent in the settlement, including on the nature of arbitration. There is definitely evidence that Dobbs and others seemed to rely, at times, rather naïvely on Olson's assurances. Dobbs's account of all of this in his rightly well-regarded 1972 book *Teamster Rebellion* is, undoubtedly, coloured by hindsight and understates the extent to which he himself was somewhat taken in by the Farmer-Labor Governor. This was of a piece with the Communist League of America's reluctance, in this period, to call for the formation of a workers' party, a reticence rooted, once again, in the 'dog-days' factionalism that plagued Trotskyism in the early 1930s. Shachtman had promoted the view, based on the Workers' (Communist) Party's opportunistic flirtations with the LaFollette movement in the 1920s, that virtually any call for a labour-party in the United States was destined to result in a reformist formation. This mechanical rejection of the labour-party, posed amidst

---

16. The above paragraphs rely on and quote from Dobbs 1972, pp. 98–9; Walker 1937, p. 127; Korth 1995, pp. 96–7; 'Minneapolis Shows the Way', *The Militant*, 26 May 1934; 'The Minneapolis Strike: Editorial Note', *The Militant*, 9 June 1934; C. Forsen, 'Browder "Exposes" Strike "Sell-Out" in Minneapolis', *The Militant*, 16 June 1934; James P. Cannon, 'Minneapolis Strike – An Answer to its Defamers', *The Militant*, 16 June 1934; C. Forsen, 'Role of the Stalinists in the Minneapolis Strike', *The Militant*, 23 June 1934; Dunne and Childs 1934; Kramer 1942, p. 394. For Charles Rumford Walker's illuminating collection of Communist Party leaflets and flyers distributed during the teamsters' insurgency, calling on workers to resist the employers and the state, and implicitly or explicitly critical of the strike-leadership, see File 'Communist Party, Minnesota, Flyers and Bulletins, 1934–1936', Box 1, CRW Papers, HMNS. Walker also drew up a five-page typescript (without page-numbers) in which quotes from the *Daily Worker* chronicle the Communist Party attack on the Trotskyist strike-leadership in July and August 1934. See File 'American City Incomplete Notes and Articles', Box 1, CRW Papers, MNHS. As late as 2009, the Communist Party, through its aged spokesman, Gus Hall, was still claiming that it alone had rescued the Minneapolis teamsters' strikes from the jaws of a 'Trotskyite' defeat. Hall claimed that the Communist Party 'assigned' him 'to give leadership to the strike', and that he and others developed the 'confrontation tactics' that ensured a victory for the truckers and turned back the Trotskyist penchant for 'playing footsie with the governor of the state of Minnesota who was out to break the strike with the use of the National Guard'. See Gus Hall Action Club 2009. This Stalinist political fantasy contains not one shred of substantiation, resting on assertions that cite no evidence. A convincing repudiation of Hall's claim to have been involved in the Minneapolis strikes, with discussion about the one identifiable Local 574 member affiliated with the Communist Party and his lack of any leadership role, is Shaun (Jack) Maloney's interview with David Riehle, 1 October 1988, Transcript, especially pp. 1–32, Box 1, File 'Maloney, Shaun Oral History Transcript, Tape 1', Riehle Papers, MNHS.

the factionalism leading up to 1934, thus limited the American Left Opposition, hobbling it at a time when working-class mobilisations suggested the possibility of new political breakthroughs. At precisely the point that it needed to be able to assert decisively that Olson's cross-class Farmer-Labor Party was not, in fact, a labour-party, but rather a third-party adjunct to the Roosevelt Democrats, the Communist League of America was handcuffed in its political critique. It could not bring itself to negotiate a creative path between the Scylla of opportunistic accommodation to the Farmer-Labor Party and the Charybdis of an altogether too wooden and sectarian rejection of the very possibility of American workers sustaining a genuine labour-party. As such, the Left Opposition was unable to pose any political alternative to the Olson-led, cross-class Farmer-Labor Party, even abstractly. Ironically, this reduced the Trotskyist critique of Olson and Minnesota Farmer-Laborism to the limiting perspective that Olson, who proclaimed his neutrality in the class-struggle, was inevitably a helpmate of the bosses. This inadequate political critique, which avoided declaring unequivocally that Olson was, indeed, a capitalist politician, albeit a 'progressive' and 'reformist' one, and Farmer-Laborism a capitalist political formation, left the small and isolated Communist League of America as the only available alternative to the ensconced 'alliance of trade unions and farmers' organizations' leavened by urban middle-class support that Olson headed in 1934. This may well have conditioned Dobbs's failure to treat Olson with a sufficient number of grains of salt, and Bill Brown's radicalism (as opposed to Trotskyism) increased the likelihood of the Farmer-Labor Governor being given too much of the benefit of the doubt by revolutionaries. More importantly, the pressures of all of these developments culminated in curtailing the *political* gains that the Communist League of America was able to consolidate on the back of the teamsters' rebellion.[17]

Yet, on balance, the Trotskyist leadership of the teamsters, in spite of their failure to counterpose the need for a workers' party to Olson's governing Farmer-

---

17. Note especially the post-strike evidence from hearings before the Regional Labor Board, quoted in Korth 1995, p. 103, where Dobbs, when challenged by trucking-company officials about the issue of who was included in understandings of 'inside workers', replied, as against the company's interpretation of the settlement that, 'The Governor assured us [Section 8] would be interpreted to give us jurisdiction over these people.... He said it would be the legal and logical interpretation.... We considered the Governor had a good legal mind and accepted his advice'. Contrast this with the account in Dobbs 1972, pp. 96–7, 102, which also has indications of Dobbs's understanding of the amorphous class-content of Farmer-Laborism, as on pp. 44, 178. Also note 'Strikers Defy Olson Militia: Local 574 Issues Call for a Protest General Strike,' and 'Protest the Military Terror in Minneapolis', *The Militant*, 4 August 1934. On Olson as a neutralist helpmate of the bosses, see Hugo Oehler, 'A Demagogue at Work: Olson's Role in the Strike', *The Militant*, 11 August 1934. For more on the issue of LaFollette, Farmer-Laborism, the labour-party, and CLA factionalism in the 'Dog Days', see Cannon et al. 2002, pp. 37–40, and Abern, Glotzer and Shachtman 2002, pp. 253–5.

Labor formation, nonetheless acted astutely in pressing a successful strike-strategy.[18] The Dunne brothers, Skoglund, and their CLA comrades understood exactly where Olson stood as a radical petty-bourgeois element, reliant on working-class support but committed to maintaining capitalist law and order. They steered a class-war course through the minefield of federal mediators, recalcitrant and reactionary bosses organised in the Citizens' Alliance, and a 'progressive' Governor whose charges included bayonet-wielding National Guardsmen. As Cannon recognised, 'the government, its agencies and its institutions' were brought 'into the center of every situation' in the class-conflicts of the 1930s. He would later write in *The History of American Trotskyism*:

> All modern strikes require political direction.... A strike leader without some conception of a political line was very much out of date already by 1934. The old fashioned trade union movement, which used to deal with the bosses without governmental interference, belongs in the museum. The modern labor movement must be politically directed because it is confronted by the government at every turn. Our people were prepared for that since they were political people, inspired by political conceptions. The policy of the class struggle guided our comrades; they couldn't be deceived and outmaneuvered, as so many strike leaders of that period were, by this mechanism of sabotage and destruction known as the National Labor Board and all its auxiliary set-ups. They put no reliance whatever in Roosevelt's Labor Board; they weren't fooled by any idea that Roosevelt, the liberal 'friend of labor' president, was going to help the truck drivers of Minneapolis win a few cents more an hour. They weren't deluded even by the fact that there was at that time in Minnesota a Farmer-Labor Governor, presumed to be on the side of the workers.... Consequently, they expected from the start that the union would have to fight for its right to exist; that the bosses would not yield any recognition to the union, would not yield any increase of wages or reduction of the scandalous hours without some pressure being brought to bear. Therefore they prepared everything from the point of view of the class war.

For the Trotskyist leadership of Local 574, the fundamental principle guiding their actions was that 'power, not diplomacy, would decide the issue.... In such things as the conflict of class interests one must be prepared to fight'.[19]

The Stalinist response to the strike and its settlement refused to address the extent to which former comrades in the Communist League of America were

---

18. Trotsky's later 1938 statement, in which he situated the drafting of the transitional programme within an understanding of prior political activity, is thus relevant: 'One can say that we didn't have a program until this day. Yet we acted'. See Trotsky 1973a, p. 137.

19. Cannon 1944, pp. 147–8.

following this kind of class-struggle course. Their repudiation of the Trotskyist leadership of Local 574 proved shrill and ineffective. It won them little in the way of support among the working-class combatants of the teamsters' rebellion. A typical Third Period concoction of sectarianism and adventurism, the Communist Party's anti-Trotskyist diatribe undoubtedly registered with many militants as a divisive harangue that seemed the mirror-image of the denunciations of the strike-leadership that were also soon forthcoming from the *Minneapolis Tribune*, Dan Tobin's International Brotherhood of Teamsters' headquarters, the Citizens' Alliance, and the truck-operatives' consolidating Employers' Advisory Committee (EAC). When strikers read Communist attacks on leaders whom they had seen tested in difficult circumstances and regarded as selfless builders of Local 574, they often reacted with forceful repudiation, replying dismissively that such critics 'must be in the pay of the bosses'. They placed no credence in wild accusations and personal attacks, which seemed 'too far from the truth'. It was just this kind of distortion and disingenuous misrepresentation of the Minneapolis strike and settlement that prompted non-Trotskyist General Drivers' Union President Bill Brown to read one leaflet and exclaim, 'The Stalinists have not only discredited Communism out here; they've discredited the mimeograph machine'.[20]

Yet for all their recognition that the Communist Party critique of the strike-leadership was little more than self-serving sectarianism, the Trotskyist leadership of Local 574 never wavered in its principled defence of Stalinist adversaries. For the ideologues at the helm of the Citizens' Alliance, not to mention mainstream newspapers and other conventional opinion-makers, were relentlessly anti-communist at the same time as not being overly careful about discriminating among obviously differentiated sections of the Left. In Minneapolis in 1934, a 'Red' was simply a 'Red', and everyone from Olson to the Dunne brothers to Communist Party spokesmen was tarred with the same anti-communist brush. When the Communists' bookstore was broken into in the mid-1930s, the premises ransacked, pamphlets torn up, books stolen, and petty cash pilfered, the perpetrators left a sign in the window proclaiming, 'modern/BOSTON TEA PARTY/NO REDS/Wanted in Minneapolis'. It would have been easy for Local 574's leadership to let this act of anti-communism go unnoticed in their circles, but they responded with a call to all workers to put a stop to ugly attacks of this kind: 'There are many workers in Minneapolis who are out of sympathy with the C.P.' noted one statement,

---

20. Dobbs 1972, pp. 98–9; Tselso 1971, pp. 234–5; F.K., 'Minneapolis Shows the Way', *The Militant*, 26 May 1934; C. Forsen, 'Role of the Stalinists in Minneapolis Strike', *The Militant*, 23 June 1934; 'Minneapolis Notes: The "Rank-and-File Opposition"', *The Militant*, 23 June 1934; Herbert Solow, 'War In Minneapolis', *Nation*, 8 August 1934, p. 160.

But it would be a short-sighted policy to abstain for this reason from register-
ing a vigorous protest.... To-day they will strike the Communists – tomorrow
it will be the Socialists – the next day the trade union halls.... If the police
will not stop the plundering of the workers by lawless vultures, the workers
will. STOP THE VIGILANTES!'

In the years to come, the Trotskyists guiding the radical wing of Minneapolis
labour would establish a Union Defense Guard to protect basic freedoms of association and speech from threats and dangerous incursions coming from right-
wing, and even fascist quarters.[21]

Cannon departed Minneapolis for New York in early June 1934, stopping off
in Chicago. There, he gave two lectures on the teamsters' organising drive and
the strikers' battles against the Citizens' Alliance, speaking to a hundred and fifty
workers at the Communist League of America headquarters on Friday 8 June and
to five hundred black and white workers, two nights later, at a Sunday forum in
Washington Park. The club that sponsored the evening open-air talk, chaired
by a Stalinist sympathiser, was enthusiastic about hearing an account of Local
574's organisational accomplishments, and voted unanimously to make Cannon
a life-long member of the radical assembly. One week later, back in New York,
Cannon addressed a crowd of five hundred workers in Irving Plaza on the Minneapolis events. He was at pains to address frontally 'the slanderous attacks of
the Stalinists on the strike leaders as betrayers and the settlement as a sell-out',
prompting a number of questions from leftists aligned with 'all groups and tendencies'. Minneapolis was, apparently, the talk of the New York Left, as Cannon
fielded an array of queries: 'What was the role of the CP?'; 'Are the strike-leaders
known in Minneapolis as Communists?'; 'How can a Communist say that Governor Olson was undecided as to whether to use the National Guard or not?'; 'Why
do you attack the Communist Party?'; 'Why do you propose to allow Local 574 to
remain in the AF of L?' Answering these and other questions, Cannon called on
all revolutionaries to support the Communist League of America and to work to
build a new communist party that would 'give the entire American working class
the same militant and intelligent leadership that was given the truck drivers in
Minneapolis'.[22]

---

21. See 'Brief Miscellaneous Notes' in File 'Notes Local 574 and Strike', Box 1, CRW
Papers, MNHS, the document seemingly relying on material drawn from *The Organizer*
from 1934.

22. 'Chicago Hears Report on Minneapolis Strike', *The Militant*, 16 June 1934; 'Cannon
Lecture on the Minneapolis Strike', *The Militant*, 23 June 1934.

Chapter Eleven
Interlude

As *The Militant* headline announced boldly, 'Strike Wave Sweeps Country', with articles detailing the class-conflict looming in Toledo and the longshoremen's tie-up of Pacific Coast ports, trucks moved unimpeded in Minneapolis. The strike ended officially on Saturday, 26 May 1934. It was anything but over, however, and the shouting certainly continued. Bill Dunne and the Communist Party denounced the Trotskyists and assailed Floyd Olson, the Farmer-Labor Governor, as a strikebreaker. When a Stalinist 'Rank and File Committee' leafleted a mass meeting of Local 574, attacking the Union's leadership, denouncing the recent strike's conduct and its ostensibly botched settlement, two members of this committee, sporting General Drivers' Union buttons but unable to produce union-cards and proof of their membership in the Local, were escorted from the hall. Only Bill Brown's pleas from the podium to allow the 'oppositionists' safe conduct from the meeting, reinforced by a union-guard, secured their exit without serious injury. Both the *Minneapolis Journal* and the *Minneapolis Labor Review* suggested in editorials that Olson, rather than acting against the strikers, had, in fact, mobilised the National Guard 'as a weapon to make unfair employers come to time'. These voices of diametrically opposed class-interests, however, had an entirely different perspective on the merits of the Governor's actions. The press had a field-day with third-party hyphenation. 'The Governor will bare his strong right arm in defense of the Farmer', declared the *Journal* editorially, 'so long as the gesture does no harm whatsoever to Labor'. Police-Chief Johannes, denouncing May's events as 'a disgrace', demanded a 100 percent increase in his budget. Additional funding, he fumed, was needed to pay for 400 new officers, establish an academy to train the cops '*just like an army* to handle riots', and purchase motorcycles, machine-guns, rifles with bayonets, and steel-helmets.[1]

Amidst the din of conflicting *post-mortems*, the Citizens' Alliance regrouped, acknowledged that it 'had been caught napping in May', raised a $50,000 war-chest, and dug in its heels for a future fight. Over the course of June and into July 1934, the employers' group unleashed a barrage of propaganda, all of it aimed at discrediting Local 574. Throughout the summer of 1934, Minneapolis was inundated with the Citizens' Alliance anti-union message: radio-airwaves were clogged with fifty thousand words denouncing teamster-militancy and Local 574's leadership, while paid advertisements totalling thirty newspaper-pages and pliant reporting in excess of two hundred and fifty columns hammered home the same hostile sentiments. Attacking the leadership of the Union as Communist, Alliance statements grew more and more strident in their insistence that Minneapolis was being pushed towards a Red revolution and the implementation of tyrannical Soviet forms of governance. Headlines in the *Minneapolis Tribune* screamed: 'MUST MINNEAPOLIS BE PARALYZED BY A STRIKE TO SATISFY A HANDFUL OF COMMUNIST AGITATORS WHO DREAM OF MAKING MINNE-APOLIS THE BIRTHPLACE OF A NEW SOVIET REPUBLIC?' Such hyperbole drew on International Brotherhood of Teamsters' leader Dan Tobin, who claimed that 'Communists and radicals' were behind the truckers' discontent in Minneapolis, and that responsible workers in the industry should 'beware of these wolves in sheep's clothing'. Firms publicly proclaimed that drivers in their pay were satis-fied with working conditions and wages, and needed to rise up and repudiate their misleaders. Another strike would ruin the city, which could ill afford the cost of yet more violent conflict, May's bill for class-battle having come in at a whopping $1.9 million.[2]

It was not long before interpretations of the settlement-agreement, with regard to who was and who was not represented by the General Drivers' and Helpers' Union, resulted in a clash of wills irreconcilably separating labour and

---

1. 'Strike Wave Sweeps Country', *The Militant*, 2 June 1934; C. Forsen, 'Role of the Stalinists in Minneapolis Strike', *The Militant*, 23 June 1934; 'The Rank and File Opposi-tion', *The Militant*, 30 June 1934; S [Max Shachtman], 'The Record of Bill Dunne: The Man on the Flying Trapeze', *The Militant*, 7 July 1934; 14 July 1934; 'The Governor's Candid Friend', *Minneapolis Journal*, 2 June 1934; 'And Now He "Repels Invasion"', *Minneapolis Journal*, 4 June 1934; 'What Other People Think', *Minneapolis Journal*, 5 June 1934; Walker 1937, p. 158.
2. Walker 1937, pp. 155–7; Bernstein 1970, pp. 239–40; Tselos 1971, pp. 234–5; Anne Ross, 'Labor Unity in Minneapolis', *The New Republic*, 25 July 1934, p. 283; 'Daniel Tobin Goes to Bat for the Bosses', *The Militant*, 14 July 1934; Cannon 1944, pp. 153–4.

capital. Within weeks, Local 574 claimed seven hundred cases of discrimination against union-members. '[T]he Gordian knot of the inside workers had not been cut by the ambiguous section written into the agreement', wrote Charles Rumford Walker. Claiming that the Union was breaking the agreement by widening understanding of union-members, the employers routinely insisted that the actual rights of union-representation extended to very few workers. They attempted to argue, based on a highly dubious telephone-survey, that only 309 drivers were members of Local 574. Refusing to entertain demands from the General Drivers' Union made on behalf of employees whom the trucking bosses claimed to have made no direct indication to them that they had either complaint or a desire to be represented by Local 574, the employers' spokesmen broke off relations with what they consistently claimed were only 'a handful of alien agitators'. Olson squirmed, and, under pressure from the Regional Labor Board to clarify what his ambiguously-written clause on union-representation in the settlement-document actually meant, backtracked. The Governor proposed restricting membership in Local 574 to drivers and helpers, receiving and shipping clerks, stevedores, and freight-elevator operators, before eventually withdrawing from the fray. Olson's final word was that the disputes between the Union and the employers should be submitted to the Regional Labor Board for arbitration. The result was a denial of the rights of representation of the 'inside workers'. Local 574 responded to the ruling with a sarcastic rejection: 'The Labor Board has "generously" ruled that Local 574 shall have the right to represent almost half of its membership'. As discussions at the Labor Board spiralled downward, it was becoming apparent that it had no authority to enforce compliance with its rulings, even if it proved able to reach decisions, which it often could not. When a federal commissioner of conciliation, Eugene H. Dunnigan, was parachuted into Minneapolis in the first week of July 1934, charged with reviewing the Board's handling of Local 574's arbitration-requests, he found the situation dysfunctional and hopelessly deadlocked. An eleven-person panel divided between five union and five employer-representatives, with the 'neutral' chair refusing to get past the ritual stalemate by casting his tie-breaking vote. The sticking point was always the issue of 'inside workers' and the Union's right to represent them.[3]

All of this suited Dan Tobin and the International to a tee. The Teamsters' bureaucracy had never wanted Local 574 to organise all of those involved in the trucking industry, and it pounced on the dissident Minneapolis union. Making no allowances for the expenses that the General Drivers' Union had borne

3. Citzens' Alliance, 'The So-Called Truck Drivers' Strike', *Special Weekly Bulletin*, 3 August 1934 in File 'Miscellaneous Papers, 1934, 1936', Box 1, CRW Papers, MNHS; Walker 1937, p. 155; Korth 1995, pp. 135–9; Dobbs 1972, pp. 102–3; Blantz 1982, pp. 111–13; Blantz 1970; Herbert Solow, 'War In Minneapolis', *Nation*, 8 August 1934.

entirely on its own during the February and May strikes, Tobin and Teamster headquarters demanded immediate payment of the initiation-fee tax of one dollar per member. This was a crippling financial blow to a local that had taken in thousands of new members while receiving no support from the IBT's treasury. In conjunction with the added material burden of what appeared to be the certainty of yet another strike, Local 574 had no option but to withhold this new-member-initiation tax, leaving it vulnerable to sanctions, and eventually expulsion from the American Federation of Labor by the Teamster officialdom.[4]

Local 574 was, nevertheless, not to be deterred. It widened networks of support and agitation. Establishing a section of the Union composed of the unemployed, it quietly rallied a contingent of five thousand jobless people to its cause. Planning began for a conference on the 'unemployment problem', to be held later in the summer. A new union-headquarters was opened at 225 South Third Street, and Friday-evening classes on trade-union history and strike-strategy were initiated. The work of the Women's Auxiliary, which had been developed to such good effect during May 1934, was now broadened and formalised with regular meetings discussing what needed to be done and recruiting new women to the fight for trade-unionism. Many families suffered the loss of a male bread-winner's pay-cheque as a consequence of the strikes. Some pickets had been injured in the violent street-battles, while others were jailed or sentenced to workhouse-terms. The Women's Auxiliary did what it could to aid these casualties of class-war, visiting hospitals and securing public relief for the needy. As the Citizens' Alliance victimisation of union-members increased in mid-to-late June 1934, more and more families grew desperate and required help from Local 574. Women's Auxiliary members took the initiative with Wobbly-style fundraising tag-days, through which money collected on street-corners, in parks, and by canvassing working-class neighbourhoods and shopping districts was distributed to those in need, easing the growing financial distress. The Auxiliary also organised a benefit-dance to launch Local 574's new building, featuring three union-bands, kegs of beer donated from unionised breweries, and bartenders affiliated with the labour-movement. This netted the General Drivers' coffers $700. Women's Auxiliary members also approached other Minneapolis unions, in search of material contributions.

Finally, on 25 June 1934, Local 574 launched *The Organizer*, a weekly tabloid of four pages issued in a print-run of 5,000. It aimed 'to weld a solid band of understanding between...members, to carry a message of hope to all non-union men, and to hold a beacon light of progress before all organized labor'. Mrs. Yeager, a Women's Auxiliary activist and 'a little butterball of a woman',

---

4. Dobbs 1972, p. 103; Miles B. Dunne, 'Story of 544', *Northwest Organizer*, 27 February 1941.

was put in charge of the distribution of this publication, and *The Organizer* was soon on sale 'in every tavern in town that had working class customers'. Consciously seeking to 'refute the lies of the boss press, give the true facts about [the Union's] aims and policies, and expose the antilabor schemes of the bosses and the government', the creation of the newspaper marked a new stage in the Minneapolis truck-drivers' struggle. The working-class paper drew the immediate ire of the Citizens' Alliance, which threatened to prosecute those responsible for *The Organizer* with 'criminal syndicalism' charges. Print-shops that agreed to put out editions of the strike-organ faced pressures from the Minneapolis establishment, causing delays in publication as fearful businesses declined to take on contracts with Local 574. On one occasion, Citizens' Alliance-allied opponents of the strike tried to hijack an edition of the bulletin as it was being trucked from the print-shop, but the union-driver and his helpers 'cleaned house on the finks'. Eventually, these attempts to suppress *The Organizer* stopped, and the paper was left relatively free to defend the cause of the General Drivers' Union. Establishing that the truckers' leaders had their own networks of 'intelligence', *The Organizer* announced that it had secured a list of names, addresses, hours logged, and 'amount of cheese due each rat'. It asked Local 574 members if they wanted this complete account of those 'Slimy creatures . . . who served as special police' during the May strike published in their newspaper.

Doing its best not to replicate the problems it had experienced with farmers during the May strikes, the General Drivers' Union established a committee to secure an arrangement with the militant Farmers' Holiday Association, the National Farm Bureau, and the Market Gardeners Association. Farm-trucks would be allowed into Minneapolis in the event of a work-stoppage, but only if they displayed permits from Local 574 and the farm-organisation to which they belonged. Farmers' committees were set up to picket the roads leading into Minneapolis, and the Union leased a large parking lot a few blocks away from the Market District so that gardeners and farmers could conduct business with small grocers in rent-free stalls, the latter being allowed to take produce from the area in cars, but not trucks. The close connections established between farmers and workers widened understandings of collectivity and solidarity, and increased the quantity and quality of food-donations made to the General Drivers' Union in the weeks to come. All of this, in the words of one Minneapolis streetcar-motorman, Howard Carlson, 'radicalized people'. As yet another conflict appeared inevitable in June 1934, Carlson could see that the leadership of Local 574 'really knew what to do. . . . It wasn't a private affair. Everybody came. Everybody was welcome'.[5]

5. The above paragraphs draw on Korth 1995, pp. 135–6; Dobbs 1972, pp. 103–5, 108–9, 122–3; Scholl 1975, p. 22; 'Minneapolis Notes: The Organizer', *The Militant*, 23 June 1934; 'Unions and the Unemployed', 'Ladies Auxiliary Give Benefit Dance', 'Union Study Class',

Cannon summed up the accomplishments of the Trotskyists in Minneapolis, evident in May–June 1934. He situated the Minneapolis strike as arguably the most important in a series of labour-battles that followed on the heels of the first wave of strikes that greeted the introduction of the National Recovery Act. Among the upheavals that figured prominently in this upsurge of class-conflict were two nationwide automobile-strikes, generalised strikes in the steel and coal-industries, and numbers of smaller industrial disturbances involving hundreds of thousands of workers. These class-conflicts, in the words of Charles Rumford Walker, 'were scotched before they began'. Government-appointed mediators orchestrated agreements that left workers no better off than 'where they started'.[6]

Something of this was at work in the Labor Relations Board-mediated settlement between Local 574 and the trucking employers. The situation in Minneapolis nevertheless had some unique characteristics: the extraordinary organisation of the Union; its startling expansion and embrace of thousands of workers previously unrecognised in any collective-bargaining procedures; the militancy expressed in the streets; and its decidedly left-wing leadership. Minneapolis thus seemed to Cannon a harbinger of a new, second wave of class-conflict under the Roosevelt administration:

> Standing by itself, the magnificent strike of the Minneapolis truck drivers would merit recognition as an extraordinary event in modern American labor history. Its connection with the second wave of labor struggles to sweep the country since the inception of the N.R.A., however, and its indubitable place as the high point of the present strike wave, invest the Minneapolis demonstration with exceptional interest.... The native militancy of the workers, so impressively demonstrated on every strike front in recent months, needs only to be fused with an authentic leadership which brings organization, consciousness and the spirit of determined struggle into the movement. Minneapolis was an example of such a fusion. That is what lifted the drivers' strike out above the general run.[7]

'You are "The Organizer"', and 'Finks!', *The Organizer*, 25 June 1934; Cannon 1944, p. 159; Skoglund interviewed by Halstead, 24 April 1934, Transcript, pp. 29–30, Box 2, Riehle Papers, MNHS; Walker, 'The Farmer Holiday Convention', in File 'Farmer-Labor Party, Chapter 5'; File 'American City: The Organizer Notes'; File 'Local 574 Strike. 1934', Carlos Hudson, 'Chains Wear Thin in Minneapolis: Notes and Sketches on the Recent Strikes', a 31-page typescript, Box 1, CRW Papers, MNHS. Under the title 'Strike Deputies', *The Organizer*, 2 July 1934, began publishing an alphabetised list of the names and addresses of the 'blackjack artists' who had tried to break the May strike.
6. Cannon 1934b; Walker 1937, pp. 161–2.
7. Cannon 1934b.

Of paramount importance in appreciating what the militancy of the American workers in 1934 was about, Cannon suggested, was the need to situate realistically the state of working-class consciousness, both in terms of what it was striving for and thought possible, and what it had yet to bring into view.

Preparing and researching his study of the rank-and-file history of Minneapolis, *American City*, Charles Rumford Walker concluded that the truckers whom he interviewed were growing politically more aware and more militant day-by-day: the conditions of their work, as well as the presence of leftists of various kinds among them, awakened prospects of radical protest and class-struggle. Yet these workers, as Cannon and his comrades in the strike-leadership of Local 574 grasped, were a long way from recognising the necessity of an all-out struggle against class-forces committed to retaining power for themselves and keeping those whom they exploited oppressed and subordinated. Walker captured the unevenness of class-consciousness in Minneapolis in 1934 by drawing a composite-portrait of the 'mythical average' trucker. On the one hand, this worker had little difficulty in seeing the state as an instrument of class-domination, and was especially agitated by acts like calling in the militia 'to break the drivers' strike'. On this point, Walker insisted, his composite-teamster had learned well, through experience, Lesson One of the Class Struggle: the power of the state was often used to suppress labour and keep capital ascendant. '[H]e believes that principle passionately, and talks on that point like a Communist', Walker wrote in his notes. Yet, on the other hand, this very same apparent advocate of class-struggle 'still votes for Olson', who had called on the National Guard to restore order, 'denies being a Communist, and has even beaten up a few in his day'. In assessing the situation in this way, revolutionaries were forced to acknowledge how contradictory and constrained class-consciousness in Minneapolis was, and, consequently, the instability of the foundations of class-struggle on which mobilisations of the working class in the city, not to mention the United States as a whole, rested.[8]

As unmistakable as the trend of the conflict between labour and capital was, it was also evident that absolute working-class victories were few and signs of mature class-consciousness faint. It was from this vantage-point that Cannon insisted that the compromises of the May 1934 settlement in Minneapolis were, nonetheless, 'a victory of the first order':

> The first and foremost demand in every struggle is: *Recognition of the union*. With unerring instinct the workers seek first of all the protection of an organization.... The outcome of every strike is to be estimated primarily by its

---

8. Walker, 'Notes for Life-Story of a Truck-Driver', pp. 1–4, Box 1, File 'American City Preliminary Prospectus and General Notes', CRW Papers, HMNS. See also Smemo 2011, pp. 42–3.

success or failure in enforcing the recognition of the union. And from this point of view the results in general are not so rosy. The workers manifested a mighty impulse for organization, and in many cases they fought heroically. But they have yet to attain their first objective.... The New York hotel strike failed to establish the union. The New York taxi drivers got no union recognition, or anything else. Not a single one of the 'Red' unions affiliated to the Trade Union Unity League has succeeded in gaining recognition. Even the great battle of Toledo appears to have been concluded without the attainment of this primary demand. The American workers are on the march. They are organizing by the hundreds of thousands. They are fighting to establish their new unions firmly and compel the bosses to 'recognize' them. But in the overwhelming majority of cases they have yet to win this fundamental demand. In the light of this general situation the results of the Minneapolis strike stands out pre-eminent and unique.

Such a perspective placed the Stalinist critique of Minneapolis, and, in particular, the judgemental attacks made by Bill Dunne, squarely in Cannon's sights. Against Dunne's insistence that Governor Olson was 'the main enemy', and that a general strike should have been proclaimed and any strike-settlement rejected until 'the state troops were demobilized', Cannon offered a more sober assessment. The CLA leader stressed that the Stalinist call for a general strike in May 1934 was premature precisely because not only would such a mass upheaval have had to have been implemented, in Dunne's words, 'over the heads of the Central Labor Council and the State Federation of Labor', it would effectively have had to have been called 'over the heads of the workers also, including the truck drivers'.

> The workers of Minneapolis, like the striking workers all over the country, understood the 'central objective' to be the *recognition of the union*. The leaders were in full harmony with them on this question, they stuck to this objective and, when it was obtained, they did not attempt to parade the workers through a general strike, for the sake of exercise or for 'the defeat of Governor Olson'. For one reason, it was not the right thing to do. And, for another reason, they couldn't have done it if they had tried.

Cannon thus concluded that the critique made by Bill Dunne and the Communist Party of the Minneapolis events of May 1934 erred in construing 'the situation as revolutionary, and aimed at an insurrection'. In the United States in 1934, this was a farcical reading of the political realities. Cannon suggested that his old friend Dunne, whom he bitingly dismissed as 'more at home with proverbs than with politics', needed to recall that 'every vegetable has its season'. Noting that much had rightly been demanded of the Trotskyists in Minneapolis, Cannon was confident that their spring-season had planted vitally important seeds that would give rise to new developments of great importance in the historical transformation of the labour-movement. 'On a local scale, in a small sector of the labor movement', he closed his assessment of the first phase of the teamsters' rebellion, 'the Minneapolis comrades have set an example which shows the way. The International Communists have every right to be proud of this example and to hold it up as a model to study and to follow'.[9]

---

9. Cannon 1934b. For further comment on the Communist Party's attack on the Trotskyist leadership of the 1934 strikes, extending into 1935, see Strang 1935; Skoglund interviewed by Halstead, 24 April 1955, Transcript, pp. 31–2, Box 2, Riehle Papers, MNHS.

Chapter Twelve
Toward the July Days

Cannon's enthusiasm notwithstanding, the May settlement was unravelling even before its terms appeared in print. His point, however, was confirmed. Having achieved a *de facto* recognition of the General Drivers' Union, the May 1934 strike-settlement, however much it would be skirted and evaded by the trucking bosses, proved resilient enough to allow the Union to grow, to educate its members and a broader working-class constituency, and to open out into possibilities for another, more decisive round of labour-capital conflict. In the process, the meaning of unionisation expanded, the political perspective of the Minneapolis working class widened, and labour's potential agenda grew to the point that calls for a general strike were soon echoing in Central Labor Union halls. Local 574 was building itself into a formidable agent of broad working-class struggle.

The General Drivers' and Helpers' Union had come out of the May 1934 confrontations as an established presence on the Minneapolis industrial scene, securing itself an invaluable breathing space. By the end of June 1934, it was well-prepared to battle the trucking bosses once again. Even Tobin conceded that there was little he could do to stem the rising tide of class-conflict, confessing to New Deal labour-reform architect Senator Robert F. Wagner that the Local 574 insurgency had reached the point where there was little the IBT head could do to keep things under control: 'the truckers', he confessed with a combination of fear and loathing, 'had organized themselves and were making their own battle'. This recognition of the realities of the situation did not, however, keep the IBT hierarchy from doing its utmost to clamp down on teamster-militancy in Minneapolis.[1]

A mass meeting of the Union decided to press forward its demands around honouring the original strike-settlement, raising wages, and cutting back hours. It convened a strike-conference of all unions associated with transportation in the city of Minneapolis, threatening 'to call the Employers' bluff' and back up the claims for justice with 'a city-wide tie-up'. From February's strike in specific coal-yards to May's struggle for union-recognition, 1934 was now shaping up as a wider class-war over the very nature of social relations in Minneapolis. As Local 574's *The Organizer* declared:

> The Employers, following custom [that] has been popular among them in the past, continue to dodge, stall, and chisel.... These bosses are now attempting to reorganize their forces to swindle the members of 574.... the trade unions as a unit must move on to the battle front prepared for a finish fight. The issue is clear. A Union city where men and women can feel and enjoy the benefits of Union security, and a decent standard of life – or Minneapolis ruled by Black reaction in the hands of the profit mad Bosses.

The truck-firms denied that they were subverting the agreement. For its part, the Regional Labor Board proved unable to untie the knots of an implacable impasse. Cannon, barely back at work in the New York National Executive Committee, reported on Minneapolis and pressed for a League organiser to be seconded from Chicago and dispatched to what was now, clearly, the CLA's largest industrial-union success. The Left Oppositionist soon found himself, once again, *en route* to Minneapolis.[2]

Aware of what was at stake in the ongoing teamsters' rebellion, the local CLA leadership of Local 574 relied on the full participation of the League's Minneapolis branch, which now constituted a substantial, and growing, fraction in the Union. Both the Trotskyist leadership of Local 574 and the New York-based National Executive Committee of the CLA decided early in July 1934, with a

---

1. Smemo 2011, p. 33, quoting 'Washington Sized Up Truck Driver Strike', *Minneapolis Labor Review*, 29 June 1934.

2. Clem Forsen, 'Tactics at Minneapolis', *The Militant*, 30 June 1934; 'Local 574 Calls Strike Conference', *The Organizer*, 25 June 1934, reprinted as 'Minneapolis Union Forcing Wage Demands', *The Militant*, 30 June 1934; 'Truck Firms Deny Evading Agreement', *Minneapolis Journal*, 1 July 1934; 'Truck Union Says Firms Ignore Pact', *Minneapolis Journal*, 2 July 1934; 'US Moves to Avert New Truck Strike', *Minneapolis Journal*, 3 July 1934. Cannon reported on the organisational needs of Minneapolis at the National Executive Committee meeting of 20 June 1934, moving a motion that the Chicago branch raise funds to send John Edwards as an organiser. See CLA, National Executive Committee Minutes, 20 June 1934, Box 32, File 14, GB Papers.

strike obviously pending, that the League should 'concentrate all its efforts on the Minneapolis situation, every member to be asked to give a full day's pay and that we speed up the raising of the necessary means with all funds received to be recorded for the organization and press campaign'. To this end, the NC was unanimous in its agreement that League members who were 'especially qualified to play key assisting roles' should proceed to Minneapolis immediately. Cannon left New York at the end of the first week of July 1934. A few days later, a number of other East-coast-based CLAers were enlisted in the Minneapolis campaign. Max Shachtman and the experienced and talented journalist Herbert Solow, later to be an editor of *Fortune* magazine, were brought in to edit *The Organizer*. Solow would so impress rank-and-file truckers that he was made a lifetime honorary member of Local 574. While Dobbs was listed on the Local 574 publication as the editor, he was, in fact, too busy with other tasks to undertake this responsibility, for which, in any case, he had no particular training or experience. Shachtman and Solow were helped in their editing of *The Organizer* by Cannon and Carlos Hudson, a Minneapolist Trotskyist of some journalistic aptitude. The Union's paper was, in effect, produced by way of consultation among union-leaders, 574 volunteers, and CLA journalists and writers. Albert Goldman, recently recruited to the League from the Communist Party in Chicago, came on board as Local 574's lawyer. A jocular masthead, ostensibly from an August issue of *The Organizer*, but in fact printed in a few copies for the benefit of the editorial staff and their loyal supporters, captured something of the personnel behind the paper. Dobbs was listed as 'Fall Guy', and Hudson as 'End Man'. Cannon and Shachtman sported the pseudonyms of Jim McGee and Max Marsh, being listed respectively as 'Office Boy' and 'St. Paul Correspondent'. Albert Goldman was the predictable 'Mouthpiece' and Herbert Solow the 'Guest Conductor'. Marvel Scholl Dobbs was assigned the tag of 'Military Reporter'. Bill Brown, 'the Three Dunne Sisters', and Carl Skoglund were simply 'Stooges'. Hugo Oehler also made his way to Minneapolis, where he was assigned to work in the unemployed-movement, the League having established an important presence in the Minneapolis Central Council of Workers.[3]

NRA-sponsored negotiators met with Governor Olson, Regional Labor Board officials, and representatives from both the Union and the employers, but little headway had been made by the end of the first week of July 1934. The Employers' Advisory Committee, engaging in a piece of public grandstanding, offered the

3. Dobbs 1972, pp. 105–6, which depicts the joke-masthead, mistakenly states that it appeared in *The Organizer*, 25 August 1934: however, this is not the case. For a copy, see File 'American City: The Organizer Notes', Box 1, CRW Papers, MNHS. See also Cannon 1944, pp. 154–5; Wald 1987, pp. 104–5; Drucker 1994, pp. 72–3; CLA, National Executive Committee Minutes, 5 July 1934, File 14, Box 32, GB Papers.

General Drivers' Union $1,000 if it could convince a panel of three judges that the trucking firms were in violation of the May settlement. The Union declined to participate in any such proceedings, hammering away at what it took to be the fundamental issues needing resolution: wages and inclusion of 'inside workers' in all collective-bargaining activities. In addition, Local 574 was organising a massive parade of protest for six o'clock on the evening of Friday, 6 July 1934, to be followed by a huge meeting at the Municipal Auditorium. The speakers' list for the public rally at the Auditorium included A.H. Urtubees, Chairman of the Local Building Trades Council; Roy Weir of the Central Labor Union; Emery Nelson of the Teamsters' Joint Council; Farmers' Holiday Association leader John Bosch; garment-workers' spokeswoman and Women's Auxiliary member Myrtle Harris; and W.J. McGaughren of the Railway Clerks' union. The parade, organised under the slogan 'Make Minneapolis a Union Town', was attracting widespread endorsement and support, with organisations like the State University's Social Problems Club seeking a place in its ranks, promising to send a delegation.[4]

The 6 July 1934 parade and Municipal Auditorium rally was an impressive event, arguably 'the largest mass meeting in the history of Minneapolis'. Thousands participated, their numbers including dozens of union-delegations, farmers' associations, and left-wing organisations. Leading the parade was a squadron of motorcycle-couriers from the May strike, whose job it was to clear traffic for the working-class throng, whose orderly columns stretched well past the eighteen-block route of the march. Then came Grand Marshal Ed Hudson, a Farmer-Labor Party alderman astride an impressive white steed. Dobbs recalled that, in placing Hudson on such 'prominent display', Local 574 was mindful that this would 'make it harder for him to chicken out on us when the going got rough'. A musicians' union band struck a note both festive and defiant, and behind it marched Local 574, its red bunting banner flying overhead, and the Women's Auxiliary. Supportive trade-unionists, farmers, ex-servicemen, and students rounded out the massive march, their placards proclaiming 'We Support 574', 'Down with the Citizens' Alliance', and 'Bosses Do Not Want a Union, We Workers Do'. Among the labour-contingents present, besides the General Drivers' Union, were street-railway employees, laundry and dry-cleaning workers, building tradesmen, electricians, brewery-workers, printers, petroleum-workers, upholsterers, municipal employees, iron-workers, railroaders, men and women of the garment-trades, and unemployed people affiliated with the united-front oriented Minneapolis

4. 'Truck Dispute Meeting is Set for Tomorrow', *Minneapolis Journal*, 4 July 1934; 'Truck Dispute Parlay Friday', *Minneapolis Journal*, 5 July 1934; 'Dunnigan in Closed Meet with Union', *Minneapolis Journal*, 6 July 1934; Dobbs 1972, pp. 109–11. On Myrtle Harris, who figured prominently in organising women-workers and in Farmer-Labor campaigns throughout the 1930s, see Faue 1991, pp. 106–7, 120, 125, 142, 161.

Central Council of Workers and the Communist Party-led Unemployed Councils. Two airplanes circled the parade-route, emblazoned with the huge numbers '574'. Estimates are that some six thousand onlookers, most of them sympathizers, cheered the parade from the pavement, alleys, and adjacent buildings. As many as twelve thousand people crowded into the Auditorium to hear a variety of labour-advocates, and thousands more congregated outside, where loudspeakers had been set up to transmit the speeches to those who could not make their way into the packed hall. From the podium, there came a torrent of attack on the trucking bosses, the Citizens' Alliance, and calls for the entire labour-movement to rally around the standard of Local 574. There was widespread belief that the employers were failing to live up to the terms of the May settlement, and that only a staunch fight would resolve the ongoing conflict. Miles Dunne addressed the issue of Local 574's 'Red' leadership, not to deny the charge, but to put the question on an entirely different footing:

> They have now raised the red issue and accused us of being reds and radi- cals . . . of wanting to substitute a new form of government and I say to you here frankly. . . . when a system of society exists that allows employers in Min- neapolis to wax fat on the misery and starvation and degradation of the many, it is time that system is changed, it is high time that the workers take this from their hands and take for themselves at least a fair share of all the wealth they produce.

General Drivers' Union President Bill Brown drew applause from the crowd when he declared that Minneapolis was not big enough for both the Citizens' Alliance and the union-movement, and the latter had no intention of moving. He warned, alluding to the May strike, that working-class taxpayers had no inten- tion of allowing the police-department to be used against them in any future conflict. As for the employers, he chortled, 'I want to say there is not a fair employer unless we are burying them', a remark that drew laughter throughout the Auditorium. Brown concluded by reading a resolution declaring that, 'as a united body the unions accept the challenge of the Citizens' Alliance, prepare for decisive action, and proceed to a common victory'. Setting a deadline of 11 July 1934, the mass meeting unanimously resolved that Local 574 represented all workers in the trucking sector, including 'inside workers'; that the entire membership of the Union should receive a wage-increase backdated to 26 May 1934; and that the bosses should be compelled to sign an agreement with the General Drivers' Union. To wild applause, the gathering endorsed the notion that 'An injury to one is an injury to all workers from *now on!*'[5]

---

5. Dobbs 1972, pp. 109–11; Walker 1937, pp. 159–60; 'New Truck Drivers Strike Impends in Minneapolis', *The Militant*, 7 July 1934; C.H., '10,000 March in Big Labor Parade', *The*

Between the mass march and rally of the Friday evening and a Wednesday, 11 July 1934 formal strike-vote among Local 574's membership, federal mediator Eugene H. Dunnigan continued to try to pull a rabbit out of the badly crushed labour-relations 'hat' that constituted the Regional Labor Board's mediation of negotiations between the employers and truck-drivers. His magic wasn't working. Cannon always insisted that trade-unionists needed to keep their distance from the likes of Dunnigan, 'slick rascals' and 'confidence men' whose purpose was to leave workers 'outmaneuvered and cut to pieces, ... their strike broken by the "friends of labor"' in the Roosevelt administration. Dunnigan's stock had never, in fact, risen very high with the leadership of Local 574. Dobbs recalled him showing up at strike-headquarters, 'cocky as hell, with a black ribbon on his pince-nez and four cigars showing in the pocket of his coat', boasting of the 'many strikes he had settled' and claiming that he was on the workers' side. Women's Auxiliary leader Marvel Scholl and head-nurse Vera 'Mac' McCormack had some fun at Dunnigan's expense. Making him wait to meet the Organizing Committee, the two women sat and drew up an order for hospital-supplies, embellishing the enlarging list with gruesome accounts of how various items would be needed in the weeks of battle to come. As the federal mediator heard the women nonchalantly tally up the medical requirements of what was being casually touted as the necessary physical toll of class-struggle, Dunnigan's 'eyes began to pop'. Sweating profusely, squirming in his chair, his patrician umbrella tapping nervously on the floor, the federal mediator was finally ushered into his meeting with the Trotskyist strike-leadership, the two women laughing until their sides ached. Recovering his usual airs of superiority, Dunnigan tried to parlay this bombast into union-endorsement, requesting that he be made Local 574's 'representative in all negotiations with the bosses'. Those at the helm of the insurgent teamsters were having none of this. When Brown, Dobbs, the Dunne brothers, and Skoglund said they were happy to have the federal mediator take their demands to the bosses, and return to them with answers so that they could tell Dunnigan what to do next, the confident and well-outfitted official 'left in a huff'. What Dunnigan then managed to piece together through discussions with Regional Labor Board officials and employers' representatives amounted to very little, and nothing that was of sufficient substance to mollify Local 574's leadership. Bill Brown and Farrell Dobbs insisted that statements hatched at the Regional Labor Relations Board were impossible to understand and that the

Militant, 14 July 1934; 'Truck Parley goes on After Labor Meet', *Minneapolis Journal*, 7 July 1934; 'Mass Demonstration of Unions, Friday July 6, Bridge Square to Auditorium', *The Organizer*, 2 July 1934; Tselos 1971, p. 236; Carlos Hudson, 'Chains Wear Thin in Minneapolis: Notes and Sketches on the Recent Strikes', pp. 10–12, File 'Local 574 Strike, 1934', Box 1, CRW Papers, MNHS.

truck-drivers' demands, in contrast, were clear enough. When one Board official at a July sit-down offered to provide a lawyer for the Local 574 team, one militant with twenty years of experience as a teamster quipped, 'Why – we can all speak English'. (This may well have been Carl Skoglund, whose criticisms of IBT locals hiring lawyers in the later 1930s organising drive of interstate truckers supposedly resulted in the Bar Association of Minneapolis 'talking about starting a suit' against him for 'discrediting a profession'.) Raising wages, recognising 'inside workers' as members of the General Drivers' Union, and signing a clear-cut agreement were what the Union asked of the employers; these demands, not ambiguously worded missives, were what needed to be addressed if a strike was to be avoided. That strike, said union-leaders, might well make May events 'look like an ice cream social'.[6]

As the Wednesday, 11 July 1934 strike-vote meeting approached, employers and their allies in the Minneapolis newspaper-business upped the ante in the anti-strike propaganda-war. They promoted Dan Tobin's views that the Teamsters did not endorse either the leadership of Local 574 or the use of sympathetic or general strikes, nor would Tobin 'approve the violation of a signed contract'. The *Minneapolis Journal* then quoted the conservative 'craft'-conscious leader: 'The reason we have raised our union from an organization which was the lowest rung in the ladder of trade unions, is because we have kept our world and our bond with our employers, with our membership, and with the public'. It also went on to denounce the 'Communist' leadership of the Minneapolis General Drivers' Union, claiming it had adopted a 'program of disorder and violence' for its 'own anarchistic purposes'. Calling on all 'law-abiding and liberty-loving workingmen' to refuse to be a part of 'such an evil conspiracy', the *Journal* castigated Local 574's plan to enlist all the trade-unions of Minneapolis in a sympathetic strike waged under its 'red flag for a regime of blood and violence'. Proclaiming their 'ostensible object to be the unionization of all of the city's industries and business enterprises', the leadership of the General Drivers' Union was, according to this mainstream newspaper, intent on enlisting 'Minneapolis in the revolution they hope to start in this Country for the overthrow of the Constitution and the laws of the land, for the violent transformation of our democratic-representative system of government into a Communist dictatorship'. As a solution to this

6. Dobbs 1972, pp. 112–14; 'Labor Board Acts to Settle Truck Strife', *Minneapolis Journal*, 8 July 1934; Skoglund interviewed by Halstead, 14 May 1955, Transcript, p. 37, Box 2, Riehle Papers, MNHS; 'Truck Union Accepts Board Helper Ruling', *Minneapolis Journal*, 9 July 1934; and, for Cannon's caustic comment on federal mediators, Cannon 1944, pp. 156–8; Untitled typescript fragment, pp. 24–5 in File 'Notes Local 574 and Strike', Box 1, CRW Papers, MNHS. For a clear public statement by Local 574 on the role of the Regional Labor Board, see 'What the Labor Board Means to the Union', *The Organizer*, 2 July 1934.

tyranny, the *Minneapolis Journal* called on Governor Olson to tolerate no interference with the public's use of the streets, insisting that he 'use every means
in his power to guarantee and protect the freedom of the streets for transportation'. This would ensure that any strike-movement in Minneapolis was stopped
in its tracks, and that liberty would be secured and saved in Minnesota and the
United States. Some conservative trade-union officials exhibited signs of vacilla-
tion. Robert Fleming, Bill Brown's equivalent as president of the St. Paul General
Drivers' and Helpers Union, Local 120, was quoted in the *Minneapolis Journal*, in
what was surely a statement made under pressure from Tobin, that his organisation would not be supporting 574 in a sympathetic walkout. He also claimed
that in St. Paul, inside workers had never been welcomed into the ranks of the
International Teamsters. 'Brotherhood' had its limits. 'No chicken pluckers', he
explained. Two days later, Fleming appeared at a Central Labor Union forum
and did something of an about-face, insisting that the General Drivers' Union in
St. Paul had similar grievances to Local 574, and 'we are for common action'. He
claimed that he had been misinterpreted in the pages of the *Minneapolis Journal*,
and that a strike-vote would be conducted within days, thus ascertaining the
views of his membership. Fleming also repudiated Tobin's Red-baiting.[7]

Metaphorical chicken-pluckers were, apparently, out in force on the night of
11 July 1934, as Local 574 met at the Eagles Hall in East Minneapolis. A parade of
General Drivers' Union leaders – Brown, Dobbs, the three Dunnes, Skoglund –
struck a militant tone, assailing the employers, the Citizens' Alliance, Red-baiting,
and the Regional Labor Board. Dan Tobin came in for a particular thrashing, the
official strike-call drafted by Local 574 and drawing on discussions that came out
of the three-and-a-half hour meeting declaring:

> We note with the greatest indignation that D.J. Tobin, President of our Inter-
> national organization, has associated himself with the diabolical game of the
> bosses by publishing a slanderous attack on our leadership in the official

---

7. 'What is Behind the Strike?' and 'St. Paul Strike Threat Vanishes; Drivers Say They
are Satisfied', *Minneapolis Journal*, 10 July 1934; 'Daniel Tobin goes to Bat for the Bosses',
and 'Red Herring Cover for Real Issues', *The Militant*, 14 July 1934; 'Twin Cities Transport
Strike Looms', and 'Red Scare Raised in Attempt to Break Union', *The Organizer*, 9 July
1934; James P. Cannon, 'Central Labor Union Backs Drivers' Local', *The Militant*, 14 July
1934. In contrast to Fleming's claims with regard to limiting membership in the International Brotherhood of Teamsters, see 'St. Paul and Minneapolis Station Attendants
Merge with 120 and 574', *The Organizer*, 9 July 1934; and, for Fleming's backtracking, see
'Labor Board Still Seeks to Avert Strike', *Minneapolis Journal*, 11 July 1934. For Tobin and
IBT resistance to the militancy of Local 574, see Smemo 2011, pp. 34–5; Cochran 1977,
p. 163; 'Fight with Tobin and Teamsters' Joint Council', File 'American City: Minnesota
Miscellaneous Notes (2)', Box 1, CRW Papers, MNHS. For an interesting discussion of
the relative quietude of St. Paul workers compared to the militancy of Minneapolis, see
Wingerd 2001.

magazine. The fact that this attack has become part of the 'ammunition' of the bosses in their campaign to wreck our union, is enough for any intelligent worker to estimate it for what it really is. We say plainly to D.J. Tobin: If you can't act like a Union man, and help us, instead of helping the bosses, then at least have the decency to stand aside and let us fight our battle alone. We did it in the organization campaign and in the previous strike and we can do it again. We received absolutely no help of any kind from you. Our leadership and our guidance has come from our local leaders, and them alone. We put our confidence in them and will not support any attack on them under any circumstances.

An Auxiliary speaker received a rousing round of applause when she declared that the women would 'fight side by side with the men to the finish'. Herbert Capelis, a youth-leader of the Communist League of America from New York, in Minneapolis as a consequence of his organising efforts on behalf of the Dental Technicians' Council of America, thought the meeting inspiring, and was struck by both its resolve and its militancy. Cannon reported to *The Militant* that the spirit of solidarity in Minneapolis was rising to new heights, and that many trade-unionists gathered outside the Eagles Hall to hear the outcome of the strike-vote. When, by a unanimous standing vote, the assembly endorsed job-action, strike-talk quickly spread to other unions, among them organizations of building tradesmen, barbers, car-mechanics, retail-clerks, dental mechanics, upholsterers, street-railway workers, and other drivers in the transport-sector. In the Central Labor Union, delegates pledged full support to the cause of the General Drivers' Union; the strike-resolution of Local 574 was adopted without dissent. Local 574 ended the meeting with instructions to its organising committee and its Executive Board to meet and develop a strike-strategy. With federal mediator Dunnigan pleading for a five-day extension of the strike-deadline, midnight on the evening of Monday, 16 July 1934, was established as the time when the walkout-clock would start ticking. This gave Local 574 five days to elect a Strike Committee of 100 and to schedule a final meeting at which a secret strike-ballot, mandatory under IBT union-bylaws, could be conducted. 'The lines are drawn', concluded one of many articles on the Minneapolis situation in *The Militant*, adding, for good measure, that even 'King' Tobin seemed incapable of putting a lid on the local class-struggle. 'The strikers are determined.... The unions have pledged their support'.[8]

---

8. Dobbs 1972, pp. 114–16; 'Strike Call of Local 574: Unanimously Adopted at General Membership Meeting, Wednesday July 11', and Herbert Capelis, 'A Trade Unionist Views the Strike Meeting of Local 574', *The Organizer*, 16 July 1934; 'Tobin Goes to Bat for the Bosses', and Cannon, 'Central Labor Union Backs Drivers' Local', *The Militant*, 14 July

The July 1934 confrontation between the General Drivers' Union and the trucking employers was thus shaping up entirely differently than the strike of two months earlier. Capital's heels were dug in; labour was now far more willing to test its newly-established strength; and the state, whether through use of the carrot or the stick, had learned that in Minneapolis, trucking unionism was not to be easily deterred. With Local 574 again exhibiting its capacity for organisation, preparing for an all-out battle, both capital and the state launched vehement pre-strike campaigns to discredit the Union, erode enthusiasm for strike-action, and impress upon working-class militants that 'law and order' would be 'rigidly enforced' in Minneapolis.

Joseph R. Cochran of the Employers' Advisory Committee, representing 166 transport-bosses, insisted that Local 574 was in violation of the May settlement-order drafted by the Regional Labor Board. Cochran claimed that appropriate avenues of dispute resolution by arbitration were open. Arguing that the Employers' Committee had always been 'ready to negotiate with chicken pickers or any other workers through any representatives whom they may select', Cochran's public statements clearly implied that the company-owners did not recognise Local 574's claims to be the rightful bargaining agents of the 'inside workers'. This issue, moreover, blurred into the employers' unambiguous Red-baiting of the leadership of the General Drivers' Union and its aims. 'So long as communists in control of the truck drivers' union are determined that there shall be a strike in the hope that victory will greatly enhance their personal power and create one big union with all trades grouped into one body – vesting power in the hands of a few communist leaders completely to paralyze all industry', Cochran declared in a 12 July 1934 statement, 'so long as this determination exists, avoidance of a strike is difficult'. These employer-missives were matched by announcements from Police-Chief Johannes that a recently-increased municipal force was committed to protect life and property in the event of a strike, and that 'every man in the police department will be put in uniform to see that law and order is upheld'. There was no talk, in mid-July 1934, of relying on 'special deputies'. Instead, Johannes, Mayor A.G. Bainbridge, and Sheriff John Wall declared that 'the minute the strike is called we will ask the Governor to send the National Guard to aid us in our duties'.[9]

Finally, within the unions, conservative forces began to mobilise against the rising working-class sentiment for sympathetic, general strikes, throwing cold

1934; 'Leaders in Truck Dispute Define Stand on Terms', *Minneapolis Journal*, 9 July 1934; 'Labor Board Still Seeks to Avert Strike', *Minneapolis Journal*, 11 July 1934.

9. 'Mayor and Sheriff to Demand Troops When Strike is Called', *Minneapolis Journal*, 13 July 1934; 'An Outlaw Strike', 'Truck Strike Gets 3 Hard Jolts in Day', and 'Communist Control of Strikes', *Minneapolis Journal*, 13 July 1934.

water on the fires of labour-movement grievances. Next door to Minneapolis, pressure was put on the Brotherhood of Teamsters Local 120 to backtrack from President Fleming's seeming commitment to stand with his counterparts in Minneapolis, and trucking unions in other Minnesota locales – Duluth, Superior, and Fargo-Moorhead – were leaned on by IBT vice-president, John Geary, to avert strike-action if at all possible. Geary was quick to proclaim that Local 574's strike-call was undertaken without the sanction of the International and was 'illegal under union laws and ... if the strike went into effect it [would] be an outlaw strike from the standpoint of the national organization'. Tobin's emissary Geary then decreed that any Teamster local supporting the Minneapolis strikers would also be engaged in illegal activities. At a four-hour meeting of the St. Paul truckers, the oratory of which was described as 'bitter', Bill Brown, Miles Dunne, and Ray Dunne locked horns with Geary and other conservative union-leaders, pleading with rank-and-file truckers to support the strike-movement. They pointed out that whatever gains workers in the Twin Cities trucking industry had registered since May had been a consequence of the audacious fighting spirit of the Minneapolis local. The Minneapolis militants won the battle for the hearts and minds of the workers, but they lost the procedural war. In a highly contentious decision opposed by many, a secret ballot was conducted after the hall of five hundred was cleared of all but St. Paul Local 120 members. The vote was 167 to 128 in favour of supporting the strike-actions of their fraternal General Drivers' Union members in Minneapolis, but Geary insisted that the IBT's constitution required a two-thirds majority to call any strike-action, and so the proposal was lost. Disappointed that barely three hundred of the Union's fifteen hundred members voted, Local 120 President Robert Fleming announced he would be seeking a second meeting, in which another vote would be conducted.

A grandiosely-named Committee of 25, led by conservative trucker Robert E. Johnstone, echoed the sentiments of the employers and the mainstream press, demanding that Bill Brown, the Dunne brothers, and Skoglund 'resign their positions'. Claiming to speak for the majority of Local 574 members, this group met with the established leadership of the General Drivers' Union at the Central Labor Union hall and raised all of the usual allegations and criticisms emanating from both the Employers' Advisory Committee and Dan Tobin's International Teamsters' officialdom. Johnstone pontificated: 'There won't be any strike. You can bank on that'. Claiming that the existing leadership of Local 574 was too radical, that it was 'tainted with communism', and that it had 'mismanaged' relations with the employers, precipitating the membership into an 'outlaw strike' that threatened their union-charter, Johnstone broke decisively with the entire strategic orientation of the Minneapolis teamsters' insurgency. Recognising that a variety of groups worked within the trucking industry, Johnstone claimed that there should be one union of drivers and helpers, but that each sector of employment should 'handle its own problems'. For all the *chutzpah* of this dissident union-faction, and the extensive coverage it received in the employer-sympathetic press, it could rally no substantial strength within Local 574. President Bill Brown and his leadership-team easily defeated this initial challenge.

Amidst increasingly vitriolic newspaper-coverage denouncing the so-called 'outlaw strike', the 'self-respecting, upstanding men of Organized Labor' were thus bombarded with calls to break from Local 574's leadership. Depicted as an 'evil conspiracy' intent on a 'harvest of hardships' and a 'probable sequel of violence and bloodshed', Vincent Raymond Dunne and others were placed in the metaphorical stocks of a relentless public excoriation. Lacking 'respect for its pledges, no pride in keeping its covenants', the 'traitorous leaders' of the General Drivers' Union were represented as doing no less than the devil's work among the 'real union men of Minneapolis', for whom 'honor' and 'solemn agreements' mattered. With a language of demonisation such as this, small wonder that on the Sunday afternoon before the strike was to begin, Reverend William Brown convened a three o'clock meeting to voice discontent with the Reds at the helm of the General Drivers' Union, and to demand a strike-vote by secret ballot. Some in Local 574 were convinced that this 'rump'-mobilisation originated with the bosses, one journalist claiming it had been organised by the clergyman Brown 'and a scab'. Truckers associated with it included the resolute Robert E. Johnstone. Those gathered to follow Reverend Brown's crusade into the promised land of righteous trade-unionism were soon outnumbered, and the minister's ostensible words of welcome were drowned out by interruptions and interjections from the crowd. When the chairman of the truckers' committee that had called the church-meeting, Jack Soule, tried to open the proceedings, he was heckled by the 'noisy and restless audience' of five hundred. With cries of 'yellow' and 'stool pigeon for the employers' flung at the pulpit, Soule, who could not be heard beyond the first three rows of pews, was soon elbowed off the rostrum by Grant and Ray Dunne and Carl Skoglund. Taking charge of the proceedings, Grant Dunne castigated the 'underhand effort...to split the union', and criticised 'the conducting of a meeting in a church or at any place outside the regular union headquarters'. The meeting was now firmly in the hands of the Local 574 leadership. Bill Brown explained to all of those present, some of whom accepted the employers' claims that 'One Big Union' in the trucking industry was a subversive endeavour, that this was, in fact, exactly what was at stake in the union-struggle: 'The charge had been made that the leaders planned to build a union so large and powerful that it could control industry. That was precisely the intention'. When International Brotherhood vice-president John Geary rose, predictably, to speak out against general and sympathetic strikes, so-called illegal job-actions, and the obligations of trade-union officials, he was roundly jeered by the now increasingly agitated audience. Grant Dunne had to appeal for 'more respectful' behaviour, insisting on conduct that 'befitted a house of worship'. One of the organisers of the anti-leadership event was eventually escorted to the speakers' stand, where he repudiated his role in calling the meeting and confessed that it had been 'a big mistake'. Motions were passed expressing confidence in the leadership of the Union. As five hundred workers filed out of the church, the General Drivers' Union was given an unambiguous vote of support. As M.E. Carlson wrote in *The Organizer*, with the Communist Party, Dan Tobin, and the employers all castigating the Dunnes, Dobbs, Skoglund, and Brown, 'No one loves the poor leadership except the truck drivers'.[10]

---

10. The above paragraphs draw on 'An Outlaw Strike', and 'Truck Strike Gets 3 Hard Jolts in Day', *Minneapolis Journal*, 13 July 1934; 'Group from Union Signs Call for New Strike Vote Tomorrow', *Minneapolis Journal*, 14 July 1934; 'Union Revolt Threatens Strike Chiefs – Group Asks Leaders Quit; Anti-Strike Meeting Called', *Minneapolis Journal*, 15 July 1934; 'As Zero hour for Walkout Nears', *Minneapolis Journal*, 16 July 1934; '"Sunday Opposition" Meeting Becomes Strike Demonstration', *The Organizer*, 17 July 1934; Skoglund interviewed by Halstead, 24 April 1955, Typescript, p. 30, Box 2, Riehle Papers, MNHS; Carlos Hudson, 'Chains Wear Thin in Minneapolis: Notes and Sketches on the Recent Strikes', pp. 13–14, File 'Local 574 Strike, 1934', Box 1, CRW Papers, MNHS; Anne Ross, 'Labor Unity in Minneapolis', *New Republic*, 25 July 1934; Herbert Solow, 'War In Minneapolis', *Nation*, 8 August 1934; Dobbs 1972, p. 116; Tselos 1971, p. 237; Korth 1995, pp. 144–5; M.E. Carlson, 'Nobody Loves 'Em', *The Organizer*, 16 July 1934.

Chapter Thirteen
A Strike Declared; a Plot Exposed

Marathon mediation-sessions at the Regional Labor Board produced little in the way of progress on the issues separating the 166 trucking firms and Local 574. An attempt on the part of the Employers' Advisory Committee to secure access to union membership-rolls and to arbitrate the wages of 'warehouse employees' of 22 market-firms betrayed a crack in the wall of resistance to recognising 'inside workers' as members of the General Drivers' Union. Nonetheless, this minor backtracking came with strings attached: it was not to be considered a precedent for any of the remaining 144 trucking operations and, from the Union's point of view, it sacrificed too much. 'We show no membership books to bosses or their agents, so that they may establish a blacklist against Union men', replied Local 574. At the final Eagles Hall strike ratification-vote on Monday evening, 16 July 1934, over two and a half thousand trade-unionists voted unanimously to strike. 'It was a hot night', recalled Farrell Dobbs, 'and the hall was packed with sweltering workers who were in a fighting mood'. They rejected outright the necessity of conducting a secret ballot, and affirmed confidence in their leaders, condemning the Citizens' Alliance-orchestrated Red-baiting campaign, insisting that, as workers, they had a fundamental right to belong to an independent organisation and to determine its policies. A Committee of 100 was elected, integrating Teamster Executive Board officials like Cliff Hall into a larger body that was constituted a strike-committee and charged with having full authority to make any and all executive decisions in the midst of the walkout. The usual nucleus of Trotskyists and trucking militants was supplemented by workers who had proved their mettle during the May strike. Farrell Dobbs and Vincent Raymond Dunne were elected as a contact-committee of two, responsible for all direct meeting and negotiating with employers, but their actions were subject to ratification by the larger, hundred-strong strike-committee. In this way the conservative influence of the Executive Board, beholden to Tobin and the IBT, was negated for the duration of the strike. Union-strategy and all dealings with the bosses and/or mediators appeared firmly in the hands of the three Dunne brothers, Dobbs, Skoglund, and their staunch ally, Local 574 president Bill Brown.

The Organizer, with Cannon, Shachtman, and Oehler contributing the bulk of its copy, was converted to a daily strike-bulletin, its pages a source of information, humour, political education, and spirited defence of working-class interests. In a matter of days, its print-run was approaching twelve thousand, 'sold' for what consumers could cough up, be it a slap on the back and wishes of good will, some small change, or as much as five dollars. The newspaper more than paid its way, underwriting the expense of the union-commissary as well as the cost of its own production. 'The morale of the strikers was kept up by' *The Organizer*, Cannon recalled a decade later; but, above all, the role of this 'powerful instrument' was as an educator. Day after day, the workers had their own source of information, a printed account of what had happened, what was coming, and what should be done. 'The striking workers were armed and prepared in advance', noted Cannon, and 'The *Daily Organizer* covered the town like a blanket'. An unambiguous success-story, *The Organizer* was heralded as the first such union-newspaper in the history of the American labour-movement to appear on a daily basis during a protracted strike. This exaggeration aside, workers relied on the paper for accounts of strike-developments and events, realising that what they might read in the mainstream media was likely to contain misinformation and purposeful falsehoods. Cannon thought publication of the daily strike-bulletin 'the greatest of all the weapons in the arsenal of the Minneapolis strike. I can say without any qualification that of all the contributions we made, the most decisive, the one that tipped the scale to victory, was the publication of the daily paper'. Writing at the end of 1934, contrasting the experience of strike-organisation in Minneapolis with that of the Southern mill-operatives, Cannon commented: 'the textile workers, half a million strong, had to depend on the capitalist press for information – Local 574 of Minneapolis published *a daily paper of its own!*'[1]

---

1. The above paragraphs draw on Korth 1995, pp. 145–6; Dobbs 1972, pp. 116–22; Anne Ross, 'Minnesota Sets Some Precedents', *New Republic*, 12 September 1934, p. 121; 'The Strike is On! Members Cheer Confidence Vote in Union Heads', and 'Jobless Support Strike', *The Organizer*, 17 July 1934; Cannon 1944, pp. 158–60; Cannon 1934a. Cannon

The strike was declared, as announced beforehand, at midnight on Monday, 16 July 1934. As Anne Ross wrote in the pages of the *New Republic*, 'The real issue of the strike is now: not merely the right of higher wages for men who ride the trucks, but the right of labor unity'. Herbert Solow put the matter similarly in *The Nation*: 'How, asked the union leaders, can we compromise? Either we have a right to represent our members or we have not; if the bosses say we have not, we'll go out'. The most clear-cut declaration of what was at stake in the strike came, predictably, from the General Drivers' Union itself:

> Ours is the cause of the whole labor movement. Should we be defeated, we who are intrenched [sic] in the key industry of transportation, the other unions in Minneapolis would be chopped down one by one. Every labor organization would be endangered. Should we be victorious, it means a strengthening of the whole labor movement, it means a tremendous step forward in making Minneapolis a Union town.

As Solow concluded, Local 574 was engaged in nothing less than 'making labor history in the city of Minneapolis'.[2]

Much, then, was at stake. Little had been left to chance. A legal staff consisting of trusted CLAer Albert Goldman, Rand Tower, Irving Green, and Fred A. Ossanna of Ossanna, Hall, and Hoaglund was assembled. Close ties with other unions had long been consolidated. The jobless, affiliated with the Unemployed Councils and the MCCW, were brought into the strike-movement, issued buttons identifying them as supporters, and assigned duties. As in the May strike, Local 574 secured a two-storey garage-building and outfitted it with loudspeakers, vehicle-bays, beds, a commissary, and an infirmary. Many of the same

---

and the Trotskyist Dunne brothers must have known that their claims about the *Daily Organizer* were exaggerated, since none other than William F. Dunne had edited a daily newspaper in the midst of a violent metal-trades strike in Butte, Montana in 1917–18. Dunne was the chairman of the Joint Strike Committee, and, in this capacity, edited the *Butte Daily Bulletin*, official organ of the Montana State Federation of Labor and the Butte Central Labor Council. Four years later, in a 1921 speech to the Workers' Party Convention, Dunne recalled the importance of this daily newspaper, and stressed that it was defended against corporate attack by an armed workers' defence-guard: 'for four weeks at a time 30 to 40 armed men slept in the composing room and the office of the "Butte Bulletin", had their sentries out covering eight city blocks, threw out lines of communication, did everything but dig trenches. And so the paper kept on being published, but it was only published because the mercenaries of the corporation knew that there was a penalty attached to an attack on the plant'. See 'Speech of William F. Dunne, of Butte, Montana, before the Workers Party Convention on Monday, December 26th, 1921', provided by David Riehle; and discussion of Dunne and the Butte paper in Draper 1957, p. 316.

2. Anne Ross, 'Labor Unity in Minneapolis', *New Republic*, 25 July 1934, p. 286; Herbert Solow, 'War In Minneapolis', *Nation*, 8 August 1934; 'The Strike is On!', *The Organizer*, 17 July 1934.

sympathetic personnel, including Dr. McCrimmon and Nurse McCormack, who had supported the strikers at 1900 Chicago Avenue, were back on the job in July. Located at 215 South Eighth Street, the new strike-headquarters was across the street from the Minneapolis Club, 'a swank set-up patronised by the "best families"'. The Union's Eighth Street larder was better stocked with foodstuffs and local produce, thanks to the improved relations and increasingly close connections with rural producers and their organisations. There was the usual attention to dispatching flying pickets, under the supervision of Kelly Postal, Ray Dunne, Harry DeBoer, and Dobbs. Once again, 'nightly meetings were held at the strike headquarters for the workers to hear reports on the day's events, listen to guest speakers, and enjoy some form of entertainment'. The Women's Auxiliary was now on a firm footing, destined to play as crucial a role in the third strike as it had in the second. Procedures were set up, and a committee headed by Ray Rainbolt established, to monitor requests from individuals and firms seeking permission to move goods and conduct trucking business in Minneapolis during the strike. Hospitals, orphanages, and public works were supplied with necessities; oil-trucks and filling stations were handled with more leeway than had been evident in the May strike; taxis and unionised brewery, ice, milk, and bakery-drivers were allowed permission to drive. In a novel exercise of strike-advertising, International Harvester was granted passage of some new trucks to a Chicago World's Fair display, provided they were paraded through city-streets emblazoned with large banners declaring 'Moved with Local 574's Permission'. Harvester also made a donation to 574's cafeteria. The July strike was, like its May predecessor, a model of union-preparation and organisational foresight.[3]

If the trade-unionists were on guard, so, too, was the Citizens' Alliance.[4] It had apparently convinced the owner of the garage rented by Local 574 to lock his new tenants out of their rented premises on the eve of the declared strike. Undeterred, the Strike Committee of 100 broke into the Eighth Avenue building and began to plan Tuesday's picket-activities. By four in the morning, pickets had been established around the city, 'all streets being guarded to prevent entrance or departure of trucks not excepted in the strike order'. Local 574 would soon learn that Governor Olson, while proclaiming his neutrality in the strike and seemingly straddling the fence, was, instead, acting quickly, if incompletely, in acceding to Mayor Bainbridge's written request to provide troops to protect

---

3. Dobbs 1972, pp. 119–21; 'Jobless Support Strike' and 'Legal Staff for Strike', *The Organizer*, 17 July 1934; 'Commissary to Move', *The Organizer*, 18 July 1934 (on the Women's Auxiliary); Korth 1995, p. 146; Tselos 1971, pp. 238–9; Anne Ross, 'Labor Unity in Minneapolis', *New Republic*, 25 July 1934, p. 285; Le Sueur 1934, pp. 330–2.

4. For a thorough account of the Citizen's Alliance and the 1934 strikes, see Millikan 2001, pp. 264–87.

citizens and property from harm during the strike. Olson mobilised one battalion of the Minnesota National Guard, having it assemble at the Fourth Avenue and Sixth Street armoury 'awaiting orders'. Refusing to be cowed, the General Drivers' Union declared defiantly, 'No truck is going to be moved. By nobody'.[5]

As in May, the first few days of the strike were quiet. Skoglund and Dobbs counselled the strikers not to provoke violence or make precipitous demands on other unionised workers. Workers walking strike-lines, many of them more than willing to physically engage the police, scabs, and others opposed to the work-stoppage, were dissuaded from taking clubs or weapons of any kind, euphemistically referred to as 'picket–equipment', with them onto the streets. Union-leaders requested firmly that all such materials be brought to the strike-headquarters and left there for the time being. Aside from a few arrests of pickets for disorderly conduct, Minneapolis streets were tranquil, if tense; scarcely a truck was on the road.

Federal mediator Father Francis J. Haas arrived from Washington to bolster the flagging efforts of E.H. Dunnigan. The press waxed enthusiastic about Haas and his hopes for a settlement. The founder of the Catholic Conference on Industrial Problems and director of the Carnegie Peace Union came highly recommended, and was hailed in the *Minneapolis Journal* as 'a consistent worker for old age pensions, for the rights of labor, [and a student] of crime and criminal injustice'. But the Trotskyist leadership of the strike put little faith in this less-than-divine intervention. Referring to Dunnigan, Haas and their ilk, Cannon insisted

> they never negotiated two cents out of the Trotskyist leaders of 574. They got a dose of negotiations and diplomacy which they are still gagging from. We wore out three of them before the strike was finally settled.[6]

Indeed, as Haas was praising the 'attitude of frankness and open mindedness shown by both sides', Local 574 was being given a taste of the deceit of constituted authority.

---

5. 'Last Minute Flash', *The Organizer*, 17 July 1934; 'Truck Drivers Walk Out Again: Troops Called to Maintain Order – Picket Line Thrown out to Circle City', 'Guard Unit Mobilized to be Ready for Strike Call', and 'Governor Promises to Protect Citizens', *Minneapolis Journal*, 17 July 1934; 'The Basis for Settlement', 'Employers Plan to Shatter Line Flops Miserably', and 'Citizen's Alliance Threatens Violence', *The Organizer*, 19 July 1934.

6. The above paragraphs draw on 'Strike is 100% Solid: Troops in Minneapolis for What?' and 'No Scab Trucks Moving Around in Minneapolis', *The Organizer*, 18 July 1934; 'Attempted Frame-Up Flops', *The Organizer*, 20 July 1934; Dobbs 1972, pp. 119–20; Blantz 1970, p. 9; 'Truck Strike Negotiations Wait Arrival of New U.S. Mediator', *Minneapolis Journal*, 18 July 1934; 'Truck Strike Accord Near, Haas Believes', and 'The Strategy of the Strike', *Minneapolis Journal*, 19 July 1934; Cannon 1944, p. 157.

On Thursday, 19 July 1934, Police-Chief Johannes staged a cop-escorted 'running' of the picket-lines, in which a mere 150 pounds of canned and bottled goods, ostensibly bound for the strike-constrained hospital, was transported in a single five-tonne truck guarded by eleven squad-cars and 44 shotgun-toting police. The entire cargo consisted of five boxes. Dispatched from the recently war-torn Market District, the delivery-truck was outfitted with banners proclaiming 'hospital supplies'. Photographers and movie-cameramen were on hand to record the truck's departure, and they were expecting fireworks from the union-pickets. Newspapers had, apparently, already been fed 'the story', and had printed what Charles Rumford Walker referred to as 'a full and dramatic account of an episode *which was about to take place*'. This 'hospital-convoy' was the first attempt to move goods in the now three day-old strike, in a deliberately constructed and unnecessary drama that was orchestrated to end in politically useful tragedy.

There was no need to escort hospital-supplies under armed guard. Johannes and the Citizens' Alliance types who concocted the scheme were well aware that Local 574 allowed free passage of supplies of all kinds to Minneapolis Hospital Council outlets. The goodwill between the General Drivers' Union and the city's hospitals was a matter of public record. Yet Johannes had instructed his officers to move the goods and to resist any union-attempts to thwart the delivery. 'Don't take a beating', he reportedly instructed his men, 'you have shotguns and you know how to use them. . . . . When we are finished with this convoy there will be other goods to move'. *The Organizer* claimed that behind this postured farce lay a more sinister design: 'The plan was to provoke a riot so that the cops would shoot down pickets, and Mayor Bainbridge and the bosses could howl for the militia to be brought out to move trucks'. Local 574 had been informed of the plot by a sympathetic 'inside worker'. Ray Dunne telephoned Police-Chief Johannes to instruct him that the pickets were not interested in impeding the progress of the truck and to suggest that the sham-convoy be called off. Outsmarted by the General Drivers' Union, the Police-Chief muttered that a messenger would be sent to stop the truck, but this never happened.

As the Minneapolis dailies proclaimed the picket-lines broken, Dunne, Dobbs, and *The Organizer* broke the real story: 'We refused to fall into the trap. All our cruising squads were recalled from the scene, and the delivery was allowed to go through without interference'. Selling some ten thousand copies on 20 July 1934, the daily strike-bulletin assured its readers that while 'The boss press . . . reports the whole incident as a serious break in the strike front . . . [this is] an attempt to save something out of the failure of the plot. . . . The picket lines are unbroken! The fight goes on!' Outraged that 'The whole thing was a fake!', strikers responded with resolve to the hospital-convoy fiasco. William Brown called a mass meeting of Local 574 for that evening, capitalising on labour's outrage that Minneapolis's senior law-enforcement officer would be guilty of attempting to provoke a bloody riot in the interests of the bosses. Haas clearly had his work cut out: Dunne and Dobbs cancelled a negotiating meeting, complaining of the Police-Chief's possibly deadly disingenuousness.[7]

7. The above paragraphs draw on Dobbs 1972, pp. 124–5; Korth 1995, p. 147; Walker 1937, pp. 164–6; '22 Armed Cars in Convoy for Two Loads of Food', *Minneapolis Journal*, 20 July 1934; '150 Cops Convoy 150 Pounds of Freight in Five-Ton Truck', and 'President Wm Brown Calls Big Meet of 574 Tonight', *The Organizer*, 20 July 1934; Shaun (Jack) Maloney, interviewed by Duffy and Miller, 16 August 1979, Transcript, pp. 20–6, File 'Minneapolis Teamsters' Strike 1934', Box 2, Maloney Papers, MNHS.

Chapter Fourteen
Bloody Friday

Thursday's 'hospital-convoy' made it abundantly clear that Johannes was following a more aggressive course than he had charted in May. The police were now committed to moving trucks through picket-lines, and were obviously working in tandem with the Citizens' Alliance and Employers' Advisory Committee. Using *The Organizer* to good effect, Cannon and others responded to police-provocation, determined both to bolster the fighting spirit of Local 574's members *and* keep the strikers and their sympathetic supporters from being drawn into senseless and counterproductive confrontation. One way this was done was through the humour-column authored by Cannon, in which a fictional worker, Mike Ryan, wrote daily 'letters to dere emily', his 'sweetheart'. Written in the vernacular of the 'working stiff', this regularly-published correspondence promoted the General Drivers' Union and labour solidarity, scaffolding the cause of trade-unionism on a sense of basic human needs and a commitment to justice and fairness. All of this was effectively translated to readers through the everyday correspondence between young lovers. As tensions rose in the first days of the July strike, for instance, with Johannes proclaiming to the press, 'We are going to move trucks for those who want them moved, and our men are not going to be permitted to be hurt without "striking back"', boasting that the Department had 200 shotguns at its disposal and 300 more had been secured for that evening, Cannon had Mike writing to Emily:

i sorta feel calm and peaceful now – and strong and determined somehow to. i feel like i could fite on forever. You probably dont like so much to hear only about the strike and our Union all the time, but to tell the truth kid that seems to me about the biggest thing in my life right now. You probly cant see how a union means so much to a fella, but old 574, well i guess we all feel that it's the only thing now that's ever goin to do us any good, to get enough dough each week so as to live like human beings ought to live.... when i think of the way the guys at the Union stand by me and all, i get a lump in my throat. The other day VE, thats one of the Dunne brothers, comes up to me and asks in the kindest way that i shouldnt drink now while the strike is on. we got to be sober so we can fite harder and think faster he says, and so none of us are getting drunk now while the strike is on. honest, emily, i could crawl 5 miles on my belly through broken glass for guys like we got in our Union, and all the rest feels the same way to ... i feel like i could fite on and on forever, through Hell and Brimstone until the strike is one for good and all and when thats done im coming up some weakend to see you.

With striking workers receiving letters from trucking employers demanding that if they did not return to their jobs within three days they would be replaced, Mike's letters to Emily were clearly intended to consolidate solidarity during a period when Minneapolis's labour-insurgency faced intensified opposition.[1]

As newspaper-headlines warned that the San Francisco general strike had reached 'Zero Hour', with the Embarcadero barricaded, patrolled by sentries armed with bayonets and machineguns, and guarded by tanks, the Minneapolis Market District was, as in May, taut with tension.[2] Mediation-efforts by Father Haas and Governor Olson came to a dead-end, with Chief of Police Mike Johannes refusing to back down on his commitment to provide police-convoys for those trucking operations that insisted on moving goods. 'It's law and order with me', was Johannes's blunt retort. Vincent Raymond Dunne and Bill Brown replied by strengthening picket-lines and insisting that 'The trucks will not move.... You can depend on that'. Dunne and Brown also worked to restrain rank-and-file

---

1. Dobbs 1972, pp. 124–5; '22 Armed Cars in Convoy for Two Loads of Food', *Minneapolis Journal*, 20 July 1934; 'letters to dere emily', *The Organizer*, 20 July 1934; Tselos 1971, p. 241. As indicated earlier in a previous chapter, I attribute authorship of this humour-column to Cannon partly on the basis that it began and ended with Cannon coming to and leaving Minneapolis. It certainly fit well with Cannon's understandings of both the need to build the Women's Auxiliary and to bolster elementary trade-union principles. The column's colloquial style also seems stamped with Cannon's authorship; but, more importantly, the 'letters to emily' often contained reference to places such as Turtle Creek that were reminiscent of Cannon's boyhood. See my discussion of Cannon's youth and Turtle Creek in Palmer 2007, pp. 31–5.
2. 'Green Says Frisco Strike is Outlaw to Federation', and 'Trappings of War Create Zero Hour in Frisco', *Minneapolis Journal*, 18 July 1934.

militants, whose anger at armed police flaunting their weapons and providing
escorts to truck-movements threatened to boil over in violent retribution. The
weather was not helping, either. A July heat-wave was pushing temperatures to
98 degrees Fahrenheit, and high humidity-levels were making it worse; within
the converted garage strike-headquarters, the thermometer climbed to 115, and
Cannon's fictional Mike Ryan complained to his 'dere emily' that inside the
building, things were 'plenty hot'.[3] The stage was set for Bloody Friday.[4]

Unlike May 1934, the blood spilled in the July Days of Minneapolis class-
conflict would largely be that of union-men. At around two o'clock on the afternoon of Friday, 20 July 1934, the Market District became animated. Unusual
activity in a wholesale grocery-store, and Local 574's 'intelligence-forces' suggested that there was going to be an attempt to move produce by truck. This
had been confirmed by National Guard Commander General Ellard Walsh, who
let strike-leaders know that the police were going to move a truck and that they
would be well armed. Extra pickets were dispatched from strike-headquarters,
bringing the total pro-union force marshalled in the area to about five thousand.
With the ultra-left, Third Period Communist Party ostensibly clamouring to take
over the Court House rather than oppose truck-movements,[5] a foot-patrol of
fifty armed police arrived, outfitted with revolvers, clubs, sawed-off shotguns,
and riot-guns. Soon, a scab-truck pulled up to a loading dock, its license-plates
removed, all identifying markings painted over, and its windows covered in wire-
mesh. Accompanying it were a hundred more police in squad-cars, with gun-
barrels protruding from the windows like 'quills on a porcupine'. A few small
cartons were loaded on to the truck, the crowd of pickets jeering menacingly
as the police stood guard, forming a gauntlet through which the truck could
drive. As the rig, carrying no more in the way of cargo than could have been
loaded into the backseat of an ordinary car, inched away from the platform and
proceeded slowly up the street, it was apparently rammed and blocked by an
open-bed picket-truck, in which no more than a dozen strikers were standing.
With the escorted scab-truck stopped, its large police-guard immediately – and
apparently without warning – fired shotguns at the pickets in the opposing truck,
none of whom had the time to climb off the vehicle into the street. As strikers
fell wounded from the truck-bed, pickets rushed to their aid. Bending over their
brothers, they were sprayed with buckshot. It was, by all reliable accounts, little

3. '22 Armed Cars in convoy for Two Loads of Food', and 'Heat Kills 62 in Nation, 3 in
State', *Minneapolis Journal*, 20 July 1934; Le Sueur 1934, pp. 330, 332; Tselos 1971, p. 241.
4. An excellent documentary-film with much useful material on the Minneapolis
strikes of 1934 contains a first-hand account of Bloody Friday's events by Shaun (Jack)
Maloney. See De Graaf 1980.
5. Skoglund interviewed by Halstead, 24 April 1955, Transcript, p. 32, Box 2, Riehle
Papers, MNHS; Korth, 1995, p. 171.

short of a massacre, and was reported as such in the first newspaper-accounts of the carnage.

Even a later Red-baiting account in the *Minneapolis Journal*, in which one of the pickets shot is depicted as a youthful, unemployed dupe of Local 574's 'communist leadership', nonetheless conveys well the nature of the market-melée. David Eugene Crocker of St. Paul, Minnesota, responded to prodding questions from the police, noting that he had been dispatched to the market from strike-headquarters, and that he was one of the men aboard the union-truck blocking the path of the police-escorted delivery-vehicle:

> [F]inally we saw a truck moving over there and one of our squad cars came and they told us we should drive into the driveway and wait until the truck comes out. We waited there a while and after a while the truck started out and we came out and drove up in front of them and smashed them but didn't do much damage. Q – You smashed the truck? A – No; he smashed into us, but didn't do much damage; but then the cops – two or three of them – fired into us. They didn't have any reason at all, to my knowledge. Several men got hurt. I jumped off and the policeman told me to go up on the curb; then without warning one of the policemen took a long shotgun and shot me in the legs, and after that they told us to move along. I started to move along and started to run; and there was quite a few guys firing all over there; and we started to move along, and a policeman turned around and fired on us and he hit me in the arm and hit quite a few other guys.... Q – You were in the battle when they were beating the police officer? When the trucks came together, weren't you in that mob? A – I got in the mob, but I ran around the truck.... I didn't see whether a policeman was beaten up.

Returning to strike-headquarters with the aid of a union-car, Crocker had his wounds attended to and spent the night there, later being transferred to a hospital, where he was interrogated by police.

Harry DeBoer, a picket-captain and Local 574 Executive Committee member, remembered the ambush-like nature of what happened:

> They started to move the truck and that's when they fired first; they just fired point blank. They just went wild. Actually they shot at anybody that moved.... There were several pickets in the truck and they all got shot.... There were even shots coming from the second and third story windows in the warehouse. They really loaded the whole area up with police and guns and whoever was in the warehouse upstairs, we don't know if they were police or what, but the bullets came from all over. It really was organized.... [T]here were at least five thousand to six thousand pickets there by the time they started shooting. You can visualize almost a whole block of pickets. So they shot at random,

anywhere; anywhere there was a worker moving they shot. They just didn't shoot at the truck and then quit, they kept on shooting until all the pickets had either hid or got shelter somewhere. Oh, they meant business.

Later press-coverage introduced rationales and misinformation, but a subsequent inquiry into the events of Bloody Friday established unequivocally that 'Police took direct aim at the pickets and fired to kill; physical safety of police was at no time endangered; no weapons were in the possession of pickets in the truck; at no time did pickets attack the police, and it was obvious that pickets came unprepared for such an attack; the truck movement in question was not a serious attempt to move merchandise, but a "plant" arranged by the police'.

Meridel Le Sueur's account was more gruesomely lyrical:

> The truck drew up at the warehouse, was loaded, began slowly to move surrounded by police, by pointed shot guns. The picket truck moved forward to stop it, jammed into the truck and the picketers swarmed off; but instantly stopping them in mid-movement, the cops opened fire.... The swarm broke, cut into, whirled up, eddied, fell down soundlessly. The eyes closed as in sleep, and when they opened men were lying crying in the street with blood spurting from the myriad wounds buckshots make. Turning instinctively for cover they were shot in the back. And into that continued fire flowed the next line of pickets to pick up their wounded. They flowed directly into that buckshot fire, inevitably, without hesitation as one wave follows another. And the cops let them have it as they picked up their wounded. Lines of living, solid men, fell, broke, wavering, flinging up, breaking over with the curious and awful abandon of despairing gestures, a man stepping on his own intestines bright, bursting in the street, another holding his severed arm in his other hand.... Standing on the sidewalk, no one could believe that they were seeing this. Until they themselves were hit by bullets.... The wounded were arrested for being shot. They were searched. Not a picket was armed with so much as a toothpick.

A block away, police fired into a crowd of union-supporting workers, with four pickets wounded. According to a report written in *The Militant*, likely authored by Cannon, these battles, while short-lived, saw unarmed workers restrain the police in hand-to-hand combat that saved lives by limiting the cops' capacity to deploy their firearms in the close quarters of physical confrontation. Two police were sent to hospital as a result of this skirmishing, which saw one sergeant suffer a beating and a patrolman shot in the leg, a victim of the ricocheting buckshot of chaotic 'friendly fire'. But the blood spilled was overwhelmingly that of the Minneapolis working class. A young Eric Sevareid, on assignment for the *Minneapolis Star*, was deeply shaken by what he saw on Bloody Friday, especially as he visited a city-hospital in search of the 'story' of that day. He referred to the police setting 'a deliberate trap', and recalled that, while one policeman had been hurt, the nurses explained to him that 'nearly all the injured strikers had wounds in the backs of their heads, arms, legs, and shoulders: they had been shot while trying to run out of the ambush'. To Sevareid, it smacked of fascism, and he went home 'as close to becoming a practicing revolutionary as one of my noncombative instincts could ever get'.[6]

The insignificant truck-cargo did, indeed, eventually get through picket-lines. After Bloody Friday's one-sided war involving a lone scab-truck, its escort of armed police, and the weaponless workers ended in a rout of the picket-line, four truckloads of National Guardsmen arrived from the armoury. They carried bayoneted rifles, sub-machine guns, and bomb-guns; trucks mounted with machine-guns patrolled the streets. Thirty minutes later, the market was cleared of pickets and the ostensibly 'food laden' truck made a rushed exit. Olson threatened to declare martial law if there was any further escalation of violence.[7]

Bloody Friday had lasted a matter of minutes. But its meaning would leave a mark on the very fabric of Minneapolis socio-economic relations, given the indelible class-outrage. The brief events of 20 July 1934 polarised class-alignments in the city, proving beyond any doubt that 'a class battle did exist . . . . it made Minneapolis people take sides either actively or in their hearts'. Eric Sevareid's father, an advocate of an almost religiously-sanctified sense of 'public order', was deeply shaken as he read the newspaper-headlines and heard his son mouth support for an insurgent working class. 'This – this is – *revolution!*', he stuttered in pale-faced disbelief. Citizens' Alliance employers and the civic and commercial clubmen of Minneapolis reacted similarly, defending the police, who had become quite scarce on city-streets in the aftermath of the massacre. Picket-captain Shaun (Jack) Maloney recalled, 'For two or three days it was pretty hard

---

6. The above paragraphs draw on Dobbs 1972, pp. 126–7; Korth 1995, pp. 147–50, with DeBoer quoted on pp. 171, 178; Walker 1937, pp. 166–9; Walker 1936, pp. 620–3, 633–4; '50 Wounded in Riot Still in Hospitals', and 'Mediator Given Secret Call from National Capital', *Minneapolis Journal*, 21 July 1934; 'Few of Pickets Wounded in Riot Are Union Drivers, Police Learn', *Minneapolis Journal*, 22 July 1934; 'Victims of the Murders' and 'Victim Denounces Police Lies', *The Organizer*, 21 July 1934; Le Sueur 1934, pp. 333–4; Maloney interviewed by Duffy and Miller, 16 August 1979, Typescript, pp. 26–32; 23 August 1979, Typescript, pp. 2–16, File 'Minneapolis Teamsters' Strike, 1934', Box 2, Maloney Papers, MNHS; Herbert Solow, 'War In Minneapolis', *Nation*, 8 August 1934, p. 160; Sevareid 1976, pp. 58–9; 'Cops Fire on Unarmed Pickets', *The Militant*, 21 July 1934. See also A Picket, 'The Minneapolis Massacre: An Eye Witness Account of Bloody Friday', *The Organizer*, 24 July 1934; Jerry Kotz, 'Minneapolis Sidelights – by an Eye-Witness', *The Militant*, 4 August 1934.

7. Le Sueur 1934, p. 334; *New York Times*, 21 July 1934; 'Cops Fire on Unarmed Pickets', *The Militant*, 21 July 1934.

to find a harness bull'. Advocates of law and order deplored the weak-kneed initiatives of the Farmer-Laborer state-governor, Floyd B. Olson; the Roosevelt administration and its Regional Labor Board apparatus of appeasement; and the 'progressive' rhetoric of mediators like Dunnigan and Haas. They were unapologetic in their praise of 'Bloody Mike' Johannes, distrusted the intervention of the state-deployed National Guard, and offered no concessions or 'compromise with Communist propagandists or agitators'. Such class-conscious advocates of bourgeois rights and freedoms were adamant that what was needed, in Minneapolis in 1934, was a 'permanent settlement', one in which the strike and Local 574 were decisively defeated, even at the price of bloodshed. As Walker, who interviewed a number of these pillars of the community, reported in 1937,

> If one believes passionately that unionism is a blight to an American city, it is romantic to count the cost of human life in annihilating it; and besides, the Citizens' Alliance correctly sensed that this was no ordinary strike and no ordinary trade union. Under the pother about a soviet in Minneapolis and Red Revolution there was a good grain of class sense. It was a strike and a union which promised to actually change the lives of tens of thousands of persons in Minneapolis, to the employers' detriment.[8]

The mood was entirely different, of course, at strike-headquarters.

It was there that many of the wounded retreated to be tended by sympathetic volunteers. In the case of the critically injured, they were transported to safety by makeshift 'union-ambulances'. All told, some 47 injured pickets and bystanders lay on the improvised cots of Local 574's garage-'hospital'. Strike-headquarters' 'chief-surgeon', Dr. McCrimmon, was soon aided by two other volunteer-physicians; meanwhile, 25 registered nurses made themselves available, as knowledge of the human carnage spread throughout Minneapolis. Many injured workers avoided the hospitals, rightly fearing arrest, but some found their way to municipal institutions, where Women's Auxiliary members made the rounds, assisting the wounded and trying to cheer up those confined to emergency-room beds. Hundreds lined up outside hospitals in case their blood was needed for transfusions. It is impossible to establish with certainty the numbers of Local 574 members and supporters who succumbed to police-fire on 20 July 1934; but, at a minimum, it included at least 67 men, of whom a dozen or so were almost certainly bystanders gathered at the Market Square to witness strike-developments.

One of the seriously wounded was rank-and-file strike-leader and future Trotskyist Harry DeBoer. A bullet lodged in his leg, DeBoer crawled under a market loading dock until he could cajole a youth passing by to call strike-headquarters

---

8. Walker 1937, pp. 171–3; Sevareid 1976, pp. 58–9.

and have a truck sent to take him back to the union-hospital. Once there, he insisted that others worse off than he was be looked after, but eventually he was transported to a local hospital, where he was placed under the watch of National Guardsmen. DeBoer almost lost a limb, but managed, after a series of operations, to survive intact, his leg-bone secured with wire and steel-pins, the healing process involving six months of traction and three months of casting. Over the course of his convalescence, DeBoer, not known as much of a 'reading man' at the time, pored over the pages of Marx's *Capital*. Oscar Coover, Sr., a Communist League of America member, brought the injured striker the book as a gift and, like other Left Oppositionists, visited DeBoer in the hospital and talked politics. With guards outside his recovery-room, ensuring that he could not escape, DeBoer was converted to Trotskyism and joined the CLA.

Not all the wounded recovered in this way, but many faced the recriminations and reprisals of the state. At least sixteen pickets and strike-supporters, many of them suffering gunshot-wounds that were treated at various city-hospitals, found themselves charged with criminal offences, including 'failing to move for an officer' or 'disorderly conduct'. They ranged in age from the 19 year-old student and friend of Eric Sevareid, the 'rabelaisian' Dick Scammon, to unemployed and union-men barely out of their teens or as old as fifty. None of the criminal charges stuck in court. Amidst the bloody chaos of the immediate aftermath of the mass shootings, strike-headquarters was tense with talk of retribution and gasps of 'Murder!' Angry strikers drove all police from the vicinity of the strike-headquarters, and pickets assumed the responsibility of directing the increasingly heavy traffic in and out of the building. 35 structural-iron workers, armed with lengths of lead-piping, came to the converted garage determined to defend it against attack. Hundreds of other workers pledged to spend the night with the strike-leaders and the wounded, committed to stand guard against any assault. As people from various walks of life came to the headquarters with cookies, fruit, and reading material for the wounded, militant workers talked of arming themselves and settling scores. *The Organizer*, its headlines screaming 'Workers Blood is Shed!', denounced the police in bold print: 'Johannes The Butcher Uses Shotguns to Mow Down 48 Unarmed Workingmen'. Attacking the police as 'the Uniformed Protectors of Profits', the strike-bulletin deplored the provocation of Friday, 20 July 1934, as nothing less than 'A cunningly conceived, diabolically planned and cold-bloodedly executed massacre'. Women's Auxiliary member Maud Carlson penned a tribute to 'Our Union': '574 with brave defiance/Threw the ire at the Citizens alliance,/They even put Tobin on the mat,/These brave boys can go to bat'. Reporting that a thousand unemployed people had registered to fight for Local 574, the increasingly popular workers' daily challenged the purchased press's propaganda-claim that the streets of Minneapolis had been taken over by communists, with the rhetorical query, 'How Do You Like Having Our Minneapolis Streets in Control of Murderers'.[9]

Almost immediately, charges surfaced claiming that the strike-leaders had been 'irresponsible' in challenging the police breaking picket-lines. Subsequent commentators, from Olson's biographer George H. Mayer to Irving Bernstein, have suggested that Local 574's Trotskyist strategists 'deliberately sought the shedding of blood to reinforce working-class solidarity'. Bernstein implies that the Dunne brothers, Skoglund, and others, like Cannon behind the scenes, wanted 'slain martyrs', explaining this with an ideological assertion that 'The Marxist doctrine of class war, with its inversion of ordinary means and ends, presumably justified in their minds the decision to send unsuspecting pickets into the rain of police gunfire'. There is, however, no evidence that this was the case. Indeed, DeBoer offers a more realistic assessment of the thinking of the strike-leadership, which had no experience of police having the proclivity to 'shoot to kill':

> Before the police had night sticks. This was the first time we encountered the police shooting. The time we were going over the deputy run, then they used night sticks. They probably had guns, but they didn't have instructions to shoot just then.... Naturally we didn't expect them to shoot like that, right at you, not even a chance, no warning at all.

Dobbs, in a roundabout way, concurred, noting that since the police were now armed with riot-guns, it would have been foolhardy to arm pickets with clubs, as had been done in the May 1934 Battle of Deputies Run: 'We knew we couldn't challenge the riot guns, and it was our intention to conduct a peaceful mass protest against the anticipated strikebreaking move'. If Dobbs's notion of peaceful protest rings rather hollow, his belief that unarmed workers would not be subject to a spontaneous police-fusillade is understandable, if tragically naïve. It also draws credibility from the fact that as late as the morning of Bloody Friday, the dialogue between the police and the strike-leadership seemed to be working towards mutually-agreed arrangements that would limit the prospects of unnecessary clashes. Condemnation of Local 574 and its Trotskyist leadership for leading the unsuspecting workers to an ideologically convenient slaughter appears

9. The above paragraphs draw on Dobbs 1972, pp. 127–130, 187; Korth 1995, pp. 150–1, 175–8; Le Sueur 1934, p. 334; Maloney interviewed by Duffy and Miller, 23 August 1979, Typescript, pp. 2–16, File 'Minneapolis Teamsters' Strike 1934', Box 2, Maloney Papers, MNHS; '50 Wounded in Riot Still in Hospitals', *Minneapolis Journal*, 21 July 1934; Sevareid 1976, pp. 57–8; 'Victims of the Murderers', and 'Workers Blood is Shed!: Johannes The Butcher Uses Shotguns to Mow Down 48 Unarmed Workingmen', *The Organizer*, 21 July 1934; File 'Civil War in July (Ch. 10)', Box 1, CRW Papers, MNHS.

not only to lack any basis in evidence; it seems a classic case of letting the perpetrators of violence off the hook and blaming the victims and their supporters.[10]

This, of course, was not the tenor of the Minneapolis working class. At an
evening open-air meeting of protest immediately following the afternoon's
bloodletting, the city's trade-unions deplored the actions of the police and their
seeming Citizens' Alliance masters. According to *The Organizer*, this 'tempes-
tuous' gathering was attended by 'Workers of every craft, thousands of unorganized and unemployed, women as well as men, people of every nationality
and many political faiths, bound in a mighty block to curse the names of their
exploiters who have shed the blood of innocent strikers...'. Estimates of the
crowd varied from the Union's claim of fifteen thousand to the *Minneapolis
Journal's* understated suggestion of five thousand attendees. With Central Labor
Union (CLU) figurehead and *Minnesota Labor Review* editor Bob Cramer chair-
ing the meeting, the large crowd heard fiery talks from Local 574 president Bill
Brown, as well as remarks from the three Dunne brothers, Farrell Dobbs, most
of the city's trade-union leaders, and representatives from farmers' organisations and the independent grocers' association. The Mayor and Chief of Police
came in for a particular dressing down, denounced as 'would-be Hitlers'. Having
stormed Mayor Bainbridge's office immediately following the afternoon's police
shooting spree, demanding the ousting of 'Bloody Mike' Johannes, the CLU
now spearheaded a drive for his dismissal and the impeachment of Bainbridge.
The petition, circulated by local fraternal societies, unions, veterans' groups, and
the Farmer-Labor Party, soon carried twenty thousand signatures. Many more
later followed, endorsing sanctions against these two prominent civic figures.
Within the City Council, the Welfare Committee eventually initiated an investigation of the allegations associated with the call to impeach Mayor Bainbridge,
and armed sentries were posted outside of the crowded room where these delib-
erations took place. Though calling for a thoroughgoing tie-up of all transport in
Minneapolis, a Saturday protest in reaction to the events of Bloody Friday, Local
574 was, nonetheless, not yet advocating 'a general strike at this time'. Brown
hinted, however, that it could well be necessary to pull out all the stops at some
future date, for the Minneapolis truckers were fighting for basic trade-union
principles, and if they were defeated, the entire labour-movement would suffer
a death-blow. 'You thought you would shoot Local 574 into oblivion', declared a
defiant *Organizer* editorial, 'but you only succeeded in making 574 a battle cry
on the lips of every self-respecting working man and woman in Minneapolis'.

---

10. See Tselos 1971, p. 242; Mayer 1951, pp. 209–10; Bernstein 1970, p. 243; Korth 1995,
p. 176, quoting DeBoer; Dobbs 1972, p. 126; Maloney interviewed by Duffy and Miller,
16 August 1979, Typescript, pp. 19–21, File 'Minneapolis Teamsters' Strike, 1934', Box 2,
Maloney Papers, MNHS.

Conservatives in the labour movement did their best to contain the widening mobilisation of workers associated with the rebellious truckers. The American Federation of Labor's president William Green, for instance, pressured Laundry and Dry Cleaning workers not to walk off the job in sympathy with the General Drivers' Union, while Dan Tobin's conventional caution undoubtedly played a role in holding back the Minneapolis milk-drivers and other transport-workers from full-fledged sympathetic job-actions. All of this helped to defeat a 25 July 1934 Central Labor Union motion favouring a massive one-day strike in support of Local 574. The death of one of the victims of Bloody Friday, however, brought workers into the streets of Minneapolis in their thousands.[11]

---

11. '15,000 Workers at Mass Meeting Condemn Johannes', and 'Workers Bloodshed: Johannes The Butcher Uses Shotguns to Mow Down 48 Unarmed Workingmen', *The Organizer*, 21 July 1934; 'Workers Blood is Shed', *The Militant*, 28 July 1934; 'Mediator Given Secret Call from National Capital', *Minneapolis Journal*, 21 July 1934; 'Green Warns Sympathetic Strike Illegal', *Minneapolis Journal*, 24 July 1934; Walker 1937, p. 174; Tselos 1971, pp. 243–6; Dobbs 1972, p. 134. On impeachment-proceedings, see the photograph 'Sentries posted at entrance to council chamber when public welfare committee of the city council began an investigation of impeachment charges against Mayor Bainbridge', available at Minnesota Historical Society, Photographs/Collections On-Line, 10729345; Maloney interviewed by Duffy and Miller, 23 August 1979, Typescript, p. 14, File 'Minneapolis Teamsters' Strike, 1934', Box 2, Maloney Papers, MNHS claims that the petition to oust Bainbridge secured a hundred thousand signatures, but this is clearly an exaggeration.

Chapter Fifteen
Labour's Martyr: Henry B. Ness

Of those shot on Bloody Friday, five were critically hurt: Henry B. Ness; John Belor; Nels Nelson; Otto Lindahl; and Ole Shugren. Ness and Belor were among the first casualties brought to strike-headquarters. The latter was unconscious, but Ness, his shirt cut away to reveal a badly disfigured torso, suffered visibly before collapsing and being rushed to St. Barnabas Hospital, where a series of blood-transfusions failed to revive him. The *Minneapolis Journal* reported on Monday, 23 July 1934, that the striker had died on the Sunday morning, attributing his demise to 'the attack on the police convoyed truck'. This was to accent a certain dimension of Ness's shooting, suggesting that, in being part of a picket-group that opposed the transit of the symbolic strikebreaking vehicle, Ness was responsible for what ensued. That was one perspective. The facts of the tragedy, however, could well be interpreted differently. The decoy-truck was obviously meant to lure Local 574 strikers and supporters into a confrontation with the cops, who were heavily armed and itching for a bloody confrontation. On the frontlines of this staged, and decidedly unequal, battle, the unarmed Ness had been shot, from point-blank range, in the chest. He was, almost certainly, the striker that Harry DeBoer described as having a packet of cigarettes embedded in his lung from being hit directly in one of the first police-volleys. Staggering from the blow, Ness then turned to escape the police-guns, only to have his back riddled with buckshot. His upper body was a mass of blue welts where he had been sprayed with shotgun-fire. The doctors removed 38 slugs from his body. Less than two days later, Ness died, his death-bed injunction repeated word-of-mouth among the strikers: 'Tell the boys not to fail me now'.

A 49 year-old father of four young children, Ness was a veteran of the First World-War and a trade-unionist of 16 years' standing, being a member of the General Drivers' Union, Local 574, and a personal friend of Bill Brown. Ness was, indeed, a trucker-militant. He was the first arrested in the early skirmishes of the July Days, charged, convicted, and fined $10 for disorderly conduct as a consequence of an altercation on 17 July. The Union erected a temporary monument at the street-corner where Ness was first shot, flying a flag at half-mast.

Local 574 organised a massive funeral for Ness, in which his body lay in public visitation for two days, before a Tuesday, 24 July 1934 private family-service followed by a mass march of thousands to strike-headquarters. Bill Brown tried to deliver an oration, but broke down in tears. CLA member and Local 574 lawyer Albert Goldman offered an eloquent eulogy to Ness, quoting his dying words:

> Brothers, Sisters, as we leave this demonstration we must bear in our hearts a fierce resolve to carry on Brother Ness's struggle. We must not fail him! We must avenge his murder. This we shall do if we struggle to win this strike, if we struggle to throw the exploiters from off our backs and to establish a new social order in which the worker may enjoy the fruits of his toil.

As Ness's slow-moving hearse moved away from strike-headquarters, over which flew a black flag of mourning, thousands of people lined the streets, and thousands more accompanied the corpse to the cemetery. A plane flew overhead, a flying escort for Ness's funeral-cortege. The burial was conducted with full military honours, a squad of soldiers from nearby Fort Snelling assembling at the grave to fire the last volley over Ness's coffin. Marvel Scholl of the Women's Auxiliary helped outfit Ness's widow and children for the funeral, the family being destitute and dependent on relief.

More than forty thousand men, women, and children paid their respects to Ness, who was hailed as the martyr of the General Drivers' Union. Minneapolis trade-unionists came out in force, as did the unemployed. It proved impossible to tally the total number of strike-sympathisers who participated in the funeral-procession, gathered to hear the eulogies at strike-headquarters, lined the streets of the cortege in mourning, or made the miles-long trek to the cemetery. Labour-movement sources estimated that between fifty and a hundred thousand people participated in the sad day's events. With traffic brought to a standstill during the proceedings, not a cop was to be seen along the funeral-route, where union-vehicles and marshals directed the flow of automobiles, trucks, and marchers with discipline and respectful order. Fearing the worst, Police-Chief Johannes concentrated a corps of armed police in the municipal court-house, fortifying the edifice with machine-guns. It was an unnecessary and truculent display of armed authority. Charles Rumford Walker concluded that 'The workers of Minneapolis display a certain genius for public demonstrations. In the funeral of Henry Ness they outdid themselves both in drama and solemnity'. Cannon described the Ness funeral in his 'dere emily' column:

> kid, ya should a seen Harry Ness' funeral yesterday. 40,000 or so people took part. It was the biggest funeral every held in this part of the country. at 3 o'clock the procession began to leave the undertakers. first comes the casket with the color guard. then our officers from 574. then some vets. then come us, about 5000 members of 574, marchin along, not saying a word…. after us comes about 500 womin auxiliary members, then comes lots of unions, and about 7,000 of these M.C.C.W.ers. and behind all of us marchers was thousands of cars. we stopped up traffic for an hour and a half.

'So magnificent and startling a demonstration has not been seen in Minneapolis in years', concluded an account in *The Organizer*, reprinted in *The Militant*.[1]

The death of Henry B. Ness cast a sombre pall over strike-torn Minneapolis. Mediators Haas and Dunnigan and Governor Olson clearly feared that the violence would escalate, especially given that Police-Chief Johannes was unrepentant and the trucking bosses, through their Committee, remained adamant that they had the absolute right to move goods throughout the city. Local 574, for its part, was committed to maintaining picket-lines.

Haas and Dunnigan struggled to put together terms of settlement, while Olson, insisting that the mediators be allowed a chance to bring the warring sides of labour and capital together in a peaceful resolution, engaged in almost daily skirmishing with the Mayor, the Police-Chief, and Citizens' Alliance and Employers' Advisory Committee spokesman Joseph R. Cochran. The Farmer-Labor Governor hit hard at what he designated a small clique of reactionary Citizens' Alliance employers, who, he claimed, were responsible for somehow

---

1. The above paragraphs draw on 'Speech by William S. Brown', File 'American City Notes: Local 574 and Strike', Box 1, CRW Papers, MNHS; Smemo 2011, p. 36; Dobbs 1972, pp. 128–34; Korth 1995, p. 176; Walker 1937, pp. 174–6; '100,000 in Tribute to Ness – Protest Johannes Butchery', *Minneapolis Labor Review*, 27 July 1934; 'Peace or a Breakup in Sight as Guarded Trucks Move Necessities', *Minneapolis Journal*, 23 July 1934; 'The Fight Has Just Begun: The First Martyr of 574', *The Organizer*, 23 July 1934; 'Rally Tonight By Workmen's Circle for 574', *The Organizer*, 24 July 1934; '40,000 Attend Ness Funeral', 'Ness Has Aviation Escort', 'A Pledge to a Martyr: Excerpts from the Funeral Address of Attorney Albert Goldman', and 'dere emily', *The Organizer*, 25 July 1934; '574's Attorney Reports on Status of Prisoners', *The Organizer*, 27 July 1934; '40,000 Join Mass Funeral for Harry Ness', and 'Goldman's Speech', *The Militant*, 28 July 1934; 'Workers Pay Respects to Ness at Public Funeral', *Minneapolis Journal*, 25 July 1934.

issuing Bloody Friday's orders for the police to fire on strikers. Olson refused to countenance approving 'the shooting of unarmed citizens of Minneapolis, strikers and bystanders alike, in their backs, in order to carry out the wishes of the Citizens' Alliance'. He added, furthermore, that he disagreed with employers responding to the 'plea for a living wage by a family man receiving only $12 a week' by 'calling that man a communist'. Yet Olson also had a martial-law declaration drafted in case civil order was threatened. Four thousand National Guardsmen were stationed throughout Minneapolis, bivouacked at the State Fair Grounds, some of them deployed throughout the city. For their part, Citizens' Alliance stalwarts were unmoved. EAC chair Cochran challenged Olson for having prepared the ground for martial law to be used to enforce a settlement of the dispute between the employers and truck-drivers, insisting that barely ten percent of workers in the industry had joined Local 574. Instead, Cochran called on Olson to use troops to aid the civil authorities in 'maintaining law and order', declaring it an 'outrage when individuals assume authority by force to say who shall use our streets and who shall not'. No advocate of a martial-law imposed settlement of the conflict, Cochran and the Citizens' Alliance demanded the use of military aid to open the streets and, in effect, break the strike. 'A handful of dissatisfied workers, aided and abetted by communists, imported disturbers and local unemployed', Cochran wrote, 'are now menacing nearly a half million citizens and jeopardizing the employment of thousands of faithful workers'.

After Mayor Bainbridge urged Johannes not to have police escort-trucks on Sunday, 22 July 1934, convoys resumed during the weekdays leading up to and immediately following the Ness funeral. The Trotskyist leadership of the strike, conscious that rank-and-file pickets were angry and prepared to arm themselves to do battle with the now truly hated police, understood that overt armed struggle could only precipitate a bloodbath and culminate in the defeat of the Union. Dobbs, Skoglund, and the Dunnes, as well as picket-captains such as Kelly Postal, Ray Rainbolt, and Shaun (Jack) Maloney, reluctantly disarmed strikers, but continued militant picket-lines, urging the use of peaceful methods. Strikers were, of course, also urged to 'defend themselves against any attacks'. Johannes was forced to send about forty police squad-cars, packed with armed cops, to convoy a single truck through even larger detachments of Local 574's cruising pickets. The strikers did not try to molest or impede the scab-traffic, but their numbers and actions meant that it was tiresome and expensive for employers to undertake the movement of any commercial goods. As *The Organizer* reported jocularly, 'Yesterday at about 9 a.m. the coppers moved a truck containing three wheelbarrows and a tool box. Sixteen squad cars were needed. The job cost about $1.00. The protection cost the taxpayer about $200.00'. Trucks were, indeed, being used. The situation, however, was anything but business-as-usual. The ranks of the Trotskyist-inspired unemployed-group, the Minneapolis Central Council of Workers, swelled as 'make-work' Emergency Relief Administration (ERA) projects were struck by five thousand jobless people. They demanded trade-union rates of pay and the thirty-hour working week, coordinating their efforts with Local 574's strike-committee. Also growing was the Women's Auxiliary, where new recruits joined the ranks of those supporting the strike and selling *The Organizer*. Charles Rumford Walker concluded that 'The strike was coming alive'.[2]

By mid-week, the Haas-Dunnigan plan had been drafted, conceding a number of essential issues demanded by Local 574 with respect to minimum wage-rates and defining inside workers more precisely than May's vague agreement. It placated employers' claims that the General Drivers' Union did not actually represent the vast majority of workers, by providing for elections. After some back-and-forth parleys, the strike-leadership offered its acceptance, and with the *Minneapolis Journal* at first reporting Local 574's rejection, the General Drivers' Union voted overwhelmingly (1866 to 147) to accept the terms laid down by Haas and Dunnigan. Submitted at noon on Wednesday, 25 July 1934, the plan called for the strike to end; all workers to be reinstated; and union-elections to be conducted by the Regional Labor Board. Negotiations on wages, hours, and other conditions were to be undertaken once elections confirmed employee-representation; but if no agreement was reached, a five-person board of arbitration would set wages and determine other issues. In a clear victory for the Union, the Haas-Dunnigan plan stipulated that drivers' wages could not be arbitrated below 52.5 cents an hour, while other workers were to receive minimum hourly compensation of 42.5 cents. This controversial provision had been opposed by Lloyd Garrison of the National Labor Relations Board in Washington; Olson had, nonetheless, insisted that it be included in the settlement. The Governor also threw his weight behind the mounting pressure to end the strike, declaring that if the Haas-Dunnigan plan was rejected, martial law would be proclaimed, and trucks would move only with special military permits, ending the practice of armed police escorting strikebreaking trucks through picket-lines. Neither Local 574 nor the EAC wanted martial law declared, but Olson's willingness to toss

---

2. The above paragraphs draw on Dobbs 1972, pp. 132–8; 'Few of Pickets Wounded in Riot Are Union Drivers, Police Learn', and 'Official Statements on Strike Riot Controversy', *Minneapolis Journal*, 22 July 1934; 'Peace or a Breakup in Sight as Guarded Trucks Move Necessities', *Minneapolis Journal*, 23 July 1934; 'Martial Law Decision Waits Action on Mediation Plan', *Minneapolis Journal*, 24 July 1934; 'Military Aid to Civil Officers Seen', *Minneapolis Journal*, 25 July 1934; 'Governor's Statement', and 'Employers Letter to Governor', *Minneapolis Journal*, 26 July 1934; *The Organizer*, 25 July 1934; Walker 1937, p. 173.

the dice of military governance into the mix of the embattled Minneapolis class-forces of July 1934 was a bold gamble destined to fail in its attempt to bring the strike to a mediated end.[3]

The Citizens' Alliance and the Employers' Advisory Committee were having no part of any enforced settlement. Rejecting the notion that all workers had to be rehired, they insisted that those 'guilty of violence' must be excluded from any back-to-work protocols. There was routine quibbling about a range of issues, including election-procedures and the selection of the Arbitration Board's chair, but the language of the employers was quite categorical in refusing the wage-rate minimums, and linking this basic material question to what was the central concern of the trucking firms, the leadership of Local 574 and the militancy that it had demonstrated: 'to fix an increased wage scale by a vicious strike, and then arbitrate from that point upwards, only paves the way for a repetition of the same lawlessness a few weeks or months hence, which would plunge our city into new turmoil, if the demands of ... agitators were not complied with'. At issue was nothing less than a repudiation of the General Drivers' Union, which was assailed for its use of 'rioting and disorder' and for engaging in strikes premised on 'false statements and misrepresentations by communistic leaders':

> Under the circumstances we cannot deal with this communistic leadership; as it represents only a small minority of our employees. It does not represent the principles of a majority of its eligible membership, nor those of the International Truck Drivers union as clearly expressed by D.W. Tobin, international president. This whole strike is the result of misrepresentation, coercion, and intimidation. The strike is being manned by pickets drawn from the ranks of local and imported communists, and local unemployed, who have been given paid-up membership cards in the union, and who do not, in any way, represent the real truck drivers of Minneapolis.

The Citizens' Alliance/EAC thus scuttled the settlement. Olson responded with an acrimonious public rejoinder, in which he placed responsibility for the ongoing strike squarely on the shoulders of the 'small clique' at the helm of the Citizens' Alliance, men consumed by their 'hate' for 'organized labor', and who were 'determined to crush it'. Privately, he admonished Cochran and his collaborators to 'discover some noun that you may use to describe those

---

3. Blantz 1970, p. 11; 'Both Sides Reject Proposals Advanced by Federal Mediator', *Minneapolis Journal*, 25 July 1934; 'National Guards Will Move Into City at Once; Strikers Vote Acceptance; Employers Object to Meeting with Reds', *Minneapolis Journal*, 26 July 1934; 'No Trucks to be Moved! By Nobody!', *The Organizer*, 26 July 1934; Dobbs 1972, pp. 145–9.

under-paid workers and perhaps describe me, other than the terms "Red" and "Communist"'.[4] Ironically, Olson's response set in motion a new and complicated round of class-antagonism, in which martial law and unmediated state-power were supplemented by an intensified 'Red Scare'. Cannon and Shachtman would find themselves hoisted on Olson's petard.

---

4. Walker 1937, pp. 176–80; Tselos 1971, pp. 246–8; Korth 1995, pp. 151–3; 'Employers' Reply', and 'Governor's Statement', *Minneapolis Journal*, 26 July 1934. There is much raw material on Olson's predicament and his resulting oscillations in Files 'Farmer-Labor Party (Ch. 5)' and 'American City (Ch. 5): Olson's Order to Haycroft, 1934', Box 1, CRW Papers, MNHS.

Chapter Sixteen
Martial Law and the Red-Scare

At one o'clock on the afternoon of 26 July 1934, most
Minneapolis citizens were finishing up their lunches.
Almost two thousand members of General Truck
Drivers' Union Local 574 made their way back to
picket-lines, strike-headquarters, or their homes after
a three-hour Eagles Hall meeting that ended with
an overwhelming vote agreeing to the terms of the
Haas-Dunningan 'peace-plan'. Employers held firm in
their opposition to specific provisions, and objected
strenuously to 'meeting with Reds'. The impasse continued. True to his word, Governor Olson ordered
4,000 National Guardsmen into the streets. Later that
evening, Olson declared martial law. According to
the Farmer-Labor Governor, 'a state of insurrection
exist[ed] in the City of Minneapolis and the County of
Hennepin', the populace threatened by 'tumult, riots,
and mob violence'. Civil authorities were demonstra-
bly unable to restrain 'Bodies of men [that] together
by force have attempted to commit felonies and to
offer violence to persons and property . . . and by force
of violence to break and resist the laws of [the] State,
imperilling the lives, health, and property and general
welfare of the citizens'. Olson aimed to make Minneapolis 'as quiet as a Sunday School picnic'.[1]

---

1. Korth 1995, pp. 153–4; 'The Duty of the Hour: Obey Orders', *Minneapolis Journal*,
27 July 1934.

This was not to be, but the atmosphere did change. Martial law meant that no truck-movements were to take place except by military license, and, within a day, thousands were lining up to secure permits for the transportation of milk, ice, fuel, breadstuffs, petrol and other essentials, including newspapers. 'Officially, Minneapolis is on a bread and milk diet', quipped the *Minneapolis Journal*. The martial-law embargo effectively ended the police-escorts of trucks, but it also banned picketing, an edict which strike-headquarters said would be complied with, although sporadic reports of striking workers blocking traffic surfaced from day to day. Brigadier General Ellard A. Walsh was put in charge of the National Guard, whose forces patrolled thoroughfares, monitoring and guarding all per-mitted truck-movement. Walsh warned pickets that their actions would be met with the requisite force of the Guardsmen, who were ordered to countenance no violence. Defiance of the ban on pickets would result in 'a trip to the military stockade'. Businesses were free to conduct their affairs, but theatres, dance-halls, and public amusement-places were to close down by midnight and could not reopen until eight o'clock the next morning. Any outdoors gathering of one hun-dred or more people required a permit signed by the troop-commander, which effectively ended Local 574's practice of holding massive open-air meetings at strike-headquarters. Tampering with permits or documents of any kind would subject the offender to punishment. Uttering alarmist reports was specifically singled out as an offence, as was carrying arms of any kind or 'the indiscriminate operation of commercial trucks', an act that was judged unusually likely to 'cause violence and precipitate riot'. With this militarisation of civil society, the Minne-apolis Church Federation decided to get in on the act, running a newspaper ad, 'Martial Law vs. The Will of God', in which spiritual authority was invoked as the foundation of all true justice: 'The will of God, accepted with the same docility as martial law, will turn any people from jungle paths to summits of vision, under-standing and peace', declared a 'United in Service' statement. 'It will develop the "Kingship of Self-Control" which is the foundation of all law, and order, and civilization worthy of the name'. Above the material fray of capital versus labour, the Church Federation invited 'all classes to seek God's will and do it'.[2]

Martial law was buttressed less by faith-based inspiration than by an ideologi-cal crusade, albeit one that had a certain religious, 'fire and brimstone' cast to it. The anti-communism cultivated by the Citizens' Alliance and the Joseph R. Cochran-led Employers' Advisory Committee flared into a bellicose Red-scare.[3]

---

2. 'Military Rule Ordered: Extra – National Guards Will Move into City at Once', *Min-neapolis Journal*, 26 July 1934; 'On Bread and Milk Diet, Troops Patrol Streets, Seize Reds', *Minneapolis Journal*, 27 July 1934; 'Military Regulations Governing Minnesota', and 'Mar-tial Law vs. The Will of God', *Minneapolis Journal*, 28 July 1934; Dobbs 1972, p. 149.

3. For a later, October 1934, statement on the strikes that revealed the intensity of the Employers' Advisory Committee's anti-communism, see Joseph R. Cochran, 'The Truth

Civic authorities such as Police-Chief Johannes bombastically added fuel to the growing anti-communist conflagration. Charles Rumford Walker's research-notes contain commentaries declaring that Johannes told a gathering of businessmen that 'the strike had been financed by Communists', promising that a repeat of the events of May would not be tolerated. 'We'll run ... bayonets up the rumps of these red agitators and then pull the triggers', boasted the Chief. Applause greeted his Red-baiting tirade. Conscious of the extent to which the American working class was simultaneously discontented and 'dominated in important respects by bourgeois ideas, aspirations and loyalty', Walker, like the Minneapolis Trotskyists he respected, understood that among the masses of workers there were few 'politically conscious proletarians'. Most labouring people, Walker's notes insisted, accepted a variety of misconceptions about communism, including that it was 'un-American' and associated with foreigners, especially Russians and Jews; that it was dictatorial; and that it involved the wanton shedding of blood, violence for its own sake, and a general destruction and terroristic chaos. 'Of the vast masses,' Walker's notes stated, 'those not consciously opposed to the idea of a collective society are so ignorant of the meaning of revolution as to be unprepared for the polemics of the counter-revolutionary'. With the 'average worker' largely oblivious to 'the distinction between a revolutionary and a Stalinist', Walker understood that 'ignorance of the meaning of Communism and impulsive unfriendliness to it ... makes possible the "Red Scare" so often effectively used by the capitalists and their labor lieutenants to break up workers' struggles'. In Minneapolis, then, it was no surprise that anti-communism was unleashed with such vehemence in 1934: 'The bosses use the Red Scare much as armies use a gas attack. Under its poisonous cover they launch the attack proper; hoping that the poison will have incapacitated the workers' vanguard, they plan to sweep forward and force the surrender of the main body'. What was somewhat unexpected, however, was that the Red-scares concocted in the midst of intense class-struggle had so little effect on rank-and-file teamsters and their supporters. Walker concluded that the strike leaders were remarkably successful in beating back the anti-communist attacks, and that 'their methods and their success contrasts vividly with those of any other strike leadership during the present phase of American labor struggles'. If the capitalist *coup de grace* of Red-baiting largely failed in Minneapolis in 1934, however, it was not for want of ideological and coercive effort.[4]

About the Truck Drivers Strikes', Typescript, 19 pages, 20 October 1934, in File 'American City: Employers Side', Box 1, CRW Papers, MNHS. This document concluded by expressing the belief that 'every employer in the state of Minnesota' would support 'opposition to Communist domination of business and industry'.

4. Johannes quote from Lou Gord, 'Minnesota Offers a President, Olson After Roosevelt, America Watches Minnesota', typescript in File 'Three Men and the Destiny

Headlines in the *Minneapolis Journal* on 26 July 1934 twinned the declaration of martial law with bold assertions, running at the top and bottom of page one, that 'Raid Reveals Communists Run Strike from New York Offices' and 'N.Y. Communists Direct Local Strike Through Vincent Dunne'. From the moment that Minneapolis was threatened with military rule, it was rumoured that 'military intelligence agents were reported ... doing "undercover" work to learn about the reported activity of communists in the strike'. The immediate targets were Jim Cannon and Max Shachtman, who had been in Minneapolis for some time advising and discussing all manner of things with the strike-committee, writing material for *The Organizer* and putting the strike-bulletin out on a daily basis, making themselves generally useful to Local 574. Cannon noted that the two leading figures in the Trotskyist Communist League of America had deliberately kept their public personas low-key during the strike, but that they were, nonetheless, followed by detectives when they left strike-headquarters on the night of 25 July 1934. Suggesting that Shachtman's flamboyant taste in headgear – 'a great big ten-gallon cowboy hat' – might well have made him conspicuous, Cannon recounted how the two were taken into police-custody at about ten o'clock in the evening. In search of a bit of diversionary entertainment, the CLA leaders had wandered down Hennepin Avenue and found themselves facing a burlesque-show at one venue and a movie-theatre in the building next door. They opted for the cinema and, as Cannon later recounted, a good thing it was, too. 'What a narrow escape from being arrested in a burlesque show. What a scandal it would have been. I would never have lived it down, I am sure'.[5]

The next day, the Minneapolis papers bristled with accounts of a police 'raid in which they took two communist workers from New York into custody', the duo supposedly 'seized on a loop street'. Naming Cannon and Shachtman as the 'two captured communists', the press revelled in reports of a 'loaded pistol found in the baggage of one of the communists', detailing that the hotel-rooms of 'the agitators' yielded an incriminating seizure of bundles of *The Militant*, telegrams, and correspondence, in which Cannon, Vincent Raymond Dunne, and Swabeck discussed the nature of the Minneapolis strike and its significance. 'The correspondence showed the country is dotted with communist agents and agitators and that they fomented trouble in the San Francisco strike', insisted the

---

of a City (Ch. 11)', and Red-scare quotes from the untitled typescript, pp. 1–2, File 'American City: Incomplete Notes and Articles', Box 1, CRW Papers, MNHS. See also Thane 1934, pp. 435–6.
   5. 'Raid Reveals Communists Run Strike From New York Offices', and 'N.Y. Communists Direct Local Strike Through Vincent Dunne', *Minneapolis Journal*, 26 July 1934; 'On Bread and Milk Diet, Troops Patrol Streets, Seize Reds', *Minneapolis Journal*, 27 July 1934; '2 Troop Officers Granted Release, Meat Runs Short', *Minneapolis Journal*, 28 July 1934; Cannon 1944, pp. 162–3.

Minneapolis Journal. 'Having been defeated on the west coast by the prompt action of citizen vigilantes, they pinned their hopes for revolution on the Minneapolis strike'. Cannon, Shachtman, and Swabeck were depicted as the communist brains-trust directing the events in Minneapolis from afar, with the eldest Dunne brother as little more than their pliant, local dupe. Herbert Solow wrote in the *New Leader* that the arrest of Cannon and Shachtman arrest marked a new stage in the intensifying Minneapolis class-struggle: 'Press, pulpit, and radio howled for blood'. [6]

After having been hauled down to police-headquarters, Cannon and Shachtman were fingerprinted and lodged in a city-cell. No charges were laid, and repeated inquiries as to what criminal offence they were being held under went unanswered. (Herbert Solow reported in *The Nation* that Cannon and Shachtman had been arrested for 'disorderly conduct by criminal syndicalism', but this information was not included in his original article in *The Organizer*.) The raid on Cannon's and Shachtman's hotel-rooms was then conducted by a squad of detectives, who ransacked the men's personal possessions without 'the formality of a search warrant'. Finding nothing more than a legally-published newspaper, *The Militant*, and sheafs of relatively innocuous correspondence, Shachtman later wrote that 'The whole thing was a flop, and didn't even have the groundwork material for a good-sized frame-up'. Interrogated by Detective Ohman and the infamous 'Bloody Mike' Johannes, Cannon and Shachtman insisted that their lawyer, Albert Goldman, be present, but they were not permitted contact with him and he was not summoned to the police-station. Thirty-six hours after their arrest, Cannon and Shachtman were finally booked on the ludicrous offence of vagrancy (they had hotel-rooms and money) and paraded before a judge. Goldman and another Local 574 lawyer were on hand with a writ of *habeas corpus*, demanding their release. Johannes readily agreed, and then proceeded to place Cannon and Shachtman in the hands of National Guardsmen, who promptly put the two men under military arrest. A guard-sergeant entered the courtroom armed with a sub-machine gun, and marched Cannon and Shachtman outside, where they were flanked by bayonet-brandishing troops. The National Guard then delivered the dangerous 'Reds' to an armed military truck, which

6. 'Raid Reveals Communists Run Strike from New York Offices', *Minneapolis Journal*, 26 July 1934. and, for a complete page-long reproduction of some of the routine correspondence seized, see 'Patrol Takes 2 Communists from City Jail', *Minneapolis Journal*, 27 July 1934; 'Troops Rule Minneapolis: Police Arrest Cannon and Shachtman', *The Militant*, 28 July 1934.; Herbert Solow, 'The Great Minneapolis Strike', *New Leader*, 8 September 1934. Consistent with the low profile kept by Cannon and Shachtman, note that *The Organizer*, which they edited, largely kept their arrests out of the paper. For a short, rather cryptic note on the arrests, which accents the anti-communist meaning of the victimisation of Cannon and Shachtman, but avoids naming them, see A 574 Man Since February, 'The Worker's Voice', *The Organizer*, 27 July 1934.

184 • Chapter Sixteen

transported the 'prisoners' to the make-shift stockade at the State Fairgrounds. As they were hustled out of the courtroom and into the truck, which was surrounded by a posse of soldiers, Cannon and Shachtman heard Bill Brown, sitting at a third-floor window, shout down at them, 'Look out for those bayonets'.

Cannon and Shachtman were thus the first military prisoners to be taken under Olson's declaration of martial law, even though they could not possibly have violated any of its provisions, since they had been in police-custody for all the time that military rule had been in effect. Awaiting their transit to the guardhouse, Cannon and Shachtman heard their sentinels given orders to 'Shoot to kill if they make a move to escape!' Once again given no explanation of why they were under arrest, the two New York revolutionaries were told that they were to be released under a deportation-order. Cannon and Shachtman, anxious to get back in touch with strike-leaders, decided they had better things to do than 'make a test case of our deportation'. Rather than challenge their unjust incarceration, they played the system, accepting an offer of release that merely stipulated that they were to leave Minneapolis. Let go after six hours under military arrest, Cannon and Shachtman dashed off a blistering letter of protest to Governor Olson, demanding that as journalists associated with the labour-press (Cannon was editor of *The Militant*, while Shachtman occupied a similar post at the *New International*), they be accorded the same rights as out-of-town correspondents from the capitalist press. This done, the two CLA leaders set up shop in nearby St. Paul. There, they conferred with the leadership of the General Drivers' Union, including President Bill Brown. Soon, Olson issued a public statement that, as far as he was concerned, those associated with the radical *Militant* should have the same freedoms of speech and movement as journalists in the pay of the Tory *Chicago Tribune*. Cannon and Shachtman moved back into their Minneapolis hotel and resumed their close connections with the strike-committee. Cannon recalled that

> every night we had meetings of the steering committee as long as any of the leading comrades were out of jail. The steering committee of the strike, sometimes with Bill Brown, sometimes without him, would... talk over the day's experiences and plan the next day. There was never a serious move made during the whole strike that was not planned and prepared for in advance.[7]

7. 'Patrol Takes 2 Communists From City Jail', *Minneapolis Journal*, 27 July 1934; 'Frame-Up Against League Leaders a Complete Collapse', *The Militant*, 4 August 1934; Herbert Solow, 'War In Minneapolis', *Nation*, 8 August 1934, pp. 160–1, dated Minneapolis, 25 July 1934, and appearing in slightly different form in *The Organizer*, 4 August 1934; 'Deported Editors Return to Minneapolis', *The Organizer*, 29 July 1934; Drucker 1994, pp. 73–4; Dobbs 1972, pp. 149–50; Cannon 1944, pp. 163–4; 'New Strike Peace Proposal Ready; Cruising Pickets Attack Trucks', *Minneapolis Journal*, 30 July 1934.

Local 574 and its Trotskyist leadership never flagged in its opposition to both martial law and the intensified anti-communism that paralleled its implementation. *The Organizer* was a forum for repeated criticism of Olson, the calling in of the National Guard, and the Citizens' Alliance-orchestrated Red-scare. Both the Women's Auxiliary and the Minneapolis Central Council of Workers rallied housewives, daughters, and the unemployed to the same positions, their ranks growing as the strike progressed. A Parade Grounds rally of fifteen thousand trade-unionists and strike-supporters on Friday, 27 July 1934, heard Vincent Dunne denounce martial law as state-sanctioned strikebreaking, and Albert Goldman warn that the incarceration of Cannon and Shachtman was the thin end of a wedge of repression that would soon open the door to the arrest of local strike-leaders. The animated crowd was hailed by *The Organizer* as 'a mighty display of determination and solidarity', an indication that Minneapolis workers had responded to 'the first day of the city's new military dictatorship' with a demonstration of their 'intention to fight for [their] rights and interests to the bitter end and against all foes'. As *The Militant* stated unequivocally at the end of July 1934, 'Despite all provocations, murders, red baiting, and martial law, the strike of drivers still remains as solid as granite, gaining new strength with every new day'. Minnesota's Farmer-Labor paper, the Rochester-based *Midwest American*, pleaded with Olson to 'Call Off the Tin Hats'. It found that the 'ordering of newspapermen out of town even if they happen to be communists, is getting a bit boresome'. The Communist League of America organized Sunday-evening protest-meetings at New York City's Irving Plaza Hall on 29 July and 5 August 1934, calling attention to the murder of strikers, the arrest of Cannon and Shachtman, and the use of martial law to break the resolve of the Minneapolis truckers. Shachtman, returning east to attend to his duties as editor of the *New International*, addressed the latter gathering. Cannon remained in Minneapolis, where his 'dere emily' column struck the same note, albeit in the dialect of the dispossessed:

> Well kid, here it is eleven days we been on strike now, and me and the boys is just getting into the swing of tings agin. Yesterday the Governor sent in the national guards, and now marshall law is declared. I think that's a rotten trick, but nottin is going to keep us from winnin this here strike.[8]

---

8. 'The Talk About Martial Law', *The Organizer*, 25 July 1934; 'Martial Law Declared by Olson', *The Organizer*, 26 July 1934; 'dere emily', *The Organizer*, 27 July 1934; 'The Right to Picket is the Right to Organize!', '15,000 Rally to Support the Strike Cause', and 'An Attorney's Views: Remarks of Albert Goldman at the Parade Rally', *The Organizer*, 28 July 1934; 'Local 574 on Martial Law', and 'Troops Rule Minneapolis: Police Arrest Cannon and Shachtman – Drivers Ranks Solid Despite Provocation', *The Militant*, 28 July 1934; Drucker 1994, p. 74; Announcement, 'Max Shachtman: The Minneapolis Strike: An

Local 574's insistence that the strike was holding firm was an affirmation of hope against reality. It was increasingly obvious that martial law was ineffective as a means of policing the movement of goods in Minneapolis and restricting truck-deliveries to actual necessities. As the number of applications for military permits to transmit essentials continued to rise, and as the National Guard forces deployed to monitor the movement of goods dwindled (over two thousand had been withdrawn only days after the declaration of martial law, in what was announced as a cost-saving measure), more and more trucks were on Minneapolis streets, moving a variety of products. The General Drivers' Union ascertained that much of this truck-movement went unmonitored, and many of the goods transported only dubiously fitted into Governor Olson's categories of the kinds of things that needed to be delivered in the midst of the strike. As the Citizens' Alliance-friendly press complained vociferously about the lack of meat and other shortages, the definition of what was included on the 'necessities'-list expanded. On 30 July 1934, 'All wholesale meat trucks, hotel and restaurant and sausage trucks started moving' at noon 'under military permit'. A ban on the delivery of eggs and all dairy-products, including ice-cream and cheese, was also lifted. Thousands of permits to move produce and other items were being issued, covering an estimated 7,500 trucks. Martial law and the National Guard were obviously breaking Local 574's strike. Estimates were that, by 1 August 1934, sixty-five to seventy percent of normal commercial-trucking traffic had been restored; but conditions were anything but tranquil. Sporadic and spontaneous picket-violence broke out as angry strikers attacked and tipped over trucks, assaulted scabs, and vandalised commercial vehicles. A National Guard squad-car, driven by an eighteen year-old recruit, was speeding to a site where pickets were supposedly dumping a truck's 'illicit' load, when it ran a stop-sign and crashed into a passenger-vehicle. The civilian-motorist was immediately killed, a passenger injured, and three of the troopers taken to hospital for treatment. The more conservative union-officials in the Central Labor Union began to draw back from their appearances at the mass rallies of Local 574, causing notable rifts in the labour-movement. From the perspective of the Strike Committee of 100, things were moving in the wrong direction.[9]

Eyewitness Account, Sunday August 5 8 PM, Irving Plaza', *The Militant*, 4 August 1934; 'Martial Law a "Mistake"', *Minneapolis Journal*, 9 August 1934.

9. Tselos 1971, pp. 248–9; '2 Troop Officers Granted Release', *Minneapolis Journal*, 28 July 1934; 'New Strike Peace Proposal Ready; Cruising Pickets Attack Trucks', *Minneapolis Journal*, 30 July 1934; '15,000 Rally to Support the Strike Cause', *The Organizer*, 28 July 1934; 'Crashes Sedan, Kills Driver – Passenger Near Death; 3 Troopers Also Injured', *Minneapolis Journal*, 31 July 1934; and, for a another account of the crash, indicating that it had nothing to do with monitoring strike and picket-activity, see '574 Man Tells Truth of Crash: Cop Threatens Witness of Auto Accident', *The Organizer*, 1 August 1934.

By this time, a Communist League of America strike steering committee had been formed, composed of Ray Dunne, Skoglund, Dobbs, Al Goldman, and Cannon. This group exercised considerable influence over strike-strategy, directing the day-to-day activities that sustained the teamsters' insurgency. Cannon's style could increasingly be discerned in front-page editorials in *The Organizer*, urging the workers to hang on and to stay true to their union and its cause.[10] Local 574's leadership moved to right the course and re-establish union-control of truck-movements. Olson was confronted with a four-point ultimatum, in which his declaration of martial law and its relation to the class-forces within strike-torn Minneapolis was challenged fundamentally. The General Drivers' Union demanded that open-air meetings at strike-headquarters be allowed without molestation; that peaceful picketing, which included the stopping of trucks, be reinstated; that the Governor withdraw all troops from the streets of Minneapolis, and leave the monitoring of permitted truck-movement to union-pickets; and that to allow the transition to this new régime, a 48-hour halt in all truck-movement be declared. A union-delegation met with Olson, and Carl Skoglund went toe-to-toe with the Governor, pointing out that if martial law had not been declared, the employers could have been forced to accept the Haas-Dunnigan strike-settlement plan. Now that things had worsened, Skoglund insisted, all martial-law-issued permits should be withdrawn for two days and any permits allowed thereafter should be granted only on the condition that employers receiving such passes agree to conditions stipulated in the earlier mediators' recommendations, which the General Drivers' Union had accepted. If implemented, Local 574's demands would effectively have created a system of dual power in Minneapolis, with union-authority taken to a level entirely unprecedented in a strike-situation.[11]

Olson, predictably, refused the General Drivers' Union's ultimatum, but promised to tighten up the monitoring of trucking activity and limit the issuance of permits. The press and the employers upped the decibel-level in their increasingly noisy Red-baiting. A showdown was set for 1 August 1934, with Local 574 mobilising 'for a continuation of the fight'. Strikers and all union-supporters and sympathisers were called to another Parade Grounds mass rally on the evening of Tuesday, 31 July 1934. Twenty-five thousand showed up to cheer Bill Brown when he declared, 'the Farmer-Labor Administration is the best strikebreaking force our union has ever gone up against'. The loudest and longest applause

---

10. A very incomplete collection of some of Cannon's articles in *The Organizer* appears in Cannon 1958, pp. 75–94. On the 'Party Steering Committee', see Dobbs 1972, p. 176.
11. Skoglund claimed that Olson later made important concessions, including roping off the market, using National Guardsmen to restrict vehicle-movements. See Skoglund interviewed by Halstead, 24 April 1955, Typescript, p. 31, Box 2, Riehle Papers, MNHS.

was reserved for Albert Goldman, who was supplementing his legal acumen and long experience as a left-winger by taking on the trappings of an old-style Wobbly agitator. Goldman assailed Olson's undermining of the labour-struggle, unambiguous in his damnation of the Governor's false claim to be trying to help working people. 'The zero hour is nigh!', thundered the CLA lawyer-agitator, 'If we submit without a struggle, then we deserve the fate of submissive slaves. We can not, we dare not, submit. We call upon the workers, organized and unorganized, to clench their fists, shout defiance of the bosses, and struggle until victory or death'. It was left to Ray Dunne to close the meeting with the assertive declaration that picket-lines were being reorganised. 'Submit to the governor', he declared emphatically, 'and the strike is lost. *The militia is moving trucks*'. In defiance of martial law, the Union summoned all pickets to assemble at strike-headquarters at four o'clock on the morning of 1 August 1934. The gloves were off. Local 574 was about to take its stand against Olson and his militarisation of the streets of Minneapolis.[12]

Olson decided to get in the first licks, although he would later have cause to regret his precipitous actions. On the grounds that the General Drivers' Union lacked a military permit sanctioning its mass meeting the night before (a claim that would later be challenged), and in response to statements that were undoubtedly 'in direct defiance...of military order', the Minnesota Farmer-Laborite ordered the National Guard to occupy strike-headquarters and arrest the leadership of the General Drivers' Union. At 3:55 a.m., before pickets had been dispatched, eight hundred troops surrounded Local 574's Eighth Street and Second Avenue strike-headquarters, occupied it, and placed a number of union-leaders and members under arrest. 'The coup', as it was proudly described in the mainstream press, was not exactly waged on a level playing field. Commanded by Colonel Elmer McDevitt, the National Guardsmen had at their disposal fifty huge army-trucks, six large machine-guns trained on the strike-headquarters, teargas-squads, their knapsacks bulging with canisters, and detachments of bayonet-bearing Guardsmen. Inside strike-headquarters, the troops seized a dozen lead-pipes and clubs and a few sharpened ice-picks, outfitted with grip-sized wooden handles. About a hundred and fifty union-men were milling around the

---

12. The above paragraphs draw on '...If it Takes All Summer', *The Organizer*, 29 July 1934; 'State Troops as Harming Strike', *The Organizer*, 28 July 1934; 'Workers Mass to Back 574', *The Organizer*, 30 July 1934; 'Pickets to Report at 4 AM', '574 to Go on Fighting for Right to Live', 'We Will Not Submit', and 'Bosses Again hiding Behind Red Scare', *The Organizer*, 31 July 1934; 'Employers Statement', 'Governor's Statement', and 'Grocery, Tobacco and Beer Carriers are Given Permits; Men Threaten More Picketing; Employers Refuse to "Sell Out City to Communism"', *Minneapolis Journal*, 31 July 1934; Walker 1937, p. 183; Dobbs 1972, p. 151; '25,000 Pledge Support to 574', and 'With Clenched Fists! From Last Night's Address by Albert Goldman', *The Organizer*, 1 August 1934; Bernstein 1970, p. 246.

headquarters, awaiting picket-orders, while some Women's Auxiliary members served coffee and prepared toast. Dr. Enright was tending to a few of the victims of Bloody Friday. Like dozens of others, the volunteer-physician found himself arrested and hauled down to the stockade. He was later the subject of a malicious prosecution for practicing medicine under ostensibly unsanitary conditions, a slap-on-the-wrist that was meant to remind the doctor that offering his services to workers, on their terms, was out of line with 'professional standards'.

Yet the martial-law proceedings directed against the General Drivers' Union were not without their lighter moments. An irreverent striker managed to purloin McDevitt's helmet, which the somewhat nervous and overheated Colonel had removed to wipe his balding head and have a brief parley with the surrendering Vincent Raymond Dunne, who immediately made himself liable to arrest by acknowledging his responsible leadership of the strikers. The rank-and-file prankster burst the bubble of solemn authority by donning the Colonel's 'tin hat' and, taking over the strike-headquarters' formidable sound-system, led Local 574's evacuation of its building with a rousing rendition of *The Daring Young Man on the Flying Trapeze*. Colonel McDevitt was not amused, and his troops, according to one report, expressed an air of demoralisation.

The Trotskyist leaders of 574, with the exception of Skoglund, who was in Chicago raising money for the strike, were napping in picket-cars parked at the rear of the headquarters, when they were awakened with word that 'the army' had descended on them. Bill Brown and Miles Dunne were not yet present, but were taken into military custody later, and, along with Ray, transported to the makeshift 'holding pens' at the Fairgrounds. Farrell Dobbs and Grant Dunne managed, by subterfuge, to slip away from the National Guard, and, along with many secondary leaders of the strike, wasted no time in establishing beefed-up picket-lines throughout Minneapolis. They set up a series of 'control-points' around town, using friendly gas-stations and public pay-phones to direct flying pickets to 'hotspots'. An astute picket-dispatcher, Henry Schultz, took charge of monitoring the Guardsmen's takeover of union-headquarters, demanding a detailed list of all 'property' seized, cajoling McDevitt into allowing the commissary to move to the Central Labor Union/American Federation of Labor headquarters at First Avenue, which would, later in the day, be raided by another three hundred troops after some two thousand strikers and their supporters congregated there. Indeed, the military assault on working-class institutions seemed rather indiscriminate, and, besides the CLU building, Guardsmen also raided a Cooks' and Waiters' Union hall and 574's regular meeting rooms on South Third Street. All of this was supposedly orchestrated in order to decapitate the strike-leadership and undermine its capacity to coordinate activities out of specific physical sites.

The Union, forced to go underground, used guerrilla-tactics that left Minneapolis awash with 'hit-and-run' devastation. As Dobbs later recalled,

Trucks operating with military permits were soon being put out of commission throughout the city. Within a few hours over 500 calls for help were reported to have come into the military headquarters. Troops in squad cars responded to the calls usually to find scabs who had been worked over, but no pickets.... Despite everything the military tried to do...the supposedly headless strike was full of life. The pickets were battling furiously and they were doing it skillfully.

Dobbs undoubtedly exaggerated the number of calls, many of which could well have been made by strikers and their sympathisers to draw the National Guard away from actual confrontations. But there was no denying that Olson's pre-emptive strike on trade-union strongholds unleashed the hounds of proletarian fury. The *Minneapolis Journal*'s evening-edition listed 25 separate troop-dispatches, in which trucks were overturned, stopped, vandalised, or hijacked, scab-drivers beaten and their deliveries smashed or dumped in poor neighborhoods, where they could be appropriated by those in need. Dozens of other clashes were also reported, many of them leading to the arrests of strikers and their sympathisers. The chaos of the day was recorded in newspaper-accounts, later reproduced in Walker's *American City*: 'Marauding bands of pickets roamed the streets of Minneapolis today in automobiles and trucks, striking at commercial truck movements in widespread sections of the city.... The continued picketing was regarded as a protest over the military arrest of Brown and the Dunnes, strike leaders, together with sixty-eight others during and after Guardsmen raided strike headquarters and the Central Labor Union'.

To add further to the now-inflamed mix of working-class grievances, John Belor, an unemployed member of the MCCW who had been seriously wounded during the Bloody Friday shootings of pickets by police, died during this day of rampage. Unmarried, his family wanted a quiet funeral. Local 574 paid all of the expenses associated with his burial and made sure that union-men and women turned out in force to pay their last respects.[13]

---

13. The above paragraphs draw on Dobbs 1972, pp. 151–5, 164; Korth 1995, p. 155; Walker 1937, pp. 204, 207–9; 'Force of 800 Moves Under Cover of Night in Coup that Breaks Up Early Morning Picket Plan', 'Three Hundred Guardsmen Raid Second Strike Headquarters on First Avenue N. After 2,000 Gather', 'Walsh Statement', 'Governor Deplores Defiance by Union', and 'Second Striker Dies from Wound in July 20 Rioting', *Minneapolis Journal*, 1 August 1934; 'Workers to Attend Funeral of Belor', *The Organizer*, 2 August 1934; 'Bosses Prosecute Strikers' Doctor', *The Organizer*, 5 September 1934.

Chapter Seventeen
Governor Olson: The 'Merits' of a Defective Progressive Pragmatism

Olson had, as Cannon was fond of self-deprecatingly describing himself, the merit of his defects.[1] As a self-proclaimed Farmer-Labor 'progressive', he was rather loose in understanding his principled commitment to what he regarded as the producing classes. This, no doubt, allowed him to sleep easily in proclaiming his loyalties to working people at the same time as he was willing to declare martial law in a strike-situation, implementing procedures that banned picketing and permitted the transport of goods in a *de facto* act of strikebreaking. With the abuse of the military-permit system, licensing the movement of many items other than necessities, the General Drivers' Union declared that it was going to do what was necessary to put a stop to this deteriorating state of affairs. The Governor and the strikers found themselves on an inevitable collision-course. Olson moved decisively to arrest the leadership of Local 574 and to intimidate its members. In what was surely a confused and inappropriate reference to his brief tenure in the Industrial Workers of the World, and that organisation's approach to the class-struggle, Olson was quick to rationalise his actions: 'The problem with these leftists and ritualists', he explained pompously, is that 'they want to ride in

---

1. Jeanne Morgan, 'Journal from James P. Cannon's Office, 1954–1956 (Notes Kept by Secretary for Personal Memento, without Cannon's Knowledge)', entry 26 January 1954, copy in possession of author, with thanks to Jeanne Morgan and Alan Wald: 'Jim asks if I am familiar with the phrase, "He has the defects of his qualities". He notes that in his own case it is reversed, for he has the merit of his defects'.

on a white horse with a pennant flying hell bent for the barricades. My method is a different one. "Boring from within", which I learned from the Wobblies'.[2]

Charles Rumford Walker suggests that Olson's abrupt about-face of 1 August 1934 can be explained only through understanding that the Farmer-Laborite had long been a political captive of the kind of electoral pragmatism that was always willing to make a 'swift accommodation of political principles' to the demands of keeping oneself in office and in power. This shifted Olson's pressure-point, at the end of July 1934, away from what he referred to as a small clique within the Citizens' Alliance and towards the Trotskyist leadership of the teamsters' insurgency. Olson appreciated that his longstanding alliance with 'Labor' was unravelling as he confronted militants such as Ray Dunne, working-class advocates who were willing to defy him, even though he was an ostensibly 'radical' head of state. No labour-leader had ever done this in Olson's illustrious career. Faced with this challenge, Olson retreated into a position that seemed, pragmatically, to offer the Farmer-Labor governor both his cake and the opportunity to eat it as well. If he had the leadership of the General Drivers' Union arrested, Olson demonstrated that he would tolerate no challenge to his declaration of martial law *and* removed an intractable obstacle that the Employers' Advisory Committee had placed in the way of settling the strike on the basis of the Haas-Dunnigan peace proposal, namely the absolute refusal of the trucking operatives to meet with 'communists'. This accomplished, the Governor could then call for the election of a 'rank-and-file' committee that was 'truly representative' of Local 574's membership (again, buttressing the employers' position), meet with this body, and settle the strike, to the applause and lasting gratitude of capital and its servile state-officialdom. In this, he could count on the support of conservative American Federation of Labor officials ensconced in the Central Labor Union, such as Roy Weir, as well as ostensible radicals like the editor of the *Minnesota Labor Review*, Robley D. (Bob) Cramer. Weir addressed Local 574 in July 1934, contrasting Olson's role in Minneapolis with that of the governors of Ohio and California: 'we have a Governor in the State of Minnesota', he bellowed, 'who did not call out his militia to kill people and put fear in them'. Indeed, labour-movement figureheads such as these colluded with Olson in an attempt to displace and discredit Dunne, Skoglund, and other Trotskyists who had so successfully guided the General Drivers' Union and its effective 1934 strikes. The fly in this attractive ointment, applied to the gaping wounds of class-war in Minneapolis, was that

---

2. Charles Rumford Walker, 'The Farmer-Labor Party of Minnesota, Part II: Governor Olson's Last Interview', *The Nation*, 20 March 1937, p. 319, in File 'Magazine Articles, Farmer-Labor Party and Floyd B. Olson, 1933, 1937', Box 1, CRW Papers, MNHS, cited in Smemo 2011, p. 78.

the rank and file of Local 574 would not sacrifice union-leaders on the altar of an unprincipled strike-settlement.[3]

When a committee of two, the Sioux Nation member Ray Rainbolt and the veteran of the February 1934 coal-yards strike, Kelly Postal, was elected to meet with Olson, they were anything but conciliatory. As Olson 'talked and talked', harping on about the need 'to settle this thing', the two strikers were adamant about one point: 'First you let out our leaders; after that we'll talk'. From there, the conversation went downhill, with Olson being called a few 'choice' names and Rainbolt advising him 'Governor, you're right in the middle, on a picket fence. Watch your step or you'll slip and hurt yourself bad'. Olson kept talking, but his dizzying spin did not phase Postal and Rainbolt, whose more polite interjections included the query 'Why don't you start a school for strikebreaking governors?' Eventually tiring of this charade, Olson concentrated on locating Farrell Dobbs and Grant Dunne, who had managed to successfully evade arrest by Guardsmen, even though troops had ransacked apartment-buildings looking for them. Making use of his labour-movement friends, Olson managed to get one of his supporters, Bob Cramer of the *Minneapolis Labor Review*, to put him in touch with Grant Dunne. The Governor promised to rescind the outstanding warrants on Dobbs and Dunne if they would talk with him. The two fugitives agreed, and, together with Rainbolt, Postal, and two other members of the Strike Committee of 100, they met with Olson and convinced him that unless the strike-leaders were released from the military stockade and the strike-headquarters evacuated

---

3. Walker 1937, pp. 204–9; Dobbs 1972, pp. 156–8. For the escalating attack of the strike-leadership on Olson's declaration of martial law and its claim that the Farmer-Labor Governor was strikebreaking, see 'Strikers Demand Troop Removal: Committee Sees State Troops as Harming Strike – Scab Trucks Roll Under Military Protection', *The Organizer*, 28 July 1934; 'More Interference by National Guard', *The Organizer*, 29 July 1934; '574 to Go On Fighting For Right to Live: Olson's Position Unsatisfactory to Committee', *The Organizer*, 31 July 1934; 'Answer Military Tyranny by a General Protest Strike! Olson and State Troops Have Shown Their Colors! Union Men Show Yours! Our Headquarters Have Been Raided! Our Leaders Jailed! 574 Fights On!', *The Organizer*, 1 August 1934; Hugo Oehler, 'Olson's Role in the Strike: A Demagogue at Work', *The Militant*, 11 August 1934. In contrast, the *Minneapolis Labor Review* and powerful elements within the Central Labor Union, like Weir, took great pains to defend Olson, claiming that his unleashing of the National Guard was an attempt to curtail *illegal* picket-activity, thus protecting the strike and preserving public support for the workers' cause. See 'Governor is Peacemaker in Driver Strike', *Minneapolis Labor Review*, 1 June 1934; 'Troops Will Not be Used to Break Strike', *Minneapolis Labor Review*, 3 August 1934; Smemo 2011, pp. 34–8, quoting Roy Weir, Manuscript 848, Box 15, Folder 6, 'Membership Meeting Minutes, Teamsters Local 574, 6 July 1934', Farrell Dobbs Papers, State Historical Society of Wisconsin, Madison, Wisconsin. The most sympathetic account of Olson remains Mayer 1951, pp. 184–222.

by the troops occupying it, and returned to Local 574 in the same condition as it was originally seized, 'The strike [would] go right on, picketing and all'.[4]

Indeed, the conflict threatened to escalate to new levels, as calls for a general strike reverberated in union-halls across Minneapolis, rebounding to good effect inside the Central Labor Union. Even the most conservative layers of American Federation of Labor officialdom were outraged at the thought of trade-union buildings being overrun by militiamen. *The Organizer* upped the rhetorical ante with a barrage of criticism of Olson, demanded that he search and seize the offices of the Citizens' Alliance to determine what incriminating evidence was being harboured in its headquarters, and called for the complete withdrawal of the National Guard from Minneapolis. As Olson opened the 1 August 1934 issue of the daily strike-bulletin, he winced as he read words of condemnation directed at him personally:

> Military tyranny has reached its peak in Minneapolis. For the first time in decades, a trade union headquarters has been occupied by military forces and trade union leaders have been arrested and imprisoned in a military stockade. Picket cars are ordered off the street while every scab truck gets a free permit.... A dastardly blow has been struck at the very heart of the labor movement by military forces under the command of Floyd B. Olson, Governor of the State of Minnesota.

If the Governor had expected Local 574 to be cowed by the occupation of its headquarters and the arrest-warrants issued against union-leaders, the workers' newspaper disabused him of any such illusions. Cannon and others putting out *The Organizer* reminded Olson that he would pay a large electoral price for his campaign of repression:

> We have been dealt heavy blows – first by the bosses of the Citizens Alliance, then by their murderous tools in the Police Department. Now Floyd Olson's National Guard points bayonets and machine guns at us and tells us to give up our fight and go back as beaten slaves. They ordered us to to quit picketing. Our answer is the right to picket has been conquered and defended by the labor movement for a hundred years. We shall never give it up. They raided our headquarters with a thousand National Guardsmen, equipped with field machine guns, the latest model tear gas bombs, bayonets and pistols,

---

4. Walker 1937, pp. 208–12; 'No Decision on Injunction: 574 is Ready for Anything', 'The Real Issue and the Fake Issues', and 'Open House at Strike G.H.Q.', *The Organizer*, 10 August 1934.

commanded by the 'friend of labor,' Floyd B. Olson.... Let him run for office now on the platform, 'I raided the headquarters of Local 574. I flung their leaders into the military stockade. I broke a strike which Johannes couldn't break. Therefore, workers and farmers vote for me'.

'Resistance to tyranny is the beginning of freedom', declared the defiant voice of Local 574 strikers, whose leaders called on all Minneapolis trade-unionists to form a solid wall of defence around the beleaguered General Drivers' Union. 'Answer Olson's military tyranny with the General Strike of Protest!'[5]

Cannon used his 'dere emily' column to convey colloquially how working-class resentment against Olson was rising, and how the Governor was perceived not only as a strikebreaker, but also as aligned with the bosses, and himself in need of the protection of the National Guard: 'I never herd guys rave against a man, like what I herd workers all over the city rave against Olson today, and I guess he nos just how the workers feel becuz this afternoon he went over to the radison hotel to have a little get-together with the bosses, and darned if about 800 nashunal guards didn't line the streets on both sides and keep people from getting anywhere near the hotel'.

Meanwhile, roving pickets continued to harass and stop trucks, the campaign to remove the Mayor and the Chief of Police continued, Women's Auxiliary members organized a tag-day to raise money for striking families, and the Saturday, 4 August 1934 funeral of John Belor had constituted authority thinking that things could go from bad to worse very quickly. One Farmer-Labor newspaper claimed that Olson's use of martial law against strikers and dissidents was 'costing the governor thousands of votes daily – and it is also jeopardizing the success of the splendid farmer-labor program'. The Farmer-Labor Party Club at the University of Minnesota sent Olson a blunt telegram: 'This is to notify you that you have been expelled as honorary Chairman of our organization'.[6]

5. 'Answer Military Tyranny by a General Protest Strike!', 'Troops Take Over Labor Headquarters', and '574 Asks CLU to Call General Strike', *The Organizer*, 1 August 1934; 'Strikers Defy Olson Militia: Local 574 Issues Call for a Protest General Strike', *The Militant*, 4 August 1934. See also Skoglund's interview with Halstead, 24 April 1955, Typescript, p. 31, Box 2, Riehle Papers, MNHS.

6. 'dere emily', *The Organizer*, 1 August 1934; 'Removal Pleas Are Taken Up: Brown Testifies Before Welfare Committee', *The Organizer*, 31 July 1934; 'Tomorrow's 574's Tag Day', and 'John Belor, M.C.C.W.', *The Organizer*, 3 August 1934; 'John Belor Buried', *The Organizer*, 4 August 1934; '574 at Belor Funeral', and 'Tag Day a Success', *The Organizer*, 6 August 1934; Dobbs 1972, pp. 156–7; 'Martial Law a "Mistake"', *Minneapolis Journal*, 9 August 1934.

Olson, ever the pragmatist, realised that his plan to split the union-ranks from their militant leadership and engineer a quick settlement had actually backfired. Picketing was now resulting in more violence than ever, and scab-truckers were not above arming themselves and unloading shotguns into strikers who blocked their path. The Governor, thinking that fresh discretion was in order, agreed to all of Grant Dunne's conditions. On 2 August 1934, Ray Dunne, Micky Dunne, and Bill Brown were back in strike-headquarters, celebrating their release, discussing the strike and its strategy, and orchestrating picket-activities. Lists of requests for military and police-aid to trucks halted by strikers continued to be published in the newspapers, and Cochran and the Employers' Advisory Committee largely stuck to their guns, while offering proposals for a settlement that they knew would be unacceptable to the General Drivers' Union. Before Ray Dunne was released, he and General Walsh, in charge of the National Guard, exchanged a few acrimonious words, with Olson acting as an Olympian referee. The Governor did what he could to salvage his reputation as a progressive by claiming that the required permit for the General Drivers' Union mass meeting that had supposedly not existed had, in fact, turned up, negating the validity of the arrest-warrants for the strike-leadership. He also ordered a raid on the Citizens' Alliance headquarters. Documents seized, according to Olson, vindicated his allegations that this body 'dominates and controls the Employers Advisory Committee', that stool-pigeons in the pay of the Alliance had infiltrated unions, and that the reactionary clique had a long history of coercing other employers and operating in defiance of the United States Department of Labor and Roosevelt's National Recovery Administration. Charles Rumford Walker concluded, 'A blow to the left, softened by a blow to the right – classic and time-honored formula for reformists "put in the middle" by class forces!' In revisiting the role of Olson in the Minneapolis class-struggle, Hugo Oehler wrote: 'The Farmer Labor Governor of Minnesota is pressed between two warring camps – between the workers and the capitalists, represented by Local 574, and by the Citizens' Alliance. Whoever exerts the greatest pressure will force this radical petty bourgeois to alter his course'. Oehler detailed Olson's original use of martial law to break Local 574's picketing power, raid its strike-headquarters, and arrest its leaders and militant supporters. But with the outcry from union and progressive forces against this repression, Olson seemingly reversed gears, releasing the strike-leaders, directing his ire at the Citizens' Alliance, and revising the terms of transport through the permit-system. The result was that Olson 'regained some of his lost prestige' among workers. Oehler suggested that, in being susceptible to mass pressure from strikers, Olson, while definitely not on the side of the working masses,

presented possibilities for their militant leadership, precisely because his contradictions produced a 'division within the camp of the enemy' that could be
exploited.[7]

---

7. 'Leaders of 574 Released', and '574 Promised Walsh Nothing: Leaders Said Picket-
ing Would not Cease', *The Organizer*, 2 August 1934; 'Strikers Back at Old Stand After
Parley', 'Employers' Proposal', and 'Order Release of 2 Dunnes and Brown', *Minneapolis
Journal*, 2 August 1934; 'Truck Driver Fires on Pickets', *Minneapolis Journal*, 4 August 1934;
'Drivers Force Release of 4 Leaders', *The Militant*, 4 August 1934; 'Strikers Elated by New
Gains: Union Rejects Employers' New Proposal', *The Organizer*, 2 August 1934; 'We Have
Won the Fight on the Picket Line! We Shall Not Lose It in the Settlement! Dunne Speaks
on Bosses Plan, Says It Contains Several Ridiculous Proposals', *The Organizer*, 3 August
1934; 'The Road to Victory', *The Organizer*, 4 August 1934; Dobbs 1972, p. 167; Walker 1937,
pp. 210–13; Hugo Oehler, 'Once Again on the Role of Governor Olson', *The Militant*,
18 August 1934.

Chapter Eighteen
Standing Fast: Satire and Solidarity

With the state clearly handcuffed, militia-courts began to hand down sixty-to-ninety day sentences of military labour for those taken to the stockade for picket-line violations; truck-firms upped 'scab-pay' to $35 weekly, when strikers were struggling to secure wages of less than $20; and rumours circulated that the bosses were importing 'pug uglies' from New York, these specimens of 'underworld humanity' provided by the Bergoff strikebreaking agency. The employers' ranks nonetheless exhibited some fractures. Firms not wedded to the Citizens' Alliance/Employers' Advisory Committee/Cochran leadership made noises about settling on the basis of earlier suggestions by mediators. The EAC, angered by Olson's raid on Citizens' Alliance headquarters, and increasingly bellicose in its criticism of the Farmer-Labor Governor's actions,[1] turned to the federal courts for relief, petitioning for an injunction against martial law, which was depicted as denying freedoms of movement and inhibiting lawful business-activity. Conservative American Federation of Labor figureheads clamoured for a settlement, and precipitated yet another flurry of activity on the part of federal mediators Father Haas and E.H. Dunnigan.

---

1. Walker assembled a voluminous body of evidence detailing the increasingly irrational hostility of employers to Olson. See Files 'American City: Employers Side', 'American City: Incomplete Notes and Articles', and 'Miscellaneous Papers, 1934–1936', Box 1, CRW Papers, MNHS. This material includes quotes from the Minneapolis press, EAC circulars, the Joseph Cochran/EAC authored typescript, 'The Truth About the Truck Drivers Strike'; and Citizens' Alliance of Minneapolis, 'The So-Called Truck Drivers' Strike', *Special Weekly Bulletin*, 3 August 1934. See also Millikan 2001, pp. 281–5.

Meanwhile, these Washington wise men were being advised by the Roosevelt administration to turn to influential elements in the Minneapolis banking milieu to twist the arm of the Employers' Committee. The Stalinist Communist Party carped from the sidelines that Local 574's leadership was urging 'the workers to depend on Governor Olson', and that they were little more than 'Trotzky-ites for Martial Law'. Led by Sam K. Davis, the Communists tried to muscle in on the four-thousand-strong Minneapolis Central Council of Workers, the local unemployed-movement that was now firmly aligned with the General Drivers' Union strike and its leadership. Such efforts merely led to Davis being rebuffed. At mass rallies called by 574, the Stalinists had to be restrained from carrying banners denouncing the Local's leadership. *The Organizer* did its best to keep the rank and file from harming these Communist Party malcontents, explaining that as offensive as these sectarian critics were, their leaflets should not be torn up, nor should they be subjected to serious physical attack: 'They are not stool pigeons – at least, not conscious ones; they are just a little bit nutty and what they need is a friendly boot in the posterior. Maybe the shock will bring them to their senses'. Amidst these developments, the employers continued to blast away at the leadership-question from the depths of their ideological bunkers, claiming that, 'Communism is still the real issue in this strike. The employers will not surrender to Communism'. The *Minneapolis Journal* editorialised that the city was on the brink of anarchy, and that the General Drivers' Union's refusal to comply with martial law constituted 'The Beginning of the End'.[2]

Cannon used his humorous, vernacular style to lampoon the anti-Red hysteria fomented in Citizens' Alliance circles and propagated by the servile mainstream press. 'Spilling the Dirt – A Bughouse Fable', appeared in *The Organizer*, supposedly a stenographer's transcript of testimony wheedled out of the daily strike-bulletin's editor before a kangaroo-court convened by the Employers' Advisory Committee chair, Joseph Cochran. In this raucous exposé, Cannon both poked fun and made serious comment, his revolutionary pedagogy eliciting laughter as well as sober political reflection:

> The editor of *The Organizer* was picked up and taken before the kangaroo court for questioning. The examining officer had been eating onions and drinking scab beer, and his breath was so strong that it overcame the editor and he broke down and confessed everything.

---

2. 'Militia Court Sentences Six', *The Organizer*, 4 August 1934; 'Bosses Import "Pug-Uglies"', and 'Fink Rate Up Due to Pickets', *The Organizer*, 3 August 1934; 'A Touch of Comedy', *The Organizer*, 7 August 1934; Korth 1995, pp. 156–60; Tselos 1971, pp. 254–65; 'Labor Unions Take Hand to Bring Peace', 'The Beginning of the End', *Minneapolis Journal*, 2 August 1934; Dobbs 1972, pp. 164–7; Dunne and Childs 1934, pp. 42–7; Old Timer, 'Drivers' Strike Reveals Workers Great Resources', *The Organizer*, 11 August 1934.

OFFICER: You might as well come clean now. Give us the whole dope.

EDITOR: O.K., officer, I'm willing to tell everything. But, would you mind turning your breath the other way for a minute. I'm a bit sick.

OFFICER: Who's dis guy called Father Haas? What's the tie-up between him and Governor Olson and youse guys?

EDITOR: His real name is Haasky. He's a Russian Bolshevik, brought over here by the Brain Trust to put across a modified form of communism through the NRA. Cochran got the goods on him, all right. His proposal of 42 1/2 cents an Hour is practically the same thing as communism. He writes editorials for the *Militant* under an assumed name.

OFFICER: Spill the rest of it. What about Dunnigan, Olson, Brown, and the Dunne brothers – how many of these here Dunne brothers is there all told?

EDITOR: Their real name is Dunnskovitsky. They are Irish Jews from County Cork, smuggled into the country about six months ago disguised as sacks of Irish potatoes. There are 17 of them in Minneapolis, all the same age, and they all holler for 42 1/2 cents an hour. They say that's beginning of communism, and they are all strong for it. They have a brother in New York who is a famous acrobat. He inspired the popular ballad, 'The Man on the Flying Trapeze'. Mr. Dunnigan's right name is Dunnigansky – a cousin of the Dunne boys and hand in glove with them on the 42 1/2 cents an hour racket.

OFFICER: What about Brown?

EDITOR: He's a Jew named Bronstein, a fish peddler from the east side of New York. He came here a few weeks ago and tried to sell Bismark herring down at the market. Then he lined up with the Dunnskovitskys and muscled into the union racket. He's sitting pretty now and doesn't have to peddle herring any more. By the way, he is a son of Leon Bronstein – that's the original name of this guy Trotsky that started all the trouble over in Russia.

OFFICER: How about Governor Olson? He's in wit youse guys in the communist racket, ain't he?

EDITOR: Sure! That's the slickest part of the whole game. That guy's a card. His right name is not Olson, and he's not a Swede either – that's just a gag to get the Scandinavian vote. He's a Russian importation – direct from Moscow – and his real name is Olsonovich. He's been a big help to the strike. That raid he pulled off at the union headquarters, and the throwing of the pickets into the stockade, was all a trick to get sympathy for the strikers.

OFFICER: This is getting' too deep for me. Who cooked up this whole scheme, anyway?

EDITOR: Well, to tell the truth, it was planned out in Constantinople a few months ago. Some of the boys worked a week driving trucks and saved up enough money to take a trip to Europe. They went over to Constantinople to

see Trotsky and get instructions for their next move. Trotsky said: 'Boys, I want a revolution in Minneapolis before snow flies'. They said, 'O.K.', and started to leave. Just as they were about to take the boat, Vincent Dunne stepped up to old man Trotsky and said, 'What's your last word of advice before we go?'
OFFICER: What did Trotsky say?
EDITOR: He said, 'Boys, keep your eye on Olsonovich. He is liable to double cross you any minute'.

Walker's *American City* described Cannon's article as the most effective of many forays into 'imaginative political satire' undertaken by the Trotskyists handling the activities of the striking teamsters. 'Anything for a laugh in Minneapolis', was how Cannon remembered this leadership grappling with the violence and intransigence of redoubtable class-adversaries.[3]

The mass meeting at the Knoll of the Minneapolis Parade Grounds on the evening of Monday, 6 August 1934 was, however, no laughing matter. Local 574's largest ever rally was organised against a complex backdrop of developments. Olson continued to pressure for a strike-settlement, threatening to revoke permits for the transport of all goods except absolute necessities *and* use the militia to crack down on 'forcible picketing'. Indeed, he was already doing this, with scores of pickets confined in the military stockade; by the time thousands of workers and their supporters had convened at the Parade Grounds, Olson's Executive Order limiting truck-movement had rescinded the nine thousand permits previously issued, and a thousand new licences had been handed out. As employer-proposals continued to harp on about communism, the right of scabs to be employed in any back-to-work scenario, and trucking firms' refusal to take back onto their payrolls any workers who engaged in 'illegal acts', the General Drivers' Union made no concessions. It remained insistent that any strike-settlement had to be premised on the original Haas-Dunnigan proposals. A handful of firms adhering to the Citizens' Alliance stand against the terms of this original mediated settlement-plan now broke ranks and accepted these conditions, allowing them to move goods. The number of firms not adhering to the Employers' Advisory Committee, and willing to sign on to the Haas-Dunnigan terms, apparently approached fifty. As *The Organizer* published a list of 'The 166 Tyrants', enterprises that had precipitated the strike into its third week, it effectively called for a boycott of these anti-union holdouts: 'The mass of the population, which likes to know where it spends its money, will be interested in reading the names of these 166 tyrants'. Countering this trade-union attack on the Citizens' Alliance,

---

3. Cannon, 'Spilling the Dirt – a Bughouse Fable', *The Organizer*, 8 August 1934, and reprinted in Cannon 1958, pp. 84–6; Dobbs 1972, pp. 169–70; Walker 1937, pp. 215–16; Cannon 1944, p. 163.

newspapers like the *Minneapolis Journal* ran full-page advertising propaganda-statements extolling the virtues of the recalcitrant employers' association. Great umbrage was taken at the Olson-ordered militia-raid on the Citizens' Alliance, conducted by a dozen Guardsmen (rather than the eight hundred deployed to take over strike-headquarters): 'This invasion of our constitutional rights climaxes the campaign of insult, abuse and misrepresentation which Governor Olson has for some time waged against the Citizens' Alliance'. Unions such as the milk-drivers made substantial donations to the coffers of Local 574, but on the streets, 574 Women's Auxiliary members distributing *The Organizer* were harassed and persecuted by Guardsmen, while Trotskyists selling *The Militant* were subject to arrest. In this volatile situation, forty thousand people turned out at the Parade Grounds to hear Bill Brown, Miles Dunne, and Albert Goldman call on the strikers to stand firm; to continue to enforce picketing; to extend the struggle into a battle for a new, and more militant, industrial unionism; to depend on their own strength and resilience and to oppose the idea that the National Guard could possibly be a substitute for picket-lines staffed by workers; and to protest against martial law's curtain of repression, lowered on the truckers' insurgency, leaving 120 Minneapolis workers incarcerated in a military stockade. Cannon put the message in the language of solidarity. Mike wrote to 'dere emily': 'if they is one thing us workers has got to lern, emily, it is this. it wont never do us no good to be ambishus for ourselfes only. we got to be ambishus for ALL our workin class brothers and sisters, and rise with our whole class'.[4]

In an almost daily swirl of shifting developments, the curbs on trucking proclaimed one day seemed to ease the next; more and more trucking firms were willing to abide by the conditions of the originally suggested Haas-Dunnigan

4. Leaflet, 'Minneapolis Workers and Friends of the Strikers', File 'Notes Local 574 and Strike', Box 1, CRW Papers, MNHS; 'Governor Demands Strike End by Midnight: Threatens to Bear Down on Both Sides', *Minneapolis Journal*, 3 August 1934; 'Union Holding Out for Original Haas Plan', *Minneapolis Journal*, 4 August 1934; 'Time to End the Strike', 'Truck Permit Withdrawal Is Next Step', 'Strong Explains Aims of Citizens' Alliance', 'What is the Citizens Alliance?', *Minneapolis Journal*, 5 August 1934; 'Dunne Speaks on Boss Plan', *The Organizer*, 3 August 1934; 'Strike Rally Breaks Record: 40,000 Turn Out to Support 574', 'The Fight of 574: Excerpts from Addresses on the Parade', 'The President in Minneapolis', 'News and Views', 'Here Are the 166 Tyrants! Union Reveals Holdout List', and 'Oil Workers Hold Meeting', *The Organizer*, 7 August 1934; 'Tyrants Ring Shows Signs of Crack Under Mass Blows: Four of Infamous 166 Accept Terms', 'Jewish Workers Aid 574', and 'Milk Drivers Give $6000: Brother Unions Rallying as Fight Goes On', *The Organizer*, 8 August 1934; Dobbs 1972, p. 175; 'Using Permits for "Bootleg"', *The Organizer*, 9 August 1934; 'Martial Law and the Strike', *The Organizer*, 11 August 1934; 'Drivers Ranks Hold Firm as Bosses Committee of 166 Begins to Crack: 574 Backed by Workers in Mass Meet', *The Militant*, 4 August 1934; 'Ban Halts All But Necessities', 'Two Sides Locked Over Terms of Re-Employment', and 'Governor's Executive Order Limiting Trucks', *Minneapolis Journal*, 6 August 1934; 'dere emily', *The Organizer*, 13 August 1934.

settlement; and Cochran and the Citizens' Alliance-led Employers' Advisory Committee continued its quest to end martial law through the courts. Postponed hearings proclaimed the justice-system's preference for prevarication. With the streets relatively quiet, the General Drivers' Union insisted that any dramatic change in the *status quo* would be met with a revival of picketing, and that truck-movement would be opposed vigorously. As newspaper-headlines complained of 'Peace Moves at Standstill', Cochran continued to bang the drum of anti-communism at all opportunities, repudiating the original Haas-Dunnigan settlement-plan which, it was claimed, opened the door wide to the collapse of 'free-enterprise' relations between labour and capital:

> If the 'Haas-Dunnigan proposals' were accepted by the employers, it would enable Local 574 to claim a victory for communist leadership in this strike, having obtained an increase in wages without or before arbitration, and thereby give prestige to the communistic leaders of the strikers. Such a victory would be followed, naturally, by a campaign to get more men into that union and commit that many more to taking orders from the communists. With this accomplished, other unions would be seduced by the communists and, shortly, all or most of Minneapolis union labor would be communized. Thus communism, after all, is still the real issue in this strike. The mediator's proposal is that the employers surrender. The employers will not surrender to communism.

Ralph M. Beckwith, a member of the Employers' Advisory Committee, used a radio-address on 8 August 1934 to make the same point, arguing that 'The communists are boring from within, wherever they can get an entry into union labor. Their intention is to take possession of labor organizations here and everywhere, and with that foothold, to upset the whole American economic and government system and replace it eventually with the soviet state'. Beckwith insisted that the original Haas-Dunningan proposal, which Local 574 had agreed to reluctantly, was nothing more than 'the entering wedge to a recognition of communistic leadership for a working man in Minneapolis'. Other employer-representatives used the airwaves (their texts printed in the Minneapolis press) to claim that communist-led unemployed workers had conspired to wreck the Union City Mission and Salvation Army shelters. Sabotage, it was argued, would strengthen the demand of the jobless for a cash-allowance in lieu of food and shelter. Often confusing the strike-leadership and specific Stalinist spokesmen, such as Sam K. Davis, these anti-strike tirades tended to represent the Trotskyist leadership of the General Drivers' Union, and even the more united-front-oriented organisation of the unemployed, the Minneapolis Central Council of Workers, as 'a branch of the Communist Party'. With Cochran and the stalwarts of the Citizens'

Alliance/Employers' Advisory Committee waving this banner of 'No Surrender' to the invading Soviet threat, it was not entirely surprising that Father Haas and his mediation-ensemble, encouraged by the Roosevelt administration (with the President conveniently appearing in Minnesota on 8 August 1934 to dedicate a plaque honouring the Mayo brothers), worked overtime to placate the employers and reconfigure an acceptable mediated 'peace-plan'.[5]

5. 'Court Postpones Martial Law Hearing: Curb on Permits to Trucks Eased, 4,100 Get Papers; 351 Operators Sign Haas-Dunnigan Agreement; Peace Moves at Standstill; Employers' Chairman Says Communism is Still Issue', *Minneapolis Journal*, 7 August 1934; '100,000 Cheer Roosevelt . . . Truck Strike Peace Moves At Standstill', and 'Employers Strike Views Given In Cochran Talk', *Minneapolis Journal*, 8 August 1934; 'Beckwith Gives Employer Views on Strike', *Minneapolis Journal*, 9 August 1934; 'Text of . . . Address on Strike Controversy', *Minneapolis Journal*, 10 August 1934; Korth 1995, pp. 157–60; Dobbs 1972, p. 171; Walker 1937, p. 217; 'Bosses Find Rev. Haas Red', *The Organizer*, 9 August 1934.

Chapter Nineteen
Mediation's Meanderings

With the Citizens' Alliance-led quest for an injunction against Olson's declaration of martial law finally squashed late in the second week of August, Haas came under increased pressure to revise and reinvigorate a mediated settlement.[1] Having met with the employers' committee, only to find it virtually unmovable, Haas and Dunnigan agreed, under pressure from Washington to end the strike in Minneapolis, to try to put the new proposal before a wider Local 574 body than the General Drivers' Union negotiating team of Farrell Dobbs and Vincent Ray Dunne. Dobbs and Dunne, well aware that the new settlement-plan was a retreat from the terms of the first Haas-Dunningan proposal – in that it altered the conditions under which men would or would not be hired back by the trucking firms, backtracked on wages, and contained other concessions – refused to recommend the new plan. Confident that the Strike Committee of 100 would find the revised settlement-terms equally unacceptable, the General Drivers' Union negotiating duo agreed that Haas and Dunningan could speak to the larger committee at the General Headquarters. This meeting took place on the evening of Monday, 13 August 1934.

As Cannon later noted, Dobbs and Dunne were not bulldozed by Haas's claims that, 'The bosses won't give

---

1. 'Enforcing of Law Held Job of Governor', 'Text of Decision', 'Strike Stirs Washington Into Action' and 'Why Not Order Elections, Father Haas?', *Minneapolis Journal*, 11 August 1934; 'Injunction is Refused', *The Organizer*, 11 August 1934; 'Conspire to Break Strike! Bosses Claim Haas Support', *The Organizer*, 13 August 1934; Bernstein 1970, p. 249.

in so you must...The strike must be settled; Washington insists'. As for the meeting with the larger Strike Committee of 100, it was 'planned and prepared in advance'. Haas, according to Cannon, 'got a meeting that he never bargained for'. After having the floor to outline the settlement-proposal, Haas was assailed by the strikers. The meeting took on the tone of an inquisition. As *The Organizer* reported, 'Man after man arose and either asked a question which made the Federal men squirm, or threw in their teeth defiant refusals to consider the new rotten scheme'. Questioning why Haas and Dunnigan were recommending that pickets sign an agreement that could well bar them from a job because they had committed illegal acts, the strikers also queried how it was that the mediators approached them over the head of their negotiating committee when they had failed to 'force the 166 bosses to get together and take a secret ballot on the *original* Haas-Dunnigan plan?' A Catholic worker rose to address Haas, calling it 'a crying shame when a man wearing the cloth of the Church as you do stands up before his brother workers and attempts to swindle them into acceptance of such a sell-out as you are giving us'. Haas and Dunnigan protested that the proposals were not theirs, and that while they recommended them, they did not endorse them. This hair-splitting language merely inflamed antagonisms, especially with Haas, who was visibly uncomfortable, 'pale as a ghost and sweating'. It was left to Local 574 President Bill Brown and negotiating-team member Vincent Ray Dunne to sum up the Union's position. Brown's words drew rousing applause:

> We have been fighting for four weeks; all of us have sacrificed and struggled; two of our brothers lie dead at the hands of the bosses agents. We accepted your first plan. And now you ask us to bow our heads and go back to the old slavery and you would speak of fairness and honor? I tell you that when we accepted the Haas-Dunnigan proposal we gave up all we mean to give up. We will not budge another inch.

No less enthusiastic was the ovation given to Dunne, who said:

> You ask us to give the bosses a licence to discriminate especially against our pickets for the very activity that builds the Union and wins a strike. We will not dishonor ourselves by delivering up our best men to these vicious employers. If we did we might as well abandon unionism. And you give us no wage guarantee. What do you mean 'present wage scales'. There are none.... Are you going to put us in the position of rejecting this rotten proposal.

Haas and Dunnigan were apparently united on just this point, and the Committee of 100 was unanimous in turning back their recommendation of these terms of settlement. After consulting with those members of the strike-committee locked up in the military stockade, Local 574 rejected what it designated the 'bosses' offer'. Herbert Solow later reported that, 'Haas and Dunnigan were crucified by the rank and file'. When Haas left the hall, a young Roman Catholic ripped a cross off his neck and hurled it at the shaken, exiting priest. Cannon thought the ecclesiastic mediator looked 'physically sick'.[2]

Cannon offered a terse *post mortem* on this round of meanderings by the mediators: 'Dunnigan was finished, Father Haas was finished'. Their parting shot was to recommend to the National Labor Relations Board (NLRB) in Washington that elections be held in the 166 firms organised by the Employers' Advisory Committee to fight Local 574. These elections would then ascertain employee-representation. Local 574, understandably, opposed any such elections. First, the very list of firms where elections were to take place was the creation of the employers; the Union had no members whatsoever in 21 of these 166 firms, and its original strike had been waged against a mere eleven trucking companies. The General Drivers' Union thus placed the accent on its right to represent its membership, rather than having its existence defined by a list of firms constructed by its trucking adversaries. Second, *The Organizer* pilloried the call for these 'fake elections' as nothing more than a strikebreaking ruse, pointing out that the employers would be escorting scabs to the polling booths and providing election-monitors with padded lists of employees. Third, Bill Brown and Mick Dunne continued to try to widen the support for the strike, working with connections in the Minnesota State Federation of Labor to promote the idea of a 48-hour sympathetic general strike. The labour-fakirs in the American Federation of Labor bureaucracy, while content to offer empty commitments in principle, were not about to actually call workers into the streets in support of Local 574. Both William Green and Tobin had long been opposed to the militant truckers' insurgency, and were, at this point, actively involved in various manoeuvres to undermine the Trotskyist leadership's efforts at building an inclusive industrial union in the trucking sector. It was at this point, according to Carlos Hudson, a young Trotskyist playing a key role in getting *The Organizer* out on a daily basis, that the Stalinists upped the decibel-level of their criticism of the strike-leadership. Communist Party spokesmen argued that the rank-and-file should have been pushed to go over the heads of the mainstream trade-union officials and Governor Olson, to whom

2. 'Haas, Dunnigan Hear Rank and File Flay "New" Boss Scheme; Deny Endorsing It', and 'Union Rejects Offer', *The Organizer*, 14 August 1934; Walker 1937, pp. 217–18; Dobbs 1972, pp. 171–2; Cannon 1944, p. 165; 'Federal Mediators Push Strike Truce', and 'The Haas-Dunnigan Plan', *Minneapolis Journal*, 13 August 1934; 'Negotiators Indicate Only One Question Left to Solve', *Minneapolis Journal*, 13 August 1934; Herbert Solow, 'The Great Minneapolis Strike', *New Leader*, 8 September 1934; 'Peace Plan Failure Deadlocks Strike', 'Employers' Statement', and 'Text of Employers' Proposals for Peace', *Minneapolis Journal*, 14 August 1934; Tselos 1971, pp. 259–60; Blantz 1970, pp. 13–14; 'Conspiracy to Break Mpls. Strike Smashed by Committee of 100: Haas and Dunnigan Exposed as Aiding Bosses in Fake Agreement', *The Militant*, 18 August 1934.

these labour-bureaucrats looked for guidance, mounting a general strike to bring the employers to their knees and force a change of government. Skoglund also claimed that it was in this period, after Bloody Friday, that Stalinists adopted increasingly other-worldly demands, their strategic ultra-leftism tending toward tactical stances pressuring militants to 'set up a workers' rule of the city' that would have necessarily left the Trotskyists in charge of developments vulnerable to state-victimisation; striking workers subject to violent repression; and the teamsters' insurgency and its *raison d'être*, the winning of union-rights for all workers in the trucking industry, resolutely routed. The attacks on Local 574 and its leadership's project of opposing an NLRB 'electoral' solution, then, were coming from almost all directions. As the General Drivers' Union's coffers dried up on account of the costs it had to bear in the ongoing battle, and as the odd striker broke ranks and returned to work, there was some fear that the strike was on the skids. Yet if the edifice of solidarity built by Local 574 over the course of the strike-torn months from February–August 1934 was, indeed, exhibiting some signs of strain and fissure, there were, equally, indications of cracks in the wall of employer-intransigence. It was in this context that a new federal mediator, P.A. Donoghue, appeared in Minneapolis on 15 August 1934. Fresh from a stint in San Francisco, where he orchestrated an election-process that resulted in the end of the tumultuous longshoremen's strike, Donoghue was 'getting a press buildup as a hotshot'.[3]

Within the Communist League's five-person strike-committee, Albert Goldman initially aired the view that the strike was lost, and that it was necessary to concede defeat. He urged calling the strike off, in order to 'save our pieces'. Apparently influenced by signs of demoralisation among strikers whose children were hungry, whose electricity, gas, and water were being shut off for non-payment of bills, and whose landlords were evicting their tenants for missing rent-payments, Goldman noted the rising number of trucks moving under military permits, the ease with which the National Guard arrested resisting pickets, and the

3. Cannon 1944, p. 165; Dobbs 1972, pp. 175–6; Korth 1995, pp. 161–3; Tselos 1971, p. 261; 'Lawson Talk on City Truck Strike', *Minneapolis Journal*, 14 August 1934; 'Employers Ask F.R. To Order Vote', and 'Text of Strike Talk by Rathbun', *Minneapolis Journal*, 15 August 1934; 'Donoghue to Select Day Upon Arrival', *Minneapolis Journal*, 15 August 1934; 'A New Strike-Breaking Scheme', *The Organizer*, 16 August 1934; "The 'Elections' are a Fraud! Bosses' Scheme to outlaw Unionism by Scab Votes and Padded Lists; Secret Circular of Employers Advisory Committee Reveals Vile Plot", *The Organizer*, 17 August 1934; 'All Unions Asked to Support 574 by 2-Day General Strike Demonstration', and 'Election Call is Boss Trick', *The Organizer*, 18 August 1934; 'Two Day General Strike Asked: Truckers Seek Sympathy Tie-Up', *Minneapolis Journal*, 20 August 1934; 'Rift Seen in Truck Driver Ranks: AFL Rejects General Strike', *Minneapolis Journal*, 21 August 1934. Hudson, 'Chains Wear Thin in Minneapolis', Typescript, p. 26, File 'Local 574 Strike, 1934', Box 1, CRW Papers, MNHS; Skoglund interviewed by Halstead, 24 April 1955, Typescript, p. 31, Box 2, Riehle Papers, MNHS.

threat that Donoghue and Washington's promotion of 'union-elections' posed to Local 574. In the heated discussion that ensued, Goldman crossed swords with V.R. Dunne, Carl Skoglund, and Farrell Dobbs. Skoglund was particularly incensed. He regarded Goldman's assessment, and its corollary that the strike must be wound down, as nothing more than concession of 'a complete defeat and a rout'. Insisting that, 'No pieces could be saved', if Goldman's advice were followed, Skoglund told the Chicago attorney that 'he would never put that proposal over as long as I was alive'. Cannon listened. As the authoritative figure on the Communist League of America committee, he eventually sided with 'the leaders in closest touch with the ranks', suggesting that if they thought the strike could be victorious, there must still be some fight left among the truckers, helpers, and inside workers.

Writing under the pseudonym 'Old Timer', Cannon penned an article in *The Organizer* that was undoubtedly influenced by this inner-circle discussion. It presented Local 574 as blazing new trails out of the tired accommodations of craft-unionism, towards a fresh start for workers and their organisations. What was different about Local 574, Cannon insisted, was that it was premised on new ideas of class-mobilisation that combined militant leadership and an approach to organising the working class that was inclusive rather than exclusive. All workers, Cannon suggested, were drawn into struggle by 574, be they organised or unorganised, male or female, employed or jobless. Unified by a powerful idea, Local 574's unique power and fighting capacity, Cannon claimed, was its recognition that all workers must be brought together in an unbreakable solidarity forged in the ongoing, relentless, war against capital.[4]

4. Dobbs 1972, pp. 176–7; Skoglund interviewed by Halstead, 24 April 1955, Typescript, p. 30, Box 2, Riehle Papers, MNHS; Old Timer [Cannon], '574 Strike Methods Are Blazing New Labor Paths', 18 August 1934, reprinted under the title 'The Secret of Local 574', in Cannon 1958, pp. 89–92.

Chapter Twenty
Sudden and Unexpected Victory

From this point in mid-August 1934 onwards, things moved rapidly. Elections and their nature were now, in some ways, inevitably bound up with whether terms of settlement could possibly be acceptable to both employers and union-members.[1]

A new pace seemed to have been set by Donoghue, whose marching orders had come directly from President Roosevelt, concerned to end the strike as soon as possible. With Olson and the Farmer-Labor Party supporting the New Deal agenda, Roosevelt was apparently adamant that the strike be over and long done with by the time of the November 1934 elections. Since Local 574 had already accepted one mediation-plan, Donoghue's obvious stumbling block was the Employers' Advisory Committee. An approach had to be concocted that would essentially settle the strike on the previously-elaborated terms of the original Haas-Dunnigan proposal, but that would also give the trucking firms a way of saving face vis-à-vis their now oft-repeated claims that the General Drivers' Union did not necessarily represent all employees. The Citizens' Alliance, its class-conscious head very much in the sand, was still referring in its propaganda, as late

---

1. On the complicated, meandering mediation-process, in which the election-issue was now centrally posed, see 'Board Orders Speedy Strike Vote: Donoghue to Select Day Upon Arrival', *Minneapolis Journal*, 16 August 1934; 'Labor Board Man Arrives to Rule Strike Election', *Minneapolis Journal*, 17 August 1934; 'Objections Hold Up Vote Rules: Strike Chiefs Call Proposed Election Fake', *Minneapolis Journal*, 18 August 1934.

as August 1934, to the 'so-called truck drivers' strike'.[2] Donoghue met with Citizens' Alliance 'guiding spirit' and Employers' Advisory Committee member, A.W. Strong. Behind the scenes, Strong was being pressured by Minneapolis magnates John W. Barton and Clive Talbot Jeffrey, conservative Republican bankers who held posts in federal financial institutions and were known to have been on the receiving end of millions of dollars of loans from Roosevelt's Reconstruction Finance Corporation. They undoubtedly let Strong know that the lid had to be put back on Minneapolis's volatile labour-capital relations. Donoghue pushed Strong to give in on two crucial matters that Haas and Dunnigan had made clear were never going to be acceptable to Local 574. First, the employers had to drop their insistence that they had the right to refuse to rehire any striker 'guilty' of 'violence' or 'illegal acts'. Second, there had to be a stipulation of specific hourly wage-rates as a starting point for arbitration. That done, Donoghue proceeded to put in place protocols governing the employee-representation elections, which were to be held within ten days, organised by the Regional Labor Board. To appease the General Drivers' Union, only those who had been on trucking-firm payrolls as of 16 July 1934 were eligible to vote; there was no vote given to 'scabs', or what the Employers' Advisory Committee referred to as 'loyal employees'. On the issue of 'inside workers', so pivotal to the industrial-union sensibilities of Local 574, the breakthrough made in the original Haas-Dunnigan proposal was maintained: in the 22 market-firms that were the centrepiece of strike-action, those allowed to vote included a broad canvas of all those employed in the trucking sector, including drivers, helpers, platform-workers, and inside workers. Those workers who devoted sixty percent of their time to the actual selling of goods were deemed ineligible to vote. For the employers, Donoghue engineered a wider vote than Local 574 would have liked, designating that all 166 Employers' Advisory Committee firms would conduct elections, even though the vast majority of such firms had not even been formally struck by the General Drivers' Union. This, Strong and his Citizens' Alliance cronies well knew, would result in election-results in which a significant number of firms, their employees mostly unaffiliated with Local 574, would almost certainly vote against being represented by the General Drivers' Union. Even if Local 574 essentially won all that it had struggled to achieve (a minimum hourly wage of 50 cents for drivers and 42 cents for helpers, with arbitration-boards instructed that these rates could be adjusted *upwards*; union-recognition; and the right to represent all of

---

2. The EAC and the Citizens' Alliance refused to concede, even in the face of demonstrations of tens of thousands of workers and pitched battles between masses of strikers and various forces of authority in July-August 1934, that there were more than a few hundred workers involved, insisting that there were 'only 309 workers actively on strike'. See Citizens' Alliance, 'The So-Called Truck Drivers' Strike', *Special Weekly Bulletin*, 3 August 1934, in File 'Miscellaneous Papers, 1934–1936', Box 1, CRW Papers, MNHS.

its members, including inside workers), employers could claim that they had been right and many of the workers in the industry did not want to be represented by the Union. Meanwhile, the General Drivers' Union insisted that before any elections take place there had to be a written agreement relating to the establishment of arbitration-boards. The rank-and-file of the General Drivers' Union received a thorough education in what constituted fair and fraudulent election-terms. Local 574 also petitioned Governor Olson to draw on a select list of strikers in monitoring truck-movements under the permit-system, and continued to advocate a two-day general-strike protest, waged by all organised labour in support of the strikers. Pickets incarcerated in the workhouse and military stockade, now disparagingly referred to as 'Olson's Resort', waged a hunger-strike in protest of their conditions.[3]

The Organizer proved an indispensable weapon in Local 574's propaganda-war, not only against the bosses, but against the inclination of federal mediators to compromise on essential, and hard-fought-for, trade-union principles. Donoghue, no doubt briefed by Haas and Dunnigan, did not only have the mainstream Minneapolis press to inform him of the prevalent state of mind with regard to the strike and its settlement. He also had to pick up the daily strike-bulletin. In reading it, he could not possibly misunderstand Local 574's resolve. His understanding of what needed doing in Minneapolis was framed, in part, by *The Organizer*, which proclaimed in bold headlines: 'No Union Man to Participate in Any Election Unless Union Agrees to It: Bosses Preparing Election Fake by Threats and Tricks'. Cannon no doubt exaggerated Donoghue's willingness to implement a plan beneficial to the General Drivers' Union, but he captured something of the surprising suddenness with which the 'man from Washington' put together terms that, in Ray Dunne's view, gave Local 574 'substantially what we have fought and bled for since the beginning of the strike'. Cannon suggested that Donoghue 'had obviously learned from the sad experiences' of his counterparts Haas and Dunningan 'not to try any shenanigans'. Instead, he 'got right down

3. 'Strikers Ask Authority to Check Trucks', *Minneapolis Journal*, 19 August 1934; 'Two Day General Strike Asked: Truckers Seek Sympathy Tie-Up', *Minneapolis Journal*, 20 July 1934; Korth 1995, pp. 161–2; Cannon 1944, p. 165; Dobbs 1972, pp. 178–80; Tselos 1971, pp. 259–65; 'All Unions Asked to Support 574 by 2-Day General Demonstration Strike', and 'Bring Up the Labor Reserves', *The Organizer*, 18 August 1934; 'Members Meet Tuesday: 574 Will not Stand for Fake Elections', 'Strike Body Will Report on Elections', and 'Market Open All Morning – Olson Again Breaks His Promise; Troops and Loading', *The Organizer*, 20 August 1934; 'Late Flash: All Prisoners of Olson's Militia Hit Conditions by Hunger Strike', 'How About Leaders', 'Union Busters Busted', *The Organizer*, 21 August 1934; 'Stockade Dance', *The Organizer*, 12 September 1934.

to business and in a few days worked out a settlement which was a substantial victory for the union'.[4]

Donoghue had the election and settlement-package in place by Monday, 20 August 1934, and presented it to Local 574's negotiators, Dobbs and Dunne, both of whom had been part of the Communist League of America strike-committee that had discussed how the struggle was flagging. The terms, on the whole highly favourable to the Union, caught the Trotskyist duo somewhat off-guard. So unexpected was Donoghue's authoritative and straightforward insistence that he had convinced Strong to 'call off the fight', that Local 574 President Bill Brown was not even in Minneapolis when the federal mediator made his proposals to the Union's negotiating team. Brown and Miles Dunne were attending the State Federation of Labor convention in International Falls. They were informed of the situation by phone, through which, as part of the Strike Committee of 100, they were briefed by the Union's chief negotiators. With these two layers of Local 574 – the small negotiating team of two and the larger Committee of 100 – agreed that they would recommend acceptance of the terms of settlement and the future Labor Board-run elections, a ratification-meeting was called for the evening of Tuesday, 21 August 1934. As one last element of the General Drivers' Union's demands, a small committee of strikers visited Governor Olson and secured from him a commitment to release all 167 pickets confined in the military stockade.[5]

Minneapolis awoke on Wednesday, 22 August 1934, to the surprising news that the strike was over. 'Martial Rule Ends, Troops Go Today', read the bold headline of the *Minneapolis Journal*. The subheadings told the story of the unanticipated and abrupt end to 36 intense days of class-struggle: 'Finish of 5-Week Walkout Comes with Startling Swiftness on Concessions by Both Sides; Board to Decide Date for Employee Elections; Employers will Take Back Men Regardless of Activities – Voting to Be by Firms'. The Employers' Advisory Committee had voted 155 to 3 in favour of the settlement; Local 574, in spite of some strong statements by militants on the need to continue the struggle to secure all that the insurgent truckers demanded, endorsed the recommendation of the Dobbs-Dunne

---

4. 'No Union Man to Participate in Any Elections Unless Union Agrees to It: Bosses Preparing Election Fake By Threats and Tricks', *The Organizer*, 21 August 1934; Walker 1937, pp. 218–19; Cannon 1944, p. 165. Dobbs 1972, p. 179, is more guarded in its assessment: 'Although the settlement provided much less than the workers deserved, it was as much as we could get at the time'.

5. Korth 1995, pp. 161–2; Dobbs 1972, pp. 178–80; Walker 1937, p. 221; 'Fought for All Workers: Dunne Says Unionism Gains Victory', 'dere emily', and 'The Settlement Terms', *The Organizer*, 22 August 1934; 'F. of L. Hails End of City's Truck Strike', *Minneapolis Journal*, 22 August 1934. Olson did not immediately make good on his commitment to release the pickets from the stockade. In September, those still under guard in the makeshift military prison held a dance: 'Stockade Dance', *The Organizer*, 12 September 1934.

negotiating team and the larger Committee of 100 that Donoghue's terms of settlement be accepted.

Meanwhile, the Citizens' Alliance crowd was silent, nursing a sense of resentment that would fester for some time. 'If we had only held out for a few days, we would have won', a strategist of this hardcore group complained to Charles Rumford Walker two years later. E.G. Hall, President of the Minnesota State Federation of Labor, managed to be petulant and prescient. His craft-union nose rubbed in the success of an industrial-union organising drive, Hall took a swipe at the audacity of the Trotskyist vanguard of Local 574: 'The leadership in the Minneapolis truck strike had caused turmoil by seeking to include other crafts in the drivers' union, and by promising the impossible'. If this kind of statement had the stamp of sour grapes all over it, Hall also suggested, in what was truly a hint of things to come, that the AFL was gearing up for a fight against 'communistic tendencies' in the labour-movement. Among the truckers, however, the taste of victory was sweet indeed. Rank-and-file strikers were jubilant; they embarked on a 'victory "celebration" that lasted for twelve hours'.[6]

In his articles in *The Organizer*, Cannon crowned Local 574's victory with recognition of what had been won and what remained to be achieved. Recognising that not all that the General Drivers' Union wanted had been secured, Cannon nonetheless championed the fighting spirit of 574. The strike had succeeded, he insisted, and Minneapolis had been emblazoned on the banners of trade-unionism across the United States, because Local 574 successfully fought bosses, a Farmer-Labor governor, police and National Guardsmen, a reactionary mayor and a bevy of federal mediators. This refusal to be cowed heralded the dawn of a new day for American labour. At the Eagles Hall, where the strikers ratified the settlement, Cannon claimed 'the walls...shook...with the fighting song of 574, "Solidarity Forever"'. Against Mayor Bainbridge's 'serving notice here and now that our fight on communism has just begun', pledging 'to rid our city of those who defy law and order [and] seek only to tear down our government', Cannon offered a counter-pledge:

> Mayor Bainbridge has started to yap about driving 'Communists' out of the city. We know what he means. He means framing up every worker who fights for his rights.... We warn all enemies of labor: Local 574 is going to take a hand in the fight against any kind of frame-up.

It was a short step from this position to Cannon's call on all workers in the trucking sector to rally around 574 and, in the forthcoming Labor Board elections, 'roll

---

6. Korth 1995, p. 161; Dobbs 1972, p. 184; Walker 1937, pp. 219–20; 'Martial Law Ends, Troops go Today...', *Minneapolis Journal*, 22 August 1934.

up such an overwhelming vote for the union that the question [of union affilia-
tion] can not be raised again'.[7]

The lead-up to the representation-vote saw Local 574 exercising vigilance with
regard to the election-procedures. Articles in *The Organizer* raised a series of
questions about employer-padding of payroll-lists with ineligible office-workers
and salesmen; excising union-men from compilations of voters; and placing
union-members on slates of the company-union counterpart to Local 574. Mass
meetings on the Parade Grounds and at the Eagles Hall drew the now-routine
crowds of thousands of workers.[8]

When the votes were finally counted, the result was of the kind that Donoghue as a federal mediator must have appreciated. Both sides scanned the tally
and proclaimed victory. The Minneapolis daily press was quick to stress that in
the 166 firms where votes could take place, the trucking firms won more com-
pany-votes than did the union-alternative. Therefore, the Employers' Advisory
Committee was declared the unequivocal victor, the conclusion being drawn
that the workers had rejected the General Drivers' Union in most firms. As coverage in *The Organizer* made clear, however, capital's 'mathematical acrobatics'
obscured some basic realities, all of which reflected trade-union victories rather
than defeats. Trucking employers made the election-results into a statement of
'vote by firm', but this construction, as well as the list of 166 local businesses, was
the creation of the Citizens' Alliance. For Local 574, 'Representation by firms was
not the issue'. Fully 21 of the 166 firms held no vote, most likely because some of
these firms had failed during the strike, or the number of workers employed was
exceedingly small and the bosses had intimidated them to such an extent that
no ballots were even cast. In 15 firms, most of them again quite small, the barely
more than one hundred votes registered resulted in a declared tie between Local
574 and the Employers' Advisory Committee as the representative voice of the
workers. Under the rules of the Labor Board election, the Union secured the right
to represent those workers in such deadlocked firms who voted for the General
Drivers' Union and joined its ranks. The employers won the vote in 68 firms, and

---

7. Cannon certainly wrote 'Victory! Settlement Goes Through!', *The Organizer*,
22 August 1934; as well as 'What the Union Means', *The Organizer*, 23 August 1934,
reprinted in Cannon 1958, pp. 92–4. See also 'Workers Will Vote for 574: Ballot to be
Secret – All Out!', *The Organizer*, 23 August 1934; and, for a more general statement on
the Minneapolis events, Herbert Solow, '574's Struggle Has Great Significance for U.S.
Labor', *The Organizer*, 25 August 1934.
8. 'Ballot Shows Two Tickets: Workers Should Get Registry Checks', and 'We Declare
Independence', *The Organizer*, 24 August 1934; 'Instructions for Voters', 'Bosses Draw
Phony Lists ... Union Takes Steps Against Fraud', '6000 Mass at Parade Rally: Workers
Turn Out at 574's Call', and 'What the Elections Mean', *The Organizer*, 25 August 1934;
'Tonight's Meeting Public', and 'Brown Sure 574 Will Win', *The Organizer*, 27 August
1934.

the General Drivers' Union, Local 574 was chosen by a majority of workers at 62 companies. What allowed Local 574 to claim victory was that an absolute majority of votes cast – 724 of 1362, or 53 percent – went for the Union's side of the ballot. Even allowing for the disenfranchisement of many strikers, this vote was also decisive proof that far more than the 309 workers that the Citizens' Alliance had steadfastly claimed to be the total number of employees taking job-action were directly involved in the July–August work-stoppage.

Equally important, among the larger firms the General Drivers' Union was undeniably successful, the claim being that workers voted roughly three to one in favour of Local 574. In the key trucking firms that had always been the target of the union-drive, those located in the Market District which had witnessed violent clashes between pickets and special deputies, police, and National Guardsmen, Local 574 won decisively, claiming 69 percent of the votes cast. Given that the first strike launched in May 1934 had targeted only eleven key firms, Local 574 had accomplished much in four months, coming out of the 'secret-ballot' elections with representation-rights in 77 individual firms. It also had a toehold in the trucking sector in scores of other small firms, where workers affiliated with the Union were now steeled in the solidarity of class-struggle, even if they were a minority in their particular company. All of this was done against a united front of employers as anti-union and anti-communist as any in the land. The General Drivers' Union managed, in addition, to battle a reactionary municipal leader, a viciously-hostile Chief of Police, and a reformist Governor who sugar-coated his willingness to use martial law and the arsenal of state-repression in the interests of property-rights and law and order. Finally, Local 574 also stared the agents of federal mediation down, refusing to blink in the face of a variety of pressures and manoeuvres. Arbitration, and reliance on the Labor Board, which had figured so centrally, and with such disingenuousness, in the May settlement, was decisively displaced. Trade-unionism in Minneapolis could declare its principles victorious.[9]

The teamsters' rebellion, and its many successes, registered forcefully in the consciousness of the Minneapolis working class and its trade-unions. As the *Minneapolis Labor Review* rightly concluded in the immediate aftermath of

---

9. See, for instance, a number of articles in *The Organizer*, including 'Elections Clinch Victory: Market Solid for 574', and '574 Protests Used', 5 September 1934; 'Local 574 Wins Majority: Daily Press Buries Truth'," 12 September 1934. Note that with respect to arbitration, Trotsky would later outline, in his discussion of a transitional programme for class-struggle militants in the unions, how critical it is to fight 'uncompromisingly against any attempt to subordinate the unions to the bourgeois state and bind the proletariat to 'compulsory arbitration' and every other form of police guardianship....' See Trotsky 1973a, pp. 77–8. Note as well Shaun (Jack) Maloney's comments on arbitration in an informal note appended to Specktor 1984 in File 'Miscellaneous Notes and Clippings, 1940s–1980s', Box 4, Maloney Papers, MNHS.

the August settlement: 'Winning of this strike marks the greatest victory in the annals of the local trade union movement.... It has changed Minneapolis from being known as a scab's paradise to being a city of hope for those who toil'. James P. Cannon certainly appreciated this local breakthrough. But he also saw what unfolded in Minneapolis in 1934, especially in the July and August days of what many described as a 'civil war', against a wider backdrop. For him, Minneapolis's meaning reached far beyond the particularities of place. 'In Minneapolis we saw the native militancy of the workers fused with a politically conscious leadership', he later wrote. 'Minneapolis showed how great can be the role of such leadership. It gave great promise for the party founded on correct political principles and fused and united with the mass of American workers. In that combination one can see the power that will conquer the world'. This somewhat visionary understanding of 'Minneapolis and its Meaning' was, however, uniquely connected with a practical recognition of the actual state of working-class political awareness, aspirations, and existing levels of organisation. Unlike the sectarian, ultra-left postures of the Stalinist Communist Party, more than evident in the attacks on the Trotskyist leadership of Local 574 that saw its every move as yet another manifestation of 'permanent counter-revolution', Cannon and his Minneapolis comrades were attuned, on the one hand, to the necessity of militant, determined, struggle, and, on the other, to a 'realistic appraisal of the relation of forces and the limited objectives of the fight'. Yet they were caricatured in attacks coming at them from opposing directions. The Citizens' Alliance strained at every opportunity to depict strikes in the trucking sector as a revolutionary attempt to create Soviet-style socialism in one city. At the same time, advocates of socialism in one country declared Cannon and Co. nothing more than apologists for Olson's pale reformism, defenders of martial law, and misleaders of an instinctively insurrectionary American working class.[10]

Cannon appreciated that what had happened in Minneapolis was highly significant, but that it was also both constrained by the historical context and defined by future tasks:

> The strike was understood to be a preliminary, partial struggle with the objective of establishing the union and compelling the bosses to 'recognize' it. When they got that they stopped and called it a day. The strong union that has emerged from the strike will be able to fight again and to protect its membership in the meantime. The accomplishment is modest enough. But if we want to play an effective part in the labor movement, we must not allow ourselves to forget that the American working class is just beginning to move on the path of the class struggle and, in its great majority, stands yet before the first

---

10. Strang 1935.

task of establishing stable unions. Those who understand and accomplish it prepare the future.

Having spent more than two months away from the National Office of the Communist League of America, immersed in the struggle of Local 574 and its multitude of daily developments, Cannon returned to New York in early September 1934. One of his first public acts was to present an Irving Plaza Sunday-evening lecture on 'The Message of Minneapolis'. Invigorated by his Midwestern sojourn amidst the struggles of a militant working class, Cannon stressed what was unique about the coming together of Trotskyists and teamsters in 1934. Minneapolis, Cannon insisted, revealed a unique dialectic in which the revolutionary leadership of the class-struggle harnessed the militancy of the masses to an exemplary organisation, a resolute will to fight to win, *and* a realistic assessment of the needs of the hour and the limitations of the specific historical context. 'In other places ... strike militancy surged from below and was checked and restrained by the leaders', Cannon wrote, but 'In Minneapolis it was organized and directed by the leaders'. The strike-wave of 1933–4 had often seen strike-leaders blunt the edge of the fight or head it off altogether, preaching reliance on Roosevelt's National Recovery Act. As the Minneapolis struggle unfolded, however, 'the leaders taught the workers to fight for their rights and fought with them'. Yet, 'This spirit of determined struggle was combined at the same time with a realistic appraisal of the relation of forces and the limited objectives of the fight. Without this', Cannon concluded soberly, 'all the preparations and all the militancy of the strikers might well have been wasted and brought the reaction of a crushing defeat'. It was this dialectic of leaders and led that constituted the meaning of Minneapolis.[11]

Cannon, staring the defeat of the Southern textile-workers in the face in the autumn of 1934, contrasted the success of the Minneapolis strikes with the record of limited accomplishment evident elsewhere. Deploring the fatal weakness of trade-union officialdoms that often compromised and prevaricated, the tragedy of 1934 as a national uprising of the working class, Cannon insisted, was that labour's leaders had too-often squandered militant mobilisations. And they did so without having to face the organised resistance of the rank-and-file. Minneapolis, Cannon stressed, was 'the one magnificent exception':

11. The above paragraphs draw on Dobbs 1972, p. 190, quoting *Minneapolis Labor Review*; Cannon 1944, p. 167; Cannon 1934b, p. 4; Walker 1937, pp. 219–20; Dunne and Childs 1934; 'An Interview with the Managing Editor of the Minneapolis Truck Drivers' Strike Bulletin', *The Militant*, 8 September 1934; James P. Cannon, 'The Message of Minneapolis', *The Militant*, 15 September 1934. It is likely Cannon left Minneapolis around 5 September 1934, as did Herbert Solow. See 'Solow Returns to New York', *The Organizer*, 5 September 1934.

There a group of determined militants, armed with the most advanced political conceptions, organized the workers in the trucking industry, led them through three strikes within six months and remain today at the head of the union. It was this fusion of the native militancy of the American workers, common to practically all of the strikes of this year, with a leadership equal to its task that made the strikes of a few thousand workers of a single local union events of national, even international, prominence: a shining example for the whole labor movement.... What miracles will the workers in the great industries be capable of when they forge a leadership of the Minneapolis caliber!

A Minneapolis striker and Committee of 100 member summed the situation up succinctly by drawing on a military metaphor. He recalled decades later that 'The rank-and-file was really the power of the whole movement, but they still needed that leadership to lead them. I don't care how good the army is, without a general they're no good'. And the general in the Minneapolis truckers' strikes was Trotskyism.[12]

---

12. Cannon 1934a, p. 68; Korth 1995, quoting Committee of 100 member, Moe Hork, p. 184. See also, 'The Strike Triumphant', *The Militant*, 25 August 1934.

Chapter Twenty-One

After 1934: the Revenge of Uneven and Combined Development

The *By-Laws of General Drivers, Helpers and Inside Workers Union*, probably drafted and circulated among Local 574's membership in 1935, spoke legions about how a different kind of unionism had been brought into being by the 1934 teamsters' rebellion. The preamble struck decisively against entrenched notions of craft-exclusiveness and class-accommodation:

> The working class whose life depends on the sale of labor and the employing class who live upon the labor of others, confront each other on the industrial field contending for the wealth created by those who toil. The drive for profit dominates the bosses' life. Low wages, long hours, the speed-up are weapons in the hands of the employer under the wage system. Striving always for a greater share of the wealth created by his labor, the worker must depend upon his organized strength. A militant policy backed by united action must be opposed to the program of the boss. The trade unions in the past have failed to fulfill their historic obligation. The masses of the workers are unorganized. The craft form has long been outmoded by gigantic capitalist expansion. Industrial unions are the order of the day. It is the natural right of all labor to own and enjoy the wealth created by it. Organized by industry and prepared for the gruelling daily struggle is the way in which lasting gains can be won by the workers as a class.

Each member of Local 574 pledged to be true, not just to their particular trade-union, but to 'the entire organized labor movement'. The struggles of 1934 had given rise to a 'new unionism', one predicated on promoting 'unity of action of all workers in the class struggle'.[1]

In the immediate aftermath of the final Minneapolis strike-victory in August 1934, Trotskyists and teamsters worked together to build Local 574 into a powerful and democratic union. Traditional American Federation of Labor 'business-union' methods were scrapped, and the executive officers of the Union and its expanded staff of full-time organisers received wages comparable to the going rate for truck-drivers. Union-officials were elected for one-year terms; a vigorous network of shop-stewards, described in Charles Rumford Walker's notes as 'the cream and back-bone of the union', linked the dozens of workplaces in which Local 574 had members; freedom of speech was encouraged within large, twice-monthly meetings; and general membership-assemblies had supreme authority to determine policy and set the course of the Local's activities. The fundamental guiding principle that had animated the 1934 strikes, that all workers 'whose jobs were by any plausible definition related to trucking' must be organised by Local 574, continued, breaking with the ossified 'craft'-sectionalism so central to the Dan Tobin leadership of the International Brotherhood of Teamsters. The Trotskyist leadership of the local – the Dunne brothers, Dobbs, and Skoglund – moved from informal positions of influence won in strikes into the recognised offices of governance within the General Drivers' Union. Local 574 was soon bargaining collectively for the employees of all 166 Employers' Advisory Committee-affiliated firms; eventually, the Union negotiated agreements with some five hundred Minneapolis enterprises. As rank-and-file democracy prevailed within a vibrant and growing *industrial* union, the Trotskyist-led teamsters offered their support to other striking workers in the Twin Cities of Minneapolis-St. Paul, extended non-partisan activity in defence of labour, and broadened the 1934 strike-newspaper, *The Organizer*, into a voice for all workers in the region, *The Northwest Organizer*. Local 574 also established a Federal Workers Section (FWS) to address the needs of the unemployed. Throughout the mid-to-late 1930s, this body developed an effective apparatus to secure relief for those who found themselves out of work, drawing on the union-treasury to supplement what was available from the Welfare Board and other municipal agencies. Walker considered this component of the General Drivers' Union so 'well organized that it amounts practically to [a] closed shop'. Mass demonstrations and constant public pressure raised the relief-rates by 10 percent, before a 1939 campaign of Works Progress Administration (WPA) layoffs and wage-reductions signalled a

---

1. Local No. 574 1935, pp. 1, 3.

new round in the struggles of the unemployed. The Trotskyist-led FWS of Local 574 was active in the resistance, which culminated in a relief-workers' strike, a deadly protest in which one unemployed painter, Emil Bergstrom, was killed. The ostensibly labour-friendly New Deal administration fought back, drawing on the arsenal of legal repression. Three trials ensued. Two-thirds of the one hundred and sixty activists (including Trotskyists Max Geldman and Ed Palmquist of the FWS) indicted for conspiracy to intimidate relief-clients had their charges dismissed, but the persecution unfolding in the courts was a hint of things to come. Nonetheless, in the late 1930s, the future seemed propitious for the Minneapolis revolutionaries heading up the General Drivers' Union and its widening influence. 'All Minnesota labor was not Communized', noted Walker in winding up his study *American City: A Rank-and-File History* with a dig directed at the Citizens' Alliance, but 'the union's prestige grew prodigiously and workers all over the Twin Cities joined in a wave of organization that grew rather than diminished with the passing years'.[2]

As Walker concluded perceptively, this development reached beyond the usual boundaries of trade-unionism. The working class had seized, through its combativity, a capacity to cultivate consciousness of its distinct interests. Minneapolis workers, Walker argued, developed and put their trust in revolutionary leaders who also happened to be decidedly effective in winning what the workers wanted. These leaders showed a capacity for the development of innovative forms of organisation and successful strategies of class-struggle. They also conditioned a climate in which coal-heavers, truck-drivers, seamstresses, and proletarian housewives all began to look 'sceptically [at their] relation to society'. This was the beginning of something new and different. It confirmed, in Walker's view, Trotsky's claim that the most advanced cultural contribution of the working class was its capacity to translate the meaning of its collective productive and reproductive existence into a *politics* of recognized socio-economic differentiation. This registered in Minneapolis in the mid-to-late 1930s in economic ideas, speeches, and songs, in May Day demonstrations, in union-picnics, and in the annual commemorative gatherings held in the market where Local 574's

---

2. The above paragraphs draw on Walker 1937, p. 245; Korth 1995, pp. 162–5; Dobbs 1972, pp. 178–90; Hudson 1935; Tselos 1971, pp. 266–7; Bernstein 1970, pp. 250–1; Sloane 1993, pp. 18–28. There is much on the post-1934 organisation of Local 574 and its Federal Workers Section in various notes and documents in Walker's files. Among the most useful to consult are 'Immediate Release from Publicity Committee, Federal Workers Section, Local 574, Minneapolis', 'Open Meeting on Direct Relief, Friday, June 26, Minneapolis' and 'Organizational Structure 574' in File 'Notes Local 574 and Strike'; 'History of 574: Skoglund', and 'Second Talk with Skoglund' in File 'American City: Miscellaneous Notes'; and File 'Newspaper Clippings: Relief Measures, 1936', Box 1, CRW Papers, MNHS; Walker 1937a, pp. 32–3; Local No. 574 1935[?], p. 15. On the 1939 WPA strikes and trials, see Faue 1991, pp. 156–64; Erickson 1971, pp. 202–14.

martyr, Henry B. Ness, was shot on Bloody Friday, 20 July 1934. Walker's talks with Minneapolis workers confirmed that out of the epic 1934 battles had come a new awareness on the part of working men and women, a way of seeing 'the election of Roosevelt, the events in Spain, the latest campaign by the *Journal* for restoring the declining economy' with great acuteness 'in reference to their own lives'. The working class was beginning to grasp that it had 'its own historic contribution to make to a civilized culture'. In 1934–5, the electorate ousted the Republican mayor of Minneapolis and elected Farmer-Laborite Thomas E. Latimer. Labour followed this statement at the polls with bitterly fought strikes of automobile-mechanics, sweatshop knitting-mill operatives, iron-workers, and building tradesmen. Such class-struggles, inevitably, indicated Latimer's vacillating and compromising nature, not unlike how earlier truckers' conflicts had exposed Olson's 'progressive' Achilles Heel of 'law-and-order' accommodation to capitalist forces. If the Trotskyist leadership of the teamsters did not state clearly enough the need for a workers' party to displace the cross-class alliance of Farmer-Laborism, it had, nonetheless, helped to take Minneapolis workers to the point that this political juxtaposition could, at least, be instructively posed. As this happened, Local 574 and its leaders were rightly acknowledged by the labour-movement for their ongoing support and 'tireless and valuable assistance'. George Dimitri Tselos, arguably the most diligent researcher who has explored the history of Minneapolis labour-organising in the 1930s, explained this achievement in one succinct sentence: 'The Trotskyists were even more successful than they had hoped'.[3]

This necessarily drew a backlash. But the antiquated ideologues of the Citizens' Alliance were a spent force, and in no position, acting on their own dissipated bourgeois-initiative, to stem the tide of working-class advance. Largely defeated in 1934, the Citizens' Alliance regrouped, defined itself more narrowly to serve business-needs in the obviously highly contested field of 'employee relations' and, on 17 December 1936, adopted a new name, the Associated Industries of Minneapolis. Mainstays of the ostensibly new body were former Alliance leader George K. Belden and A.C. Hubbard, head of a company-formed organization known as the Mutual Truck Owners and Drivers' Associated Independent Union. One reflection of the extent to which the Citizens' Alliance successor, the Associated Industries, was destined to be an ineffective opponent of the Trotskyist-led Minneapolis IBT local was the politics of extremism with which it quickly came to be associated. Belden, for instance, was rumoured to have raised a war-chest of

---

3. Walker 1937, pp. 239–40, 245–58; Tselos 1971, quote at p. 356, but, for the full history of this period, see pp. 322–417. Note as well the more general discussion in Le Blanc 2010.

$35,000, to be used to pay for the assassination of three of the leaders of the 1934 insurgency. However far-fetched such schemes may have seemed, they were certainly believable in Minneapolis trade-union circles, which, as will be discussed below, had direct experience of violence and thuggery of all kinds, including a 1937 killing of a Teamster official. Belden also attended invitation-only meetings of William Dudley Pelley's fascistic Silver Legion of America, popularly-known as the Silver Shirts, on 29 July and 2 August 1938. Company-union boss Hubbard was on the Silver Legion's mailing list, as were a number of other prominent anti-communist Minnesota employers and political figures. Pelley's 'Field Marshall', Roy Zachary, aimed to recruit thousands of new members to the Silver Shirts in Minneapolis, and he took particular aim at the infamous General Drivers' Union, calling for vigilante bands to conduct an open war on militant labour. '[T]he time for the ballot was passed', Zachary pontificated angrily, 'and the only way to deal with the unions was to raid their headquarters and destroy them'. Claims that the Silver Shirts were infiltrating Minneapolis unions were made, and Zachary singled out the so-called 'Communist racketeers' of the teamsters' local for vitriolic abuse.

Guided by discussions with Trotsky, Cannon, Shachtman, and Ray Dunne were aware of the need to meet this threat of fascist attack head-on, but to do so in ways that would not isolate the ranks of armed proletarian resistance in either the Socialist Workers Party or the General Drivers' Union. This would inevitably subject these bodies to police-attack and frame-ups. Nonetheless, Trotskyist militants, through their Minneapolis union-voice the *Northwest Organizer* – successor to the daily strike-bulletin of 1934 – mobilised a Union Defense Guard (UDG) composed of six hundred men, most of whom had guns at home that they used for hunting. Formed in August 1938, the UDG was composed largely of militants in the Minneapolis General Drivers' Union, many of whom had military experience as 'former sharpshooters, machine gunners, [and] tank operators', but was constituted as an independent entity. It was open to active union-members across the spectrum of organised labor in Minneapolis, the sole consideration being commitment to the defence of trade-unions. Small squads of five, with a designated captain, facilitated rapid mobilisation in the event of an emergency. The UDG raised its own funds through sponsoring dances and other social events, and was a democratic body in which all decisions were arrived at by a majority-vote preceded by full and open discussion among the membership. Those trade-unions contributing guards did so with full knowledge of the UDG's activities, agreeing that their members could and should participate and help in the recruiting process. Ray Rainbolt was elected commander of the Union Defense Guard. A 1934 strike-veteran, Trotskyist, and Sioux Nation member, Rainbolt, who had experience as a First World-War soldier, drilled the Guard and oversaw target-shooting practice. During these manoeuvres, lectures and discussions were conducted on the tactics to be used in fighting fascist opponents of the labour-movement. Rainbolt and the UDG assembled in public to thwart gatherings of the Silver Shirts and, while pitched battles never developed, by late October 1938, the demoralised supporters of Pelley and Zachary had withdrawn from Minneapolis. Beldon and the Associated Industries backtracked. They retreated into a strategy of defeating Olson's successor, Farmer-Labor Governor Elmer Benson, supporting the Republican Party's Harold E. Stassen in his successful electoral bid to take-over Minnesota's government in 1938–9. Stassen would soon contribute to important legislation that redefined labour-capital relations in ways applauded by Minnesota employers; but the Trotskyist-led General Drivers' Union, while reeling from this blow, was hardly felled by it.[4]

Ironically enough, it was Dan Tobin and the IBT officialdom that fought back most effectively, their project complemented by a parallel attack launched by an array of powerful state-officials and agencies, at the local, regional, and national levels. Stassen would also be a factor in this unfolding attack, but he played a supplementary role, not a central one. Tobin and the IBT first manoeuvred to have Bill Brown removed from the Teamsters' Joint Council, a delegated seat he had held, to good effect, for a number of years. John Geary, Tobin's St. Paul flunky, tried to scoop the ice and taxi-drivers out of the ranks of the Minneapolis truckers' union and shift them into other American Federation of Labor organisations. Finally, having given Local 574 nothing in the way of material support during the protracted struggles and strikes of 1934, the IBT hierarchy nevertheless demanded *per capita* dues-payments on the vastly expanded membership of the Minneapolis teamsters, which was itself the outcome of the Trotskyist-led organising campaigns. Attempting to placate Tobin and requesting a reasonable amount of time to raise funds so as to be able to clear the local's backlogged debt to the national office, Local 574 correspondents received no reply. Then, on 15 April 1935, the IBT union-tops lowered the bureaucratic boom: Local 574's Charter was revoked, its delegates to the Teamsters Joint Council unseated, and Tobin went on a rampage against Secretary-Treasurer Farrell Dobbs, attacking him and other Minneapolis union-leaders for 'acting in defiance of the principles of the trade union movement . . . pulling strikes for racketeering and propaganda purposes'. Refusing to conduct any further communications with the outlawed Local,

---

4. Dobbs 1975, pp. 142–6; Millikan, 2001, especially pp. 242–3, 336–8, 344–57; Allen 2012; 'Mr Belden and the Silver Shirts', *Northwest Organizer*, 11 August 1938; 'Murder of 544 Men Planned, Is Charge', *Northwest Organizer*, 30 June 1938; '544 Answers Fascist Thugs with Union Defense Guard', *Northwest Organizer*, 8 September 1938; Harry DeBoer, 'Ray Rainbolt: Veteran Teamster Leader', *The Militant*, 19 May 1978; Trotsky 1973a, pp. 139–41. Rainbolt's affiliation with the organised Trotskyist movement would prove shortlived, lasting until January 1938.

Tobin declared emphatically, 'Better have no International Union than one composed of organizations such as Local 574'. Soon, the IBT constitution would be amended to 'bar communists from membership'. An officially-sanctioned Teamsters 'Local 500' was set up, led by Tobin strongmen from Chicago and Detroit and Patrick J. Corcoran, a conservative but somewhat malleable trade-unionist active in the Minneapolis Milk Drivers' Union and the local Central Labor Union. Farrell Dobbs reportedly mocked Tobin's man in St. Paul, IBT Vice-President John Geary, insisting that revoking the credentials of Local 574 was going to do the International Brotherhood no good. '[Y]ou have got the charter', Dobbs snorted in derision, 'but we have got the men'. Dobbs would later claim that barely fifty teamsters joined the newly-established rival Minneapolis IBT union backed by Tobin, and he and the established leadership of 574 hammered away at Teamster officialdom for undermining the collective strength of the militant truckers and their local working-class supporters. As Carlos Hudson explained in *The Nation*, this internecine union-warfare spilled over into the larger Minneapolis labour-movement. 'Actually there exist today two trade-union movements, each with its own headquarters and press', Hudson wrote.[5]

What followed was not pretty. IBT goons cajoled truckers to join the Tobin local, and threatened Trotskyists and their supporters. Ray Dunne and George Frosig, a vice-president of Local 574, were beaten with blackjacks. Dobbs had to have a bodyguard accompany him throughout his union-rounds and for much of his leisure-time. He even went so far as to carry a gun in a particularly tense period, and Dobbs's wife, Marvel Scholl, was convinced that the Trotskyist union-leader was stalked and their house broken into. Not surprisingly, Local 574 looked to the emerging Congress of Industrial Organizations to admit it to affiliation, but John L. Lewis and other CIO leaders, trying to get the fledgling industrial-union movement off the ground, had no appetite, at this time, for an all-out war with Tobin and the IBT. Supported by the local Minneapolis Central Labor Union (CLU), the General Drivers' Union was, nonetheless, the object of much attention from the national and state-level American Federation of Labor, none of it positive. George W. Lawson, Secretary of the Minnesota State Federation of Labor, informed the Executive Council of the AFL, in October 1935,

5. Dobbs 1972, p. 103; Dobbs 1973, pp. 60–1, 76; Galenson 1960, especially pp. 478–81; Smemo 2011, pp. 45–9; Hudson 1935; 'A False Rumor', *Northwest Organizer*, 8 May 1935. Tobin's acts, as well as a pattern of such behaviour in locales other than Minneapolis extending into the 1940s, prompted a vigorous attack on him by Trotskyist leader, James P. Cannon. See 'The Mad Dog of the Labor Movement' in Cannon 1958, pp. 153–8; Strang 1935. Skoglund interviewed by Halstead, 14 May 1955, Typescript, pp. 32–44, Box 2, Riehle Papers, MNHS suggests that Corcoran, originally a business-agent in the Milk Drivers' Union, at first led the goons on Tobin's behalf, but was later neutralised by Local 574's leadership, which pressured his constituency to the point that Corcoran was forced to work with the militants of the General Drivers' Union.

that the situation in Minneapolis was menacing and the CLU was in danger of 'being controlled by dual organizations and Communists'. The AFL promptly dispatched a trusted agent, Meyer Lewis, to break up the dreaded Trotskyist-led drivers' local on the grounds that it was creating 'a single labor organization that will take in everyone and anyone, regardless of jurisdictional bounds'. Lewis, known as a crack AFL 'organiser', found it especially troubling that the General Drivers' Union had 'made a great deal of progress, due to its ability to appeal to unfortunate individuals who are victims of the economic conditions of the present day'. Unaware of the timidity at the pinnacle of the CIO, the AFL hierarchy was undoubtedly fearful that it would lose Local 574 and its thousands of members to the rising alternative national labour-organisation. This eventually prodded the conservative union-officialdom to compromise, but not before Trotskyists and militant teamsters had been subjected to the ugliness of gangsterism and Red-baiting.

Local 574 and its Trotskyist leadership, in part by design and in part because of necessity, engaged in a principled and relentless campaign to remain affiliated with the AFL and the IBT, wearing Tobin down to the point that a reconstituted General Drivers' Union, amalgamating Locals 500 and 574, was readmitted to the national American Federation of Labor-affiliated union in the summer of 1936. With the membership of Local 574 voting six-to-one to rejoin the IBT, Brown, Skoglund, and Dobbs joined with Corcoran and three other Tobin supporters on the Executive Board of a renamed Local 544. Dobbs and his allies used their influence to extend union-organisation of all trucking-associated workers beyond Minneapolis and throughout Minnesota and the Northwest. Even though they were in the minority on the Union's Executive Board, the Trotskyist-radical alliance that had forged the successful organisation of Minneapolis teamsters in 1934 felt that, once reintegrated into the AFL, they could displace Tobin's thugs and push their IBT counterparts on the Executive in the direction of an aggressive and widening campaign of interstate unionisation. Dobbs, the Dunnes, Skoglund, and Brown were convinced that if those figures from Local 500 whom Tobin had placed in power continued to follow the defeatist and abstentionist policies of an outdated craft-unionism, these opponents would inevitably be repudiated by the rank-and-file. They were confident that their ideas and genuine commitment to trade-unionism would either neutralise such anti-communist Tobin loyalists or, more likely, win them over.

This was exactly what happened. Corcoran and others on the Local 500 Executive came to see their Trotskyist counterparts in the Union as dedicated to advancing the cause of the labour-movement. The Trotskyist-teamster alliance was poised for another significant breakthrough. Corcoran and Dobbs nursed into being the North Central District Drivers' Council (NCDDC). Established in

January 1937, it quickly gained ground over the course of the next 18 months, bringing together, organising, and improving the conditions and wages of over-the-road teamsters. Late in 1938, the IBT signed a contract with a group of inter-state trucking firms covering 250,000 drivers and affiliated workers in eleven states. Irving Bernstein concluded that 'the leaders of 574, with the imagination and drive they had evidenced during the strikes [of 1934], expanded the organi-zation of over-the-road drivers in the Upper Mississippi Valley as the foundation for mass unionism on a semi-industrial basis'.[6]

Dobbs, with Skoglund as a key figure behind the scenes, was the inspiration of this development, mobilising the interstate truckers whom Tobin and the Inter-national Brotherhood had long disdained, just as they had shunned the coal-yard workers in February 1934 and the inside market-workers in July 1934. As most commentators recognise, the legacy of Dobbs was his insight that while orga-nising long-distance truckers was crucial, the strategic issue in doing this was developing *'centralized area-wide bargaining designed to establish uniform wages, hours, and working conditions'*. But how to do this when the trucking workforce was dispersed and necessarily moving from one locale to another (in which organised labour might have highly different relations of strength and weak-ness with regard to specific employers) was challenging. Dobbs pioneered the technique of 'leapfrogging', through which the organised and militant teamster-base in Minneapolis was used to force employers from other centres needing to truck goods into the city to concede union-wages and conditions in their distant operations. As particular core metropolitan hubs were brought under union-control, such as Chicago and Kansas City, they were then used to leverage other cities, like Omaha and St. Louis, where recalcitrant employers held out against organised labour. Not only did the IBT expand, but this technique was also used to create networks of labour solidarity, as teamster-power proved indispensable in supporting unionisation-campaigns among relatively low-skilled workers in laundering, baking, clerking and other traditionally difficult-to-organise occu-pational sectors. Having proven that an industrial union encompassing all of

---

6. For CLU support of Local 574 in the face of pressure from the IBT, see 'Minneapo-lis Central Labor Union Supports Drivers Local 574', *Northwest Organizer*, 16 April 1935; 'Central Labor Union Votes Unanimously to Back Recommendation of Special Commit-tee to Restore 574's Charter', *Northwest Organizer*, 8 May 1935; 'Local 574 Under Fire Again', *New Militant*, 4 May 1935; and on Local 574's struggle to retain its American Fed-eration of Labor connections see Hudson 1935. On Tobin's antagonism in 1935, followed by concessions and the reconciliation/merger of the warring teamster-locals in Minne-apolis, see 'Union of 574–500 Thrills Workers', *Minneapolis Labor Review*, 17 July 1936; Dobbs 1973; Dobbs 1975, especially pp. 37–46; Dobbs 1972, p. 13; Walker 1937, pp. 258–66; Smemo 2011, pp. 49–67; Tselos 1971, pp. 356–89; Galenson 1960, pp. 478–82; Bernstein 1970, pp. 250–2.

those connected to trucking could, indeed, be successfully established in Min-neapolis, Dobbs and the Trotskyist leadership then deployed that strength to expand labour's power. Ironically, once this process was set in motion, it actually *reversed* the organisational direction that had initiated the Minneapolis cam-paign. In that mobilisation, the drivers were, of course, central, but at the same time, the Dunnes and Skoglund had insisted that coal-yard labour and inside market-workers were pivotal to the success of the union-drive. In the Dobbs-led campaign to organise over-the-road truckers, however, the fulcrum of which was the established militancy of union-labour in Minneapolis, the maxim became: 'Once you have the road men, you can get the local cartage, and once you have the local cartage, you can get anyone you want'. And so teamster-unionism spread throughout the Northwest, and in its wake labour-organisation in other sectors advanced as well.[7]

One of Dobbs's most ardent disciples in this interstate organising crusade was a young Detroit militant, James Riddle Hoffa. He would, over the years, lose his youthful idealism as he climbed the corrupt ladder of union-bureaucracy, but he never forgot what he learned from the Minneapolis Trotskyists, whom he admired greatly. 'Vince Dunne was my friend', he told two scholars decades later, his voice breaking with emotion. It was Dobbs, however, from whom Hoffa learned the most. If Hoffa distanced himself from Dobbs's 'political philosophy' and his 'economic ideology', he understood well the contribution that the Left Oppositionist had made. '[T]hat man had a vision that was enormously benefi-cial to the labor movement', Hoffa insisted, acknowledging that Dobbs 'was the master architect of the Teamsters' over-the-road operation'. Hoffa thus made a close study of the organising methods pioneered by Dobbs and those whom he directed in the union-campaigns of the later 1930s, noting in admiration, 'I was studying at the knee of a master'. By 1940, when Farrell Dobbs left his union-work to take up a full-time position with the Trotskyist Socialist Workers Party, estab-lished in January 1938, the face of Teamster unionism in the American Northwest had been transformed. Left Oppositionists like Dobbs, the Dunnes, and Skoglund were, at least in part, responsible for 'bringing about a fundamental change in the structure' of the International Brotherhood of Teamsters, whose ranks exploded

---

7. For a succinct discussion of the strategy and legacy of Dobbs see James and Dinerstein 1965, pp. 96–101. Dobbs's account appears in *Teamster Power* (Dobbs 1973). Shaun (Jack) Maloney insists that the original idea of organising over-the-road truck-ers was Skoglund's. Maloney interviewed by Salerno, Rachleff, and Seaverson, 1–4 April 1988, Transcript, p. 88, Maloney Biographical File, 1911–99, Box 2, Riehle Papers, MNHS; Maloney's note appended to Dobbs to Maloney, 28 June 1955, in Box 3, Maloney Papers, MNHS. See also Skoglund's interview with Halstead, 15 May 1955, Typescript, pp. 39–51, Box 2, Riehle Papers, MNHS.

from seventy-five thousand in the year before the Minneapolis truckers' strikes to over four hundred thousand in 1939.[8]

These historic advances had not been achieved easily. A high price was paid for such working-class victories. Pat Corcoran was murdered in November 1937; Bill Brown was killed by a deluded friend and trade-unionist six months later. Vincent Raymond Dunne and his brothers were in and out of both courts and hospitals, Ray receiving three broken ribs at the hands of police, as well as a jail-term of 15 days, for his picket-line support of striking Strutwear hosiery-workers in 1935. The Communist Party, having ostensibly jettisoned its Third Period sectarianism, thus abandoning its position that separate 'Red unions' were called for, nevertheless remained steadfast in its slanders of and relentless attacks upon the Trotskyist leadership of Minneapolis truckers. It echoed Dan Tobin in the insistence that the Dunne brothers and Dobbs had hijacked Local 574 and were leading it in ways that were anathema to genuine trade-union principles. When Corcoran was murdered, a CIO publication in which mainstream Communists had a hand declared brazenly that, 'His assassination was the logical outcome of the gangsterism and racketeering fostered in the Minneapolis labor movement by the Dunne-Brown-Dobbs leadership of 544 and their allies among the worst right wing section of the A.F. of L. fakerdom'. A 'Volunteer Committee to Drive Gangsters from Minneapolis', called on the labour-movement to get rid of Ray Dunne and his two Trotskyist brothers. While Corcoran's killers were never identified and brought to justice, a coroner's inquest ascertained that the wild Stalinist-originated allegations targeting the Dunnes and Dobbs as responsible for the killing were without a whiff of substantiation. Indeed, the ostensible 'Volunteer Committee' collapsed almost as soon as Communist sources cited its existence, many of its trade-union signatories repudiating their support and claiming that it had been obtained under false pretences. If an educated guess had to be made as to who had orchestrated the murder of Pat Corcoran, it would necessarily have pointed in the direction of a trio of Tobin goons – Eddie and Al Fiorotto and Joe Bellini – expelled from Local 544 as the Corcoron-Dobbs coalition solidified. Few in the labour-movement, however, wanted to air this dirty linen in public, preferring, instead, to suggest that employer-aligned enemies of teamster-unionism were responsible for the execution of the local IBT official.[9]

8. Dobbs 1972, p. 13; James and James 1965, pp. 102–14; Russell 2001, pp. 36–40; Hoffa 1970, pp. 105–11; Schlesinger Jr. 1978, pp. 139–40. Teamster membership-figures and other relevant comment appear in Leiter 1957, pp. 39–42.

9. Dobbs 1973, p. 142; Tselos 1971, pp. 438–41; Galenson 1960, p. 483; Hudson 1938; Ben Holstrom, 'Organizer for 544 Slain in Loop Bar', *Minneapolis Star Journal*, 27 July 1945. On Vincent Ray Dunne and the Strutwear strike, see Hudson 1935, and for the strike's nature and significance, see Faue 1991, pp. 216–22. For Skoglund's view that Corcoran's murder had been carried out by mobsters originally affiliated with Tobin, see Skoglund's interview with Halstead, 14 May 1955, Typescript, p. 34, Box 2, Riehle Papers, MNHS.

Against this background of terror and ugliness, it is not surprising that the significant advances registered by the Trotskyist leadership of the Minneapolis teamsters also masked some lapses in principled revolutionary practice. This constituted something of a revenge of uneven and combined development. For the decisive success of the revolutionary leadership of the Minneapolis teamsters owed much to the extent to which the transport-sector was overripe for industrial-union organising in 1934. This reality, as well as the fact that the ossified leadership of the IBT was essentially moribund and relatively easily marginalised, allowed a small corps of dedicated and visionary Trotskyists to vault over the arduous process of struggling against the labour officialdom. They did this by posing a series of transitional demands that linked the everyday needs of the working class to the ultimate, but clearly distanced and developing, project of displacing capitalism and constituting a proletarian order. The revolutionary Trotskyist leadership of Local 574 found itself, almost from the beginning of the Minneapolis trucking upheavals, in *de facto* control of the teamsters' mobilising initiative. With the victories of 1934, secured against employers whose conception of labour-relations was rooted in the nineteenth century, this advance-guard moved forcefully into the public and acknowledged leadership of local trade-union forces.

Under Dobbs's leadership, and within a context in which a Tobin-led anti-communist assault on Local 574 was relentless and brutalising, Trotskyists found themselves more and more aligned with progressive, but decidedly mainstream, labour-officials. Dobbs and his comrades obviously needed both contact with and support from such figures in order to pursue the organisation of over-the-road drivers. To draw elements like Pat Corcoran towards them, the Minneapolis Trotskyist leadership of the General Drivers' Union may well have soft-peddled their revolutionary politics in the interests of promoting honest, effective, militant trade-unionism. Then, as the organising drive reached beyond Minneapolis in the later 1930s, this orientation deepened. Rather than utilising ongoing struggles to build militant class-struggle caucuses in the distant locales where interstate organising campaigns were being launched, the Minneapolis trade-union leaders tended, instead, to forge relationships with established IBT union-leaderships. This was the easiest path to follow, and it produced tangible short-term gains. The result, however, was that a rank-and-file, infused with radical currents, steeled in struggle, and trusting of a revolutionary leadership, did not cohere as it had in Minneapolis in 1934. This was the only force that could actually serve as an effective brake on the anti-communism and conservatism inherent in the mainstream trade-union bureaucracy, a politics of hegemonic containment also central to the ideology of state-agencies in the field of labour-relations and intrinsic to the legalism of the courts and consolidating collective-bargaining system. Each step in this seemingly benign direction solidified the labour-movement credentials of Trotskyist union-leaders like Dobbs, but moved them further away from their capacity to promote the revolutionary politics of Left Oppositionists. Correctly calling for 'All workers into the unions and all unions into the struggle', Dobbs and the Trotskyist leadership of the eleven-state campaign moved, gradually and largely imperceptibly, into closer and closer relations with their non-revolutionary counterparts in the International Brotherhood of Teamsters and further away from the initiatives that would have been necessary to develop militant class-struggle currents within the international union, extending their influence in lasting as opposed to episodic ways. The Trotskyists in the Northwest IBT thus retained much that was militant and good, but they also sacrificed something of what they had been when they entered into the leadership of the General Drivers' Union. Their success, bred in part by the uneven and combined developments of class-formation and class-struggle on the eve of 1934, pushed them, ironically, in directions that muted their accomplishments and, arguably, contributed to a later defeat.

Even Tobin eventually found it within himself to cooperate with the Trotskyists at the head of the teamsters' rebellion, albeit only for a limited time. The Teamster boss appointed Dobbs an international organiser and actually tried to entice him to stay on with the IBT rather than leave the Union to become a full-time functionary in the Socialist Workers Party, offering him the first available vice-presidency if he would continue organising truckers. But at this point, the oppositional thrust of this SWP-affiliated union-leadership was losing some of the sharp edge of crucial principles.

It was not so much that what the Trotskyist advance-guard in the Minneapolis labour-movement did was wrong; rather it was what it did not do clearly enough that proved troubling. Channelling their energies into consolidating 'united fronts' from above with various trade-union leaders, and concentrating their activity on trade-union questions alone, Minneapolis's Trotskyists lost an important part of the revolutionary momentum that could have cultivated radicalising rank-and-file caucuses through which revolutionary politics would have been extended among insurgent workers. This, alone, could have saved and preserved the victory of 1934. But it was not to be.[10]

---

10. Witwer 2003, p. 69; and for detail on Dobbs's connections, in the later 1930s, to powerful local Teamster officials in Chicago, Kansas City, Detroit, and elsewhere, many of them quite close to Tobin, see James and James 1965, pp. 90–6. For the critical perspective developed in this paragraph, see also Knox 1998b. Knox's insights, forged in the revolutionary perspective that the Spartacist League brought to its trade-union work in the early 1970s, represents a decisive continuity with the positions elaborated in Trotsky's *Transitional Programme*, published in 1938, but drawing on fundamental Marxist principles that reach back to *The Communist Manifesto* of 1848.

Trotsky himself saw the danger of this development quite early, in June 1940.[11] In discussions with Cannon, Dobbs, founding Left Oppositionist Antoinette Konikow, and Socialist Workers Party organisers and activists such as Sam Gordon and Harold Robins, Trotsky pointed out that the distinctions between trade-union policies and Bolshevik policies had taken on a new salience as the organising drive in trucking achieved certain successes:

> We are in a bloc with so-called progressives – not only fakers but honest rank-and-file. Yes, they are honest and progressive but from time to time they vote for Roosevelt – once in four years. This is decisive. You propose a trade union policy, not a Bolshevik policy. Bolshevik policies begin outside the trade unions. The worker is an honest trade unionist but far from Bolshevik politics. The honest militant can develop but it is not identical with being a Bolshevik. You are afraid to become compromised in the eyes of the Roosevelt

---

11. Following Trotsky's critique, and in keeping with the focus in this book on teamster union-organising, the discussion below puts stress on the industrial organising led by Dobbs in this era, focusing on the Socialist Workers Party's trade-union work. But it is entirely possible that a similar critique could be posed against the Minneapolis Trotskyist leadership in the political realm, where illusions were, perhaps, cultivated in the Farmer-Labor Party. Upon Olson's death from cancer in 1936, his role in the state's attempts to suppress the 1934 strikes, for instance, was papered over in the *Northwest Organizer*, successor to the 1934 daily strike-bulletin. Olson, who had decided to run for the United States Senate and ceded his leadership of the Minnesota Farmer-Labor Party to Elmer Benson, was celebrated as 'an unswerving champion of the underprivileged and exploited'. See 'Whole State Mourns as Floyd B. Olson Passes', *Northwest Organizer*, 26 August 1936. In the 1936 election, the *Northwest Organizer* offered qualified support to the Farmer-Labor Party that translated into an unambiguous call to vote the FLP slate into office, since it was the only 'political party to which labor unions are directly affiliated'. One editorial stressed that the Farmer-Labor Party of Minnesota had written into its platform 'planks that promise the workers aid in organizing and state protection in strikes'. This constituted, apparently, grounds demanding 'the support of every worker'. But the workers of Minneapolis had seen something of the state's 'protection' of strikes in Olson's use of the National Guard in 1934. Furthermore, the compromising nature of the 1936 elections in Minnesota was complicated by the pressure to elect Roosevelt, which caused Democratic Party candidates in the state to cede the liberal vote to the FLP, dropping out of the race so that Benson could vie for the governor's position against a Republican adversary. The *Northwest Organizer* urged voters to 'Keep Faith with Floyd [Olson]', and rallied behind FLP candidates. To be sure, it also warned of the need for all trade-unionists to 'vote for the party that promises support to labor, but ... also be on the alert to see that promises made to labor are carried out to the letter'. By 1938, with the Farmer-Labor Party in power for two years, the *Northwest Organizer* was more critical. See 'Labor Set Aside by Clique in F–L Convention', 3 March 1938. On all of this, see Valelly 1989, p. 170; Gieske 1979, p. 229; 'Olson and the Party', *Northwest Organizer*, 26 August 1936; 'The Worker Vote', *Northwest Organizer*, 17 September 1936; 'The Labor Vote', *Northwest Organizer*, 15 October 1936; 'Official FLP State Ticket', and 'FLP Mass Rally in Union Hall on October 29', *Northwest Organizer*, 22 October 1936; 'The Coming Election' and 'Drivers Will Fall in with Joint Council', *Northwest Organizer*, 29 October 1936; 'The New Regime', *Northwest Organizer*, 19 November 1936. This question deserves further detailed study, but see Smemo 2011, pp. 79–89.

trade unionists. They on the other hand are not worried in the slightest about being compromised by voting for Roosevelt against you. We are afraid of being compromised. If you are afraid, you lose your independence and become half-Rooseveltian.

In reading the official organ of extending the mobilisation of truckers beyond Minneapolis, the Left Oppositionist-founded and controlled *Northwest Organizer*, Trotsky, who had praise for some of the paper's qualities, noted that this loss of revolutionary independence was evident in its pages. 'I notice that in the *Northwest Organizer* this is true', Trotsky stated unequivocally. 'The danger – a terrible danger – is adaptation to the pro-Rooseveltian trade unionists . . . we must have a policy'. The lack of such a policy might not be catastrophic in peacetime, Trotsky conceded, but in wartime, he stressed prophetically, 'They can smash us. Our policy is too much for pro-Rooseveltian trade unionists'.[12]

Trotsky's warning that repression might, indeed, be coming, and that it would be wielded as war conditioned a climate of xenophobic patriotism easily turned against revolutionaries in the trade-union movement, was soon proven all-too correct. Indeed, the 'privileges' of backwardness that Vincent Ray Dunne and Carl Skoglund had turned to such good purpose in the years 1931–4, when the uneven and combined development of class-relations in Minneapolis allowed them certain openings, had turned into their opposite by 1940–3. In the earlier context, Trotskyists had moved dramatically ahead out of positions of 'backwardness'. They organised the unorganised, challenged the hegemony of an ossified craft-unionism, and effectively mobilised a reservoir of untapped militancy to defeat a particular kind of capitalist interest, organised in the Citizens' Alliance but clearly living on the avails of an atavistic ideology of crude and totalising class-rule. Basic victories achieved, a new day had dawned. Minneapolis Trotskyists, now an advancing vanguard that had vaulted over 'backwardness' into a position of relative 'forwardness', found themselves facing the very reverse of what uneven and combined development had conditioned on the eve of 1934. There were now no 'privileges' of 'backwardness'. The ruling order saw clearly

---

12. Trotsky 1969, p. 273. See also Knox 1998b, pp. 104–14. That the *Northwest Organizer* was, indeed, controlled by the Trotskyists, although formally under the auspices of the Minneapolis-based Teamsters' Joint Council was evident in 1941, as Local 574 was engaged in battle with Tobin's IBT bureaucracy. The Joint Council apparently 'sold' the *Northwest Organizer* to the Dunne brothers for one dollar. See James and James 1965, p. 107. For background on this, see also Jack Maloney to David Riehle, n.d relating to how the *Northwest Organizer* was founded as the *Organizer* was wound down, its subscription list going to Cramer's *Minneapolis Labor Review*. With the Tobin bureaucracy attacking Local 574, Ray Dunne, Skoglund, and Cannon determined that the new press would have to be established separate from IBT officialdom, with an editor not affiliated with the General Drivers' Union. See File 'Teamsters Local 23–574, 1919–1934', Box 1, Riehle Papers, MNHS.

the danger posed by a class-struggle current in the unions that was not only guided by a revolutionary programme, but that had managed to implement portions of it in ways that were obviously threatening to lift the lid that kept labour-relations from boiling over into volatile struggles.

This registered most acutely, if obliquely, in the balance-sheet of economic and political gains: as the Trotskyist-teamster alliance marched forward aggressively and successfully, organising the trucking industry as it had never been unionised before, it did so with fewer returns for revolutionary politics. One problem, a component of the shifting class-terrain of uneven and combined development, was that the forces of opposition were no longer occupying defensive outposts that a revolutionary leadership could strike obviously effective blows against. Tobin and other AFL leaders were, for the moment at least, different in 1938–41 than they had been in 1928–31, when they were entirely and obviously out-of-touch with the organisational needs of the hour. They had been forced – and not only by the Dunnes, Dobbs, and Skoglund, but also by John L. Lewis and others in the Congress of Industrial Organizations – to accept the inevitable forward march of the respectable labour-movement into industrial organizing. The breed of Citizens' Alliance employers, reactionary paternalists who staked their all on the absolute repudiation of trade-unions and the decisive subordination of 'their' workers, had not, to be sure, entirely died out, but it was most definitely on its last, atrophied legs. As Dobbs mobilised interstate truckers, the most sustained and serious resistance came from a group of die-hard bosses in Omaha, Nebraska, organised in an anti-union Business Men's Association that bore a striking resemblance to the Citizens' Alliance.[13]

The more the Left Opposition within the IBT succeeded, then, the more it seemed to be boxed into making accommodations with forces that had, in any case, adapted to a more liberal, if often bureaucratised, stand. Unable to shift political gears sufficiently deftly and utilise the all-too-often meagre resources at their disposal to develop left-caucuses and mass support within the union-locals that they were promoting and working with, the Minneapolis Trotskyists thus found it increasingly difficult to differentiate themselves from 'progressive', but defiantly non-revolutionary, figures within established trade-union official-doms. The localised base of the Minneapolis revolutionary teamster-leadership, as important as it had become, was unable to actually reach into the kind of broad regional and national development that would have been necessary for

---

13. Knox 1998b, p. 110; James and James 1965, p. 101; Dobbs 1973, pp. 198–232. On Tobin's more conciliatory approach to Dobbs and the Trotskyist initiative to organise over-the-road truckers in this period, see 'Dan Tobin Confers on N.W. Problems', *Northwest Organizer*, 27 January 1938; 'President Tobin on the Over-the-Road Strategy', *Northwest Organizer*, 11 May 1939.

the Trotskyists among the teamsters to have been protected from the kind of attack that was entirely possible in the changed climate of Roosevelt's third, wartime, term as President. The ultimate turning of the tables of uneven and combined development meant that, by the early 1940s, the Trotskyist success-story of 1934 was, in the realm of trade-unionism, undeniable, at the same time that, in terms of building a revolutionary presence within the working class, it was about to be reversed.

The Minneapolis Trotskyists, and indeed the SWP nationally, were soon singled out for very rough treatment, not only by the pro-Roosevelt trade-unionists, but also by state-agencies dedicated to promulgating a 'Red-scare'. As Tobin and other trade-union tops signed on to the Roosevelt call for increased dedication in the impending war-effort, the Minneapolis Trotskyists waged a fight against such 'preparedness' on their home-turf of Minneapolis, successfully turning back the patriotic tide within the Central Labor Union. Yet they had not adequately nurtured the basis of a wider support for their anti-war policies within the broader regional teamsters' organising campaign. The consequence was that they could not pursue a mobilisation around their politics of opposition to war, and Dobbs could do little more, in 1940, than resign his leading role in the IBT and shift his primary activity into the Socialist Workers Party. Tobin was able to seize the momentum.

On 29 June 1940, with the United States increasingly aware that its formal entry into war was likely, President Roosevelt signed what would come to be known as the Smith Act into law. The bill, promoted by Congressman Howard K. Smith of Virginia, was debated at hearings in 1939. It was originally designated HR 5138, and referred to as 'Crime to Promote the Overthrow of Government'; later it was dubbed the Alien Registration Bill. Whatever its name, the Act, in all its components, was a peacetime anti-sedition law that criminalised even advocacy of disloyalty and the overthrow of the government. As such, it marked a decisive repudiation of the protection of free speech, making it unlawful to organise or belong to any party or group that put forward positions of this kind or to print, publish, or distribute such seditious views. The Smith Act, widely reputed to be directed at the ostensible threats that communism and fascism posed to the United States government, was, in fact, first used against 29 individuals active in the Trotskyist Socialist Workers Party (SWP) and the Minneapolis Teamsters. After raiding SWP offices, indictments were secured against important figures in the national leadership, such as James P. Cannon, Albert Goldman, Felix Morrow, and the former Secretary-Treasurer of Local 574/544, Farrell Dobbs; key organisers and officials from the Minneapolis Teamsters' union, including V.R. Dunne, his brothers Miles and Grant, Carl Skoglund, and non-SWPer Kelly Postal; and members of the Federal Workers Section and Union Defense Guard (also known as the Workers' Defense League) of Local 544. The allegations were based on both the Smith Act and an antiquated 1860s statute that had criminalized overt acts of rebellion, which the establishment of the UDG was claimed to be, leaving those under indictment facing two charges. Count I, drawing on the Civil War-era prohibition of insurrection, alleged that the defendants had been engaged in an 'unlawful conspiracy' to forcefully destroy the government of the United States. Count II, building on the Smith Act, alleged a further 'unlawful conspiracy' that, through its use of advice, advocacy, and publications, promoted the idea that overturning the United States government by force was desirable. In the end, of the 23 individuals brought to trial, 5 were acquitted on both counts. No convictions were secured on Count 1, but 18 of the defendants were judged guilty on the Smith Act-inspired second count. On 8 December 1941, they were sentenced to prison-terms ranging from 12 months plus a day to 16 months.[14]

An appeal in 1943 proved fruitless, and the Communist Party, through its leader Earl Browder, provided evidence that was used to uphold the convictions of the hated 'Trotskyites'. Former Communists like Dorothy Healey, Joseph R. Starobin, and John Gates later repented that when the Smith Act was turned on their own leadership in 1949, they were forced to conclude that, 'We had reaped the harvest of the seeds we ourselves had sown'. Healey was more forthcoming in acknowledging the ugly role Stalinism had played when the state first turned its apparatus of repression on the reviled Left Oppositionists and their teamster-supporters:

> The Smith Act, passed by Congress during the 'little Red Scare' of 1940, made it a crime to conspire to advocate the overthrow of the government by force or violence. It was first used against the Trotskyists in Minnesota during the war, and the Communists, to our discredit, not only refused to come to their support but actually organized to prevent other people from supporting them. It was a position which would all too soon be thrown back in our faces as we attempted to gather support for our own leaders on trial.

---

14. As will be noted in citation of Trotskyist sources from the 1940s and liberal journalism from the same period, the first Smith Act prosecutions have, indeed, been written about extensively. But scholarly comment on this early 1940s use of the Smith Act is overshadowed by discussion of the later, 1949 Smith Act trials targeting the leadership of the Communist Party. For brief scholarly comment on the SWP/Minneapolis case see Schrecker 1999, p. 104; Steele 1999, pp. 129–41; and Belknap 1977, pp. 38–41. Legal historian Stanley I. Kutler writes that the Smith Act prosecution of the Communist Party leadership was 'the most blatant political trial in American history', but he alludes to the previous use of the legislation against those he refers to as 'a group of Minneapolis Trotskyites who headed a local Teamster union' almost in passing, and clearly without any exploration of the nature of this earlier political prosecution. See Kutler 1982, pp. 152–3.

With the *Daily Worker* proclaiming that 'The leaders of the Trotskyist organization which operates under the false name of the "Socialist Workers Party" deserve no more support from labor... than do the Nazis who camouflage their Party under the false name of "National Socialist Workers Party"', the Stalinists provided a series of exhibits which, whatever the dubious content, helped seal the fate of the convicted revolutionaries at their appeal-trial. Pointing to the effectiveness of the Trotskyists in Minneapolis labour-circles, this legally-orchestrated exercise in odious political assassination concluded on a note of slander and vilification:

> Being a sabotage organization, concentrating upon the disruption of the war effort, the Trotskyites do not require a large organization. On the contrary, a smaller group is more easily controlled and efficient for their purposes.... The dangerous efficiency of this small group is shown by the fact that it succeeded in obtaining aid for the convicted Minneapolis traitors from the AFL and CIO unions representing 1,000,000 workers.... This core of saboteurs is small, but its underground influence is large.

Willing to align themselves with the coercive anti-communism of the state as long as the victims were reviled revolutionary dissidents of the Left Opposition, Browder and the Communist Party advised the prosecution to jail the Trotskyist leadership as a means to disable a repugnant, totalitarian threat: 'Remove the core', the Stalinists urged, 'and you wreck a strong fascist weapon in America'.[15]

Tobin's role in the persecution, prosecution, and jailing of Trotskyists and teamsters in 1941–3 preceded this Communist Party initiative. In a detailed, recent examination of the events that culminated in the conviction of Cannon, Ray Dunne, Dobbs, and others, Donna T. Haverty-Stacke has suggested the need to revise somewhat an older interpretation, promoted by liberal scholars, a contemporary report of the American Civil Liberties Union, and Socialist Workers Party publications of the time, all of which emphasised the IBT leader's central place in the Smith Act prosecutions of the early 1940s. A well-known partisan of the Democrats, Tobin had headed the campaign to win support among organised workers for Roosevelt's re-election to a third term as President. The IBT leader was also associated with Roosevelt's policies of aid to Britain before events necessitated American entry into the Second World-War. Conventional wisdom has it that Tobin essentially called on Roosevelt, who owed the powerful IBT President a political debt, to use his authority to squash an increasingly irksome and influential foe within the Teamsters. In appealing to the President of

---

15. Jaffe 1975, pp. 50–2, 174; Gates 1958, p. 127; Healey and Isserman 1990, pp. 114–15; Starobin 1972, pp. 46–7. For one account that accents the nature and extent of Stalinist attacks on the Trotskyist-led Local 574 in the later 1930s, see Dobbs 1975, especially pp. 85–126.

the United States, Tobin ostensibly solicited Roosevelt's intervention in an internal union-matter, and unleashed an investigation of the SWP and its Minneapolis trade-unionists that led to charges of sedition and the eventual incarceration of most of the Trotskyists who had proven such a thorn in Tobin's bureaucratic side since the 1934 truckers' strikes.[16]

Haverty-Stacke presents a nuanced argument, in which more weight is placed on the emergence of a small, but vocal anti-Trotskyist opposition within Local 544,[17] the independent role of the Federal Bureau of Investigation in interpreting widely Roosevelt's licensing of the need for broader domestic 'political intelligence', and the Justice Department's eagerness, under Acting Attorney-General Francis Biddle, to wage an anti-communist witch-hunt, thus downplaying somewhat the role of the IBT head, Daniel Tobin. No doubt, the state had an appetite for repression in 1940–1, although Biddle would later claim (possibly self-servingly) that he authorised a criminal case against the Dunne brothers and others under the Smith Act 'so that the law would be tested at the threshold, and taken to the Supreme Court, where it would, I believed, be knocked out'. Whatever the differences evident in the state-apparatus, Tobin had, indeed, been quick to jump into the mix. Acting on an inflammatory assessment of the SWP he received from the Justice Department, Tobin editorialised in the May 1941 issue of the *Minnesota Teamster* that Trotskyism was dangerously revolutionary;

---

16. For scholarly arguments of this kind see James and James 1965, pp. 102–9; James and James 1966; Pahl 1967; Bernstein 1970, p. 781; Galenson 1960, p. 483; Goldstein 1978, p. 252; O'Neill 1982, p. 44; Alexander 1991, pp. 820–4. Understandably, SWP publications were quite adamant that, in the words of Albert Goldman, the indictment of the Trotskyists was 'an attempt by President Roosevelt to pay political debts to Daniel J. Tobin'. See Goldman 1942, p. 6; Goldman 1944, pp. 87–92; Novack 1941a, pp. 7–18; Novack 1941b, p. 7; Cannon 1973, pp. 103, 183–5; Cannon 1975.

17. There had always been small groups opposing the Trotskyist leadership of the Minneapolis teamsters. See Dobbs 1977, pp. 80–5; Dobbs 1975, pp. 146–8. Shaun (Jack) Maloney, undated note appended to 'The Organizer: The Secret of Local 574', Box 3, Riehle Papers, MNHS, calls attention to the anti-leadership 'petty politics' that broke out in the Women's Auxiliary, supposedly necessitating its disbanding. As noted in James and James 1965, p. 103, dissidents in Local 574 petitioned the courts in 1938 to put the local union in receivership. With the Dobbs-led campaign to organise over-the-road truckers such a success, this local animosity to Trotskyist leadership did not even draw much support from Tobin, the International Brotherhood, or the Teamsters' Joint Council. But the judge hearing the case against the Dunnes was sufficiently hostile to Trotskyism that he fined the brothers $6,000 for alleged misuse of union-funds and removed Carl Skoglund as president of the General Drivers' Union on the grounds that he was not a citizen of the United States, which put him in violation of the IBT constitution. Haverty-Stacke makes much of the so-called Committee of 99–100 in the 1940s, especially James Bartlett. There appears little evidence that Bartlett, an IBT official in the Warehouse Employees' Union, and a disgruntled ex-member of the SWP who had spent little time in the movement, actually represented a substantial opposition within the General Drivers' Union, with which he had no direct connection. See Dobbs, 1977, pp. 102–6, 115, 122, 199–201, 226, 231, 251, which refers to Bartlett as 'the government's chief stool pigeon in the sedition trial'.

it needed to be banned from the IBT as the equivalent of communism. Tobin had, in fact, been schooled in 'elementary Marxism' by his AFL needle-trades counterpart, David Dubinsky. The International Ladies Garment Workers head opined that 'The Socialist Workers Party is in reality more communistic than the Communist Party.... Trotsky, when serving under Lenin in Russia was even more radical and communistic and hateful of our form of government than either Lenin or Stalin'. Brought up to speed on Trotskyism's vile revolutionism, Tobin warned those SWPers in IBT ranks to cut their Party ties or face expulsion. While he may have been prodded to act by complainants among Minneapolis Local 544 members (at least one of whom had been in the employ of the FBI), such anti-leadership elements had long been present, albeit ineffectively, in the General Drivers' Union. In any case, Tobin did communicate with the White House on 12 June 1941, warning Roosevelt that the Trotskyist-controlled Minneapolis union was extending its organisational reach throughout the Northwest. The timing of Tobin's communication was critical. For Local 544, according to the IBT patriarch, was supposedly in a position to disrupt commerce and exploit a possible war-crisis in its efforts to establish a socialist state.

All of this unfolded *before* the indictments against Trotskyists and Local 544 members were served. Indeed, as has been shown in earlier chapters, Tobin's anti-communist and bureaucratically officious assault on the Left Opposition leadership of the Minneapolis truckers had been evident even *before* the mass strikes of 1934. While there were times when Tobin and the AFL/IBT trade-union tops stepped back from their campaign of obstruction and vilification, for reasons that were entirely opportunistic and adapted to their own pragmatic assessment of a particular situation, the overall orientation of the most conservative elements of the labour-bureaucracy toward the Trotskyist teamster-leadership of Local 574/544 in the years 1933–43 was one of unambiguous, Red-baiting resistance.[18] This consistent antagonism reared its ugly head at the same time as the militant Minneapolis teamster-leadership was preparing to strike 370 trucking firms in the early 1940s. Tobin, committed to the American Federation of Labor's pro-war 'no strike pledge', summoned Local 544 representatives to Washington, where they were treated, in Vincent Ray Dunne's words, to humiliation and insult. Faced with Tobin's tyrannical and non-negotiable insistence that they were about to be put under receivership, Dunne and others opted to jump ship from the AFL/IBT and be chartered by the CIO's United Construction Workers'

18. Charles Rumford Walker assembled sufficient evidence of Tobin's anti-communist attacks on the leadership of Local 574/544 to convince him that this was a prime example of how 'the bosses find spokesmen in the workers' camp'. See 'Fight With Tobin and Teamsters Joint Council', 11-page typescript, in File 'Minnesota Miscellaneous Notes (2)', and untitled typescript, File 'American City: Incomplete Notes and Articles', Box 1, CRW Papers, MNHS.

Organizing Committee, a move they confirmed was acceptable to the rival industrial-union centre, which extended a more helpful hand than it had in the mid-
1930s. The membership of Local 544 quickly approved a resolution breaking from
Tobin's Teamsters and taking a charter from the CIO. Local 544 of the AFL/IBT
became Local 544 of the Motor Transport and Allied Workers' Industrial Union.
John L. Lewis sent the Minneapolis teamsters his personal congratulations, wir-
ing the new CIO local and stating his hopes that in joining the burgeoning ranks
of the industrial-union movement it would mount 'an intensive drive to bring all
truck drivers in the United States into a free and democratic organization'. Tobin,
who had not seen this act of defiance and disaffiliation coming, then turned to
Roosevelt, and the prosecution of the Trotskyists followed, its groundwork having been laid by other parties. Outflanked, Tobin had not been outgunned.[19]

The war that ensued over the leadership of Local 544 pitted Tobin and his AFL
officialdom against the militants and Trotskyist leadership instrumental in building Minneapolis trucking unionism from the bottom up. IBT 'organisers' from
Detroit, led by Jimmy Hoffa, flooded into the Twin Cities. Hoffa later recalled,
'I took enough men with me to make sure we could handle it'. Seizing the local
IBT office, Hoffa and his 'crack guys' also took to the streets. They were not above
using physical violence to intimidate drivers who cast in their lot with the CIO
union. A local newspaper reported that scores of Michigan-licensed cars packed
with 'labor huskies' cruised the warehouse districts of Minneapolis, accosting
those sporting Local 544 buttons. 'Very determined and very tough', these Tobin
heavies used their fists to good effect, and this 'caravan mop-up persuaded' many
drivers and helpers to 'sign up with the new AFL set-up'. Hoffa would later boast
that in the Minneapolis war waged against the Trotskyists, 'We won every battle'.
Farrell Dobbs thought Hoffa's terse assessment a tad immodest:

> Now it is true that Hoffa was among the IBT goon squads that Tobin sent
> into Minneapolis.... [H]e...says in effect...he whipped us.... [But] he was
> helped by the Minneapolis Police Department, the courts...the mayor, the

---

19. In the above, I draw on Haverty-Stacke forthcoming, which Professor Haverty-
Stacke graciously allowed me to read in unpublished form. Haverty-Stacke's stress on
the independent role of the Justice Department and the FBI, and her analytical move
away from Tobin's leading place in the prosecution of the Trotskyists, is given some
credence in James and James 1965, p. 109, where it is noted that in the mid-1960s, Dobbs,
with whom they had obviously talked, disputed 'the view of the ACLU and other liberal groups that the Justice Department's moves were political payoffs from Roosevelt
to Tobin'. Instead, Dobbs appeared to believe that 'the war and general class issues
motivated the government's attack on the Trotskyites'. See also Dobbs 1977, especially
pp. 137–8. The Dubinsky quote on Trotskyism also appears in James and James 1965,
p. 104. Biddle's statement appears in Biddle 1962, p. 151. See, as well, Witwer 2003, p. 137;
Evans (ed.) 1975, pp. 136–9; Galenson 1960, pp. 483–5, quoting the Lewis telegram. See
also *Northwest Organizer*, 3 July 1941; 11 September 1941.

governor and an antilabor law that had been rigged and put through by the Republican governor of the state, and by the Federal Bureau of Investigation, the United States Department of Justice and Franklin Delano Roosevelt, who then happened to be President of the United States.

As Dobbs concluded sardonically, 'you got to admit Hoffa had just a little help, didn't he'.[20]

A full account of the defeat of the Minneapolis Trotskyists in the early 1940s confirms Dobbs's assessment. Tobin's victory was a foregone conclusion. Even though he controlled only a phantom Local 544, the IBT oligarch had the powerful force of the state behind him. More important than the physical intimidation in the streets were the court-battles over who controlled Local 544's property, union-books, membership-rolls, and dues. These endless legal wrangles, which the deep-pocketed IBT could sustain, weakened Local 544 and tore apart the once powerful Minneapolis Brotherhood of Teamsters. Publication and distribution of the voice of Minneapolis truckers, the *Northwest Organizer*, was stopped at Tobin's request, the judge issuing the injunction declaring that 'the International ought to have stepped in sooner'. As Hoffa's henchmen patrolled the streets and alleyways of the Minneapolis Market District, a lawyer acting on behalf of the AFL and Teamster headquarters, Joe Padway, and a West Coast teamster-import, 'Dutch' Woxberg, met with civic officials – the District Attorney, the Chief of Police, and the Captain of Detectives – who promised them 'all protection and cooperation possible'. Tobin also had the backing of Republican Minnesota Governor Harold Stassen, who first defeated the Farmer-Labor incumbent, Elmer Benson, in a 1938 gubernatorial contest. Stassen supported the IBT over its CIO disaffiliate, prompting a Minneapolis state conciliator to intervene when the National Labor Relations Board refused to act on a request from the CIO to even the playing field, Tobin having imposed a national boycott on all trucks driven by the Trotskyist-controlled Local 544. The result was that the Minnesota Department of Labor certified the IBT-affiliated Local 544 as the bargaining agent for Minneapolis teamsters, a decisive blow struck against Trotskyism and militant industrial unionism. Employers applauded the decision, and collective agreements signed with the AFL Teamsters bore all the trappings of 'sweetheart contracts', concessions now being the order of the day under Tobin. In contrast, when the CIO's Local 544 attempted to negotiate with employers, it was routinely blocked by a variety of state-edicts and tribunals. The entire machinery of the conservative AFL trade-union hierarchy was mobilised to shore up Tobin's anti-Trotskyist campaign. Within the Central Labor Union, a

20. Galenson 1960, p. 484; James and James 1965, pp. 105–8; Sloane 1993, pp. 28–31, with Hoffa and Dobbs quoted on p. 30, referencing a television news-interview from 1974.

'loyalty'-inquisition unfolded, while the annual Minnesota Federation of Labor Convention voted to bar Trotskyists from AFL unions.

Whether the 'Red-scare' that descended on Minneapolis trade-union militants in the early 1940s originated with Tobin, Roosevelt, J. Edgar Hoover of the FBI, or Acting and then Attorney-General Francis Biddle, is, in some senses, beside the point. The undeniable reality was that it was an all-encompassing assault on the revolutionary leadership of what was a highly successful but non-revolutionary body, the Minneapolis-based General Drivers' Union, that had its origins in the depths of the Great Depression. Even if the Citizens' Alliance had been bested, and the trucking bosses and other employers chastened in their anti-communism and recalcitrance to trade-unionism, businessmen in Minneapolis hardly warmed to the militant leadership that had made relations with unionised workers less than ideal, in their view. They relished the invigorated repression that was visited upon their class-adversaries and that, with America's entry into the Second World-War pending, gave no sign of letting up. The 'Red-scare' of the early 1940s, much more intense and broad-ranging in its utilisation of the full weight of the state and its apparatus of attack and incarceration than anything experienced by the Minneapolis militants in the heat of the battles of 1934, reversed the tide of class-struggle in the Northwest. In this worsening climate, the Trotskyists heading up the original Local 574 decided to throw in the towel, dissolving the Union and instructing union-members, much as it would gall them, to join Tobin's Teamsters. Further victimisation was pointless, and in order to preserve something of the gains of 1934, it was necessary for all in the trucking industry to be in one organisation, from which, in the future, the fight against Tobin might possibly be waged again. It was all too much for Grant Dunne, who could not face the combined prospects of world-war and the incessant attacks on the kind of trade-unionism he had contributed so much to building. Despondent and spiralling downward in depression, Dunne killed himself on 4 October 1941, three weeks before he was to be tried alongside his brothers, fellow trade-unionists, and other SWPers for seditious conspiracy.[21]

As the trial of Local 544's Trotskyist leadership proceeded through October and November of 1941, it provided ample opportunity for Tobin's forces to Red-bait even moderate supporters of Dobbs and the Dunne brothers. With the conviction of so many Trotskyists who had contributed to the making of Minneapolis

21. On Padway, Woxberg, and other relevant details, see James and James 1965, pp. 102–8. The assault on the Trotskyist leadership of Local 574/544 is detailed at length in Dobbs 1977 and there is extensive archival material in File 'Newspaper Clippings: Local 544 Election, 1941', and File 'Newspaper Clippings, 10–20 June 1941', Box 3, and 'Scrapbook: May–December 1941', Box 7, Socialist Workers Party (Minnesota Section) Papers, Minnesota Historical Society, St. Paul, Minnesota (hereafter SWP Papers, MNHS). On Grant Dunne, see Farrell Dobbs, 'Funeral Address', *Northwest Organizer*, 9 October 1941.

teamster-unionism, a lethal blow was delivered to the now nationally famous militant workers and their identifiably revolutionary leadership. Even if most liberal opinion complained of the legal victimisation of the Minneapolis Trotskyists and teamsters, writers like F.O. Matthiessen promoting the rational and sceptical view that charges against Vincent Ray Dunne and others were based on flimsy evidence orchestrated so that a specific group could be 'railroaded to jail because of its uncompromising activities on behalf of labor', this mattered very little in the hothouse-atmosphere of intensified patriotism evident in December 1941. The Smith Act defendants would undoubtedly have gone to jail whatever the circumstances, so powerful were those forces arrayed against them, but it did not help their cause that they were sentenced to jail on charges of conspiring against the interests of the state a mere day after the Japanese bombed Pearl Harbor. In this climate, vengeance against anti-capitalist revolutionaries was a *fait accompli*.[22]

Local 544 President Kelly Postal, for instance, had managed to win an acquittal in the 1941 seditious-conspiracy prosecution. He was promptly charged and convicted of embezzlement because he refused to turn over dues and union-property to Tobin's team. Receiving the exceedingly stiff sentence of five years' imprisonment, Postal was, nonetheless, released after serving less than a year. The state bowed to a non-partisan labour-defence campaign launched by an SWP-initiated body to advocate on behalf of the Smith Act defendants, the New York-based Civil Rights Defense Committee (CRDC). It was headed by the philosophically-inclined SWPer, George Novack, and drew to its cause distinguished novelists such as James T. Farrell and John Dos Passos, the anarchist Carlo Tresca, ACLU head Roger Baldwin, and the authoritative voice of African-American radicalism W.E.B. Du Bois. Thousands of workers signed petitions calling for Postal's release, and the mobilisation elicited the support of famous class-war prisoner Warren K. Billings; the Minnesota branch of the National Association for the Advancement of Colored People; and A.J. Muste's Fellowship of Reconciliation. Small victories such as Postal's release were, then, flickers of light in a very dark time of defeat and repression. With the IBT secure in its stranglehold over Local 544, there was little that the experienced Trotskyist leadership could do, even upon release from prison. Carl Skoglund, for instance, was blacklisted from the trucking industry by Tobin, and wherever he found work, the job-site was immediately picketed by Teamsters. Lacking citizenship-papers and hounded incessantly by the Immigration Service, which wanted nothing more than to deport Skoglund as an 'undesirable alien', the Swedish revolutionary who had played such a decisive role in the 1934 strikes was eventually driven

---

22. Matthiesson 1948, p. 87; I.F. Stone, 'The G-String Conspiracy', *The Nation*, 26 July 1941.

from Minneapolis, forced to work in the SWP's summer camp in New Jersey. By the end of the Second World-War, little Trotskyist presence was left in the critically important unionised trucking industry of the Northwest.[23] The 'privileges' of uneven and combined development's 'backwardness' were definitely over, the possibilities of a seemingly distant past apparently closed down.

---

23. The demise outlined in the above paragraphs is chronicled in Dobbs 1977, which has much on Skoglund's plight, and more briefly in Alexander 1991, pp. 774–5, 818–24; Galenson 1960, pp. 484–6; Le Blanc 1999, p. 95; Lawson 1955, p. 123. Aside from his Smith Act conviction, Skoglund lived under threat of deportation for much of the 1950s. See James and James 1965, p. 110. Extensive comment on Skoglund can be found in a variety of sources in files in Box 2, Riehle Papers, MNHS; Skoglund Centenary Committee 1984. On the CRDC, see James T. Farrell, 'The Story Behind Kelly Postal's Frame-up', in Civil Rights Defense Committee, *Help Free Kelly Postal*, undated leaflet, File '1934 Teamsters Strike', Box 2, Maloney Papers, MNHS; Wald 1978, pp. 94–102; and the rich collection of material in File 'Civil Rights Defense Committee, 1941–1944', Box 1, SWP Papers, MNHS, including George Novack, 'Report of a Visit to Kelly Postal, Stillwater Prison', three-page typescript. Extensive coverage of the original Smith Act trial, and the civil-rights defence-campaign, can be found in *The Industrial Organizer*, 16 October 1941–16 May 1942, successor to the original 1934 daily strike-bulletin, *The Organizer*. The trial and its issues, including the defence-campaign and the respective roles of the Roosevelt administration, Tobin and the IBT bureaucracy, the FBI, the Attorney-General, the Communist Party, and the increasingly fractured labour-movement, are deserving of a fuller study. Both Donna Haverty-Stacke and Joe Allen have been researching this subject and book-length studies are promised. An exceedingly detailed collection of relevant documents can be found in the 'Scrapbooks' covering the 1941–3 sedition trials in Box 7 and the Files 'Newspaper Clippings', dated from 10 June to 17 December 1941, and 'Newspaper Clippings: Local 544 Election, 1941', Box 3, SWP Papers, MNHS. See also Daniel Eastman, 'The Minneapolis "Sedition" Trial', *New Republic*, 20 October 1941; and Editorial. 'The Issues at Minneapolis', *The Nation*, 13 December 1941.

Chapter Twenty-Two
Conclusion: the Meaning of Minneapolis

Was it all for nothing? Had the victories of Trotskyists and teamsters, so exhilarating in 1934, been vanquished? It is all-too easy, in a period of relative labour-quietude and working-class defeat, to regard the Minneapolis events described in this book as separated from our own times by an unbridgeable historical gulf. Yet 1934, as a profound demonstration of working-class self activity *and* revolutionary leadership, is a remarkable articulation of what can be accomplished in periods that appear decidedly bleak.

Too often, we conceive the times we live in as the most constrained, limiting, and enervating imaginable – it is easy to resign oneself to inactivity and sigh that today and the days that reach before us truly are 'the worst of times'. We see the barriers to advancing the interests of the working class and its allies as insurmountable. And, to be sure, if we scrutinise the current moment of economic restructuring that inhibits the formation and radicalisation of working-class organisations, if we look seriously at the generalised retreat of political mobilisations of dissent and the decline of the Left, and if we take judicious measure of the prospects for radical, working-class led social change – if we do, indeed, do all of this with a sober and realistic mindset – it is difficult not to conclude that the prospects for the kind of advances registered in Minneapolis in 1934 are slim.

This is, arguably, not the lesson to be drawn from consideration of what happened when Trotskyists and teamsters came together decades ago. Let us think through how we might view the Minneapolis truckers' strikes of 1934 in 2013, if we could actually shed all the ideological blinders and baggage that blinds us and weighs us down in terms of our capacities to appreciate that struggles for social change, justice, and equality – which trade-unionism at its best has always advocated and exemplified – can, indeed, be won, and that workers are a powerful force capable of seizing victories in these spheres, if only they combine together to demand a new and better world.[1]

Denials, I: that was then, this is now

A powerful arsenal of denial has been built up around the common-sense notion that victories like those achieved in Minneapolis in 1934 are simply not possible in the present day, because that was then and this is now. The historical gulf separating the past and the present is judged so wide and so all-determining that the gains of another era are alleged to be impossible in the entirely new setting of our present. This argument has many dimensions, but some of its most potent include assertions that: 1) the economic context in the current time is so depressingly bad that aggressive struggles for human betterment can not be waged successfully; 2) the complexities of contemporary life are such that the old simplicities, including the crucial importance of class-inequality as a fundamental and recognised division, no longer have the salience they once did; and 3) trade-unions as vehicles, not only of class-protest, but of wider social struggles aiming to advance humanity, are compromised by their narrowness as agents of economistic collective bargaining, to the point that they are counterproductive, and a stress on their significance and utility in the struggles of the present is thus misguided. Looking at the context in which the Minneapolis struggles of 1934 unfolded allows us a much-needed comparative perspective. It suggests that claims that we cannot successfully resist the challenges of our time are overstated and defeatist.

First, it would be difficult to imagine an economic context more brutally depressing than that of 1929–32, when the United States economy spiralled downward, resulting in sky-rocketing unemployment, widespread destitution, and a marked decline of working-class struggle. This only gave signs of lifting in 1933–4, after years of worsening material conditions that left the labour-movement emaciated and seemingly powerless to fight back. However bad today's overall economic climate may be, its constraints can hardly be regarded as more limiting than those of the early years of the Great Depression, when the seeds of the

---

1. For a similar kind of argument posed at a more general level, see Eagleton 2011.

Minneapolis truckers' revolt were planted and carefully nurtured. Even in the toughest of times, then, steps can be taken that will prove foundational in the struggle for social change, especially if they are consciously understood as part of a protracted process of fighting for improvement.

Second, while the shifts in the make-up of society and the nature of everyday life associated with the last seventy to eighty years have, indeed, brought into being many new complexities, they have by no means altered the single most basic feature of modern capitalist societies: the undeniable reality that the great social gulf separating the truly rich and powerful from the masses of people has not narrowed, let alone been transformed decisively. Whatever the changes that have taken place in the nature of productive occupations and other dimensions of the world of work and human social relations, these developments have done nothing to reconfigure the essential character of class-power – who has it and who does not – that actually determine what it is possible for anyone to do or not do in contemporary America. To be sure, we are now aware of a whole range of issues that relate to and intersect with class that are pivotally important in making individuals what they are, including race, gender, sexual orientation, age, and many other matters. In addition, there is no doubt that the fabric of working-class life has been altered by an intensification of individualism, which means that the working class in advanced capitalist society is different now than it was in the 1880s or the 1930s. Political consciousness, as well as class-identity, has, indeed, changed under the pressures of consumerism and the apparent hegemony of acquisitive individualism. There is no denying that it is, consequently, difficult to build the kind of insurgent working-class mobilisation that rocked Minneapolis in 1934.

As true as this may be, it is, nonetheless, critically important to recognise that it was never easy to bring working-class resentment to a political boil. While the challenges of our times are considerable, then, they are by no means insurmountable. Nor are they necessarily more daunting than the hurdles past advocates of class-struggle had to leap to land on their feet in the ongoing minefield of organising oppositions of various kinds. Indeed, it may be possible that roadblocks to the cultivation of solidarity that once existed in some areas could well be less restrictive now than they once were. It is possible to argue, for instance, that in spite of the destructive persistence of racism, sexism, national chauvinisms, and other divisions, all of these fragmentary forces, whatever their current debilitating impact, are, in actuality, less virulent in their contemporary forms than they were in previous times. Racism, for instance, certainly does remain a pernicious influence undermining human solidarities in modern-day life, and there is no denying its capacity to disfigure struggles that have inclusiveness, democracy, social justice, and equality as their aim. But we also live in an age quite different to the post-Reconstruction era of Gilded Age America, or even 1919, at which point labour-struggles were routinely compromised by the existence of a *de facto* Jim Crow social order. Claims that globalisation, the rise of the knowledge-based economy, and the broad shift to the dominance of more precarious kinds of labour have made working-class organisation more difficult and less likely to succeed can not be entirely dismissed. But globalisation, in some senses, is as old as Marco Polo and Columbus. Undoubtedly intensified in importance in the post-1945 years of widening capitalist integration, in which the financial order institutionalised in the Bretton Woods system has gone through various refinements, globalisation is an ever-present reality, a backdrop against which class-struggles and material transformations take place.

The suggestion that an arresting set of developments associated with this ostensibly and fundamentally 'new' capitalist order make it impossible to organise new sectors of the working class in new kinds of ways is surely wrong-headed. Globalisation, while undoubtedly erecting 'walls' inhibiting class-mobilisations, has also torn down many previously intimidating structures that have long contained voices and acts of resistance. New enthusiasms, fresh insights, and revived optimism can, perhaps, be gleaned as the potential of igniting rebellious mobilisations emerges out of newly combative sectors. We are never at the end of social evolution, and Karl Marx's old mole, revolution, while burrowing so deeply that it seems to have disappeared, may well remain thoroughgoing and methodical, obscured from view as it journeys through a historical purgatory. Out of sight, and out of mind, it can 'leap from its seat' and reclaim its right to recognition, reminding all concerned that denial of its subversive capacity is a dangerous illusion. 'In great upheavals, analogies fly like shrapnel', writes Mike Davis in the midst of what he suggests were 'the electrifying protests of 2011'. He found 'the on-going Arab Spring, the "hot" Iberian and Hellenic summers, and the "occupied" fall in the United States' comparable to the *anni mirabiles* of 1848, 1905, 1968, and 1989. 'Well grubbed, old mole', Marx might well comment from his grave.[2]

We are not used to thinking of *our times* in terms of revolutionary upheavals. What happens to us is long removed from 1789, 1848, or 1917. There are no *revolutionary teamsters*!! Nor did there appear to be any such political beings worth worrying about in Minneapolis during the fall and winter of 1933–4, either, or at least none that ruling authority treated very seriously. What role, in 2013, might new upheavals play? Are rebellions in far distant places able to stimulate uprisings in unexpected quarters, including places close to home, where class and other struggles have been written off as unlikely in the extreme? As E.P. Thompson

---

2. Marx 1968, p. 171; Davis 2011, pp. 5–6.

could write, in 1963, 'Causes which were lost in England might, in Asia or Africa, yet be won'. Davis points presciently, almost half-a-century later, to the pow-der-keg of the Far East, with its revolutionary history and claims to socialised property-forms newly-coloured by the broad brush of the world capitalist market and its transformative powers. 'Two hundred million Chinese factory workers, miners, and construction labourers are the most dangerous class on the planet', Davis notes, concluding that, '[t]heir full awakening from the bubble, may yet determine whether or not a socialist Earth is possible'.[3] Globalisation, in this context, may well be a two-edged sword, and capitalism, which has lived long and lucratively by its cuts, might now be wounded, possibly fatally, by them as well. As the Earth is moved by acts of resistance and uprisings of the downtrod-den and the dispossessed, we are freed to recognise that the distance separat-ing Athens, New York, Shenzhen, and São Paulo has been shrinking in the last decades. This may make it more likely that we can lessen the gulf separating Minneapolis in 1934 and our own times.

The collapse of the economy in 1929 and the difficulties that had to be sur-mounted to organise the previously unorganised workers whom conventional craft-unionism considered beyond the reach of labour's cause, posed challenges just as inhibiting as the many ways in which working-class self-activity seems thwarted today. To be sure, the advances registered when industrial unionism replaced craft-unionism as the wave of the future in the mid-1930s can not be replicated exactly in our own times. A new kind of trade-unionism, orienting itself to more explicitly *political* agendas and aligned more directly with other social movements, might well be where a new breakthrough will take place. Dif-ferent sections of the workforce may assume unanticipated leading roles. All of this will, of course, take time to work itself out, just as the industrial versus craft-unionism contest within the history of the working class reached from the begin-ning stages of the Knights of Labor in 1869, through the radical challenge of One Big Unionism and the Industrial Workers of the World in the era of First World-War class-struggle upheavals, and into the 1930s establishment of the Congress of Industrial Organizations (CIO), when mass-production trade-unionism was finally firmly consolidated in the United States labour-movement.

Change, of course, does happen. It complicates things. But there are also fun-damental continuities, and insights to be gained by looking at the ways in which resistance developed in the past. However different the world we live in now is from what existed in the past, this does not override the basic, determined, and overtly material reality of class-relations under capitalism. An exploited majority still confronts an exploiting minority. Power remains concentrated in the hands

---

3. Thompson 1964, p. 13; Davis 2011, p. 15.

of the very few. This is precisely the message that resonates in the – admittedly all-too loosely populist – language of 2011's Occupy movement: 'We are the 99 percent!' Ultimately, class-inequality forms an undeniable foundation affecting all aspects of what constitutes human engagement in the modern world. This is as true today as it was in 1934.

Third, the argument that trade-unions are little more than bloated, bureaucratised bodies, outmoded guild-like institutions protecting the interests of the well-heeled, governed by antiquated ways of thinking and exaggerated expectations of what constitutes reasonable demands on the part of labour, is wide-ranging. This claim, which undermines the attractiveness of trade-unionism at the very point that such working-class organisations are under fierce attack, has become something of a rallying cry, not only of the right-wing, but also for segments of the progressive milieu that think of themselves as left-leaning. Trade-union bashing is the order of the day. It has become a staple in the market-place of cheaply bantered ideas floated on talk-radio, pushed in the tabloid-press, blogged about incessantly, and justified in pseudo-scholarly tracts. Too often, such thinking can be found, albeit often in muted forms, among progressives, especially young radicals drawn to right the wrongs of environmental despoliation, racial injustice, or the oppression of those who self-identify themselves as outside the mainstream, such as transgendered people. Trade-unions can, of course, be easily dismissed as little more than guardians of apparent privilege. There is something in this critique. No leftist worth his or her political salt has ever discounted the extent to which trade-unionism, with all of its rhetoric of solidarity and its founding principle of 'an injury to one is an injury to all', can, nevertheless, descend into something very much its opposite. Trade-union leadership does, indeed, too often manifest the worst of bureaucratic, corrupt, even gangsterish inclinations. Labour-organisations have, historically, been known to ossify into little more than enterprises dedicated to advancing the interests of the few at the expense of the many. Revolutionaries have always railed against the superior airs and complacent attitudes of labour-aristocracies and trade-union officialdoms.

Once again, however, a scrutiny of what the 1934 struggle to build a different kind of trade-unionism entailed and accomplished is instructive. In Minneapolis, the Trotskyist leadership of truck-drivers, warehousemen, and market-labourers battled to expand the horizons – both in terms of thinking and of organisational activity – of a narrow, sectional trade-unionism that refused, at every step of the way, to open its institutional mind and its closed-shop union-halls to the mass of workers engaged in the trucking industry. Few trade-unions, yesterday *and* today, have ever been as bloodily narrow-minded as Dan Tobin's International Brotherhood of Teamsters on the eve of the Great Depression. Yet within this very union, premised on the notion articulated relentlessly by an ossified leadership that only the few warranted the benefits of *craft*-organisation, while the many should, on principle, be locked out of its largesse, there grew a mobilisation and an opposition premised on the inclusiveness of *industrial* unionism. In the struggle to build this kind of labour-organisation, revolutionary Trotskyists battled to sustain their vision of trade-union principles. They did so against an entrenched bureaucracy that not only refused to support specific organisational initiatives, but resisted them at every turn with officious proceduralism, disenfranchisement, and even brutal physical violence and intimidation. For almost a decade, the Trotskyist opposition to this sad obstructionism not only thrived, but actually prevailed. Thousands came to see these revolutionaries, not as dangerous Reds undermining cherished and hegemonic ideals of an American way of life, but as effective advocates of working-class needs and entitlements. Against the reigning orthodoxies of their times, masses of workers believed in and followed the leadership of these revolutionaries, and together these leaders and their working-class constituency expanded the influence of the International Brotherhood of Teamsters. They built Local 574/544 into a vibrant, democratic, industrial union with thousands of members. In this process, the reach of trade-union solidarity and organisation was extended throughout Minneapolis, Minnesota, and the wider Northwest. One meaning of Minneapolis, for our times, is that trade-unionism, for all of its sorry history of compromise and adaptation to the ethos of capitalism within which it lives and fights, can be turned in different directions. Once this is done, trade-unionism can be a vision as well as a power, a force for wide-ranging social change and a nursery of new possibilities of human relations.

Yet trade-unionism, in and of itself, while a necessary component of working-class struggles against tyranny and unchecked autocracy, is never a sufficient force in the ultimate fight to transcend the capitalist system. It is this rapacious political economy that reproduces the iniquitous power-relations sustaining a systemic undermining of human worth. Replacing this exploitative order with a different, more egalitarian, civil society in which the hierarchy of class-power is vanquished remains the necessary task of fundamental social transformation. For this to happen, trade-unions, as mechanisms in the everyday relations of labour and capital, are simply not enough. They are, necessarily, defined within a system of production organised on the basis of profit and accumulation. If the unions struggle to lessen inequality, they are not designed to overcome it nor able to eradicate it. Trade-unions exist to ameliorate such inequalities, to improve the conditions under which they are perpetuated, and to lessen the levels at which surplus is extracted from the working class in the name of the proverbial 'bottom line'. But the project of changing this system entirely, so that production is organised not for profit and accumulation, but for human worth and advance, for the use of society and its members, is something beyond the reach of trade-unions, although they and those enrolled in their ranks can, of course, contribute to this end. Moreover, while trade-union solidarity can, indeed, be widened, so that principles of working-class brotherhood and sisterhood extend through unions and beyond them, the notion that any single union can lift itself entirely above the state of working-class organisation and struggle as a whole is necessarily illusory. The wider battle, in which trade-unions are situated as essential institutions in the defensive arsenal of the working class, involves the *political* organisation of those willing to demand eradication of capitalist exploitation and an end to the many oppressions intimately related to the economics of a social order that has historically gone by the name of the 'wage-system'.

Marx put forward such views in what would become perhaps the most widely-read primer among the militant minority of the pre-WWI United States, *Value, Price, and Profit*, first published in Germany in 1849. Trade-unions, Marx argued, 'work well as centres of resistance against the encroachments of capital', but he also grasped that '[t]hey fail generally from limiting themselves to a guerrilla war against the effects of the existing system, instead of simultaneously trying to change it, . . . using their organised forces as a lever for the final emancipation of the working class'. He urged workers to widen their horizon. 'Instead of the *conservative* motto: "*A fair day's wages for a fair day's work!*"', Marx admonished labour and the trade-unions to 'inscribe on their banner the *revolutionary* watchword: "*Abolition of the wages system!*"'[4]

This was a long way from happening in 1934. Indeed, James P. Cannon, V.R. Dunne, Farrell Dobbs and other Trotskyists understood that whatever the gains registered by Local 574 in Minneapolis in 1934, one segment of the working class organised in one union local in one city could not, in and of itself, transform the nature of the unequal social relations in the United States. The arm-twisting that defined the labour-capital antagonism had only, at this point in time, reached a certain level of intensity. Cannon always accented the fact that great forward strides had been made in Minneapolis, but the accomplishment of the General Drivers' Union was the modest, if vital, one of 'compelling the bosses to "recognize" it'. Insistent that 'if we want to play an effective part in the labor movement we must not allow ourselves to forget that the American working class is just beginning to move on the path of class struggle', Cannon further stressed that 'the great majority stands yet before the first task of establishing stable unions'. This sober realism also animated Dobbs's understanding

---

4. Marx 1933, pp. 61–2.

of the ultimate defeat of the Trotskyist-led Teamsters in the 1940s. Faced with a formidable combination of foes that included employers, Tobin and the entire IBT and AFL hierarchy (with the willingness of these union-heavies to deploy all the muscle they could muster, up to and including thuggery), Franklin Delano Roosevelt and presidential authority, as well as forces associated with his office, including the FBI, the Justice Department, the Immigration and Naturalization Service, the National Labor Relations Board, and a host of lesser bodies embedded within federal, state, and municipal jurisdictions, not to mention the Communist Party, Local 574/544 was unable to sustain its militant stances. Unique in its Trotskyist leadership, and thus isolated nationally, the insurgent Minneapolis truckers and the affiliated workers had no larger political culture of dissent to reach out to for protection and support. In a climate of war, scapegoated as a seditious conspiracy of treasonous intent, one Trotskyist-led union could hardly stem the tide of reaction. It found itself, by 1941–3, 'reduced to fighting a rearguard action, doing so as skilfully as possible in an effort to minimize the losses suffered in our defeat'. In the conservatising climate that was engulfing the nation, and that would culminate in the McCarthyite Red-scare of the late 1940s and 1950s, the historic advances of 1934, and the Trotskyist leadership that charted their course, were an initial, early, casualty in a revived class-war waged from above.[5]

Just as – despite Stalinist assertions to the contrary – socialism could not be built and sustained, in the long term, in a single country, neither could one union-local stand alone as a beacon of democratic unionism and militant class-struggle when a variety of powerful forces were pressuring the labour-movement and its membership to accommodate to opposite trends. Given the defeat of the Trotskyist-led General Drivers' Union, Local 574/544, and the obliteration of the memory of what it accomplished in 1934 and its immediate aftermath, we are handicapped in our capacities to see the potential of militant and principled trade-union leadership, constituted as it was within a consciously revolutionary-socialist tradition and nurtured by non-union organisations like the Communist League of America and the Socialist Workers Party. We have trouble even imagining *revolutionary teamsters*. This leads directly into a second, and final, set of denials that infuse the political culture of acquiescence and quietude of our current political times, all of which are again usefully interrogated through an appreciation of what happened in Minneapolis in 1934.

---

5. See, for instance, Cannon 1934b, p. 4; Dobbs 1977, especially pp. 288–9.

Denials, II: goodbye to the old mole

Central to this second dimension of a contemporary politics of denial is the notion that the revolutionary Left is a proven failure, and that its advocated end, socialism, is an impossibility, if not a patent absurdity. The ideology of our current moment proclaims confidently that Marx's old mole, revolution, is dead and buried, never to resurface. We can, again, isolate some critical strands in this weave of conventional capitalist wisdom: 1) with the implosion of the Soviet Union, the long history of capitalism versus socialism has, indeed, ended with the victory of the 'free-enterprise West'; 2) the political realities of our time are defined not by revolutionary socialism and its opposition to capitalism, but by the more limited field of contestation pitting liberal capitalism against its more reactionary forms; and 3) it is always necessary, whatever one's commitments, to thwart ultimate reaction, an accomplishment that often means opting for the lesser of two political evils. Like the previous set of denials that always ended in suggesting that class-struggle of the kind that erupted in Minneapolis in 1934 is simply not possible in our current, restructured economic climate, these shibboleths invariably end in the conclusion that the politics of revolutionary socialism are outmoded and very much off the agenda of contemporary political possibilities. Developing and building revolutionary-socialist organisation is, it follows, futile. Again, the Minneapolis events of 1934 are instructive in evaluating this kind of negative, and often unreflective, thinking.

First, the implosion of the Soviet Union and the restoration of capitalism inside the territorial expanse of the former USSR has not, *pace* Francis Fukuyama,[6] ended the world-historic modern clash of capitalism and socialism, nor has it culminated in the unambiguous hegemony of capitalism. Rather, the last two decades have seen accelerating crises of capitalism. Admittedly, these episodic, but increasingly common downturns do not constitute *a fundamental crisis of capitalism* in which masses of people and specific organised movements oppose the profit-system's hegemony and are effective in challenging capital's right to rule. Capitalist crises have, so far, fuelled the drive to a more ideologically rapacious accumulative régime, one cognisant of the need to further beat back any opponents to the unfettered rule of the market. And they have served, as well, to concentrate capitalist power in fewer and fewer hands, weeding out smaller and struggling capitalists and shoring up the fortunes of the larger, global, players in the new world-order of an ever-concentrated régime of accumulation.

The faltering of 'actually-existing socialism' has, to be sure, contributed to the ideological and material advances of revanchist capitalism, resulting in particular kinds of economic and political restoration in Russia, Eastern Europe, China, and

---

6. Fukuyama 1989.

elsewhere. But this is no demonstration that socialism is forever buried under the debris of its failures, for socialism had never really managed to root itself decisively and irrevocably in such incompletely transformed societies. Indeed, the setbacks for socialism that have occurred under the recent race to capitalist restoration (successfully completed in the former Soviet bloc, if not yet realised absolutely in China and Cuba) have been counterbalanced by considerable evidence that the once-confident capitalist heartland is also less than secure. In the United States and Western Europe, market-economies have been blighted with serious blows to their economic well-being. The 2007–8 sub-prime mortgage-meltdown and the consequent bailing out of huge investment-banking consortiums taxed the political economies of Western capitalism and has brought the European Union to the point of an economically-induced dissolution in 2013. Meanwhile, in parts of the developing world, class-antagonisms – both domestically and on a world-scale, as evidenced by the spread of revolutionary ideas and organisations in Latin America and upheavals in the Arab world – remind us that the fundamental divisions of inequality have by no means been lessened or transcended in the mythical end of history promoted by late 1980s ideologues of market-ascendancy. At the high tables of capitalism, Mike Davis has recently suggested, there is now fear and panic. Events of the last half-decade have shaken the confidence, if not the hegemony, of global capital's ruling classes, at least to the point that far-seeing bourgeois elements can, indeed, grasp that their grip on the throttle of accelerating acquisition has been weakened. Davis discerns 'a spectre haunting the opinion pages of the bourgeois press: the imminent destruction of much of the institutional framework of globalization and the undermining of the post-1989 international order'.[7]

So the fall of the erstwhile Soviet Union is not capitalism's ascendant and permanent victory, socialism's ultimate end. The Trotskyist leadership of the Minneapolis strikes of 1934 was part of a small but prophetic contingent that understood that the Stalinised Soviet Union could not sustain socialism in one country, and that the contradictions in its degenerating political economy had long since sidelined the advances registered with the Bolshevik Revolution of 1917. By the mid-to-late 1930s, it was evident to Trotsky and his followers in the Communist League of America/Socialist Workers Party that the Soviet Union would eventually be convulsed by political upheaval. Two paths would lead out of this social conflagration. There would either be the revolutionary establishment of workers' democratic control of the productive apparatus, or else a restoration of capitalism. This was a long time in coming, and took a truly tortuous route that brought no joy to advocates of revolutionary socialism.

---

7. Davis 2011, pp. 5–6.

Trotskyists, then, have been battling Stalinists within the revolutionary movement for decades. Much ink has been spilled on the principled, if often difficult,
ground where criticism of the erosion of socialism under Stalinism has been
accompanied by a defence of the Soviet Union as an imperfect workers' state
that for most of the twentieth century was, nevertheless, not capitalist. If Stalinists have long pursued strategies, articulated specific positions, and saddled the
Left with particular repugnant acts, revolutionary Trotskyism has been a voice
of dissent and refusal that, if listened to, challenges the claim that all of socialism's possibilities rest precariously on a belief that the Soviet Union's history
reflected socialism's inevitable nature and preordained failure. To look at the
way the Trotskyist leadership of Local 574/544 functioned is to appreciate that
the loading up of the anti-socialist arsenal with ammunition forged in the ugliness of Stalinism is little more than a stacking of the ideological deck. Stalinist attacks on the 'permanent counter-revolution' that was allegedly evident in
the Trotskyist leadership of the epic truckers' mobilisations and strikes of 1934
indicate just how far removed from reality and from principled socialist politics
mainstream Communist thought and practice had become by the mid-1930s.
This Stalinist politics, unfolding over decades from the mid-to-late 1920s until
the 1980s, has done much to sour the very idea of socialism in the mouths of
many who would gravitate instinctively to it as an alternative to the exploitation and oppression they rightly associate with capitalism and the concomitant
rapaciousness of imperialist war.

Second, precisely because of Stalinism's easy and opportunistic equation with
revolutionary socialism, a timid and rightward moving social democracy has congealed with liberalism as the only viable option for many on the progressive Left.
At precisely the historic conjuncture where these forces are incapable of addressing capitalism's denouement, they become the spent politics that the alienated
and disaffected too-often rally around, only to be led further into the jaws of
defeat. Yet again, in Minneapolis in 1934, the truckers had to battle not only
the staunchly reactionary forces of the employers and the police, but the end-
lessly slippery and vacillating political challenge posed by a 'progressive' Farmer-
Laborite Governor, Floyd B. Olson, who was nonetheless a capitalist politician
propping up the profit-system and its last line of defence, the military suppression of strikes. Olson oscillated between speeches of support for the truckers and
back-room manoeuvres with their employer-adversaries, but he never wavered
from an ultimate willingness to call out the National Guard to break Local 574's
strikes. Just how the Troskyist leadership of the General Drivers' Union oriented
towards Olson, compared to the ultra-left but empty rhetoric of a blustering
Communist Party, is instructive. The latter orientation, sectarian and removed
from the realities of its time, claimed that workers needed to bring Olson to a

political defeat in an all-out general strike. In contrast, the Left Opposition cultivated a politics attuned to contradictions in the ruling order's understanding of the dynamics of class-struggle in the mid-1930s, using this approach to win important concessions and register specific, limited, and transitional victories. Such strategic acumen established not only a beachhead from which militancy could be further promoted; it also confirmed that revolutionaries had a contribution to make in the trade-union movement, and that they would be around another day to fight on the wider political canvas of more thorough-going social transformation. The Minneapolis truckers' strikes provide a concrete reminder that there are, indeed, alternatives when it comes to the leadership of the class-struggle. Stalinised Communists would have risked all, and lost, in a premature confrontation with the state. Trotskyists saw opportunities to exploit uncertainties in the political economy of governing authority. They thereby achieved a dual outcome, winning tangible gains *and* instructing working people in the valuable lesson that reliance on non-revolutionary liberal and social-democratic elements would inevitably result in setbacks.

Cannon summed up the meaning of Minneapolis in this regard, drawing explicit attention to the strike's limited victories as important on their own terms, but also significant because of the ways in which they advanced the consciousness of the working class.

> As in every strike of any consequence, the workers involved in the Minneapolis struggle also had an opportunity to see the government at work and to learn some practical lessons as to its real function. The police force of the city, under the direction of the Republican mayor, supplemented by a horde of 'special deputies', were lined up solidly on the side of the bosses. The police and deputies did their best to protect the strikebreakers and keep some trucks moving, although their best was not good enough. The mobilization of the militia by the Farmer-Labor governor was a threat against the strikers, even if the militia-men were not put on the street. The strikers will remember that threat. In a sense it can be said that the political education of a large section of the strikers began with this experience. It is sheer lunacy, however, to imagine that it was completed and that the strikers, practically all of whom voted yesterday for Roosevelt and Olson, could have been led into a prolonged strike for purely political aims after the primary demand for the recognition of the union had been won.[8]

One strength of the Trotskyist leadership of the Minneapolis teamsters in 1934 was the understanding that this kind of political education of the working

8. Cannon 1934b, p. 4.

class and its allies was both necessary and invariably evolved within protracted struggles and the lessons assimilated therein. Precisely because the Minneapolis events have been separated from us by time, political distance, and a cumulative set of defeats, cultivation of this essential perspective is once again critical. That a seeming progressive such as Barack Obama, far less radical than the Farmer-Laborite Olson, garnered so much support from American progressives, trade-unionists, and ostensible leftists in his successful bid for the presidency in 2008, is a measure of how much essential ground has been vacated, and needs to be recovered, in the politics of our times.[9]

Thirdly, this is not, of course, unrelated to arguments so common among progressive leftists that all political struggle must be subordinated to the defeat of the worst of all evils. In contemporary American politics, this has meant compromise and conciliation with all manner of repugnant developments, a watering down of demands, and avoidance of many positive initiatives, all in the name of keeping one particular set of – admittedly dangerous – reactionaries out of office. In Minneapolis in 1934, the Trotskyists guiding the working-class rebellion of teamsters and associated workers took aim at employers, the police, conservative craft-unionists, Stalinists and social democrats, Farmer-Laborites, Republicans, and Roosevelt's mediation-emissaries. They did not barter away their critical senses in a cat-and-mouse game of setting on one main enemy and toying with ways of making their struggle more palatable to others, with whom they had fundamental disagreements. Dan Tobin and the IBT officialdom, for instance, were never placated, even as they obstructed the every move of Local 574. Rather, the Dunne brothers, Dobbs, Skoglund, and their ally Bill Brown, waged a relentless war on Tobin's backtracking, at the same time as they cultivated a rank-and-file militancy that was able, in 1934, to simply shunt aside the trade-union tops who would have derailed the truckers' struggle. 'Out of a union with the most conservative tradition and the most obsolete structure came the most militant and successful strike', Cannon concluded in one July 1934 commentary.[10]

There is, then, much to learn from Minneapolis and its meaning. The past is never entirely buried and forgotten, unless we allow it to be. What happened in Minneapolis in 1934, as Trotskyists led teamsters to a major victory, achieved at great cost, should not be forgotten. One component of this Minneapolis achievement was to illustrate vividly just how effective revolutionary leadership can be in the trade-unions. Of course, there were lapses in judgement on the part of this leadership, and decisions were made and orientations followed that can be criticised for their limitations and short-sightedness, as I have suggested. That said, Local 574 was, from its beginnings, very much in the hands of a far-seeing

---

9. See, for one relevant statement, Ali 2011.
10. Cannon 1934b, p. 4.

contingent of revolutionary Trotskyists guided by the principles and programmatic clarity of the Communist League of America. In 'The Strike Triumphant', the *Militant* understandably laid great stress on the question of leadership:

> In the gratifying conclusion to the battle there lie the features that distinguish the Minneapolis strike from all others in recent times. For the first time in years, militants, indigenous to the industry, have entered an A.F. of L. union; converted it from a craft to an industrial union; built it up patiently and quietly; prepared carefully and struck at the proper moment; combined organization with militancy and political wisdom, and emerged from a five week's strike against insuperable odds with victory in their laps. And on top of all of this, what is almost unprecedented in such strikes – not only is the union intact but the leadership is still in the hands of the genuine militants.

This was not some inconsequential set of developments, and Trotskyists were rightly proud of what they had done, declaring, 'The example of the Minneapolis leadership will be an inspiration everywhere!'[11]

Decades later, Dobbs reiterated this point in his books relating to the working-class insurgency which he had figured in so prominently. His *Teamster Bureaucracy* concluded on the note that 'the principal lesson for labor militants to derive from the Minneapolis experience is not that, under an adverse relationship of forces, the workers can be overcome; but that, with proper leadership, they can overcome'.[12] A host of other commentators, beginning with Herbert Solow, Charles Rumford Walker, Meridel Le Sueur, and journalists writing for magazines intimately connected to American capitalism, like *Fortune* and *Time*, made a similar point in different ways.[13] Scholars as different in their orientations as Walter Galenson and Bert Cochran have essentially opted for the same conclusion.[14]

The dialectic of leaders and led

Turning to the politics of the current moment, however, a refinement is, perhaps, in order. The meaning of the Minneapolis strikes and their successes can

---

11. See Cannon 1944, pp. 139–68; 'The Strike Triumphant', *The Militant*, 25 August 1934.
12. Dobbs 1977, p. 298.
13. Herbert Solow, 'War in Minneapolis', *The Nation*, 8 August 1934; Solow, 'The Great Minneapolis Strike', *New Leader*, 8 September 1934; and much of the Solow correspondence collected in File 'Correspondence, 1934, 1936', Box 1, CRW Papers, MNHS; Walker 1937a, pp. 29–33; Walker 1937; Le Sueur 1945, pp. 289–97; 'Revolt in the Northwest', *Fortune Magazine*, 13 (April 1936), pp. 112–19; 'National Affairs: Three Little Men', *Time*, 7 July 1941; Kramer 1942, pp. 388–95.
14. Galenson 1960, p. 482; Cochran 1977, p. 88.

be appreciated, in our context of relative labour-movement quietude and the demise of the revolutionary Left, as an impressive dialectic, in which the accent is placed on the reciprocal relations of leaders and led. Our times have seen no mobilisations of labour that can be compared with that of the 1934 Minneapolis working class. The self-activity of workers, their willingness to fight to win, and their sacrifice in the face of the odds stacked against them, stand as a testimony to a rank-and-file militancy that must once again be developed among working people. Animated by the conviction that 'an injury to one is an injury to all', the Minneapolis working class, be it waged or unwaged, male or female, American-born or Native-American, rallied to the cause of the truckers, seeing in the 1934 strikes battles that affected all labour.[15] This class-resolve was evident in street-level confrontations, to be sure, but it also came to be exhibited in a changing consciousness of the routine relations of everyday life.

Charles Rumford Walker describes the working-class Baumans, Roy and his wife, always referred to only as 'Mrs.':

---

15. Little has been said in this study, or other writings on the Minneapolis strikes, about the issue of race, largely because the trucking industry in the region and in this period was relatively homogeneous racially. Walker's 'Notes for Life-Story of a Truck-Driver' p. 1, commenced with a brief statement on 'Race. Might well be Norwegian or Swedish, and the son of a Minnesota farmer, gone to the city, or of English or Irish descent. The industry racially, I gather, is predominantly Nordic', in File 'American City Preliminary Prospectus and General Notes', Box 1, CRW Papers, MNHS. There were, undoubtedly, a few African Americans who were 'inside workers', engaged in the least well-paid labour in the Market District, hauling crates and plucking chickens. Some women also worked in these less than prestigious jobs. But the vast majority of workers eventually organized in the General Drivers' Union were male and white. The apparent exception was a group of Native Americans. All indications are that they were readily accepted into both the Union and the Trotskyist milieu, where individuals of aboriginal ancestry occupied prominent positions as picket-captains, members of strike-committees, and leaders in the Union Defense Guard, and joined the Socialist Workers Party. 'A member of 574, not a Communist, but a Chippewa Indian and a real American' protested what he called the slanders of International IBT President, Daniel J. Tobin, suggesting that Red-baiting attacks on the union and its leaders provided employers with 'fuel for their fire'. See 'The Strikers' Voice', *The Organizer*, 19 July 1934. Walker's 'Notes on the Organizer' in File 'Civil War in July (Ch. 10)', Box 1, CRW Papers, MNHS, contain the statement: 'They accuse us in this local of being un-American, but how's this for some real Am. Members: Happy Holstein, Chippewa; Ray Rainbolt, Sioux; Doc Tollotson, Chippewa; Bill Bolt, Chippewa; Bill Rogers, Chippewa; Joe Belanger, Chippewa'. On Ray Rainbolt, see also Harry DeBoer, 'Ray Rainbolt: Veteran Teamsters Leader', *The Militant*, 19 May 1978. Specktor 1984 noted that Happy (Emanuel) Holstein was Ojibwa from the White-Earth reservation in northern Minnesota, that he joined the Communist League of America/ Socialist Workers Party, and that he was vilified in an anti-union scandal sheet as 'a Red amongst the reds'. Rainbolt and Holstein, both affiliated with the SWP for a time, would no longer be members by the 1940s. Ethnicity was also grounds for attack from those hostile to working-class organization and radical leadership, Skoglund being scapegoated even within Local 574/544 as a communist and an incapable foreigner who 'couldn't speak English'. See Skoglund's interview with Halstead, 14 May 1955, Transcript, p. 38, Box 2, Riehle Papers, MNHS.

Roy was one of the first of his outfit to join [Local 574]; it took a little nerve to join a Minneapolis trade union in 1933. When the strike came, Roy spent seventeen and eighteen hours a day on the picket line. He felt they *had to win the strike* or he'd lose his job and be even worse off than he was in 1932. Mrs. Bauman worked all day peeling potatoes and making coffee in the commissary, and listening breathlessly to what they said over the mike in the evening mass meetings.... When they brought in the women who had been beaten up by armed guards in the *Tribune* alley, and laid them out in rows at Strike headquarters, Roy went and got himself a club.... On the day of the battle of Deputies Run...Roy was at it all day – in the battle and in the mop-up. He fought with a kind of delighted fury, and has gotten a kick ever since out of his memories. He sent three cops to the hospital.[16]

It is not the masculinist bravado of this recollection that merits attention, although some will see Roy Bauman in this way. Rather, it is that Roy and Mrs. Bauman were drawn to the truckers' struggle in 1934 wholeheartedly, the experience determining their outlook on the world and forever stamping them with a perspective unique to their class.

This was repeated thousands of times over, as Minneapolis workers flocked to the cause of Local 574. Carlos Hudson captured something of this process when he described how, one year after the momentous 1934 strikes, the General Drivers' Union had emerged as the focal point of working-class life in Minneapolis. One part of this was support for other workers and their struggles. 'Besides rescuing the strikes of iron workers and the hosiery workers', Hudson wrote, 'members of 574 have appeared on the picket lines in the Arrowhead steel strike, the Minneapolis-St. Paul mechanics' strike of last January, the Fargo drivers' strike of last winter, and the New England building trades strike. In each instance the truck drivers gave a good account of themselves', concluded Hudson, adding for good measure: 'A picket detachment from 574 is bad news for both the employers and the police'. Beyond this contribution to overt class-struggle, however, Hudson noted how the headquarters of the militant teamsters, located in 1935 in a former roller-skating rink in the heart of a working-class neighbourhood, epitomised a cultural/political change in workers' lives:

At any hour of the day or night one finds some sort of meeting in progress. On Monday the full membership of the General Drivers' Union gathers, on Tuesday the taxi drivers, on Thursday the independent truck owners. A large unit of federal workers recently organized by Local 574 meets each Friday evening in the third-floor auditorium. Every Saturday night there is dancing. A workers' forum is held Sunday afternoon. In one or another of the numerous halls

16. Walker 1937, pp. 152–3.

a stewards' meeting is usually in session; or a group of raw workers is busy organizing itself, with the help of 574. On the second floor is located what must be the most popular bar in town, where every evening crowds of workers with their wives and sweethearts sit around the tables gossiping, or dance to the music of a mandolin and guitar. It is doubtful whether, since the 1890s, a union has come to mean so much to so many thousands of workers.[17]

Meridel Le Sueur, observing the truckers' insurgency of the summer of 1934 with a determination to make this kind of class-upheaval central to her artistic endeavours as a writer, wrote in her notebooks that 'A civilization becomes transformed when its most oppressed element the humiliation of the slave, suddenly becomes a value, when the oppressed ceases to attempt to escape this humiliation and seeks his salvation in it, when the worker ceases to escape this work and sees in it his reason for being'.[18]

This was the rank-and-file strength of working-class self-activity in Minneapolis in the mid-1930s. An old Socialist, jailed as a war-objector two decades before the teamsters' rebellion of 1934, and not active in the movement since his incarceration, dropped into the General Drivers' Union headquarters in 1935, enthused by what he had heard was happening. 'I've just made the rounds of the country, and Minneapolis is the hope of the movement', he reported. 'I heard things were breaking wide open here, and I've come to see the fireworks'.[19]

Inseparable from the emergence and growth of this galvanised working class was the Trotskyist leadership that had burrowed into the Minneapolis coalyards, propagating the message of trade-unionism among individual workmates and small, isolated, fearful groups of two or three. For years, Ray Dunne and Carl Skoglund kept the embers of potential union-breakthroughs glowing in the cold and inhospitable climate of craft-union complacency, the dominance of harsh anti-union employers, and the vicissitudes of the capitalist business-cycle. They managed to convince a few followers of the righteousness of their cause, but, along the way, they were jeered at by workers and bosses alike, and, in the worst of times, fired for their public political stands. Biding their time, these patient revolutionaries gambled that those workers they had managed to draw into their circle of militants were but the tip of an iceberg of proletarian discontent. Their wager, backed by the knowledge that they had won some staunch figures like Farrell Dobbs, Marvel Scholl, Harry DeBoer and others to their ideas, and shored

17. Hudson 1935.
18. Meridel Le Sueur, 'Notebooks, Volume 8, 1934–1935', undated entry, but relating to the July events of 1934, preceded by the exclamation, 'I was marching', Box 26, Le Sueur Papers, MNHS.
19. Hudson 1935.

up by a judicious sense of the temper of the drivers and others associated with trucking in Minneapolis, paid huge dividends.

A February strike catapulted trade-unionism in Minneapolis into the mix of class-relations, in what had been a bastion of the open shop, thus altering forever the nature of political and economic life in the transportation-hub of the American Northwest. What started with less than a dozen Trotskyists and militants, soon encompassed thousands of Local 574 members and tens of thousands of allies among other trade-unionists, unorganised workers, and the unemployed. In developing a sense of strike-timing and strategy, in preparing, organising, and building not only a union, but a vast infrastructure supporting Local 574's activities, Minneapolis Trotskyists drew on their own experience as class-struggle militants and their understanding of revolutionary politics. They also benefited immensely from the aid and support of an impressive continent of editors, organisers, theorists, and like-minded advocates from New York and elsewhere, figures such as James P. Cannon, Max Shachtman, Hugo Oehler, and Herbert Solow, all of whom contributed the skills of agitators and editors, and perspectives enriched by wider experience in the class-struggle. These committed participants in the Minneapolis story were affiliated with the small, but resolute, revolutionary organisation, the Communist League of America. This Left Opposition leadership led the rank-and-file truckers' insurgency, orchestrating working-class self-activity in ways that harnessed basic class-instincts, angers, and needs to the dynamic drive for union-recognition. Out of this dialectic of leaders and led came innovative strike-tactics like the flying pickets, first proposed by a trucker who was not at that time a Trotskyist,[20] and critically important creations, such as the Women's Auxiliary, the organised movement of the unemployed, and the daily strike-newspaper, *The Organizer*. Leaders relied on and learned from the rank-and-file; the rank-and-file relied on and learned from the leaders.

Revolutionary teamsters: 'the Earth shall stand on new foundations'

The victories achieved out of this reciprocal pooling of resiliency and resources, propaganda and perspective, militancy and moxie – all filtered through the sophisticated understanding of revolutionary politics that had germinated in the Left Opposition's confrontation with Stalinism – was an unprecedented

---

20. See the discussion of the origins of the flying pickets in 'The Coal Strike of 1934 – Birth of a Great Union', *Northwest Organizer*, 24 February 1938; 3 March 1938. Shaun (Jack) Maloney maintained that it was Harry DeBoer who developed the idea of roving pickets. See Maloney's interview with Duffy and Miller, 4 June 1979, Transcript, p. 15, File '1934 Teamsters Strike', Box 2, Maloney Papers, MNHS.

advance for militant class-struggle trade-unionism in the United States of the early 1930s. It pioneered approaches to organising and industrial unionism that would become associated with the Congress of Industrial Organizations. Indeed, the dialectic of leaders and led in Minneapolis, a fusion of revolutionary Trotskyists and insurgent workers, resulted in a union-mobilisation within one of the most reactionary enclaves of the American Federation of Labor. All of this, especially the push for militant industrial unionism, *anticipated* the CIO at its very best. This validated revolutionary leadership within the labour-movement and consolidated significant trade-union advances, inoculating, for a time, many workers against the infectious germ of anti-communism.

This was an accomplishment of considerable magnitude, and one not to be forgotten even as it was undermined in later years of concerted assault. It has many lessons for our own era. Among them are a sense of both the necessity *and* possibility of rebuilding the kind of revolutionary organisation that can simultaneously nurture a creative leadership *and* encourage and develop the militant combativity of the working class. Struggles that secure gains in new causes have to be fought through, planned, and mobilised in order to be won. The desperate need of our particular times is to revive the kind of dialectic of leaders and led that was evident in Local 574's historic achievements in the 1930s. In this lies the possibility of victories. Out of such advances, and only out of this kind of forward movement, will it be possible to make new inroads in the struggle for emancipation and equality that has long been associated with the best traditions of the American labour-movement.

The gains fought for and won by Minneapolis Trotskyists and teamsters in 1934 wrote an important chapter in the history of the possibility of class-struggle. These pages need to be read and appreciated. The longevity and continuity of oppression and exploitation breed, partly at least, in the recesses of a social amnesia that wipes the collective human consciousness clean of recollection of events like Minneapolis. Those who would arise in belief that 'A better world's in birth', and that 'Justice thunders condemnation', can see in Minneapolis in 1934 the small seeds of a potentially large transformation, in which 'the Earth shall stand on new foundations', and we who have been *naught* shall finally be *All!* When this happens *revolutionary teamsters* will, once again, be a living reality, rather than the apparent contradiction-in-terms this coupling may seem in our own jaded times.

Appendix
Trotskyism in the United States, 1928–33

What was this Trotskyism that led the Minneapolis truckers and their working-class allies to victory in 1934? Who were the Trotskyists that managed to emerge out of the coal-yards in which they had worked for years, rising from obscurity to the point that they would be written about in the pages of publications like *Fortune, Time*, and *Harper's Magazine*? Answers to these questions will have emerged as the narrative of events in Minneapolis in 1934 unfolded in the chapters above. But for some readers, to understand adequately the great leap forward that this episodic confrontation in Minneapolis represented, not only for American labour, but for American Trotskyism, it is necessary to outline the obscure and modest origins of this particular revolutionary current in the United States in the years reaching from its founding in 1928 through the early-to-mid 1930s.[1]

Trotskyism, also known as the Left Opposition, was a dissident-component of the international communist movement. It was born of realisation that the transformative politics associated with the creation of the world's first workers' republic in 1917, the Soviet Union, had succumbed to a constraining renunciation of any commitment to world-revolution. As Joseph Stalin consolidated power inside Russia and extended this hegemony into the Communist International, its animating goal of world-revolution was jettisoned, the

---

1. A useful introduction to Trotskyism in the United States is Breitman, Le Blanc and Wald 1996.

new orientation invoking the possibility and priority of building 'socialism in one country'. This was a contradictory aim that was both impossible to realise, on the one hand, and, on the other, a decisive retreat that subordinated potential advances of the world's revolutionary forces to the needs of an increasingly bureaucratised Soviet régime. Internationally, the failure of the socialist revolution in Europe (and especially in Germany), on which the healthy continuity of the Russian Revolution depended, first in 1919 and then in 1921–3, limited Soviet possibilities.[2] This conditioned an internal régime in the Soviet Union that consolidated Stalin's power, weakened and marginalised his potential opponents – Leon Trotsky foremost among them – and, ultimately, culminated in the decimation of the Leninist Communist Party that had registered such gains in 1917 and during the years immediately following the Revolution. The resistance to this process inside the Russian Communist Party took various forms, involving some of Lenin's closest comrades. All, including the most sustained and consistent efforts of Trotsky, were overwhelmed by the bureaucratic apparatus. Originating in the years 1923–9, this process wrote *finis* to the promise of the first experiment of a workers' government.

The practical consequences of this constellation of obstacles and setbacks, both inside and outside the Soviet Union, were thus formidable. Within the degenerating revolutionary Soviet society, the ruthless elevation of the *líder máximo*, Joseph Stalin, produced an autocratic state. Stalin ordered the first Bolshevik shot in 1923, and, between 1927 and 1940, orchestrated the trial, exile, or execution of virtually the entire original revolutionary Bolshevik leadership. Trotsky himself was increasingly targeted by Stalin, first marginalised and then stripped of all power. The once-revered leader of the Red Army failed to gain election to the Executive Committee of the Communist International, and Stalin was voted into the seat instead. As early as 1924, Stalin rigged elections to the Thirteenth Russian Communist Party Congress. The Soviet Thermidor had begun. Eventually, Trotsky, as the Left Opposition's leading figure and theoretican, would be assassinated. This final, murderous act of suppression took place in Mexico in 1940, but had been preceded by a decade in which Trotsky was driven from the Soviet Union and forced to wander the globe in search of some limited refuge. Over the course of the 1920s and early 1930s, however, the full meaning of this reactionary turn within a Stalinising Soviet Union was only incompletely and partially understood, even by its Left Opposition critics. Trotsky's fullest elaboration of the degeneration of the Soviet Union in these years, *The Revolution Betrayed: What Is the Soviet Union and Where Is It Going*, was only written in 1936, and appeared in English translation the next year. His most developed articula-

---

2. On the German Revolution's defeat, see Broué 2006.

tion of a strategic orientation for revolutionaries, working in mass movements and in trade-unions in times when the actual seizure of state-power was not a realistic possibility, was not published until 1938, appearing as the founding document of the Fourth International in September 1938. Entitled 'The Death Agony of Capitalism and the Tasks of the Fourth International', this statement emphasised the necessity of using *transitional* demands to advance the interests of the working class, at the same time as revolutionaries' posing of these issues would relentlessly expose 'the destructive and degrading tendencies of decadent capitalism' and draw forces to the ranks of the Left Opposition. In many ways, with a few significant lapses, the conduct of the revolutionary leadership of the Minneapolis teamsters' strikes anticipated (and, undoubtedly, informed) Trotsky's development of this 'transitional programme'.[3]

Trotsky and his international allies spent the late 1920s and much of the early 1930s constituting themselves an external faction of the Communist International, appealing constantly to their former comrades to accept their analysis of the mistaken political turn of Stalinist degeneration, struggling to win the established forces of Bolshevism back to the politics of world-revolution. Finally, in 1933, Trotsky called for a break from the Communist International, rallying his small global forces to the standard of a new, Fourth International. As critical as this new International was of Stalinist degeneration, it nonetheless insisted that it was the duty of all proletarian revolutionaries to defend the Soviet Union from capitalist attack, preserving the gains of 1917, which had abolished the exploitative essence of the wage-profit system and done away with private property. Meanwhile, beyond the boundaries of 'socialism in one country', a series of defeats and international misadventures plagued the revolutionary Left, and confirmed Trotsky's assessment of the Communist International as politically degenerated beyond rehabilitation. Beginning with the rout of the Chinese Revolution in 1925–7, and reaching through the debacles of fascism's rise to power in Germany and the bloodletting of the Spanish Civil War in the 1930s, these events, in conjunction with the purge-trials and domestic reign of terror inside the Soviet Union, condemned Stalinism as the antithesis of a politics of revolutionary possibility.[4]

---

3. Trotsky 1937; 1973, which contains a section addressing the importance of an event like Minneapolis in influencing Trotsky's strategic sensibilities, 'Completing the Program and Putting it to Work', written 7 June 1938: 'In this sense the draft program doesn't presage a new invention, it is not the writing of one man. It is the summation of collective work up until today' (p. 137).

4. Much could be cited on Stalinism, the degeneration of the Russian Revolution, and the early Left Opposition. See, for example, Nove 1975; Löwy 1982; Broué 1988, especially pp. 640–54; Carr 1979; Lewin 2005; Medvedev 1971; Rogovin 2009. The best account of Trotsky remains Isaac Deutscher's trilogy, *The Prophet Armed, The Prophet Unarmed* and *The Prophet Outcast* (Deutscher 1954; 1959; 1963).

In the United States, those who gravitated to the revolutionary politics of Trotsky's International Left Opposition were originally led by James P. Cannon, Max Shachtman, and Martin Abern. This trio, disparagingly referred to as 'Three Generals with No Army',[5] was expelled from the American Communist Party that they had helped to build over the course of the 1920s. Jay Lovestone led the move to drive Cannon and his allies from the Workers' (Communist) Party in October 1928, and then, before he himself was also expelled, Lovestone heavy-handedly purged scores of rank-and-file communists who refused to simply toe the line of denunciation and condemn Cannon and all others who embraced Trotskyist politics. The other major leader of the American communist movement and ally of Cannon in earlier internal disputes, William Z. Foster, aligned his faction with the leading Lovestone group in attacking the embryonic Left Opposition. By the end of November 1928, the nascent ranks of American Trotskyism probably numbered about 125 individuals, some 27 of these expelled communists being in Minneapolis. Most of this Minneapolis contingent, including Vincent Raymond Dunne and Carl Skoglund, key figures in the Trotskyist organising of truckers in 1934, gravitated quickly but somewhat uncertainly to Cannon, Shachtman, and Abern. They knew little of Trotskyism at this point, but were outraged by the lack of democracy and ham-fisted behaviour of those in the Workers' (Communist) Party leadership who tried to bludgeon them into recanting positions they had never embraced and did not understand. Soon, however, they would be schooled in the elementary politics of the Left Opposition. Their Trotskyism developed as they read translated works being published by the organisation they were now affiliated with, the Communist League of America (Opposition), founded in May 1929. Like all in the United States Left Opposition, these Minneapolis Trotskyists tested the orientations of the CLA against the increasingly barren and sectarian stances of the Communist International and its futile Third Period (1929–34) calls for separate, revolutionary 'Red' unionism. As these budding Trotskyists looked around the world, moreover, they saw the Communist International failing to combat the rise of fascism in Germany and squandering opportunities at home to bring together potentially revolutionary forces to turn back the tides of reaction in the trough of the Great Depression.[6] By the early 1930s, this steeled cohort of Minneapolis Trotskyists was the proletarian backbone of the American Left Opposition. In 1935, Paul Jacobs, a New York student who had joined the Trotskyist movement, was introduced to the Minneapolis

5. Bertram D. Wolfe, 'The Three Generals with No Army', *Daily Worker*, 27 November 1928; Wolfe 1928.
6. For an account of how the Workers' (Communist) Party organized the first wave of recruits to American Trotskyism, see Palmer 2007, pp. 344–9.

milieu, and was immediately struck by its 'toughness' and 'hard, spare ascetic' intensity.[7]

The numerically insignificant but increasingly politically prescient forces of the Communist League of America appeared to enter the Great Depression riding success after success. This dissident political current emerged out of the American communist movement with much fanfare, and its leading figures, especially James P. Cannon and Max Shachtman, seemed to capture, between them, much that was good and promising in the American revolutionary tradition. Cannon epitomised the best of American proletarian militancy, and had been an exemplary class-struggle militant and hobo-rebel associated with the Industrial Workers of the World. Throughout his years in the United States communist movement, he was an admired orator, a leading figure in the trade-union-oriented wing of the Party, second in stature only to William Z. Foster, the famed organiser of the post-WWI steel-workers' strike. Cannon had proven himself, by 1921, something of a master-organiser of disparate strands of the communist weave, and he was the founding chairman of the first legal, above-ground American communist party. Few figures of Cannon's generation had such an evident capacity to bring together American-born radicals and immigrant, foreign-language revolutionaries. He was the pre-eminent force bridging old divisions among fractious revolutionary groupings, ushering American communism out of the wilderness of its clandestine underground-period, and into the Party's years of legality and potential mass growth in the mid-1920s, drawing on and extending into practice the advice of pillars of the early Comintern like Lenin, Radek, and Trotsky.

Many young recruits to communism saw Cannon as an experienced cadre from whom they had much to learn. Shachtman and Abern had each been just this kind of Cannon protégé. The precocious and irrepressible Shachtman and the organisationally-minded youth-functionary Abern worked closely with their mentor throughout the 1920s, building the Party's most important mass agitational body, the International Labor Defense. Led by Cannon, it mobilised against the deportations of alien radicals, fought lynch-law in the American South, and organized street-protests and rallies to protest the railroading of the Italian anarchists Nicola Sacco and Bartolomeo Vanzetti to the electric chair in 1927. Shachtman, in particular, had an aesthetic sensibility put to good use in the ILD's monthly magazine, the covers and internal photo-montages of which were striking expressions of avant-garde techniques. In addition, the urbane Shachtman brought to his communist activism a mastery of languages that was critically important in translating International Left Opposition texts, and that allowed

---

7. Sam Gordon in Evans (ed.) 1976, pp. 63–5; Jacobs 1965, pp. 52–3.

him to integrate seamlessly into the European ranks of Trotsky's followers. The Cannon-Shachtman-Abern alliance thus seemed to weld together important and complimentary components of the American revolutionary forces; the prospects for Trotskyism in the United States seemed propitious.[8]

In fact, a series of developments reduced significantly American Trotskyism's capacity to intervene effectively in either the Communist Party or any larger politics of mass struggle. By late 1929, and into 1930–1, the Communist League of America had passed through the euphoria of its initial founding, which included the publication of an impressive Left Opposition newspaper, *The Militant*, as well as a series of translated pamphlets bringing the basic positions of Trotsky to the American workers' movement. Two years into its young life, the US Left Opposition appeared listless and without political influence. 'We were stymied', remembered James Cannon, who referred to this period as 'the real dog days of the Left Opposition'. For Cannon, writing in 1944, these 'were the hardest days of all in the thirty years' he had been in the revolutionary movement, the 1929–32 downturn recalled as 'years of ... terrible hermetically sealed isolation, with all the attendant difficulties'.[9]

One part of this worsening political context was outside the control of the Trotskyists themselves. No sooner had Cannon, Shachtman, and Abern been expelled from the ranks of the ostensibly revolutionary communist movement, than the economy collapsed, and the American working class was thrown into disarray. For the best part of a decade, the balance of class-forces had, in fact, been tending towards capital, with workers facing Red-scares, state-trials, deportations of radical 'aliens', open-shop drives, vigilante-assaults, trade-union defeats, declining working-class militancy, and the growing conservatism of the labour-movement. The class-upheavals associated with opposition to war, attraction to the Bolshevik Revolution of 1917 and its calls for workers' soviets and the dictatorship of the proletariat, and the socialist strike-wave of 1916–19, culminating in general strikes and a widespread proletarian insurgency, were, by 1929, little more than a distant memory. Four million workers undertook job-actions in 1919, but a decade later that impressive figure had shrunk to fewer than three hundred thousand. Indeed, the aggressive labour-movement that spawned claims of a 'new unionism' and demands for 'industrial democracy' in the combative 1916–19 era was brought to its knees by 1924, the victim of a virulent class-war waged from above. The number of organised workers plummeted to 3.5 million by the mid-1920s, down from a highwater mark of 5 million in 1920. Thereafter, the ranks of the trade-unions stagnated. Entering the Great Depression, the United States working class was led by an increasingly ossified

---

8. See, for instance, Palmer 2007; Drucker 1994.
9. Cannon 1944, pp. 94–5.

and conservative American Federation of Labor, a mainstream body that was far more reticent than it was radical.

With the precipitous collapse of the economy in 1929, things only worsened. From 1929–33, the ranks of organised labor wilted by almost half a million. Strikes fell off in numbers, declining to an annual count of only 637 in 1930. Most of these were defensive skirmishes, small struggles to stave off wage-cuts, which had become endemic. By 1930–1, almost three million manufacturing workers had been forced to accept reductions in pay amounting to roughly ten percent. Pioneer Hungarian-American Left Oppositionist, New York's Pauline Gutringer, wrote to *The Militant* in 1930, deploring the nationalistic, labour-aristocratic outlook of the AFL unions, which reduced unskilled labour to 'rabble, an undesirable, disloyal element'. With the circle of craft-unionists shrinking and the numbers of unskilled, semi-skilled, and unorganised workers growing daily, Gutringer insisted it was up to the communist movement to organise all workers 'under the banner of internationalism'.[10]

Yet the Communist League of America was too small and too marginal to capitalise on the labour-movement possibilities of the moment. When they developed, working-class struggles seemed to be something of a property-right of either the American Federation of Labor union-bosses or, far to their left, the established Communist Party (CP). The CP still retained within its ranks a corps of dedicated labour-organisers and a presence in a number of unions, where it was often the voice of the 'left wing'. The Left Oppositionist CLA simply could not compete with the much larger and more established official Communist Party.

Moreover, much of the pre-1929 Trotskyist critique of mainstream communism accented its rightward drift over the course of the 1920s, such as its – ultimately disastrous – prevaricating and waffling in the face of the revolutionary situation that arose in China in 1925–7. But as Stalin moved to outflank his rightward-leaning Bukharinite Opposition in the late 1920s, he orchestrated a Third Period left-turn. The history of contemporary capitalism was now said to be divided into three periods: the revolutionary offensives of the era of the First World-War and immediately after had shaken the global order, divided the international workers' movement, crystallised a Bolshevik tendency resolutely opposed to both imperialist war and capitalist exploitation, ushering into being the world's first proletarian state; then followed a second period, substantially covering the mid-to-late 1920s, that achieved a 'relative, partial, and temporary stabilisation of capitalism's hegemony'; finally, a third period was commencing in 1928–9, and it was predicted that as mass radicalisation unfolded and workers went on the

---

10. Pauline Gutringer, 'Nationalism and Internationalism', *The Militant*, 4 January 1930. On the state of the labour-movement and workers in the years 1920–33 see Bernstein 1960.

offensive, mounting militant strikes and mobilising the unemployed to shake the House of Capital to its foundations, communists would reap the benefits. In this new and ultra-revolutionary Third Period, according to Stalin and his growing chorus of sycophants, the Communist Parties of the world, alone, were able to speak for and lead the masses of insurgent workers. There could thus be no conciliation with those radical forces choosing not to affiliate with the communist 'vanguard'.[11]

At the very moment of the birth of the Communist League of America (Opposition), then, at which point it was struggling to convince the rank-and-file of the Communist Party that Stalinism represented a reactionary repudiation of fundamental revolutionary principles, the Communist International lurched to the left, undercutting, albeit superficially, the critique made by Cannon and others that world-revolution had been abandoned. The ultra-leftism and sectarianism of the Stalinist Third Period did, indeed, bear out the Left Opposition's criticism that fundamental Bolshevik principles had been abandoned. The basic, tried-and-tested Leninist united-front orientations of the 1920s were sacrificed at the altar of the demand that communists alone should lead the insurgent masses in an ultimate battle against capitalism. This dealt a harsh blow against those struggling left-wing elements within American trade-unions, since the call to create 'Red-led' labour-organisations sacrificed militants in the mainstream unions to the reactionary and apolitical leaders of the American Federation of Labor. Internationally, this Third Period sectarianism, espoused in shrill attacks on all 'social fascists' of the Left who did not recognise the absolute leadership of Stalin's Communist International, handcuffed those forces inside and outside of Germany who could have united to defeat Hitler's rise to power and, possibly, halted the drift towards war. By 1935, even the Communist International recognised the huge price that the world's labour and left-wing movements had paid for this adventurism, and it replaced its 1928 leftist lurch with a right-turn into Popular Frontism. Calls were made to unite with bourgeois forces to stop the death-march of reaction. Communists who had, in 1932, insisted that revolution was around the corner and no alliance was possible with any but those committed to an ultimate class-conflagration were, in 1937, happy to align with almost anyone. They then suppressed the politics of revolution in the interests of a broad coalition in which the distinct interests of the working class were too-often sacrificed in active maintenance of progressive bourgeois order.

If this Stalinist trajectory did, indeed, eventually confirm Trotsky's critique of the bureaucratisation and degeneration of the Communist International, in the

---

11. See, among other Comintern statements, 'Theses and Resolutions: The International situation and the Tasks of the Communist International', *International Press Correspondence*, 23 November 1928, pp. 1567–8; ECCI 1929.

immediacy of the early years of the Great Depression, the Third Period lurch to the left undercut the Left Opposition's argument that the established Communist Party was incapable of leading workers in militant struggles against capitalism and reaction. Especially in the United States, with its relatively weak traditions of revolutionary internationalism, the Communist Party appeared to most radicals to be espousing revolutionary demands. Both entering the Great Depression, and at its lowest points in 1931–2, mainstream Communists appeared to be leading most of the militant battles of labour, such as the struggles of mill-workers in the Piedmont in 1929; Communists led the way in forming Unemployed Councils and championing the rights of the jobless to relief and wages; and it was the Communist Party that seemed to address most decisively the defence of racist victims of American lynch-law such as the Scottsboro Boys. All of this made it extremely difficult for Trotskyists to intervene effectively, to convince rank-and-file communists that their Party was misleading them. Limited by what it could do as an external faction of the Communist Party, the CLA was also too small to mount any effective, independent leadership role in mass struggles. Cannon and his allies were largely confined to being propagandist critics of Stalinism, and *The Militant* and Left Opposition public forums reflected this.

Moreover, whenever the forces of nascent American Trotskyism appeared to gain ground in their criticism of the Communist Party, whether reflected in sales of their newspaper outside of their former comrades' mass meetings or in campaigns that began to expose the limitations of the Communist International's Third Period sectarianism, the small and beleaguered Communist League of America found itself subject to Stalinist thuggery and hooliganism. Many a League member was physically assailed after rising to speak the message of Trotskyism at a public forum; Left Opposition meetings were routinely invaded by Stalinist bullies, whose tactics of physical disruption had to be rebuffed by organised defence-guards.

Minneapolis was the site of one of these early Stalinist assaults on Trotskyism. No special plans had been made for a 23 January 1929 lecture by Cannon, which was to take place at a small local fraternity-society hall, and was entitled 'The Truth About Trotsky'. Nineteen year-old Fannie Curran, who had joined the Communist Party's Young Workers' League (YWL) at the ripe young age of fifteen, and then gravitated to the Left Opposition, remembered that 'Jim warned us that we had better come to the meeting early and be prepared'. But Cannon's claim that the Stalinists would try to smash up the meeting was brushed off as so much New York hyperbole. 'We just couldn't visualize that the comrades whom we had known and worked with for years would go so far as a physical attack', Curran remembered. Yet it was, perhaps, precisely because of Minneapolis's strength as a centre of developing Trotskyism in 1929 that the attack on the Left Opposition there would be particularly brutal. Veteran revolutionary militants and CLA members Oscar Coover and Carl Skoglund arrived at the Cannon meeting first, their job being to handle ticket-sales and admissions at the door. Alone, they were set upon by a Stalinist gang of thirty, fitted out with blackjacks and brass-knuckles. Coover required hospitalisation. With free access to the hall, Communist Party hooligans occupied all the front seats. When Cannon appeared and commenced his lecture, the howling and cries of 'counter-revolutionist' 'snivelling Trotskyite cur', and 'renegade' began. 'Then', in Curran's words, 'all hell broke loose'. In the ensuing 'free-for-all', chairs were broken and the woman managing the hall called the police. 'Arrest him, he's a counter-revolutionist', roared one Young Workers' League zealot, pointing at Cannon, betraying a rather naïve notion of the police's understanding of what constituted criminal behaviour, not to mention a repugnant reliance on the state to crush a political opponent. As the police pulled Cannon off the podium and cleared the room, the Left Opposition experienced one of its worst defeats at the hands of Stalinist thuggery. For Cannon, it was 'a rather scandalous and demoralizing thing'. The nascent forces of Minneapolis Trotskyism had, nonetheless, been taught a valuable lesson. It was now drummed into their battered heads that they, not the capitalist class, were regarded as the main enemy by their former comrades.

Cannon would not leave Minneapolis in defeat. He did not relish the legacy of Stalinist hooligans breaking up the first open Trotskyist meeting in the city's history, the shame of this hanging over militant heads for decades to come. Appealing to Minneapolis radical workers' resentment that 'a collaboration of the police and gangsters' had managed to suppress freedom of expression within the Left, the Communist League of America (Opposition) rallied broad support. The Industrial Workers of the World cancelled their Saturday-night forum and, 'as a demonstration against violation of the workers' right of free speech', rented the hall to Cannon and his comrades so that the lecture on Trotsky could actually be delivered. A Defense Guard was assembled, armed with oversized hatchet-handles purchased from a local hardware-store. Handbills circulated indicating that the talk was to take place and would be defended against attack. One Left Oppositionist boldly walked into the headquarters of the Workers' (Communist) Party and 'dared them to try to break up [the] meeting'. Over two hundred and fifty people packed the IWW hall and listened to Cannon's two-hour address. The Stalinists were a no-show. At the invitation of his Wobbly allies, Cannon appeared at their hall the next night as well, presenting a forum on 'Free Speech and the Labor Movement' to another large, and enthusiastic, audience.[12]

---

12. Fannie Curran in Evans (ed.) 1976, pp. 81–2; Vincent R. Dunne, 'The Minneapolis Meetings', *The Militant*, 1 February 1929; Cannon 1944, pp. 71–2. Myers 1977, p. 36 claims

If the early Trotskyist movement found the political terrain difficult in 1929 because of a series of factors external to the US Left Opposition, it was also the case that the Cannon-Shachtman-Abern forces soon found themselves at loggerheads internally. Shachtman, travelling to Europe in 1930, was the first CLA representative to actually meet Trotsky, who obviously hoped that the talented American revolutionary would exercise a stabilising influence in the European sections of the International Left Opposition (ILO), whose cadre had not really coalesced around principled programmatic orientations. In Germany and France, particularly, ILO figures like Kurt Landau and Pierre Naville, among others, were falling into increasingly routine habits of cliquism and opportunism, which troubled Trotsky. As the American representative on the ILO's International Bureau, Shachtman was asked by Trotsky to take a number of proposals to an international conference of Trotskyists held in Paris in April. Trotsky clearly saw the gathering as an opportunity to crystallise the politics of the ILO in ways that would place 'freelancers' in the emerging Trotskyist movement under certain political and organisational discipline. Shachtman proved a disappointment. Trotsky concluded, on the one hand, that Shachtman had 'the tendency to see things much too much from the journalistic or writers' standpoint at the expense of the political and the revolutionary', and, on the other, that the American Left Oppositionist also preferred to avoid open discussions of critical matters and 'substitute questionable personal combinations for revolutionary politics'. This manifested itself in Shachtman's 'chummy' accommodations in France to the opportunistic appetites of leadership-elements in the *Ligue Communiste* such as Naville, Alfred Rosmer, and Pierre Gourget, who congealed syndicalist sensibilities on trade-union questions with an attraction to the politics of the *salon*. One of this French cohort, M. Mill (also known as Jacques Obin or Pavel Okun), a leader of the autonomous Parisian Jewish Group of the ILO, managed to translate this political waffling to Spain, where he drew Trotsky's ire for muddying the Left Opposition waters by advocating unity with all manner of dissidents, a position promoted in other ways by Andreu Nin. Mill was eventually bounced from the Left Opposition and the *Ligue Communiste*, but not before Shachtman eased into *The Militant* two of Mill's dubious articles. Eventually defecting to Stalinism, Mill secured employment inside the Soviet Union on the promise that he could procure Trotskyist documents and expose the treacherous plot against the socialist fatherland. In Germany, Shachtman tried to soften criticism of Naville's close friend, Landau, who adapted to the French current's 'semi-syndicalist' privileging of the unions against the Left Opposition, creating, in Trotsky's view, 'a high *wall* between the League and the trade unions instead of a *link* between

---

that the Left Oppositionists 'hired strong-arm men to protect their speakers'. I am not aware of any evidence that supports this allegation.

them'. Not only did Landau embrace this politics, he 'systematically prevented the German Opposition from taking a correct position on this central question', and through 'concealment, reservations, and maneuvers' obfuscated matters inside a now-fractured Trotskyist movement. All the while avoiding an open and principled discussion of political positions, Landau waged an inexorable bureaucratic struggle for the German leadership, demoralising the Left Opposition in the process. Shachtman, in Trotsky's view, had been midwife to the birth of this European deformity. 'In the struggle that we waged... against the accidental, used-up, or downright demoralized elements', Trotsky wrote to Shachtman in December 1931, 'you... were never on our side, and those concerned (Rosmer, Naville, Landau, and now Mill) have always felt that they were backed in large measure by the American League'.[13]

These international questions resulted in considerable political debate and discussion within the leadership of the American Left Opposition, all of which divided the small forces of US Trotskyism. This was the background to a CLA pamphlet translated by Shachtman and introduced by Cannon, Trotsky's *Communism and Syndicalism: On the Trade Union Question*. It was published in March 1931 with the aid of funds raised in Cannon's home town, Kansas City, by one of his oldest comrades in the communist movement, A.A. 'Shorty' Buehler. Cannon, the experienced Seattle and Chicago revolutionary and trade-unionist Arne Swabeck, and a significant sector of the Communist League of America (Opposition), including most of its Minneapolis comrades, found little to quarrel with in Trotsky's chastisements of Shachtman's European manoeuvres. At a June 1932 gathering of the League's leading body, the National Committee, Shachtman protested that he had been misunderstood and misrepresented. His close allies, Albert Glotzer, Martin Abern, and the leading Canadian Trotskyist, Maurice Spector, largely distanced themselves from Shachtman. But the circle around Shachtman nonetheless remained unbroken: rooted in personal grievance and the 'politics' of gossip, this unprincipled factionalism was, in part, nurtured by Cannon's leadership-failings in these same years. On the surface, the international questions associated with conflicts within the European sections of the International Left Opposition were dispensed with, and, in a June 1932 document

---

13. The best discussion available on this internal crisis in the Communist League of America is Cannon et al. 2002, from which I have selectively quoted Leon Trotsky to the CLA National Committee, 25 December 1931, 'Shachtman's Personal and Journalistic Sympathies' (pp. 135–6); Leon Trotsky to Albert Glotzer, 1 May 1932, 'Personal Combinations vs. Revolutionary Politics', (p. 219); Leon Trotksy to Max Shachtman, 25 December 1931, 'You Were Never on Our Side', (p. 134). Trotsky 1973b; 1931, pp. 59–63.

penned by Cannon, there was recognition that a critically-important conflict had been liquidated with agreement 'reached on a political basis'.[14]

In fact, while the international political issues that seemingly divided the young Trotskyist movement in the United States had apparently been put to rest, the common ground that led Cannon, Shachtman, and Abern out of the Workers' (Communist) Party in 1928 and into the formation of an American Trotskyist Left Opposition was certainly weakened, if not broken. During the challenges of the years 1929–32, it would be difficult to piece this political unity back together.

Originally conceiving itself as an external faction seeking to reform rather than replace the Comintern, the Left Opposition understood that it could not go directly into the mass workers' movement, such as it was, and engage in a generalised recruitment to its politics. Rather, Trotskyists around the world determined that it was necessary 'to make the principles of the Left Opposition known to the vanguard', appealing to the 'tens of thousands of Communist Party members and sympathizers' to revive the original Bolshevik approach associated with the practice of the first years of the revolutionary Communist International. The defeatist policies of Stalinism's ultra-left and sectarian Third Period, in which attacks on all non-Party leftists as 'social fascists' and calls to form 'Red unions' in opposition to the established organisations of the working class were commonplace, had to be criticised and defeated *within the vanguard itself.* This meant reaffirming the Leninist orientation towards united fronts, accenting the necessity of working within the conservative craft-unions of the American Federation of Labor, and broadening the struggle against capitalism and its virulent programme of reaction so as both to more effectively build mass mobilisations of resistance *and* to win over non-communist workers, youth, minorities, and others to revolutionary politics. Doing this, as Cannon and others in the American Left Opposition recognised, necessarily meant – given Trotskyism's small numbers and weak influence in mass organisations of the working class – a sustained effort to convince former comrades in the communist movement to see the error of Stalinist ways. The American Left Opposition had been formed on this basis, understanding that it faced a difficult choice: 'We had to either turn our face towards the Communist Party, or away from the Communist Party in the direction of the undeveloped, unorganized and uneducated masses'. The latter orientation was, simply put, not an option. As Cannon wrote, 'We must first get what is obtainable from this vanguard group, ... [crystallising] out of [it] a sufficient cadre either to reform the party, or, if after a serious effort that fails in the end – and only when that failure is conclusively demonstrated – to build a new one with the forces recruited in the endeavour. Only in this way is it possible for us

---

14. 'Draft Statement to the Membership on the National Committee Plenum', 25 June 1932: Cannon et al. 2002, p. 311.

to reconstitute the party in the real sense of the word'. Inevitably, of course, this strategic understanding limited the Left Opposition to setting its main task as that of '*propaganda*, not *agitation*'.[15]

The dialectical reality of the origins of the American Left Opposition was thus that it found itself impaled on the horns of not one, but many, dilemmas, most of which were not, and could not have been, clearly understood at the moment of its formation in 1928–9. Cannon, Shachtman, and Abern, for instance, never imagined that their explusion from the Workers' (Communist) Party would be followed by the vitriolic denunciations, physical intimidation, and violent thuggery that descended on them and their comrades in the years 1929–33, and that revived and intensified whenever they made modest political inroads with their appeal to the Communist rank-and-file. Equally unpredictable, given the rightward drift of nascent Stalinism in the latter 1920s, was the leftist lurch that unfolded in 1928–9. To a superficial observer, it seemed to coincide directly with capitalism's collapse and the Great Depression. This provided Communist Parties around the world with a patina of 'revolutionary respectability': the Comintern had seemingly predicted and responded to capitalist crisis with a militant 'class-against-class' approach that proved its revolutionary mettle, effectively undercutting the Trotskyist criticism of Stalinism as compromised and calloused in its retreat into the constrained politics of 'socialism in one country'. Trotskyists in the United States were thus riding an apparently receding tide. As Cannon later wrote, 'At a time when tens and hundreds of thousands of new elements were beginning to look toward the Soviet Union, going forward with the Five Year Plan, while capitalism appeared to be going up the spout, here were these Trotskyists, with their documents under their arms, demanding that you read books, study, discuss, and so on. Nobody wanted to listen to us'. In the difficult years of 1929–32, then, the American Left Opposition appeared to be locked out of the politics of class-struggle. Baying at the distant and hostile Communist Party, the CLA was far-removed from those class-struggles that did unfold in this period, which all-too often seemed to be under the sway and influence of those whom the Left Opposition was determined to repudiate.[16]

The result was an isolation and marginalisation that invariably brought out the worst features of the human personnel that constituted Trotskyism's American leadership. Cannon, his personal life complicated by issues of responsibility for children arising out of the premature and unexpected death of his first wife, Lista Makimson, was burdened with financial obligations and domestic pressures that his younger cohort of Left Oppositionists – Shachtman, Abern, Spector, and the precocious Chicago youth-leader, Albert Glotzer – simply failed to

15. See Cannon 1944, pp. 86–8.
16. Cannon 1944, pp. 91–2.

comprehend. Furthermore, the situation for Cannon worsened decidedly as his partner, Rose Karsner, a dedicated communist with a long history in the revolutionary movement, suffered a series of debilitating health-problems. Feeling the adverse effects of Communist Party ostracism more acutely than her male counterparts, Karsner soon succumbed to a breakdown that left her incapable of contributing much to either the household-economy or the beginnings of the Left Opposition.[17]

Obviously finding it difficult to cope, Cannon absented himself from his leadership-responsibilities for an extended period reaching from the middle of 1929 into the early 1930s, and his failure to provide direction to the nascent Trotskyist movement eventually drew comment and criticism from his closest allies, among them Arne Swabeck, V.R. Dunne, and Rose Karsner.[18] Pouncing on Cannon's retreat, which was undoubtedly worsened by his tendency to descend into binge-drinking to avoid 'some insurmountable problem he didn't want to think about for a while',[19] Shachtman, Abern, Spector, and Glotzer waged a relentless, personalised factional war against their former comrade and leader. An extensive and ongoing gossipy correspondence was rife with denunciations of 'his royal highness' and 'Il Maestro'; Cannon's laziness was pilloried and the 'cult of worshippers' who refused to break decisively from him castigated. Their Bolshevism, Glotzer wrote in 1932, was little more than 'a veneer beneath which the shoddy paint of Stalinism is thickly smeared'. Few barbs contained as sharp and as intentional a sting among Trotskyists as such words of contemptuous dismissal.[20]

---

17. I detail this personal history in Chapter Two, 'Dog Days', of the second volume of my study of James P. Cannon, tentatively entitled *James P. Cannon and the American Left Opposition in the Time of Trotsky, 1928–1940*. For a brief introduction only, see Sam Gordon in Evans (ed.) 1976, pp. 56–62; Wald 1987, pp. 171–2.

18. Swabeck to Cannon, 5 December 1929, Box 3, File 2; Swabeck to Cannon, 8 April 1930, Box 3, File 3; Karsner to Cannon, 3 May 1933, Reel 20, James P. Cannon Papers, State Historical Society of Wisconsin, MD 92–175, Madison, Wisconsin (hereafter, JPC Papers); Swabeck to Cannon, 17 April 1933 – Cannon et al. 2002, p. 509.

19. Sam Gordon in Evans (ed.) 1976, p. 58; Roskolenko 1965, p. 178, describes Cannon in these years as 'the Big Bertha' of the Trotskyist movement, 'with more bad whiskey than good blood in him'.

20. This factional correspondence was voluminous, and is detailed in my discussion of the 'Dog Days', as well as in the already published collection of documents, Cannon et al. 2002, which also contains the Abern, Glotzer, Shachtman summary-document on the internal problems in the CLA (Opposition), 'The Situation in the American Opposition: Prospect and Retrospect': see Abern, Glotzer and Shachtman 2002. For some select examples of this correspondence only, see Shachtman to Glotzer, 11 September 1929; 30 September 1929, Reel 20, JPC Papers; Glotzer to Shachtman, 13 March 1932; Shachtman to Spector, 3 July 1932, Roll 10, Reel 3353; Shachtman to Glotzer, 26 November 1932, Roll 11, Reel 3354, Max Shachtman Papers, Tamiment Institute, Bobst Library, New York University, New York, New York (hereafter, MS Papers). See also Drucker 1994, pp. 56–8.

This personalised anti-Cannon factionalism paralleled and contributed to the controversy over international questions that saw Cannon and Trotsky pitted against Shachtman over the course of the early 1930s. It also contaminated the organisational procedures of the American Left Opposition as a whole, with Cannonists and anti-Cannonists lined up in oppositional voting blocs, and the National Committee deformed by factional jockeying for power. The general problem was exacerbated as the Left Opposition, forced inwards upon itself, 'began to recruit from sources none too healthy', such elements being 'dilettantish petty-bourgeois minded people who couldn't stand any kind of discipline, who had either left the CP or been expelled from it, wanted, or rather thought they wanted to become Trotskyists'. Cannon remembered these types in a particular way:

> They can all talk; and not only can, but *will*; and everlastingly, on every question. They were iconoclasts who would accept nothing as authoritative, nothing as decided in the history of the movement. Everything and everybody had to be proved over again from scratch.

Shachtman did not disagree, acknowledging that more than a few 'dilettantes, well-meaning blunderers, biological chatterboxes, ultra-radical oat-sowers, unattachable wanderers, and many other kinds of sociological curiosa' found their way into the CLA. Particularly in New York, where the leadership of Trotskyism was at this time concentrated, and where the non-proletarian side of the Left Opposition was developing with vigour, branches of the Communist League of America (Opposition) were 'one continuous stew of discussion'. They became, moreover, nests of factional intrigue, and endless internal squabbles created an atmosphere of acrimony, ongoing tension, and seemingly irresolvable disputes.[21]

The American Trotskyist movement almost succumbed to these problems. But it managed to transcend such difficulties. Trotsky's published writings and correspondence with the Communist League of America (Opposition) provided a common body of analytical thought and programmatic guidance that was of tremendous importance. Cannon thought this writing nothing less than 'a window on a whole new world of theory and political understanding'.[22] In 1933–4, the US

---

21. Cannon 1944, pp. 90–5; Shachtman 1954, p. 18. See Jacobs 1965, pp. 44–76, for a recollection of one young Trotskyist transferred from New York to Minneapolis in the mid-1930s. Jacobs contrasted the 'easy going radical atmosphere' of New York with its Village parties, kibitzing at Left Opposition headquarters, and 'schmoozing over coffee in cafeterias', with the harsh discipline that left 'little room for errors or weakness' in Minneapolis. 'I understood very well how it was possible for this group of men to successfully run the teamsters' union and why the Minneapolis general strike had been run like a military operation', Jacobs confessed, adding for emphasis that, 'Ray Dunne and the people around him were very serious revolutionists' (Jacobs 1965, pp. 52–3).

22. Cannon 1944, pp. 99–100.

Trotskyist movement, guided by fundamental revolutionary principles, began to dig itself out of the holes of the 'Dog Days', regardless of whether they were of its own making or not. A changed context provided the Left Opposition with new possibilities to translate its abstract understandings into concrete engagement in actual class-struggles and political campaigns.[23] The personalised factionalism of the years 1929–32 eventually gave way to productive working relations that reconfigured what had been divisions growing out of unprincipled combinations into new political solidarities.

This was done slowly and with difficulty. Common discussions on questions that had long vexed the American revolutionary movement, such as how the Communist League of America (Opposition) was to address the issue of a party of labour or confront racism and develop a strategic approach to what was, in the early 1930s, referred to as 'The Negro Question', brought warring factions of the Left Opposition closer together in 1932–3. In rejecting the mistakes that had been made in communists' past practices with regard to these important issues, both the Shachtman and Cannon camps in the League found some hint of common ground, even if it was not always recognised and appreciated as such.[24]

More importantly, perhaps, by 1933, American labour was giving signs of coming out of its Depression-induced lethargy. As the combativity of working-class forces revived, campaigns against unemployment and in defence of labour-movement political prisoners such as Tom Mooney created spaces for Trotskyists to intervene in mass struggles.[25] Even the Communist Party, struggling to offset the deleterious consequences of its Third Period sectarianism, made a half-hearted 'half-turn' in the political direction of the united front.[26] All of this not only prodded Cannon to come to life, but it showcased his best features, more or less neutralising criticisms of him from his factional opponents such as Shachtman.[27] As the Communist League of America made some important, albeit limited and transitory, inroads in the Illinois coal-districts, influencing the potentially militant Progressive Miners of America movement, further steps were taken in bridging past divisions in the ranks of the small and increasingly more coherent forces

23. There is an overly brief and often inadequate summary of this process in Myers 1977, pp. 59–82.

24. Again, the complicated development of the clarifications made on these kinds of issues can not be dealt with here, but is discussed at length in Chapter Three, 'Daylight: Analysis and Action', of my forthcoming work *James P. Cannon and the American Left Opposition in the Time of Trotsky*. For an important discussion of 'The Negro Question', see Shachtman 2003. On the labour-party, note Trotsky 1973a, pp. 113–36.

25. Rosenzweig 1975; 1976; Lorence 1996; Frost 1968; Gentry 1967.

26. Klehr 1983, pp. 97–117; Storch 2007, pp. 99–129; 'United Front Call Issued for Unemployment Insurance: Opposition Welcomes Party Turn and Warns Against Opportunistic Tendencies', *The Militant*, 14 January 1933; James P. Cannon, 'The New Party Turn', *The Militant*, 21 January 1933.

27. See, for instance, Cannon et al. 2002, pp. 413–14.

of US Trotskyism.[28] When the New York hotel and restaurant-industry erupted in a massive and bitter strike in January-February 1934, the Communist League of America was centrally involved, one of its members, B.J. Field, leading the struggle, with Cannon and his close confidant and skilled industrial organiser, Hugo Oehler, playing decisive roles. In the end, Field, a mercurial figure, led the strike to defeat, and was expelled from the League for serious breaches of discipline and a refusal to work collaboratively with the Left Opposition leadership. The Shachtman-Cannon divide seemed finally bridged, and the Communist League of America had tasted the fruit, both bitter and sweet, of influencing the mass struggles of the working class.[29]

Indicative of the coming together of the factionalised CLA forces, and the growing potential for American Trotskyism to intervene in mass movements of the Left, was the 1932–4 agitation around Hitler's rise to power in Germany. Both the ILO and the CLA stressed repeatedly the urgent need for united-front actions to derail the fascist juggernaut. In the United States, this mobilisation revealed starkly the differences between Stalinists and Trotskyists, the lines of demarcation being drawn in blood.[30] League member Harry Roskolenko recalled attending a 1932 rally at which a professorial-looking J. Louis Engdahl, leading spokesman of the Communist Party, expounded a vitriolic Third Period attack on so-called social fascists, insisting that Stalin's Comintern would alone defeat Hitler and that it was necessary to fight to the death both against 'the capitalist masters of fascism' and the 'fascist nature' of all non-Communist misleaders on the Left. Quaking in his dissident-boots, Roskolenko stood up during the discussion from the floor to denounce Engdahl's divisiveness. He spoke of the necessity of forging a 'real united front' of class-struggle opponents of fascism as the only way to defeat Hitler. Shouting over 'the cat-calls . . . from Engdhal's frontbench claque', Roskolenko insisted that 'prattling about socialist leaders being *social-fascist*' had to come to an end, and that the term was a meaningless and pejorative 'word invented by Stalin'. Engdahl fumed on the stage, interjecting with a shouted threat: 'You Trotskyists take your lives in your hands when you come here to make counter-revolutionary speeches. I am not responsible for anything that happens to you when you leave!' Roskolenko took the rejoinder as 'an invitation to beat hell out of me'. After the meeting, as he was selling *The Militant*

28. For dated studies of the Progressive Miners, see Hudson 1952; Young 1947. Cannon would appreciate both the militancy of the miners' insurgency, the weaknesses of the revolutionary forces among the miners, and the important role that the Women's Auxiliary played in the class-struggle in the Illinois coal-fields. This latter recognition would figure forcefully in developments in Minneapolis in 1934. See Cannon, 'Miners Form New Union: Raise Struggle to New Heights', *The Militant*, 10 September 1932; Cannon 1958, pp. 91–2.

29. Cannon 1944, pp. 126–30.

30. Glotzer 1989, pp. 176–9.

and urging the dispersing crowd 'to fight Hitler and not each other', Roskolenko was jumped by three leather-jacketed assailants. As they beat and kicked him senseless, onlookers former a circle around the fallen Trotskyist and egged on the violence. Roskolenko woke up in the hospital, offering a wry summary: 'Three teeth were gone and my testicles were hardly in a masculine shape'.[31]

Two Communist Party rank-and-file workers fared even worse as a consequence of Stalinist violence in a New York City Lower East Side park in August 1932. Soap-boxing CLAers regaled crowds with stinging criticism of Stalinist sectarianism and its ineffectiveness in halting Hitler's march to power in Germany. The Party hierarchy inflamed the ranks with 'a lynch spirit against the Trotskyites'. On 20 August 1932, a small agitational corps of Trotskyists plopped down some portable wooden podiums to set up their anti-fascist rabble-rousing shop as usual on the corner of Seventh Street and Avenue A. There, they readied themselves to address a gathering on the situation in Germany. Soon, they were assailed by a 'surging, singing, howling' throng. With banners flying, the larger Communist Party contingent erected a platform of the Unemployed Council right next to the reviled Trotskyists, and, before long, 'a mob of communists were going through their usual disorders'. Outnumbered Left Oppositionists were soon driven into retreat, and the street-corner belonged to the Party. But in the chaos of the confrontation, bricks and heavy granite-cobblestones had been thrown from the top of a darkened roof, apparently by a small group of Party members responding to a signal from a comrade on the ground. When the dust cleared and the shock subsided, however, it was not the hated Trotskyists who suffered, but two Communist Party members, Michael Semen and Nick Krusiuk. Both were seriously injured. Semen succumbed almost immediately, and Krusiuk was taken to the hospital, where he also later died. The two workers were ostensibly killed by their own comrades, whose blind hatred of Left Oppositionists prompted them to what became a rash, murderous act.

At the time, however, few knew for certain who was responsible for the heavy debris that rained down on the street-corner being used for soap-boxing. Initially, Left Oppositionists put forward the view that the attack was undertaken by reactionary anti-communists of the 'Black Legion' stripe. For its part, the upper echelons of the CP that knew better immediately pointed the finger directly at the sinister 'Trotskyites'. In the pages of the *Daily Worker*, and in leaflets in English, Russian, and Ukrainian, the murders were said to be the responsibility of Cannon and his renegade-group. *The Militant* claimed that 'There is taking place a general campaign of incitement for a pogrom against us which also has the elements of provocation to the authorities'. It deplored the 'vicious campaign' as

31. Roskolenko 1965, pp. 134–6.

a 'desperate last resort', in which the 'depraved Stalinist bureaucracy' had finally stooped 'to the lowest depths' of its general method of 'physical violence in place of political argumentation'. Forced, in this climate of hatred and retribution, to postpone all street-meetings and arrange for the guarding of its headquarters, the Communist League of America (Opposition) also demanded a public, open-air hearing on 'the Stalinist frame-up'. As various labour and civil-liberties organisations signed up for the proposed meeting, the Communist Party lapsed into silence, effectively withdrew its allegations of Trotskyist responsibility, and ignored the call for a workers' inquiry into the events of August 1932. But the Left Opposition's branch-organiser Hugo Oehler, and Tom Stamm, chairman of the original Trotskyist street-meeting, were summoned to appear before the District-Attorney. Prior to this, thousands of Communists and sympathisers had heard Party leaders denounce the Left Opposition at a 23 August 1932 rally. The Party's organs were filled with 'venomous lynch propaganda'. A march took place from the Lower East Side to Union Square, the inflamed Communist Party crowd raising clenched fists in the air, their slogans shouted in hate: 'Death to the Trotskyites. Death to All Renegades'.[32] Max Shachtman considered this 'the heart of darkness of Stalinism itself'.[33]

With Hitler confirmed as Chancellor in 1933, the League used its paper, *The Militant*, to propagandise relentlessly around the need to mobilise a resolute opposition to the fascist forces in Germany. Cannon sensed that 'things were beginning to break' as fresh openings in labour-struggles and the mass politics of anti-fascism brought Trotskyists more and more into contact with new and radicalising forces. The front page of the 4 February 1933 issue of *The Militant* was headlined 'Hitler in Power; Civil War Starts – Opposition's Demand for a United Front is Need of the Hour in Germany', while the bottom of the page announced a Sunday-night mass meeting held at the Stuyvesant Casino on New York's Second Avenue, sponsored by the CLA, with Cannon and Shachtman speaking on 'The Crisis in Germany'. A week later, Cannon addressed a similar mass meeting at the Hollywood Gardens in the Bronx. He also attended Party meetings and spoke from the floor, as well as travelling to Philadelphia and other adjacent population-centres to speak. The Left Opposition was, at the same time, actively engaged in making widely available its pamphlet-version of Trotsky's *Germany –*

---

32. Gitlow 1948, pp. 233–5; Oneal and Werner 1947, p. 216; Roskolenko 1965, pp. 135–6; Minutes of the National Committee, Communist League of America, #110, 25 August 1932; #111, 1 September 1932, Box 32, File 2, George Breitman Papers, Tamiment Institute, Bobst Library, New York University (hereafter, BP); 'Stalinists in Monstrous Frame-Up Against Left Opposition', *The Militant*, 27 August 1932; 'The Stalinist Bureaucrats Back Out on Murder Frame-Up Hearing', *The Militant*, 3 September 1932; 'Police Act on Stalinist Frame-Up', *The Militant*, 10 September 1932.

33. Shachtman 1954, p. 13.

What Next? Meanwhile, *The Militant* upped its publication-schedule to three times a week (halving the size of each paper) during 'the German crisis', an effort that taxed all League comrades fully. Speakers such as Abern and Oehler addressed audiences from Wilkes Barre, Pennsylvania to Des Moines, Iowa on the need to rally mass support to stop Hitler. 'Fascists Command Police; Shoot Reds!' and 'Whoever Blocks the Workers' United Front is a Traitor!', screamed *The Militant's* headlines. Throughout February and March, Cannon and Shachtman were speaking almost weekly at a variety of New York venues on topics relating to the German crisis, laying stress on the barbarity of fascism, the bloodthirsty repression of militant workers and communists, and Stalinism's bankrupt policies, the self-isolating 'united front from below' failing to galvanise workers to the solidarity and common front needed to defeat Hitler. As Cannon's surviving speech-notes indicate, when he addressed audiences about the German crisis, he highlighted the necessity of united-front action, stressing that it was crucial that all of the forces of the international proletariat must be readied to take their stand against fascism and in defence of the German working class. Hitler's triumph, the Left Opposition continually pointed out, would not only decimate the powerful German workers' movement and its strong communist component; it would also inevitably culminate in an attack on the Soviet Union.[34] If there remained a residue of personalised factionalism, with Shachtman more than willing to haul Cannon on the carpet for any political miscue that might be conjured out of the propaganda over the German crisis, it was, nevertheless, clear that the anti-Hitler/anti-war campaign of 1932–3, like the League's efforts to intersect various unemployed, trade-union, and labour political-defence causes, brought Left Oppositionists together and pointed the way to common actions.[35]

The ILO in Europe and the CLA in America failed to convince the official Communist movement to abandon its sectarian abstentionism from the struggle to build united-front resistance to Hitler's rise to power. In Germany, not only the Stalinists, but also the Social Democrats, capitulated to fascism; leaderless, the once-powerful proletariat was conquered without a fight. Trotsky had warned of the consequences of this kind of defeat, a betrayal that he insisted would demoralise workers the world over. No longer able to see the Communist

34. *The Militant*, 4 February 1933; 11 February 1933; 15 February 1933; 22 February 1933; 1 March 1933; 3 March 1933; 6 March 1933; Cannon, 'Rough Notes', 'Speech on Germany', New York, 10 March 1933 and 'Fascism (Mass Meeting), Manhattan Lyceum, 1/5/33', Reel 33, JPC Papers; James P. Cannon to All Branches, 'German Campaign – Circular # 2', 14 February 1933; Cannon 1944, pp. 105–8; CLA, National Committee Minutes, 3 April 1933, Attachment, Martin Abern, 'Report of Activity During the Period of the Three-times-a-week Militant in New German Campaign', Box 32, File 10, BP; Drucker 1994, pp. 62–5.
35. For one Shachtman-led attack on Cannon, raised in opposition to the latter's ostensible statement that the Red Army had to be readied in Russia to strike the first blow against fascism, see Cannon et al. 2002, pp. 421–8.

International and its national sections as capable of being won back to the traditions and principles of revolutionary Marxism, Trotsky concluded, on the basis of the German defeat, that the Communist Party (KPD) had passed over into a new stage of degeneration, in which its organized expression was nothing but 'the convulsion of a dying organism'. In this context, maintaining the International Left Opposition as an external faction of the German KPD was politically impossible and, by mid-March 1933, Trotsky had concluded that to remain oriented to the mainstream Communist Party in Hitler's Germany was little more than a criminal act of tying 'oneself to a corpse'.[36]

It followed, logically, that the International Left Opposition would eventually break decisively from the Communist International, declaring an end to its status as an external faction and opting, instead, to form its own International and establish affiliated revolutionary parties as its specific national sections. Trotsky called for just such a shift in perspective in August 1933. While tensions and factional animosities continued to rankle within the leadership of the Communist League of America, it was nevertheless the case that both Cannon and Shachtman embraced Trotsky's new course. Shachtman's November 1933 pamphlet *Ten Years: History and Principles of the Left Opposition* referred to the necessity of 'breaking relentlessly and completely with the decadent Stalinist apparatus'.[37]

Five months later, Cannon debated his old comrade turned adversary, Jay Lovestone, at Irving Plaza. Lovestone argued that the Communist International could be reformed and unified, but Cannon was adamant that 'Too much water had passed over the mill, too many mistakes had been made, too many crimes and betrayals had been committed, too much blood spilled by the Stalinist International'. With a catalogue of Stalinist 'error' at his fingertips, Cannon was relentless in his condemnation of the political crimes of those advocating 'socialism in one country', detailing the capitulations to imperialism from the time of the abortive Chinese Revolution of 1925–7 and outlining the price that had been paid in workers' blood as a consequence of the sectarianism of the Third Period, especially in Germany and Austria. Stalinist terror inside the Soviet Union had decimated the ranks of the original Bolsheviks, with explosions, exiles, beatings, and worse being used to ugly effect. Also within the US labour and workers' movements, Cannon insisted, the Communist Party had much to atone for. Hooliganism and violent thuggery had been imported into these milieux by Communists, and Cannon's own apartment had been burgled by Stalinist agents. 'The blight of Stalinism', Cannon proclaimed with certitude to the fifteen-hundred-strong Irving Plaza crowd, 'is world wide.... The Third International as a revolutionary

---

36. Trotsky 1972a; 1972b; 1972c.
37. Shachtman 1933, p. 5.

force is dead', he insisted. 'The revolutionary vanguard, now, as in 1914, must build new parties and a new international'.[38]

Shachtman, on national tour, was taking the same message across the United States. *The Militant* of 31 March 1934 carried the banner-headline 'For the Fourth International! Appeal of the Communist-Internationalists to the Workers of the World', in which the unambiguous call for the formation of a new revolutionary party and a new International was presented as the imperative of the hour. With imperialist war threatening and fascism already ensconced in Germany, 'The autocratic rule of the unrestrained bureaucracy' of Stalinism had elevated itself above the working masses, making 'a religion of its infallibility'. This development needed to be challenged and reversed. For the American Left Opposition, 'Trotskyism on a world scale was on the march. We in the United States were in step'. Cannon felt like it was 'old times', and the isolation and factional infighting of the early 1930s had finally been transcended. The struggle was now taking place 'on a far different, on a higher plane'. Trotsky was heartened that the situation in the American League seemed finally to be righting itself, and he wrote to Shachtman that as opportunities presented themselves in the new context of revived class-struggle and intensified Left Opposition engagement in wider public activity, 'the danger of an exacerbation of the internal struggle diminishes'.[39]

Minneapolis was just such a presentation of opportunity within an expanding framework of working-class initiative, and it allowed American Trotskyism to show a good part of what it could accomplish. This would be followed, in the September-December 1934 period, with a political fusion, uniting the Communist League of America and the American Workers' Party (AWP), led by the leftward-moving former pacifist preacher A.J. Muste. Muste and the AWP had been the animating force behind the Toledo Auto-Lite upheaval, and had pioneered new tactics in uniting the employed and the unemployed in the mass strike. Under the banner-headline 'Launch Workers Party of the U.S.', *The Militant* celebrated the formation of a new revolutionary party: 'Minneapolis and Toledo, exemplifying the new militancy of the American working class, were the stars that presided over its birth'. Dedicated to 'the overthrow of capitalist rule in America, and the creation of a workers' state', the formation of the Workers' Party was a promising leap out of Trotskyism's 'Dog Days'. It would prove a crucial step in the process of revolutionary regroupment that would culminate in the formation of the Socialist Workers Party. The Minneapolis strikes of 1934, advancing the interests of

38. Cannon 1944, pp. 136–8; 'Big Crowd at Debate: Cannon and Lovestone Discuss Internationals', *The Militant*, 10 March 1934; Cannon speech-notes, 'Fourth International: Debate with Lovestone', 5 March 1934, Reel 32, JPC Papers.

39. Drucker 1994, pp. 68–91; Cannon 1944, pp. 136–8; 'For the Fourth International!', *The Militant*, 31 March 1934; Trotsky to Shachtman, 30 January 1934, in Cannon et al. 2002, p. 606.

tens of thousands of workers and boldly proclaiming a new path for American labour, had also been decisive in bringing into being a new and more forceful revolutionary organisation. For the American Left Opposition, Minneapolis, with its modest demands for recognition of a truly industrial union and improvement in the material standards of its widening membership, would, indeed, be demonstration of the validity of Trotsky's confident 1938 proclamation that, 'The old "minimal program" is superseded by the *transitional program*, the task of which lies in systematic mobilization of the masses for the proletarian revolution'. This was the road to the ultimate realisation of the revolutionary teamsters' cause.[40]

---

40. 'Launch Workers Party of U.S.', *The Militant*, 8 December 1934; Cannon 1944, pp. 167–88; Trotsky 1973a, p. 76.

References

Abern, Martin, Albert Glotzer, and Max Shachtman 2002 [1932], 'The Situation in the American Opposition: Prospect and Retrospect', in Cannon, James P. et al. 2002, *Dog Days: James P. Cannon vs. Max Shachtman in the Communist League of America*, New York: Prometheus Research Library.

Adamic, Louis 1934, *Dynamite: The Story of Class Violence in America, Revised Edition*, Gloucester, MA: Peter Smith.

Alexander, Robert J. 1991, *International Trotskyism, 1929–1985: A Documented Analysis of the Movement*, Durham, NC: Duke University Press.

Ali, Tariq 2011, *The Obama Syndrome: Surrender at Home, War Abroad*, London: Verso.

Alinsky, Saul 1947, *John L. Lewis: An Unauthorized Biography*, New York: G.P. Putnam's Sons.

Allen, Joe 2012, 'Confronting the fascist threat in the US in the late 1930s, Part I: It can't happen here', *International Socialist Review*, 79.

Barzman, John 1997, *Dockers, métallos, ménagères: mouvements sociaux et cultures militants au Havre, 1913–1923*, Rouen: Publications de l'université de Rouen.

Belknap, Michael 1977, *Cold War Political Justice: The Smith Act, the Communist Party, and American Civil Liberties*, Westport, CT: Greenwood.

Bernstein, Irving 1960, *The Lean Years: A History of the American Worker, 1920–1933*, Boston: Houghton Mifflin.

—— 1970, *Turbulent Years: A History of the American Worker, 1933–1941*, Boston: Houghton Mifflin.

Biddle, Francis 1962, *In Brief Authority*, New York: Doubleday.

Blantz, Thomas E. 1970, 'Father Haas and the Minneapolis Truckers' Strike of 1934', *Minnesota History*, 42: 8–9.

—— 1982, *A Priest in Public Service: Francis J. Haas and the New Deal*, Notre Dame, IN: University of Notre Dame Press.

Booth, Stephane E. 1996, 'Ladies in White: Female Activism in the Southern Illinois Coal Fields, 1932–1938', in *The United Mine Workers of America: A Model of Industrial Solidarity*, edited by John H.M. Laslett, University Park, PA: Pennsylvania State University Press.

Brecher, Jeremy 1974, *Strike!*, Greenwich, CT: Fawcett Premier.

Breitman, George, Paul Le Blanc, and Alan Wald 1996, *Trotskyism in the United States: Historical Essays and Reconsiderations*, Atlantic Highlands, NJ: Humanities Press.

Brill, Steven 1978, *The Teamsters*, New York: Simon and Schuster.

Brody, David 1972, 'Labor and the Great Depression: The Interpretive Prospects', *Labor History*, 13.

Broué, Pierre 1988, *Trotsky*, Paris: Fayard.

—— 2006, *The German Revolution*, Chicago: Haymarket.

Budenz, Louis Francis 1947, *This is My Story*, New York: McGraw-Hill.

Cannon, James P. 1934a, 'The Strike Wave and the Left Wing', *New International*, 1, September-October: 67–8.

—— 1934b, 'Minneapolis and Its Meaning', *New International*, 1, July: 3–5.

—— 1944, *The History of American Trotskyism: Report of a Participant*, New York: Pioneer.

—— 1958, *Notebook of an Agitator*, New York: Pioneer.

—— 1973, *Letters from Prison*, New York: Pathfinder.

Cannon, *Cont.*
—— 1975 [1941], 'Why We Have Been Indicted', in *James P. Cannon Writings and Speeches, 1940–1943: The Socialist Workers Party in World War II*, edited by Les Evans, New York: Pathfinder.
—— 1985, 'Textile Strike Debacle', in *James P. Cannon: The Communist League of America, 1932–1934 – Writings and Speeches*, edited by Fred Stanton and Michael Taber, New York: Monad Press.
Cannon, James P. et al. 2002, *Dog Days: James P. Cannon vs. Max Shachtman in the Communist League of America*, New York: Prometheus Research Library.
Carr, Edward H. 1979, *The Russian Revolution: From Lenin to Stalin, 1917–1929*, London: Macmillan.
Cherny, Robert W. 2002, 'Prelude to the Popular Front: The Communist Party in California, 1931–1935', *American Communist History*, 1: 5–42.
Cochran, Bert 1977, *Labor and Communism: The Conflict That Shaped American Unions*, Princeton, NJ: Princeton University Press.
Crook, Wilfrid Harris 1931, *The General Strike: A Study of Labor's Tragic Weapon in Theory and Practice*, Chapel Hill, NC: University of North Carolina Press.
Davis, Colin J. 1997, *Power at Odds: the 1922 National Railroad Shopmen's Strike*, Chicago: University of Illinois Press.
Davis, Mike 2011, 'Spring Confronts Winter', *New Left Review*, II/72: 5–15.
De Graaf, John 1980, *Labor's Turning Point: The Minneapolis Truck Strikes of 1934*, Minneapolis: Labor Education Service, University of Minnesota.
Deutscher, Isaac 1954, *The Prophet Armed: Trotsky, 1879–1921*, Oxford: Oxford University Press.
—— 1959, *The Prophet Unarmed, 1921–1929*, Oxford: Oxford University Press.
—— 1963, *The Prophet Outcast, 1929–1940*, Oxford: Oxford University Press.
Dobbs, Farrell 1972, *Teamster Rebellion*, New York: Monad.
—— 1973, *Teamster Power*, New York: Monad.
—— 1975, *Teamster Politics*, New York: Monad.
—— 1977, *Teamster Bureaucracy*, New York: Monad.

Draper, Theodore 1957, *The Roots of American Communism*, New York: Viking Press.
—— 1963, *American Communism and Soviet Russia*, New York: Viking Press.
Dray, Philip 2010, *There is Power in a Union: The Epic Story of Labor in America*, New York: Doubleday.
Drucker, Peter 1994, *Max Shachtman and His Left: A Socialist's Odyssey Through the 'American Century'*, Atlantic Highlands, NJ: Humanities Press.
Dunne, William F. and Morris Childs 1934, *Permanent Counter-Revolution: The Role of the Trotskyites in the Minneapolis Strikes*, New York: Workers Library.
Eagleton, Terry 2011, *Why Marx Was Right*, London: Yale University Press.
ECCI 1929, *The World Situation and Economic Struggle: Theses of the Tenth Plenum, ECCI*, London: Communist Party of Great Britain.
Edwards, P.K. 1981, *Strikes in the United States, 1881–1974*, Oxford: Basil Blackwell.
Eliel, Paul 1934, *The Waterfront and General Strikes: San Francisco, 1934*, San Francisco: Hooper Printing.
Emery, Robert C. 1934, *Thirty Years From Now*, St. Paul, MN: R.C. Emery.
Erickson, Herman 1971, 'WPA Strike and Trials of 1939', *Minnesota History*, 42, Summer: 202–14.
Evans, Les (ed.) 1975, *James P. Cannon, Writings and Speeches, 1940–1943: The Socialist Workers Party in World War II*, New York: Pathfinder.
—— 1976, *James P. Cannon as We Knew Him: By Thirty-Three Comrades, Friends, and Relatives*, New York: Pathfinder.
Faue, Elizabeth 1991, *Community of Suffering and Struggle: Women, Men, and the Labor Movement in Minneapolis, 1915–1945*, Chapel Hill, NC: University of North Carolina Press.
Foster, William Z. 1939, *Pages from a Worker's Life*, New York: International.
Franco, Joseph and Richard Hammer 1987, *Hoffa's Man: The Rise and Fall of Jimmy Hoffa as Witnessed by His Strongest Arm*, New York: Prentice Hall.
Friedman, Allen and Ted Schwarz 1989, *Power and Greed: Inside the Teamsters Empire of Corruption*, New York: Franklin Watts.

Friedman, Samuel R. 1982, *Teamster Rank-and-File: Power, Bureaucracy, and Rebellion at Work and in a Union*, New York: Columbia University Press.

Frost, Richard H. 1968, *The Mooney Case*, Stanford, CA: Stanford University Press.

Fukuyama, Francis 1989, 'The End of History?', *The National Interest*, Summer: 3–18.

Galenson, Walter 1960, *The CIO Challenge to the AFL: A History of the American Labor Movement, 1935–1941*, Cambridge, MA; Harvard University Press.

Gates, John 1958, *The Story of an American Communist*, New York: Thomas Nelson.

Gentry, Curt 1967, *Frame-Up: The Incredible Case of Tom Mooney and Warren Billings*, New York: Norton.

Gieske, Millard L. 1979, *Minnesota Farmer-Laborism: The Third-Party Alternative*, Minneapolis: University of Minnesota Press.

Gitlow, Benjamin 1948, *The Whole of Their Lives: Communism in America – A Personal History and Intimate Portrayl of Its Leaders*, New York: Scribner's Sons.

Glotzer, Albert 1989, *Trotsky: Memoir and Critique*, New York: Prometheus Books.

Goldberg, Joseph P. 1958, *The Maritime Story: A Study in Labor-Management Relations*, Cambridge, MA: Harvard University Press.

Goldman, Albert 1942, *The Truth About the Minneapolis Trial of the 28: Speech for the Defense by Albert Goldman*, New York: Pioneer.

—— 1944, *In Defense of Socialism: The Official Court Record of Albert Goldman's Final Speech for the Defense in the Famous Minneapolis 'Sedition' Trial*, New York: Pioneer.

Goldstein, Robert Justin 1978, *Political Repression in Modern America from 1870 to the Present*, Boston: Schenckman.

Goodstein, Phil H. 1984, *The Theory of the General Strike from the French Revolution to Poland*, New York: Columbia University Press.

Green, James 1972, 'Working Class Militancy in the Great Depression', *Radical America*, 6: 1–36.

Gus Hall Action Club 2009, 'Red Heroes of the 1934 Minneapolis Teamsters Strike: Gus Hall and the CPUSA', available at <http://gushallactionclub.blogspot.ca/2009/05/red-heroes-of-1934-minneapolis.html>.

Haverty-Stacke, Donna T. forthcoming, 'Punishment of Mere Political Advocacy': The FBI, Teamsters Local 544 and the Origins of the 1941 Smith Act Case', *Journal of American History*.

Healey, Dorothy and Maurice Isserman 1990, *Dorothy Healey Remembers: A Life in the American Communist Party*, Oxford: Oxford University Press.

Hentoff, Nat 1963, *Peace Agitator: The Story of A.J. Muste*, New York: Macmillan.

Hoffa, James R. 1970, *The Trials of Jimmy Hoffa: An Autobiography*, Chicago: Henry Regnery.

Hoffa, James R. and Oscar Fraley 1975, *Hoffa: The Real Story as told to Oscar Fraley*, New York: Stein and Day.

Hudson, Carlos 1935, 'Minneapolis One Year Later', *The Nation*, 141: 512–14.

—— 1938, 'A Frame-Up That Failed', *New International*, 4, March: 73–5.

Hudson, Harriet D. 1952, *The Progressive Mine Workers of America: A Study in Rival Unionism*, Chicago: University of Illinois Bureau of Economics and Business Research Bulletin #73.

International Bolshevik Tendency (ed.) 1998, *The Transitional Program: The Death Agony of Capitalism and the Tasks of the Fourth International*, London: Bolshevik Publications.

Jaffe, Philip J. 1975, *The Rise and Fall of American Communism*, New York: Horizon.

Jacobs, Paul 1957, 'The World of Jimmy Hoffa', *The Reporter*, 7 February.

—— 1965, *Is Curly Jewish? A Political Self-Portrait Illuminating Three Turbulent Decades of Social Revolt – 1935–1965*, New York: Atheneum.

James, Ralph C. and Estelle Dinerstein James 1965, *Hoffa and the Teamsters: A Study of Union Power*, New York: Van Nostrand.

—— 1966, 'The Purge of the Trotskyites from the Teamsters', *Western Political Quarterly*, 19, March: 5–15.

Kimeldorf, Howard 1988, *Reds or Rackets? The Making of Radical and Conservative Unions on the Waterfront*, Berkeley, CA: University of California Press.

Klehr, Harvey 1983, *The Heyday of American Communism: The Depression Decade*, New York: Basic Books.

Knox, Chris 1998a [1973], 'Trotskyist Work in the Trade Unions, Part 2: Minneapolis 1934 – General Strike!', in *The Transitional Program: The Death Agony of Capitalism and the Tasks of the Fourth International*, London: International Bolshevik Tendency.

—— 1998b [1973], Trotskyist Work in the Trade Unions, Part 3: The Primacy of Politics', in *The Transitional Program: The Death Agony of Capitalism and the Tasks of the Fourth International*, London: International Bolshevik Tendency.

Korth, Philip A. 1995, *The Minneapolis Teamsters Strike of 1934*, East Lansing, MI: Michigan State University Press.

Korth, Philip A. and Margaret Beegle (eds.) 1988, *I Remember Like Today: The Auto-Lite Strike of 1934*, East Lansing, MI: Michigan State Press.

Kramer, Dale 1942, 'The Dunne Boys of Minneapolis', *Harper's Magazine*, 184, March: 388–98.

Kramer, Reinhold and Tom Mitchell 2010, *When the State Trembled: How A.J. Andres and the Citizens' Committee Broke the Winnipeg General Strike*, Toronto: University of Toronto Press.

Kutler, Stanley I. 1982, *The American Inquisition: Justice and Injustice in the Cold War*, New York: Hill and Wang.

Larrowe, Charles P. 1956, *Shape-up and Hiring Hall*, Berkeley, CA: Institute of Industrial Relations, University of California.

—— 1972, *Harry Bridges: The Rise and Fall of Radical Labor in the United States*, New York: Lawrence Hill.

Lasky, Marjorie Penn 1985, '"Where I Was a Person": The Ladies' Auxiliary in the 1934 Minneapolis Teamsters' Strikes', in *Women, Work, and Protest: A Century of U.S. Women's Labor History*, edited by Ruth Milkman, Boston: Routledge & Kegal Paul.

Latchem, E.W. 1920, 'First of May in Minneapolis', *One Big Union Monthly*, 2, June: 6–8.

Lawson, George W. 1955, *History of Labor in Minnesota*, St. Paul, MN: Minnesota State Federation of Labor.

Le Blanc, Paul 1999, *A Short History of the U.S. Working Class: From Colonial times to the Twenty-first Century*, Amherst, NY: Humanity Books.

—— 2005, 'Uneven and Combined Development and the Sweep of History: Focus on Europe', *International Viewpoint*, available at <http:///www.international viewpoint.org/spip.php?article1125>.

—— 2010, 'Radical Labor Subculture: Key to Past and Future Insurgencies', *Working USA: The Journal of Labor and Society*, 13, September: 367–85.

Lefkovitz, Herbert 1935, 'Olson: Radical and Proud of It', *Review of Reviews*, 91, May: 36.

Leiter, Robert D. 1957, *The Teamsters Union: A Study of Its Economic Impact*, New York: Bookman.

Le Sueur, Meridel 1934, 'What Happens in a Strike', *American Mercury*, 33, September–December: 329–35.

—— 1945, *North Star Country*, New York: Dull, Sloan & Pearce.

—— 1978 [1939] *The Girl*, Cambridge, MA: West End.

Levinson, Edward 1956 [1938], *Labor on the March*, New York: University Books.

Lewin, Moshé 2005, *The Soviet Century*, London: Verso.

Local No. 574, Minneapolis, Minnesota 1935, *By-Laws of General Drivers, Helpers and Inside Workers Union*, Minneapolis: Local No. 574.

Lorence, James J. 1996, *Organizing the Unemployed: Community and Union Activists in the Industrial Heartland*, Albany, NY: State University of New York Press.

Lovell, Frank [Frederick J. Lang] 1945, *Maritime: A Historical Sketch and a Workers' Program*, New York: Pioneer.

Löwy, Michael 1981, *The Politics of Combined and Uneven Development: The Theory of Permanent Revolution*, London: Verso.

Luxemburg, Rosa 1971, *The Mass Strike, the Political Party, & The Trade Unions and The Junius Pamphlet*, New York: Harper Torchbooks.

Marx, Karl 1933, *Wage-Labour and Capital/Value, Price and Profit*, New York: International Publishers.

—— 1968, 'The Eighteenth Brumaire of Louis Bonaparte', in Karl Marx and Frederick Engels, *Selected Works*, Moscow: Progress.

Matthiessen, F.O. 1948, *From the Heart of Europe: On a Lecture Tour of Central Europe, from July to December 1947*, Oxford: Oxford University Press.

Mayer, George H. 1951, *The Political Career of Floyd B. Olson*, Minneapolis: University of Minneapolis Press.

Mayhew, Henry 1968, *London Labour and the London Poor: The London Street Folk*, Vol. 1, New York: Dover.

Medvedev, Roy 1971, *Let History Judge: The Origins and Consequences of Stalinism*, New York: Knopf.

Merithew, Caroline Waldron 2006, ' "We Were Not Ladies": Gender, Class, and a Women's Auxiliary's Battle for Mining Unionism', *Journal of Women's History*, 18, Summer: 63–94.

Millikan, William 1989, 'Maintaining "Law and Order": The Minneapolis Citizens' Alliance in the 1920s', *Minnesota History*, 51: 219–33.

—— 2001, *A Union Against Unions: The Minneapolis Citizens Alliance and Its Fight Against Organized Labor*, St. Paul, MN: Minnesota Historical Society.

Milton, David 1982, *The Politics of U.S. Labor*, New York: Monthly Review.

Montgomery, David 1987, *The Fall of the House of Labor: The workplace, the state, and American labor activism, 1865–1925*, Cambridge: Cambridge University Press.

Moody, Kim 1988, *An Injury to All: The Decline of American Unionism*, London: Verso.

—— 2007, *US Labor in Trouble and Transition: The Failure of Reform from Above, the Promise of Revival from Below*, London: Verso.

Muste, Abraham Johannes 1935a, 'Strikes on the 1935 Horizon', *New International*, 2, March: 57–60.

—— 1935b, 'Some Lessons of the Toledo Strike', *New International*, 2, July: 127–9.

—— 1967a [1935], 'Sketches for an Autobiography', in Nat Hentoff (ed.), *The Essays of A.J. Muste*, New York: Bobbs-Merrill.

—— 1967b [1935], 'Trade Unions and the Revolution', in Nat Hentoff (ed.), *The Essays of A.J. Muste*, New York: Bobbs-Merrill.

Myers, Constance Ashton 1977, *The Prophet's Army: Trotskyists in America, 1928–1941*, Westport, CT: Greenwood Press.

Nelson, Bruce 1988, *Workers on the Waterfront: Seamen, Longshoremen, and Unionism in the 1930s*, Chicago: University of Illinois Press.

Novack, George 1941a, *Witch Hunt in Minnesota: The Federal Prosecution of the Socialist Workers Party and Local 544-CIO*, New York: Civil Rights Defense Committee.

—— 1941b, *The Bill of Rights in Danger! The Meaning of the Minneapolis Convictions*, New York: Civil Rights Defense Committee.

—— 1972, *Understanding History: Marxist Essays*, New York: Pathfinder.

Nove, Alec 1975, *Stalinism and After*, London: George Allen and Unwin.

Odets, Clifford 1937, *Waiting for Lefty: A Play in Six Episodes*, London: Victor Gollancz.

Oneal, James and George E. Werner 1947, *American Communism: A Critical Analysis of its Origins, Development, and Programs*, New York: E.P. Dutton.

O'Neill, William L. 1982, *A Better World – The Great Schism: Stalinism and the American Intellectual*, New York: Simon and Schuster.

Pahl, Thomas 1967, 'The G-String Conspiracy: Political Reprisal or Armed Revolt? The Minneapolis Trotskyite Trial', *Labor History*, 8: 30–51.

Palmer, Bryan D. 2007, *James P. Cannon and the Origins of the American Revolutionary Left, 1890–1928*, Chicago: University of Illinois Press.

P.B. 1948, 'We Note: Henry Wallace and His Followers', *Antioch Review*, 8, Autumn: 368–76.

Preis, Art 1964, *Labor's Giant Step: Twenty Years of the CIO*, New York: Pioneer.

Quam, Lois and Peter J. Rachleff 1986, 'Keeping Minneapolis an Open Shop Town: The Citizens' Alliance in the 1930s', *Minnesota History*, 50, 3: 105–17.

Quin, Mike 1949, *The Big Strike*, Olema, CA: Olema.

Rachleff, Peter 1989, 'Turning Points in the Labor Movement: Three Key Conflicts', in *Minnesota in a Century of Change: The State and Its People*, edited by Clifford E. Clark, Jr., St. Paul, MN: Minnesota Historical Society Press.

Rayback, Joseph 1966, *A History of American Labor*, New York: Free Press.

Redfield, Sandra 1984, *The Great Minneapolis Strikes and the Revolutionary Potential in 1934*, New Haven, CT: Revolutionary Communist League.

Robinson, Jo Ann Ooiman 1981, *Abraham Went Out: A Biography of A.J. Muste*, Philadelphia: Temple University Press.

Rogovin, Vadim Z. 2009, *Stalin's Terror of 1937–1938: Political Genocide in the USSR*, Oak Park, MI: Mehring Books.

Rorty, James 1936, *Where Life is Better: An Unsentimental Journey*, New York: John Day.

Rosenzweig, Roy 1975, 'Radicals and the Jobless: Musteites and the Unemployed Leagues', *Labor History*, 16: 51–77.

—— 1976, 'Organizing the Unemployed: The Early Years of the Great Depression, 1929–1933', *Radical America*, 10: 37–60.

Roskolenko, Harry 1965, *When I Was Last On Cherry Street*, New York: Stein and Day.

Russell, Thaddeus 2001, *Out of the Jungle: Jimmy Hoffa and the Remaking of the American Working Class*, Philadelphia: Temple University Press.

Shachtman, Max 1933, *Ten Years: History and Principles of the Left Opposition*, New York: Pioneer Publications.

—— 1954, 'Twenty-Five Years of American Trotskyism, Part I', *New International*, 20, January–February.

—— 2003, *Race and Revolution*, edited and introduced by Christopher Phelps, London: Verso.

Schlesinger Jr., Arthur 1958, *The Age of Roosevelt: The Coming of the New Deal*, Vol. 3, Boston: Houghton Mifflin.

—— 1978, *Robert Kennedy and His Times*, New York: Houghton Mifflin.

Schrecker, Ellen 1999, *Many Are the Crimes: McCarthyism in America*, Princeton, NJ: Princeton University Press, 1999.

Scholl, Marvel 1975, 'Socialist Women and Labor Struggles, 1934–1954: A Report by Participants', *International Socialist Review*, 36, March: 20–3.

Schwartz, Stephen 1986, *Brotherhood of the Sea: A History of the Sailor's Union of the Pacific, 1885–1985*, New Brunswick, NJ: Rutger's University Press.

Selvin, David F. 1996, *A Terrible Anger: The 1934 Waterfront and General Strikes in San Francisco*, Detroit: Wayne State University Press.

Sevareid, Eric 1976, *Not So Wild A Dream*, New York: Atheneum.

Silverberg, Louis G. 1941, 'Citizens' Committees: Their Role in Industrial Conflict', *Public Opinion Quarterly*, 5, March: 17–37.

Skoglund Centenary Committee 1984, *Carl Skoglund, 1884–1960: Remembered in Struggle*, Minneapolis: Skoglund Centenary Committee.

Sloane, Arthur A. 1993, *Hoffa*, Cambridge, MA: MIT Press.

Smemo, Kristoffer O. 2011, 'The Politics of Labor Militancy in Minneapolis, 1934–1938', MA thesis, University of Massachusetts, Amherst, MA.

Specktor, Mordecai 1984, 'Militant Minneapolis: Strike Remembered', *Guardian*, 8 August.

Spielman, Jean E. 1923, *The Stool Pigeon and the Open Shop Movement*, Minneapolis: American Publishing Company.

Stanton, Fred (ed.) 1981, *James P. Cannon, Writings and Speeches, 1928–1931: The Left Opposition in the U.S., 1928–1931*, New York: Monad.

Starobin, Joseph R. 1972, *American Communism in Crisis, 1943–1957*, Berkeley, CA: University of California Press.

Steele, Richard W. 1999, *Free Speech in the Good War*, New York: St. Martin's.

Steinbeck, John 1947, *In Dubious Battle*, Cleveland: World.

Storch, Randi 2007, *Red Chicago: American Communism at its Grassroots, 1928–1935*, Chicago: University of Illinois Press.

Strang, Harry 1935, 'A Labor Lieutenant and Top-Sergeant', *New International*, 2, August: 165–6.

Streeter, Edward 1918, *Dere Mable: Love Letters of a Rookie*, New York: Frederick Stokes Co.

Swabeck, Arne 1935, 'The A.F. of L. Begins to Face Issues', *New International*, 2, December: 212–15.

Thane, Eric 1934, 'The "Red Menace" in Minnesota', *The Nation*, 17 October: 435–6.

Thompson, Edward Palmer 1964 [1963] *The Making of the English Working Class*, New York: Random House.

Thoreau Weick, David 1992, *Woman from Spillertown: A Memoir of Agnes Burns*

Weick, Carbondale, IL: Southern Illinois University Press.

Trimble, Steven (ed.) n.d., 'Interviews with Strikers', *Red Buffalo*, 2/3.

Trotsky, Leon 1931, *Communism and Syndicalism: On the Trade Union Question*, New York: Communist League of America (Opposition).

—— 1932, *The History of the Russian Revolution: Volume 1 – The Overthrown of Tzarism*, New York: Simon and Schuster.

—— 1937, *The Revolution Betrayed: What Is the Soviet Union and Where Is It Going*, New York: Doubleday, Doran.

—— 1939, 'Marxism in Our Time', in *The Living Thoughts of Karl Marx: Based on Capital: A Critique of Political Economy*, New York: Longman's, Green and Company.

—— 1969, 'Discussions with Trotsky, 12–15 June 1940', *Writings of Leon Trotsky [1939–1940]*, edited by Naomi Allen and George Breitman, New York: Pathfinder.

—— 1972a 'Hitler's Victory', in *Writings of Leon Trotsky [1932–1933]*, edited by George Breitman and Sarah Lovell, New York: Pathfinder.

—— 1972b, KPD Or New Party (I)', in *Writings of Leon Trotsky [1932–1933]*, edited by George Breitman and Sarah Lovell, New York: Pathfinder.

—— 1972c, 'KPD Or New Party (II)', in *Writings of Leon Trotsky [1932–1933]*, edited by George Breitman and Sarah Lovell, New York: Pathfinder.

—— 1973a, *The Transitional Program for Socialist Revolution*, New York: Pathfinder Press.

—— 1973b, 'The Crisis in the German Left Oppositon', 17 February 1931, in *Writings of Leon Trotsky [1930–1931]*, edited by George Breitman and Sarah Lovell, New York: Pathfinder.

—— 1977, *The First Five Years of the Communist International*, Vol. 2, New York: Monad.

Tselos, George Dimitri 1971, *The Minneapolis Labor Movement in the 1930s*, Unpublished PhD dissertation, University of Minnesota.

United States Senate 1936, 74th Congress, Second Session on Senate Resolution 266, *Violations of Free Speech and Assembly and Interference with Rights of Labor*, Washington, DC: Government Printing.

Valelly, Richard M. 1989, *Radicalism in the States: The Minnesota Farmer-Labor Party and the American Political Economy*, Chicago: University of Chicago Press.

Wald, Alan 1978, *James T. Farrell: The Revolutionary Socialist Years*, New York: New York University Press.

—— 1987, *The New York Intellectuals: The Rise and Decline of the Anti-Stalinist Left from the 1930s to the 1980s*, Chapel Hill, NC: University of North Carolina Press.

Walker, Charles Rumford 1936, 'Minneapolis: City of Tensions, II', *Survey Graphic*, November.

—— 1937, *American City: A Rank-and-File History*, New York: Farrar & Rinehart.

—— 1937a, 'A Militant Trade Union: Minneapolis Municipal Profile', *Survey Graphic*, January.

Weinstein, James 1969, *The Decline of Socialism in America, 1912–1925*, New York: Vintage.

Wingerd, Mary Lethert 2001, *Claiming the City: Politics, Faith and the Power of Place in St. Paul*, Ithaca, NY: Cornell University Press.

Witwer, David 2003, *Corruption and Reform in the Teamsters Union*, Chicago: University of Illinois Press.

Wolfe, Bertram D. 1928, *The Trotsky Opposition: Its Significance for American Workers*, New York: Workers Library.

Young, Dallas M. 1947, 'Origins of the Progressive Mine Workers of America', *Journal of the Illinois State Historical Society*, 40: 313–30.

Index

174–6, 185, 190, 200, 204, 224–5, 250, 267, 276–7, 285, 287, 289, 291
uneven and combined development   6, 29–39, 223, 234–9, 248
Union Defense Guard   125, 227–8, 239, 264 n.
United Relief Workers' Association (URWA)   62
Urtubees, A.H.   140

Valelly, Richard M.   34 n., 47 n., 236 n.

Wagner, Robert F.   137
Wald, Alan   139 n., 191 n., 248 n., 269 n., 283 n.
Walker, Charles Rumford   6, 7, 27, 28 n., 32 n., 33–4, 36 n., 38–9, 45, 48 n., 49 n., 52 n., 56, 57 n., 60 n., 64–7 n., 81 n., 83–4 n., 85, 86 n., 88, 89 n., 90, 92 n., 94–6 n., 99 n., 102–3 n., 105 n., 107 n., 109 n., 112 n., 121 n., 128 n., 129, 132–3, 141, 156, 157 n., 164 n., 165, 169 n., 173, 175, 177 n., 181, 188 n., 190, 192–4 n., 196,

197 n., 199 n., 202, 205 n., 209 n., 216 n., 217, 221 n., 224–6, 231 n., 243 n., 263, 264–5 n.
Wall, John   146
Walsh, Ellard   161, 180, 190 n., 196, 197 n.
Weinstein, James   35 n.
Weir, Roy   60 n., 140, 192, 193 n.
Werner, George   288 n.
West-coast longshoremen   3, 8–9, 13–18, 25, 127, 210
Wingerd, Mary Lethert   144 n.
Witwer, David   2 n., 235 n., 244 n.
Wolfe, Bertram D.   272 n.
Women's Auxiliary   Figures 7–8; 75–81, 83–5, 88, 90 n., 95, 97, 98 n., 130, 131 n., 140, 142, 145, 154, 160 n., 165, 166, 172–3, 175, 185, 189, 195, 203, 242 n., 267, 286 n.
Woxberg, 'Dutch'   245, 246 n.

Young, Dallas M.   75 n., 286 n.

Zachary, Roy   227–8

CPSIA information can be obtained
at www.ICGtesting.com
Printed in the USA
LVOW13s0840101116

512426LV00009B/29/P